FAITH AND FURY

Faith and Fury:

The Evangelical Campaign in Dingle and West Kerry, 1825–1845

Bryan MacMahon

Eastwood

First published in 2021
Eastwood Books,
an imprint of the Wordwell Group.
Unit 9, 78 Furze Road, Sandyford Industrial Estate, Dublin 18
www.eastwoodbooks.com
www.wordwellbooks.com

ISBN: 978-1-913934-12-5 (paperback)
ISBN: 978-1-913934-17-0 (epub)

British Library Cataloguing-in-Publication Data.
A catalogue record for this book is available from the British Library.

Typeset in Ireland by Wordwell Ltd
Copy-editor: Myles McCionnaith
Cover design and artwork: Wordwell Ltd
Printed by: Gráficas Castuera, Pamplona

Contents

Preface

My interest in the Protestant mission in west Kerry was first stimulated by the account written by Fr Mícheál Ó Mainín in the book *Céad Bliain, 1871–1971* (1973). I also owe a debt to the work of Desmond Bowen and Irene Whelan, who wrote short accounts of the Dingle mission.

One book in particular has been an invaluable source of information to readers with an interest in the conversion campaign in west Kerry. The author was given as 'Mrs. D.P. Thompson' and the book's full title was *A Brief Account of the Rise and Progress of the Change in Religious Opinion now taking place in Dingle and the West of the County of Kerry, Ireland*, published in 1846. This was the first comprehensive account of the early years of the Protestant mission in west Kerry, written at a time when hopes were high for the success of the enterprise. It could be called the 'foundation story' of the conversion campaign. The author was the wife of David Peter Thompson, the agent of Lord Ventry. Her name was Anna Maria (or Anne Mary), and for that reason, I have abbreviated references to her book as AMT. In a preface addressed to 'Mr. George Hitchcock, London', Thompson wrote that her book was written in response to his 'earnest request, backed by that of many friends', and that it was 'a fuller and more precise statement of the whole work than has yet been placed before the public'.[1] I have found no further information on George Hitchcock.

Two books published in the early twentieth century also have some relevant information. In the title page of Patrick Foley's *The Ancient and Present State of the Skelligs, Blasket Islands, Donquin and the West of Dingle* (1903) he is described as vice-chairman of the Dingle Board of Guardians and Rural District Council. In the copy of this book held in the Royal Irish Academy Library, Dublin, a handwritten note says that Foley was a carpenter living in Strand Street, Dingle. The other book was *Romantic Hidden Kerry* (1931) by Thomas Francis O'Sullivan, a native of Glin, Co. Limerick, who received his early education in Listowel. He was a journalist by profession.[2]

In such a bitter conflict as the religious war in west Kerry, it is understandable that many of the primary sources are biased. The editorial stances of newspapers published in Tralee were clearly drawn. The *Kerry Evening Post* was strongly conservative, unionist, pro-landlord and pro-Protestant. The *Tralee Mercury* and the *Kerry Examiner* were populist, nationalist, pro-tenant and pro-Catholic. The *Tralee Chronicle* was populist and anti-establishment, but tended to adopt a neutral stance in religious matters. Some of the other newspapers and journals cited in this book were written by authors who were supporters of the evangelical movement, and this will be obvious from their content.

Many of the contemporary books, newspapers, journals and manuscripts have not been readily available to previous researchers, and I have benefitted from the availability of digital copies of books and journals on Google Books. The digitisation of local newspapers has transformed access to this rich resource.

This book touches only briefly on the period after 1845. Readers are invited to enter the pre-Famine world and to experience the religious conflict in west Kerry as it unfolded year by year, when nobody had any premonition of the disaster that was to change the course of Irish history following the arrival of the potato blight in the autumn of 1845.

Corca Dhuibhne (Corkaguiny) is the name of the barony that comprises the whole peninsula, but the term Corca Dhuibhne is generally used today to refer to the Gaeltacht, the Irish-speaking district in the western part of the peninsula, of which Dingle (An Daingean) is the main town. The evangelical campaign was centred on Dingle town and areas to the west of it, for which Iarthar Dhuibhneach (western Corkaguiny) is a more precise term. There was no sustained proselytising activity on the north side of the peninsula, or in places east of Dingle.

For place-names, I have followed the English spelling of the Ordnance Survey, and so Ceann Trá is rendered as Ventry, Dún Chaoin as Dunquin, An Blascaod Mór as the Great Blasket, An Mhuiríoch as Murreagh, Cill Mhaoilchéadair as Kilmalkedar and Cill Chuáin as Kilquane. Dunurlin (Dún Urlann) was the name most often used for today's Ballyferriter (Baile an Fheirtéaraigh).

Spellings of personal names and place-names vary considerably in the sources. For example, Fr Michael Divine's name was often rendered as Devine, but Divine is the spelling on the plaque to his memory in St Mary's church, Dingle, and I have followed this.

In contemporary newspapers, clergymen of all denominations were generally given the title 'Rev. Mr' and 'Fr' was rarely used for priests. For clarity here, Church of Ireland ministers are termed 'Rev.' and priests 'Fr'.

As a guideline for monetary conversion, £1 in the 1840s can be taken as equivalent to €110, or approximately £100, in 2020. Twelve pence (*d*) was equal to one shilling (*s*) and twenty shillings equalled one pound (£).

Translations from Irish are my own.

Acknowledgements

I am grateful for the courteous assistance of the staff in the National Library of Ireland, National Archives of Ireland, Royal Irish Academy Library, Trinity College Library, Kerry Diocesan Archive and Central Catholic Library, Dublin. A special word of thanks is due to Tommy O'Connor, Kerry County Librarian; Michael Lynch, Kerry County Archivist; Jean Kent-Sutton, librarian of St Columba's College, Dublin; Mike Maguire, Limerick City and County Library; Bernard Mac Brádaigh of Dingle Branch Library; Lorcán Ó Cinnéide, Ionad an Bhlascaoid Mhóir; and Bryan Whelan, Representative Church Body Library, Dublin.

For biographical information on the Church of Ireland ministers who feature in this book, readers are referred to Janet Murphy and Eileen Chamberlain, *The Church of Ireland in Kerry: a record of church and clergy in the nineteenth century* (2011).

I am indebted to Dr Patrick O'Donovan for his advice on the text and for hours of discussion that helped to clarify many matters for me. I am also grateful for the advice of Dr Pádraig de Brún, former professor at Dublin Institute of Advanced Studies, whose published works have led me to source material I might not otherwise have discovered. Dr de Brún's numerous articles in the *Journal of the Kerry Archaeological and Historical Society* and his book *Scriptural Instruction in the Vernacular: The Irish Society and its Teachers, 1818–1827* (2009) have been particularly helpful. I am grateful to Ronan Colgan of Eastwood Books for his encouragement and to Myles McCionnaith for his professional advice on the text.

My sincere thanks also to Dr Breandán Mac Suibhne for his advice, and to Anne O'Connor, Micheál Ó hAllmhuráin, Marion Rogan and Tony Mahon for their advice.

Any errors or omissions are my responsibility.

I am grateful to Anthea Kennedy Gayer Mitchell of Australia, great-great-granddaughter of Rev. Charles and Catherine Gayer, for genealogical information on the Gayer family and for portraits of Charles and Catherine. A special word of thanks to Margaret Smith for drawing my attention to Seán Magee (ed.) *Ballinteer, Co. Dublin: A Local History from Rural to Suburban* (Dublin, 2017). Seán's research led me to the rich source material on Ventry in the Adare Narrative, held in the archives of St Columba's College, Whitechurch, Co. Dublin.

My thanks also to Fr Jim Sheehy of Díseart Centre of Irish Spirituality and Culture, Dingle; Rev. Phyllis Jones, rector of Dingle; Fr Michael

Moynihan, St Mary's Parish; Des McQuaid; Laurence Dunne; Richard M. Doherty; Ted Holohan; Siobhán Prendergast; Bro. Seán Aherne; Dr Conor Brosnan; Julia Barrett; Ted Creedon; Gary Delaney; Thomas McKeever; Caitríona Ní Chathail; and Cathy Griffin.

Breege Granville kindly showed me the interior of the former glebe house of Dunurlin (Ballyferriter), and pointed out the remains of the nearby church. This glebe house was the first building to be erected as part of the evangelical campaign. Oisín Lavery welcomed me into the restored and refurbished former mission church in Cloghaneduff near Kilmalkedar, the last mission building to be erected in Corca Dhuibhne.

Ba mhaith liom mo bhuíochas ó chroí a ghabháil arís le mo chaoinbhean chéile, Caitríona, as ucht an tacaíocht a thug sí dom agus mé i mbun taighde.

Abbreviations

AMH: *The Achill Missionary Herald and Western Witness*

AMT: Mrs D.P. Thompson, *A Brief Account of the Rise and Progress of the Change in Religious Opinion now taking place in Dingle and the West of the County of Kerry, Ireland* (London, 1846).

C.C.:   Catholic Curate

FJ: *Freeman's Journal*

IEG: *Irish Ecclesiastical Gazette*

JKAHS: *Journal of the Kerry Archaeological and Historical Society*

KEx: *The Kerry Examiner and Munster Observer*

KEP: *The Kerry Evening Post*

KCA: Kerry County Archives

NAI: National Archives of Ireland

NGI: National Gallery of Ireland

NLI: National Library of Ireland

P.P.:   Parish Priest

Q.C.:   Queen's Counsel

QE: *Quarterly Extracts from the Correspondence of the Irish Society*

RCB: Representative Church Body

RIA: Royal Irish Academy

TC: *Tralee Chronicle and Killarney Echo*

Introduction

Today, St James's church in Dingle is widely known as the venue for an annual music festival, Other Voices, which attracts internationally renowned performers. 'Other voices' could also be said to be the theme of this book, as it is a record of long-forgotten voices that resonated throughout west Kerry, and were heard around Ireland and Britain, over several decades in the nineteenth century. They were strident voices, and they could be judgmental, reproachful, provocative and challenging, but they could also be comforting, uplifting and inspiring. They were the voices in Irish of scripture readers and teachers who enabled people to read in their own language, and the voices of evangelical clergymen in both Irish and English. The first Irish-language printed books that circulated in Corca Dhuibhne were the school primers and scripture extracts used by these evangelicals. The opportunity of learning to read in their own language drew many people towards the scripture readers and teachers, and it is likely that these first books in Irish fostered a regard for the printed word that culminated in the extraordinary literary flowering in western Corca Dhuibhne in the twentieth century. The first chronicler of life on the Great Blasket, Tomás Ó Criomhthain, author of *An tOileánach* (1929), was probably influenced by these primers.

The scripture readers and teachers worked in association with the Irish Society for Promoting the Education of the Native Irish through the Medium of Their Own Language, which had been established in Dublin in 1818. The evangelicals in west Kerry, lay and clerical, were collectively known as 'bíoblóirí' or 'biblers', and the term was appropriate, as the Bible was central to their work. 'Search the scriptures', the clergymen advised the people, challenging Catholic priests to point to the biblical sources of their doctrines. They also told people that they had no need of priests, as Jesus Christ was the only high priest, the only mediator between God and man. The evangelical clergymen saw themselves as missionaries, while adherents of the Catholic Church, particularly its priests, saw them as proselytisers. In this remote district, the great majority of the population was Catholic, and while the Church of Ireland, the Established Church, had a presence, its clergymen had not actively sought converts. The bíoblóirí were a new phenomenon.

The relationship between the missionaries and the existing Church of Ireland diocesan structures was complicated. They won the approval of Dr Edmond Knox, who succeeded Bishop John Jebb in the diocese of Limerick, Ardfert and Aghadoe in 1834, but they operated largely independently and set up an organisation first named the Dingle Colony and later the Dingle and Ventry Mission, which received great amounts of money direct from supporters in Britain. There was a strong element of cultural imperialism in the conversion campaign, and although Irish was used initially by evangelicals as the only realistic means of communication and education in west Kerry, English was undoubtedly the preferred language – the language of civilisation, as they saw it. Irish, then, was a means to an end.

This systematic campaign of conversion was part of the 'Second Reformation', an evangelical development in Irish Protestantism from the 1820s. Historian David W. Miller identified some characteristics of evangelicalism:

> It was not a religion, a sect, a church or a denomination. It was a movement. There were dozens of organisations which identified themselves as evangelical, but the movement itself had no centre of authority comparable to that of a hierarchy of prelates or an assembly. Nor did it have a systematic theology or creed such as Calvin's *Institutes* or the Anglican *39 Articles*. Rather it had a certain style of Protestant religious behaviour.[1]

In all, some 800 people shed their traditional religious allegiance in west Kerry before 1845. It was a period when zeal turned into zealotry, passions became inflamed, language became abusive and actions became violent. In later years, veils of silence came to be drawn over the conversion campaign for fear of stirring up old passions. This book peels back the layers of history to shine a spotlight on the origins of the conversion campaign in west Kerry.

'Soupers'
In popular memory, the evangelical missionaries have been depicted as fanatics, and their work as devious, opportunistic proselytising. Converts were described by Catholics as 'perverts', 'soupers' and 'turncoats', and the

phrase 'taking the soup' referred to a shameful act of betrayal. The term 'souper' was first coined in the 1830s by a Dingle curate, Fr John O'Sullivan. 'Souper, souper, ring the bell, souper, souper, go to hell,' went one of the milder chants of the time. 'Lucht a' tsúip' (the soup people or soupers) was a common Irish expression for converts, and 'scoil a' tsúip' was the school they attended. T.F. O'Sullivan, a Catholic nationalist author of the early twentieth century, summed up the prevailing view of the Protestant conversion campaign. Acknowledging that between seven and eight hundred Catholics converted, he insisted that 'almost every one [...] was in a state of destitution, [when they] abandoned their faith and yielded to the overtures of the proselytisers.' He regarded the conversions as insincere, as indicated in his comment that 'in the course of time, however, the "converts" returned to the Catholic Church.'[2]

Some converts endured significant hardships as a result of their decision, not least the severing of familial and communal ties. Dutiful Catholics followed the advice of their priests and boycotted converts, who were depicted as receiving great benefits and rewards. It took courage and independence for converts to walk away from family and friends, to become estranged from the wider community while still living and working in it. Converts usually lost opportunities for employment, except from their new co-religionists, who could only offer a limited range of work. Certain advantages did accrue to converts, since they came under the patronage of people who were powerful, influential and wealthy, and being associated with this class brought a certain status. Their children received education in the mission schools, and some converts were provided with jobs, money and houses at low rent in the colonies of Dingle and Ventry.

Evangelical leaders and converts in general were acutely sensitive to the charges of bribery levelled against them and vehemently denied them. If some converts were attracted by material gain, for others, the losses were considerable. When accused of succumbing to bribery, one Dingle convert indignantly replied that he was no better off by the change, 'Bribed! Is it the effect of bribery to have my wife and children in want?'[3] The 1847 report of the Dingle Colony pointed out, 'It is not in our power to know unerringly what is in men's minds, and it is possible no doubt that some may have joined us from mixed or impure motives.'[4] It was argued that even if someone first converted for base reasons, it was possible that he or she could in time become a genuine believer.

In describing their first successes, the evangelicals did not always speak of conversions, but rather of 'a spirit of independent inquiry' that was taking hold among the people. Some west Kerry converts were confident, determined, stubborn, independent-minded individuals, open to challenging the dogmas of Catholicism and the power exerted by priests. With the arrival of the bíoblóirí, there was, for the first time, the prospect of joining an alternative religious system. Ordinary curiosity was also a factor in the early success of the bíoblóirí, with the novelty of their message appealing to inquisitive minds. It was the advent of religious pluralism in west Kerry. The liberating experience of learning to read books in their native language was a powerful attraction for all ages and made people well disposed to the early Bible readers. Contemporaries referred to the 'blandishments' of the proselytisers, and the word is apt.[5] There were several charismatic and persuasive preachers and teachers, such as Rev. Thomas Moriarty and scripture-reader Thomas Dowling, among the evangelicals in west Kerry. Still, many converts were sincere and conscientious in their decision and experienced conversion as John Wesley did in 1738, when he wrote, 'I felt my heart strangely warmed.'

For generations, however, the conversion campaign evoked painful memories of fractures in family and community life, when harsh, unforgiving words rang out. The spirit of community interdependence that is captured in the Irish saying 'Ar scáth a chéile a mhaireann na daoine' (People live in the shelter of each other) was undermined by the bitterly divisive events of the conflict. The taint of betrayal associated with conversion, the stigma of souperism, made it an uncomfortable and almost taboo subject. In 1973, Fr Mícheál Ó Mainín wrote about the conversion campaign, 'Mhúscail sé fuath agus fearg in measc an phobail [...] Tá iarsmaí an achrainn seo sa dúthaigh fós.'[6] (It generated hatred and anger among the people [...] The legacy of this conflict still exists in the area.) Ó Mainín welcomed the ecumenical spirit of the 1970s, and the end of religious animosity, 'Tá tuile na feirge tráite le fada.' (The tide of anger has long since ebbed.) In 2007, scholar and broadcaster Muiris Mac Conghail, a perceptive writer with an intimate knowledge of Corca Dhuibhne, wrote, 'Fuar go maith a shéideann an ghaoth ó na leathanta san i gcónaí.'[7] (It is still a cold wind which blows from those times.)

For Mac Conghail, the term 'souperism' was an injustice to genuine converts. He argued cogently, 'The religious fervour and controversy which inhabited the Corca Dhuibhne peninsula from about 1830 was a complex one and in part represented a desire for genuine moral and social reform.'[8] As one convert in Kilmalkedar explained in simple terms, 'There's no power in man as will let him run from the Lord.'[9]

Little can be known now of the inner motives of most converts, but this book reveals details of the transformation experienced by Fr Denis Leyne Brasbie, a curate in Kilmalkedar, who converted and became an Anglican minister. He left written accounts of his reasons for leaving the Catholic Church, explaining it as an act of conscience. Several converts from west Kerry went on to train as ministers of the Church of Ireland and to serve it faithfully. Their commitment to Protestantism was genuine, and there were undoubtedly other less prominent converts who also acted on conscientious principles but who could not articulate their motivation so well.

Polarisation of society

The arrival of Protestant teachers and missionaries in west Kerry from the late 1820s polarised society, and sundered social and familial bonds. Their proselytising or missionary activities left an enduring legacy that cast a shadow over the history of the region and over its religious heritage. Yet leading figures on both sides of the bitter divide – Protestant ministers and Catholic priests, and their respective supporters – saw themselves as dutifully carrying out their obligations as Christians, fostering Christian values and imparting a message of salvation. The evangelicals were following the gospel imperative that bade them to 'go teach all nations', and they sincerely believed that Irish speakers in the west of Ireland had been wilfully neglected by the clergy of the Established Church.

Many of the leading evangelicals who are profiled in this book were perceived as intruders and outsiders, and there was a strong element of class difference underlying the conflict. 'An teampall Gallda' or 'the foreign church' was how the Protestant church in Ballyferriter was referred to by the local writer Pádraig Ó Siochfhradha, whose pen-name was An Seabhac.[10] (Gallda was a euphemism for Protestant, as distinct from Gaelach, a euphemism for Catholic.) One of the leading evangelical ministers, Rev. Charles Gayer, lived comfortably in a fine house in Dingle under the patronage of Lord Ventry. Catholic priests could only look on in amazement at the financial resources available to their Anglican counterparts. With funds pouring in from supporters all over Britain, the evangelicals taught and preached and built at an astonishing pace. In the context of pre-Famine Kerry, they had all the trappings of wealth and privilege, and they associated with landlords, land agents, magistrates, professional classes, members of the Coast Guard, policemen and naval officers who lived in west Kerry. They travelled widely on fund-raising campaigns, and they welcomed a succession of visitors keen to see their progress and to learn from them. As schools, churches and parsonages were built in various parts of west Kerry, the alarm of Catholic priests escalated. It was perhaps the coffers of the bíoblóirí, as much as their Irish Bibles, that generated this alarm.

From the Catholic clergy's perspective, the evangelicals were spreading false and disruptive beliefs among a settled people who had previously been united in the one true faith. They vigorously challenged the right of the evangelicals to teach and to preach, and denigrated their motives. When Dingle-born Thomas Moriarty converted, became a Protestant minister and returned to work in Ventry, he was denounced as a traitor to his race and his religion. Moriarty, who was a fluent Irish speaker, asserted his own identity, 'Some men claim exclusive patriotism. If they are Irish, so are we. Am I not Irish, heart and soul and tongue? Have we not Irish hearts and love of country and as much Irish blood as they?'[11]

Some contemporaries saw the religious conflict in west Kerry as one between the Irish church and the Roman church. The evangelicals followed the Protestant tradition of claiming their church as Irish and catholic (meaning universal), tracing its roots back to St Patrick and early Christianity in Ireland. They depicted the Catholic clergy as 'Romanists' who deviated from biblical Christianity, particularly by virtue of papal decrees. When the last two remaining converts on the Great Blasket, Eugene and Kate Connor, filled out the census form in 1901, they described their religious allegiance as 'Irish Church' and their children as 'Roman Catholic'. When Fr Brasbie sensationally converted to Anglicanism in 1844, he told his congregation that it was because he had 'discovered that the church of Rome was not the church of Christ' and salvation could not be found within it.[12]

These are the outlines of the sectarian conflict among the Christians of west Kerry, which sowed divisions in communities and in congregations and stirred up powerful passions. In terms of numbers, there were approximately 600 converts in the area in 1841, 700 in 1844 and 800 by late 1845.[13] The number rose during the Famine years, reaching a peak of approximately 2,000. These numbers included children, and it is difficult to give precise numbers of adult converts. A convert petition of 1845 gave the names of 147 heads of households, all male except for two widows; so including wives, the total number of adults may have been under 300. In the 1841 census, the total population of Dingle and parishes to the west of it was approximately 16,200. Clearly, in numerical terms alone, the converts were a small minority, but they were nonetheless seen as presenting a threat to the existing order.

Sectarian bigotry

The evangelical ministers were not demons, but they were demonised and portrayed as showing 'the cloven foot' of Satan.[14] They lived and loved, worked and wrote, debated and disputed, married, raised families and buried their children in west Kerry, and they saw themselves as belonging to the place. They baptised, instructed, confirmed, married and buried members of their congregations. They left their mark on the area by touching hearts, raising spirits, instructing minds and inspiring the hopes of their followers. They mingled among the poor in the course of their work, and although some were aloof and arrogant, not all were so. But they, and all those who came under their influence and attended their religious services, experienced what is now referred to as 'othering', that is, the systematic stigmatisation of a minority by presenting them in a negative and threatening way. There was overt hostility towards those who chose a different path. Priests and newspaper editors instructed the majority Catholic population to shun all converts and to regard all evangelicals as outsiders and interlopers supported by money donated by gullible advocates overseas. The evangelicals were seen as a threat to the Catholic Church, regarded as the one true church, and its doctrines, regarded as absolute truths.

People on opposing sides were absolutely convinced that they adhered to the one true faith; that their beliefs would lead to salvation and others' heresies to damnation. It is difficult today to grasp fully the potency of concepts such as eternal damnation and eternal salvation in the 1830s and 1840s. The evangelicals saw themselves as saviours performing God's work, bringing words of liberation and delivering misguided Catholics from superstition and priest-craft. As one minister expressed it, 'When we see our fellow countrymen bowing down to a system of superstition [...] is it not an act of mercy to bring them before the truth?'[15] Another man expressed the same idea with more local colour, saying that when he saw a person setting out towards the cliffs at Beenbawn under the mistaken belief that he was on the road to Dingle, he had an obligation to stop that person and set him on the right course.[16]

Exchanges between Catholic and Protestant clergymen became toxic, and formal curses were routinely issued by priests, some of them to last seven generations. (If a generation is taken as twenty-five years, that particular curse of 1845 lasted until 2020.) The sombre ritual of excommunication was performed on a mother whose only offence was that she dared to send her children to a Protestant school. For Catholic congregations, such curses and sanctions from a priest carried great power. On the other hand, evangelical supporters accused Catholics of idolatry, ignorance and superstition, and sometimes mocked their traditional beliefs and rituals.

Role of the press

Rival newspapers published in Tralee aligned themselves with one side or the other and fomented the conflict with provocative journalism. The conservative *Kerry Evening Post* took the Protestant side, while the popular nationalist newspapers, the *Tralee Mercury* and the *Kerry Examiner*, followed the line of the Catholic clergy. Inflammatory editorials, articles and letters, which regularly stooped to personal abuse, stoked passions on both sides. The war of words in newspapers involved smear campaigns, false allegations, scaremongering and abusive nicknames. Rev. Thomas Moriarty of Ventry was 'Tomás an Éithigh' or 'Lying Tom', and Rev. Charles Gayer of Dingle was 'Gayer the Betrayer'. When Denis Leyne Brasbie converted to Protestantism, he was nicknamed 'Brass-boy'. The Catholic curates in Dingle, Frs Halpin and Scollard, were 'Bully Halpin' and 'Fr Scold-hard'. The latter was also known as 'the cursing curate'.

On several occasions, disputes were heard in court, most notably in the spring of 1845 when Charles Gayer won a libel case against the *Kerry Examiner*. A pamphlet with an account of the trial circulated widely. There were assaults on individuals and on property. The policy of ostracism, known as 'exclusive dealing', towards converts reached a peak in 1845, when a distraught Thomas Moriarty pleaded, 'All we ask is liberty of conscience.'[17] With his congregation enduring hunger, isolation and abuse, Moriarty posed these questions, 'Do we live in the nineteenth century? Do we live under British law? Shall we not be allowed liberty of conscience whether we are right or whether be wrong?'[18]

This book provides a detailed record of the extraordinary events and personalities in west Kerry before the Famine, based on a wide range of sources, including newspapers, journals, manuscripts, official documents and private letters. The evangelicals were inveterate self-publicists, but their writings and the writings they generated are more than a record of the religious conflicts in which they were involved. They provide a pathway into the society and culture in west Kerry before its transformation by the Famine.

As early as 1836, the Irish Society had great hopes for its work in Kerry, stating:

There is no part of Ireland which presents a more interesting appearance to the Christian world than Kerry [...] The calls from west Kerry have been so urgent that the committee has been induced, within the last quarter, to establish a new district there, in which the town of Dingle will form the central and principal station.[19]

Ten years later, the scholar Henry Joseph Monck Mason appreciated the challenge of presenting a complete account of the progress of the conversion crusade in Kerry, 'It is difficult to know where to begin the history of proceedings in this county; it is still more difficult to abbreviate it.'[20] Now, almost two centuries later, this book attempts to meet the still-daunting challenge of presenting a comprehensive narrative of these events.

In the decades before the Famine, Dingle and west Kerry resounded with voices that were sometimes shrill, sometimes seductive, sometimes scandalous, sometimes shocking and always stirring. The powerful voices of the missionaries and their converts have long been stilled. They spoke in other voices, different voices, challenging voices. *Is fiú cluas a thabhairt dóibh arís* (It is worth listening to them again) in the spirit of a saying adapted from Tomás Ó Criomhthain: *Chun go mbeidís beo agus iad marbh.* (So that they may be living when they are dead.)[21]

1. The 'Second Reformation' in Kerry

In order to understand the religious conflict that occurred in west Kerry before the Famine, it is necessary to look briefly at the origins of evangelicalism in Ireland. In the late eighteenth century, an evangelical revival took place in the Anglican Church in Britain and Ireland, and many Bible societies were founded with the objective of winning converts to Protestantism. In the 1820s, this revival movement was referred to as the 'Second Reformation', and the many Irish evangelical societies were liberally supported by donors in Britain and Ireland.[1] These included the Irish Society, founded in 1818, and the Scripture Readers' Society, founded in 1822. English evangelicals began to show 'intense interest' in Ireland and supported missionary activities, including the distribution of Bibles.[2] The Irish Bible societies also found support and patronage among sympathetic landowning families. Members of the Bible societies believed that they were saving souls from eternal damnation and rescuing people from what they perceived as the darkness and superstition of Catholicism. They saw themselves as responding to a moral imperative to win Irish converts. To Catholics, the evangelical campaign was proselytism, a devious, underhand, systematic plan to entice people away from the Catholic faith in which they had been raised and to which their ancestors owed allegiance over centuries.

British and Irish society was permeated with religion in the 1830s and 1840s. Huge numbers of publications on religious matters were in circulation, and newspapers devoted great attention to religious affairs. Christian beliefs were deeply embedded in every aspect of life, and the world-view of the great majority encompassed a deity who was directly involved in the everyday lives of the people. People believed that the 'almighty disposer of events' influenced natural phenomena such as weather and harvests, as well as the health and fortune of individuals. These deep-seated beliefs were found not just among the simple and superstitious but also among the eminent and educated people all over the Union of Great Britain and Ireland. This was evident during the Great Famine, when providentialism, the belief that the catastrophe was a visitation of the

Almighty, was espoused by some of the most powerful churchmen and government officials.

The Church of Ireland, the Anglican Church, was the Established Church, despite representing only a small proportion of the population. In the census of 1831, the population of Ireland was approximately 7,900,000; this was made up of 81 per cent Catholic, 10 per cent Anglican and 8 per cent Presbyterian.[3] The evangelical wing was not always supported by Church of Ireland clergy, most of whom traditionally tended to be more restrained and more private in professing their faith and were not overtly seeking or working for conversions. Oliver McDonagh succinctly described the shift towards more strident evangelicalism in the Church of Ireland, 'The liberal and rational tone of eighteenth-century Protestantism in Ireland, its tranquil ease of effortless superiority, its readiness to await the withering, in the natural course of things, of popish superstition and priest-craft, were widely and swiftly replaced by evangelicalism in the post-union era.'[4]

Religious divisions in Ireland were fomented by a sermon delivered by Archbishop William Magee of Dublin at his inauguration in October 1822, in which he characterised the Catholic Church as 'so blindly enslaved to a supposed infallible ecclesiastical authority as not to seek in the word of God a reason for the faith they profess'.[5] Desmond Bowen regarded this sermon as 'an open declaration of religious war – the beginning of a "Second Reformation"'. It generated spirited responses from Catholics and began 'a furious pamphlet warfare'.[6] Prominent landlords such as Lord Farnham in Co. Cavan, Lord Roden in Co. Down, Lord Powerscourt in Co. Wicklow and Viscount Lorton in Co. Roscommon enthusiastically embraced the evangelical spirit and supported proselytism in their own areas. To these can be added Thomas Mullins, who became 3rd Lord Ventry in 1827 and whose residence was in Burnham House near Dingle. The Mullins family name was later changed to de Moleyns.

Irene Whelan described two aspects of 'the vast institutional and ideological machinery that lay behind the drive to make Ireland into a Protestant country'. These were an extensive system of private philanthropy and a political doctrine which held that Ireland could never prosper until Catholicism was wiped out.[7] In Whelan's words, 'It became an article of faith among evangelical Christians on both sides of the Irish Sea that if the Catholic Irish could be "brought over" to the Protestant faith, the problems which bedevilled Irish society, such as economic backwardness, lack of respect for the law, and hatred of the Protestant establishment, would be eradicated.'[8]

Whelan gave an overview of the historical background to what she terms 'the age of moral reform' in the Protestant church, when many voluntary societies were established, with some developing into national movements. The societies had various philanthropic and religious aims, such as prison reform, education, Bible distribution, and relief of widows and orphans. The Association for Discountenancing Vice was one such, as was the Kildare Place Society, which supported education. Others were the Sunday School Society, the Hibernian Bible Society, the London Hibernian Society and the Baptist Society. When these societies secured the patronage and support of sympathetic landlords and churchmen, they were able to establish a secure foothold in an area. Making copies of the Bible (or extracts from it) available to people to read for themselves was a standard practice of all these societies, and copies were often distributed to interested groups and individuals by itinerant preachers. Whelan wrote that the most significant feature common to all the societies was 'the most basic principle of Protestantism, i.e. the insistence on the right, indeed the necessity, for individuals to read and interpret the scriptures for themselves'.[9] Whelan's study included a short section on west Kerry. Desmond Bowen's book *Souperism: Myth or Reality* (1970) remains an excellent introduction to this period, and he also devoted a brief section to Dingle and its hinterland. In a later book, Bowen outlined the social and political conflicts in Ireland in the early nineteenth century. He discussed the 'marathon controversies' and crises which showed that Ireland had 'two culturally divided peoples, whose radical differences were passionately revealed whenever circumstances or design disturbed whatever temporary and uneasy peace the two peoples had obtained'.[10]

The evangelical movement in Ireland was financed by huge amounts of money donated by supporters all over Britain. Ireland was seen as mission territory, and the missionaries were admired for their dedication and intrepidity in penetrating faraway and often hostile places, particularly areas in the west of the country where the people had never heard 'the word of God' preached by Protestant ministers. Immediately after his ordination in 1830, Rev. John Jebb, nephew and namesake of Bishop John Jebb, was appointed as a minister to Dunurlin (Ballyferriter), and he served until 1832. He was an absentee, but on first visiting his parish he described it as 'this westernmost parish in Europe, the wildest country he ever beheld.'[11]

One of the leading Irish evangelicals of the 1820s was Rev. John Gregg, who was based in the Bethesda Chapel in Dublin and who travelled around the country as an itinerant preacher. He was born near Ennis, Co. Clare, and was a fluent Irish speaker. Gregg visited almost every county in Ireland, often accompanied by one of his lifelong friends, Rev. Robert Daly, rector of Powerscourt, Co. Wicklow, or Rev. Denis Browne of Santry, Co. Dublin. John Gregg later became bishop of Cork, Cloyne and Ross. Robert Daly became bishop of Cashel and John Browne became Dean of Emly. Gregg and Browne visited Dingle in 1829 and spoke at an evangelical meeting held in a room over the Market Hall.[12] Although the attendance was small, this meeting was significant for several reasons, one of the most important being 'that it was on this occasion that Lord Ventry (who is lay-rector of Dingle) saw the necessity of opening extensively a Reformation movement there'.[13] Assuming that this account is accurate, it provides an exact moment for the beginning of the intensive campaign of conversion in west Kerry in late March 1829.

An unimpressed correspondent of the *Tralee Mercury* wrote about the visit to Dingle of 'those itinerant mountebanks, misnamed preachers, who for the first time in our recollection have displayed forth their fustian in the courthouse of this town'. Naming Gregg and Browne, he wrote that they had come 'to chase away from our polluted atmosphere the cimmerian darkness in which we are enveloped'. On seeing a placard announcing the lecture, the writer admitted to being 'struck by the novelty of the thing' and went along to listen. He was unimpressed by the 'drawling sepulchral voice and Connemara dialect' of John Gregg, and by his 'farrago of nonsense', which the writer found 'disgusting, puerile and insipid'. He did not believe that the 'half-Rev. Mr. Gregg' would ever 'succeed in alluring the humblest peasant from the bosom of our holy religion'.[14]

It is interesting to note that this writer mentions the novelty of the event as stimulating his interest. Simple, natural curiosity about visiting speakers and their performances on platforms and in pulpits was a significant factor in attracting people to the first evangelical gatherings. Another letter also made fun of Gregg's accent and mocked his mission:

Never more shall we behold pestilence or famine walking through our land. The pure and unadulterated text of the scriptures will be put into the hands of every peasant and every peasant's child, which will afford every consolation to the poor image-worshipping creatures; to them it will be the highest solace to embrace it on their return to their cabins at night, and, oppressed with hunger and toil, to refresh themselves with large potations from this never failing fountain. Already does the golden age arise before our entranced sight.[15]

In later years, this meeting in Dingle courthouse became noteworthy for the presence of a young Catholic boy who tried to disrupt proceedings. He was Thomas Moriarty, who later converted and played a leading role in the evangelical campaign in west Kerry. In 1879, John Gregg's son, Robert Samuel, wrote about his father's Dingle visit. As Rev. Gregg attempted to speak, 'an effort was made by a young man, a Roman Catholic, armed with a large stick under the platform to drown out [Gregg's] voice.' This was young Moriarty, of whom Robert Gregg wrote, 'The message penetrated the young man's heart, as the faithful labours and long ministerial life devoted to the welfare of his own people in his own land, of the Rev. Thomas Moriarty, still afford proof of.'[16]

Rev. Robert Samuel Gregg, who also became a bishop, wrote a vivid description of the state of the Established Church in Ireland in the 1820s, when his father became an active evangelical:

It cannot be denied that at this time a cold formality prevailed in the Church in Ireland. Real earnestness, conscientious discharge of duty, above all, faithful evangelical teaching were not often to be found; and about this time a new movement sprang up in the Church, of which it has been said to me that he was the life and soul, but in which at all events, he took a very active part. Men whose minds had attained to a clear perception of evangelical truth and whose hearts were warmed by the love of Christ, desired that these principles should spread throughout the land and dispel the darkness and indifference that still rested upon a great portion of the Church in Ireland, not yet awakened to its responsibilities.[17]

This account is consistent with the view that by 1835, evangelicalism 'had established itself as the most invigorating and enlivening force within the Irish Protestant world'.[18] Another historian concluded that in the early nineteenth century, 'the tone and outlook of Irish Protestantism underwent a great change, due mainly to the influence of the evangelical movement.'[19] West Kerry was one area in which the evangelical movement had a profound effect on community life, with many public conflicts and a great well of bitterness ensuing.

Social and political issues of the time included the rise of Daniel O'Connell, the campaign to repeal the Act of Union of 1801, Catholic Emancipation, the Tithe War, government support for Maynooth seminary for the training of priests, the growing confidence of the Catholic Church and the introduction of the National School system. Issues such as these impacted on the minority Protestant community and increased their sense of vulnerability and isolation, since these forces were perceived as threats to their privileged status in Ireland. The march of democracy presented a clear threat to the Protestant way of life. However, this book does not deal in detail with these national issues, concentrating instead on the religious conflicts that divided communities in west Kerry in the years 1825 to 1845.

Religious differences

The areas of controversy between the two branches of Christianity revolved around theology and history and certain beliefs and rituals. At local level, it was not so much theological differences that came into play; more relevant were the rituals that were considered by devout evangelicals to be pagan, superstitious and disrespectful towards the deity. Rev. James Goodman was born in 1828 near Dingle, where his father Thomas was a clergyman. Like his father, James spoke fluent Irish and is now honoured as the collector of over two thousand traditional Irish tunes, the manuscripts of which are kept in Trinity College. Hundreds of these tunes were passed to James Goodman by the piper Tom Kennedy, who was a convert.

James Goodman wrote a long poem in Irish in the form of a dialogue between a Catholic named Brian and a convert to Protestantism named Art. The title is 'Agallamh Bhriain agus Airt', and in the poem the men debate the merits of the two Christian belief systems. Art's criticisms of some beliefs and practices of the Roman Catholic faith give an indication of the features that Protestants found objectionable. The criticisms are directed at: Roman bulls, the rosary, holy water, miracles, brown scapulars, vestments, wax candles, last oils (or the Catholic sacrament of Extreme Unction), penance, fasting, blessed cloths, holy wells, pilgrimages, Latin, bones, stones, palm branches, skulls and worship of graven images. The writer concludes, 'Sin é, cé náireach, bhur gcreideamh marfach.'[20] (Such is your shameful, deadly faith.)

At this time the Pope was also a head of state involved in a power struggle with other states in Italy and elsewhere. The doctrine of papal infallibility had not yet been promulgated, but the power exercised by the Pope was something to which Protestants strongly objected, sometimes describing him as the anti-Christ. Goodman's poem has Art describing Roman Catholicism as a foreign faith, employing multiple synonyms for the term foreign, 'An creideamh coigríoch gallda Rómhánach/Iasachtach coimhthíoch do thriall ón Iodáil chugainn.'[21]

Evangelical Protestantism emphasised the Bible, and fostered a spirit of individual inquiry and a personal relationship with the deity without the necessity of a priest's mediation; it also rejected doctrines such as transubstantiation and the veneration of Mary and the saints. Protestants believed that 'the Roman church' was a deviation from true biblical Christianity, and that Protestantism was the true inheritor of the faith of St Patrick. In a book published in 1880, dealing with Protestantism and the Irish language, one author expressed his 'deep conviction' that Roman Catholicism was 'the really blasphemous counterfeit of God's own truth'. He added that he did not say this to irritate or vex Roman Catholics, and justified himself by stating that he spoke the truth 'in love'.[22] When the term heresy was used to characterise Protestant doctrines, they countered by stating that it was the church of Rome which was guilty of heresy. One writer pointed out that 'the ancient Christianity of Ireland was independent of the see of Rome and rejected the Pope's supremacy, auricular confession, priestly absolution and other essential dogmas of Romanism.'[23]

English Protestants particularly looked askance at some of the customs and beliefs that they encountered in Ireland, where there were many superstitions about the spirit world and priests were widely believed to have special powers. This account by a Presbyterian observer was written in 1846:

> We can have, however, no proper idea of the hold which popery has on the Irish heart unless we understand how entirely it is enslaved by SUPERSTITION. What folly can a poor superstitious Papist not be made, by his priest, to believe? Some believe that the seals along the shore are animated by the spirits of their ancestors; some that when a man offers to become a convert, all the Roman Catholic blood is drained out of him, and Protestant blood poured in, and some that the priest can punish the disobedient by changing them into goats, hares or asses.[24]

This writer was outraged that priests would demand 'a fee for saying a Mass to banish vermin or for reading and cutting the sign of the cross to cure a vicious mule!' He condemned priests who blessed salt for hire as a cure for disease in the potato crop, used the horsewhip on their flocks, badgered people from the altar, destroyed Bibles and withdrew children from schools.[25]

The Irish Evangelical Society in Kerry
One of the first missionaries to spend time in Kerry was Charles Graham,

named 'the apostle of Kerry' in a book about his life. Graham was a Methodist who founded communities in Killarney, Milltown, Killorglin and Dingle in 1790. His biographer described him as 'an angel of light' and stated that he won over two hundred people to the Methodist faith during the year he spent in Kerry.[26] The work of Graham and his associates was on a modest scale; it did not attract much controversy at the time and does not appear to have evoked any response from the Catholic clergy.

The Irish Evangelical Society (IES) was founded in London in 1814 and had a presence in Tralee two years later, with regular congregations of beween four and five hundred people. One report stated, 'Perhaps there are few places of worship in Ireland or England better attended on the weekday evenings than the Assembly Room of Tralee.'[27] By 1825, the IES was working in other parts of County Kerry, such as Killarney, Killorglin, Listowel, Castlemaine, Ardfert and Beaufort, but not in the Dingle area. Rev. John B. McCrea, an independent minister based in Tralee, was an agent of the society from 1824 to 1828.[28] He conducted his missionary activity by 'the dissemination of tracts, by the establishment and superintendence of schools, and by public preaching and private instruction'. 'Schools are the nurseries of the church', he wrote, 'and my first object in every village I visit is to encourage them where they are and try to fix them where they are not.'[29] McCrea faced opposition from some Catholic priests, one of whom described him as the anti-Christ. When he was told that the scarlet lining of his riding-coat contributed to this image, McCrea judiciously changed the lining to black.[30] One priest wrote that when McCrea first preached in Ardfert, 'the people hooted him in the street' and then challenged him with 'perplexing questions as to his mission and his authority to preach'.[31]

J.B. McCrea worked on behalf of a number of evangelical societies as well as the IES, including the Irish Society. With financial support from some Tralee ladies and a London friend, he distributed two thousand religious tracts – 'silent but insinuating little messengers', as he called them – around Kerry.[32] Copies of the Bible, covered in black canvas, were also distributed, and when McCrea heard that Catholic priests described it as 'the black book', he interpreted this as an attempt to associate it with 'the apparatus of sorcery'.[33]

In 1826, McCrea's reports were full of confidence that 'the cause of pure and undefiled religion' was making steady progress in Kerry.[34] He wrote about large crowds attending his meetings and appealed to the committee of the IES for a second minister to be appointed to the county, since '*little justice* can be done to Kerry and *little return be made to the Society* without two ministers here'.[35] Initially, at least some Catholic priests were disposed to co-operate with the Bible schools in their areas, and were permitted to do so. The teachers employed in the schools were usually Catholics, and the Catholic-approved Douai version of the Bible was used. In practice, while the Douai version of the Bible was permitted by Catholic authorities, there was always the caveat that the Bible required interpretation and that the tradition of the church had also to be taken into account.

Parents appreciated the opportunities for learning and advancement being offered to their children in these schools. But opposition from priests steadily grew, and parents who sent their children to the schools were condemned by priests from the altar, a form of public denunciation that was regarded as most solemn by Catholic congregations. Because of this resistance, some Catholics resolved to petition their bishop, Cornelius Egan, to ask for permission to continue to send their children to the Bible schools.[36] On learning that these parents could not find a suitable person to compose such a formal request, McCrea disingenuously wrote that 'he took the hint and embodied their sentiments in a petition.'[37] He did not expect the petition to succeed, but he wished that 'the appeal might reverberate through the land as the voice of Kerry upon the subject of the Bible.' Within a month, the petition was signed by 438 individuals, the parents of over 1,300 children.[38]

The key appeal of the petition, as highlighted in the printed text, was, 'Permit us to know something of the word of God.' It was ostensibly a reasonable request, which any clergyman might be slow to refuse. When the package with the petition arrived by post, the response of Bishop Egan was to return it to the sender, John B. McCrea.[39] The bishop explained that McCrea had previously insulted him and that was his reason for rejecting the petition without reading it. When he eventually read the text of the petition in a newspaper, Bishop Egan said that he knew that it was 'of Protestant manufacture', since he was addressed as 'holy father' and this was not the usual form of address to a Catholic bishop. Furthermore, he added, the petition was too well written to be 'the production of ordinary country schoolmasters'.[40]

Daniel O'Connell supported Bishop Egan and was dismissive of McCrea, 'He went there [to Kerry] first as a candle-snuffer; he then became a strolling player, and now he dubbed himself a Reverend. He was never ordained. But he was still more fortunate for he got himself a rich wife into the bargain.'[41] O'Connell drew loud cheers at a political meeting when he ended his address by saying, 'Of all the lies ever uttered by the London Hibernian Society, some of the most gross are those lies of Johnny McCrea, styling himself the Rev. John McCrea.'[42]

The petition was undoubtedly written by McCrea, but its general thrust may have accurately reflected the wishes of at least some of the people. It is noteworthy that the petition contained no objections to Catholic beliefs, and was deferential but assertive in tone. References in the petition to 'scorn and persecution' experienced by parents and 'insult and abuse' directed at their children foreshadowed the tragic religious conflict that was to come in west Kerry.

2. 'All on a blaze for the Irish scriptures'

The Irish Society

In 1818, the Irish Society for Promoting the Education of the Native Irish through the Medium of Their Own Language was founded by a group of men who were critical of, and impatient with, the approaches of other similar societies. Henry Joseph Monck Mason, librarian at King's Inns in Dublin, and Rev. Robert Daly, rector of Powerscourt, Co. Wicklow, were two prominent members. The Irish Society was based in Upper Sackville Street (O'Connell Street today) in Dublin, and its first secretary was Rev. Joseph D'Arcy Sirr, who was followed by Monck Mason. The management and inspectorate of the society was confined to members of the Established Church, but its local agents came from all denominations, and many of its teachers and scripture readers were Catholics.

The aims of the Irish Society were set out as follows:

> That the exclusive objects of this Society be to instruct the native Irish who still use their vernacular, how to employ it as a means for obtaining an accurate knowledge of English; and for this end, as also for their moral amelioration, to distribute among them the Irish version of the Scriptures by Archbishop Daniell and Bishop Bedell, the Irish Prayer Book, *where* ACCEPTABLE and such *other* works as may be necessary for school books, disclaiming at the same time, all intention of making the Irish language a vehicle for the communication of general knowledge.[1]

'Archbishop Daniell' was Uilliam Ó Domhnaill, whose translation of the New Testament into Irish was published in 1602. Some forty years later, the Old Testament was translated into Irish under the direction of Bishop William Bedell of Kilmore diocese, but this was not published until 1685. The 'Irish Prayer Book' was the Book of Common Prayer. Between 1680 and 1685, the scientist Robert Boyle funded the publication of a complete Irish Bible, combining the translations of Ó Domhnaill and Bedell. Various editions of this Bible were published in the 1820s, with the Hibernian Bible Society printing a pocket-size version.[2]

The Irish Society made very slow progress in its first years but then gained momentum – so much so that 'none of the evangelical societies penetrated the upper echelons of the Church of Ireland quite as thoroughly as the Irish Society'.[3] The Irish Society had a specific focus on teaching Irish speakers to read the Bible in their own language, and it differed from similar societies by using Irish letters rather than English letters. In his history of the Irish Society, Monck Mason wrote that its work was aimed at the 'Irish peasantry' and that 'the sole object in view from the beginning was to instruct them in reading their native language, so as to enable them to read the scriptures and to present them with the Bible in that tongue.'[4]

Teachers working with the Irish Society were directed to tell people that they were employed to teach Irish, and that if students 'wish to learn English in a short time, & to understand it well, they will first learn to read their own language'.[5] The Irish Society was not unique in directing its work towards Irish speakers, but in the words of de Brún, 'the Irish Society came in time to be regarded as the chief exponent of this "vernacular policy" and the main focus of opposition to the use of the language for evangelical purposes.'[6] The society concentrated on 'enabling illiterate Irish speakers to read the scriptures in their own language, aiming to provide them with the means of obtaining a knowledge of English in the process'.[7] Conversion was not the aim of the society, or so it appeared at first, but conversions certainly followed as a result of its work.

The objectives of the Irish Society were in keeping with the principles of Martin Luther, in providing access to the scriptures in the vernacular language and without mediation, explanation or elaboration. An advertisement for the Irish Society in 1880 cited 'the 24th article of the Church of Ireland' as one of its founding principles, 'It is a thing plainly repugnant to the Word of God and the custom of the primitive Church to have public prayer in the Church or to minister the sacraments in a tongue not understanded of the people.'[8] The logic of this policy was clear to Monck Mason. He regarded it as an obvious fact that 'there is but one medium through which the preaching of the gospel can be conveyed to the hearts or the understandings of men, and that is through the language of the hearers.'[9] Monck Mason calculated that the number of Irish speakers in the country was about three million, of whom five hundred thousand spoke only Irish.[10]

Monck Mason regretted that for centuries most Irish people had heard preaching 'in a voice to them unknown' – in English.[11] He pointed out the irony of Protestant criticism of the use of unintelligible Latin in Catholic rituals while Protestant services for Irish speakers were conducted in unintelligible English. He was critical of the attempts by governments over the centuries to crush the Irish language by legislation, seeing them as counter-productive, 'The efforts to exterminate the Irish tongue were forcible and unremitted, but every attempt was sure to destroy itself by the reaction which it occasioned.'[12]

When people were enabled to read the Bible in their own language, Monck Mason was confident that they would inevitably turn away from the errors of Catholicism to the light of the true Protestant faith. 'The primary object was not proselytism from any particular sect, yet as it was foreseen that the sure result of the study of divine truth would be the abandonment of human error [...] it could not but be hoped that the next result would be the seeking for the way, the truth and the life within the pale of some scriptural church.'[13] By steadfast loyalty to its founding principles, the Irish Society, according to Monck Mason, established 'the kind, the affectionate intercourse that at present exists between the peasant, reconciled and awakened by the use of his native tongue, and the English Protestant, from whom alone he can receive improved instruction'.[14] There was also an expectation of social and moral improvement, as outlined in a later report which stated confidently that the Bible would 'steadfastly root out prejudice, bigotry and intolerance, substituting truth, love, mercy, tenderness, forbearance and long-suffering'.[15]

Like the Hibernian Society, the Irish Society had large numbers of supporters in Britain. Monck Mason's collaborator, Robert Daly, spoke at a meeting of the Bath Auxiliary Irish Society in 1828 and outlined the reasons for founding the society:

> Although there were abundant places in which the Highlander or the Welshman might hear the word in his native tongue, there was not one on the face of the earth where the poor Irishman could hear prayer or praises or the preaching of the gospel in his vernacular tongue. He alone stood without the chance of picking up one crumb of the bread of life.[16]

Daly blamed the Protestants of Ireland for neglecting their duty in this regard. Robert Daly has been described as 'one of the most bitter anti-Catholics in the country'.[17] His attitude to the Catholic faith, undoubtedly shared by some members of the Irish Society, has been succinctly described as follows, 'Like most ardent evangelicals, he regarded Catholicism as a pernicious faith, founded on superstitions and heresies that were perpetuated by a priesthood steeped in ignorance and obscurantism.'[18]

Modus operandi of the Irish Society

The Bible was the only book to be used in the Irish Society's work, and at a later stage, the Book of Common Prayer, if it was considered appropriate. No other tracts or texts were allowed, apart from elementary language books. This was to ensure that nothing unorthodox would be taught, and that people would be 'imbibing spiritual knowledge at the fountain-head'.[19] The society employed Catholics who were native Irish speakers as scripture readers and teachers. They were regarded as being more effective than people from a different class and culture who spoke no Irish. It was also emphasised that the scriptures should be used without note or comment. The underlying rationale was that it was required only to introduce people to the scriptures in order to arouse their interest in the true Christian message. The early teachers employed by the Irish Society had a regular salary, replaced in 1824 by a system of payment by results. They were well paid, especially when compared to teachers in the 'hedge schools', which preceded the foundation of the National School system in 1831.

In 1824, a twenty-four-page primer was published under the title *An Irish and English Spelling Book; Being a Few Easy Steps to a Right Understanding of the English Language, Through the Medium of Irish*.[20] Many editions were published, some of which ran to 10,000 and 20,000 copies, with the 23rd edition published in 1852 under the imprint of the Irish Society. Pádraig de Brún wrote, 'It was thus by far the most widely circulated work of its kind.'[21] The final section of the book contained familiar, non-controversial New Testament parables such as the Prodigal Son, the Good Samaritan and the Pharisee and the Publican.

The primer was believed to have been compiled by Thaddeus (Thady) Connellan of Skreen, Co. Sligo, a well-known Irish scholar and an influential scripture reader with the Irish Society whom de Brún has described as 'almost the parent of this Society'.[22] However, de Brún has established that the book was compiled by William Conner and Peter Hanley. This primer was among the first books in the Irish language (other than the Irish Bible) to circulate in Corca Dhuibhne. One phrase from this textbook has remained in everyday speech in Corca Dhuibhne and wider afield to the present day. On page six, under the heading 'Lesson 2. In words not exceeding one syllable', a list began with 'lá fuar – a cold day', followed by 'cat breac – a cat with white spots'. (This translation was amended to 'speckled cat' in the 5th edition, 1829.[23]) The term 'cat breac' was subsequently applied to those who attended the Bible classes, and by extension to those who converted. Children who attended Protestant schools in Corca Dhuibhne were termed 'cait bhreaca'.[24] 'An cat breac' or 'an leabhar breac' was sometimes used as a term for the Irish Bible, and converts were referred to as 'lucht an Chait Bhric'.[25] In Ó Dónaill's Irish-English dictionary, the translation of *cat breac* is given as 'turncoat', which was another term used for converts to Protestantism.

Monck Mason was convinced of the wisdom of using the Irish-language Bible as a text, as it undermined Catholic objections to the Bible:

> The peasant is assiduously instructed to consider the Protestant Bible to be a heretical book, but nothing will persuade him that heresy can be uttered in his native tongue and he imagines that Satan is dumb in it, an opinion that has been industriously encouraged; when therefore the peasant is possessed of the scriptures in that language, curiosity and other motives induce him to institute a comparison of them with the supposed book of Satan. He finds them to agree and, becoming at once emancipated from some part of his former delusions, he ardently desires to possess and examine the English Bible.[26]

The *modus operandi* of the Irish Society was described by Monck Mason as follows. An able person was employed as an Irish teacher in a certain area, meeting people at times when they were free from their work. The teaching took place with small numbers, whenever and wherever the teacher could find an opportunity: there was 'no schoolroom, no tables, no benches, no apparatus, no regular collections of scholars'. 'In order to avoid discovery', the teacher would meet the scholars in a cabin or even behind a haystack or a turf-clamp.[27] This description is echoed in another history of the Irish Society which explained that 'teachers were engaged to instruct their neighbours when and how they could, by day or by night, at home or abroad, sitting under the hay-stack or on the wild mountain-side.' These arrangements for learning were 'in order to avoid exciting the notice of the priests'.[28]

In a review of Monck Mason's book, an author identified some key stages of development for the Irish Society, particularly in the Kingscourt district. (Kingscourt is in County Cavan, but the Kingscourt district of the Irish Society extended over several counties in the north-east of the country.) The reviewer highlighted as a significant moment the society's adoption in 1823 of 'an ingenious policy' that involved 'making the native Irish a SELF-INSTRUCTING PEOPLE'.[29] This policy meant that Catholics 'of respectable moral character' who could read Irish were sought out and encouraged to teach their family, relatives and neighbours. They were given a small remuneration for each pupil they presented at quarterly examinations. They would use the Bible for instruction, but they were meant to teach only 'the art of reading'.[30] If the teaching attracted learners to acquire a deeper knowledge of the Bible, that would be warmly welcomed. A contrasting perspective on the Irish Society's strategy was given by Dingle historian Patrick Foley, writing in 1907, 'The pupils were first supplied with Irish primers; these contained little or nothing objectionable, but the second or third books gave the Protestant version of the scriptures.'[31]

Speaking to a meeting in Chelmsford, England, in 1850, Rev. D'Arcy Sirr, on a visit from Ireland, related an anecdote about a man who went to see the work of the Irish Society and specifically asked to see the school. The teacher brought him around the area, meeting people in the fields and villages, and reading with them. After nine hours, the visitor said that he was very impressed by all he had seen but still wished to see the school. The teacher told him that he had been at school all day, and that it was all 'under the canopy of heaven'.[32] One member of the Irish Society appreciated the wisdom of its strategy of having no buildings, because if prevented from working in one area, the teacher could quickly move on, 'No schoolhouse has to be accounted for, no furniture to be moved, no expense of a change of position to be feared. Is one master silenced for a time? A roll and a few portions of the scriptures only are necessary to enable another to commence in a more favoured spot.'[33] This policy was referred to by Monck Mason as 'our guerrilla warfare'.[34] Elementary language books and extracts from the Bible were the only texts. After three or four months an inspector would visit and examine the scholars, giving the teacher one shilling for each student who passed a test. The work of inspection was done with small numbers 'to avoid exciting the opposition of the priest'.[35] After a year, a pupil was considered proficient at reading.

Rev. John Alcock served briefly as a curate in Tralee in the 1830s. He was supportive of the evangelical work in and around Dingle and often visited the area. He later became archdeacon in the Waterford diocese. In her biography of her father, Deborah Alcock wrote about his lifelong support for the methods of the Irish Society, and she described its nonaggressive approach as being in keeping with his gentle personality and his spirit of cultivating good relations with people of all persuasions.[36] Deborah Alcock believed it was 'a happy thought' to decide to impart the biblical message to Irish peasants using 'this hunger for knowledge and this love for their cherished mother tongue'. She approved of the Irish Society policy, which 'let in the light and trusted to the action of the light to dispel the darkness'. Like Monck Mason, she trusted in

> the singular readiness of the Irish people to receive anything that came to them in their beloved language. The mind of the Irish peasant is naturally acute and intelligent and there is in him a strain of imaginative and poetic feeling which makes him welcome all that appeals to the heroic or the ideal nature of man.[37]

Alcock's book also confirms that the Irish Society had no actual buildings, 'The Irish teacher's schoolroom was his own dark cabin, where after the day's work was done, his neighbours gathered round the hearth. Or haply it was a mountain slope or the clearing of a bog or the sheltered side of a hedge.'[38] House gatherings would have been familiar in west Kerry, where the custom of *bothántaíocht* was strong. This referred to groups of neighbours coming together in the evening in each other's houses (botháin) for conversation and entertainment.

In addition, the custom of gathering in the evening to listen to scholars reading old Irish sagas was common in many parts of Ireland. These 'scribal readings' were extremely popular, and the readers were known as 'the manuscript men'. Alcock referred to 'a class called MS. men whose pride it was to read, to study, to transcribe and to preserve any writings they could find in their beloved native tongue'.[39] In 1883, Rev. Thomas Moriarty paid tribute to 'the Irish manuscript-men, the literary peasants, the LL.Ds [Doctors of Law] in freize' for their work in disseminating Irish Bibles. Moriarty referred to these men as 'Irishians', adding that they were 'deeply versed in heathen mythology, traditional Irish history and all about Fuin MaCuil, Ossian and, to come nearer home, the Battle of Ventry Harbour'.[40]

London branch of the Irish Society

The London branch of the Irish Society was established in 1822, and at the inaugural meeting on 25 March, the bishop of Gloucester was named as president.[41] Others involved were the bishops of Durham and Norwich, and Lords Roden, Gosford, Calthorpe, Lifford and Teignmouth. Four members of parliament, including Sir Thomas Baring, the banker, and William Wilberforce, the anti-slavery campaigner, were named among its vice-presidents. The London branch noted that the society had forty-seven schools in operation in Ireland, with a total of 2,078 scholars, of whom 888 were adults.[42] The population of Ireland was stated to be 6,800,000, with two million requiring education through the Irish language.[43] It was pointed out that while 600,000 Welsh speakers had been provided with 100,000 Bibles in their own language, and 20,000 Manx speakers had received 25,000 Bibles, the two million people who spoke only Irish had been supplied with a meagre 3,000 Irish Bibles. 'What an ample field for Christian activity!', the London branch declared.[44]

The branch cited evidence that Catholic priests welcomed the Irish Society's work, 'What is offered is so decidedly valuable, the Roman Catholic pastors and gentlemen co-operate with the Society in many parts of Ireland.'[45] The committee members were aware of the great attachment of the people to their native tongue, and the fact that, in the whole country, only two Protestant ministers were fluent in Irish was regretted.[46] A preacher who could address people in Irish would have a profound effect:

> Such is the love of the native Irish for whatsoever is Hibernian that it is altogether superior to any feeling that is in his heart [...] It was long ago said in Ireland, when you plead for your life, plead in Irish – the Catholics listened willingly when they were addressed in their mother tongue; hearers frequently shed tears, and frequently sobbed aloud and cried for mercy; and in the country towns the peasantry who, going there upon market days, had stopped to hear the preacher from mere wonder and curiosity, were oftentimes melted into tears and declared that they could follow him all over the world.[47]

The London branch became an important source of funds for the evangelical work in Ireland, and by the 1840s it 'had given up active work among the London Irish and acted solely as an English bank for the Dublin committee'.[48] A Ladies Auxiliary was also set up, and this provided funding for the payment of scripture readers; although it was prohibited from raising funds publicly, it could do so by private appeals to its supporters.[49] This auxiliary became, in Bowen's words, 'a frankly proselytising body' and was active in the Dingle area.[50]

Officially, the strategy adopted by the Irish Society was to be characterised by patience, respect and non-aggression, 'a softly-softly approach'.[51] But there were many extreme evangelicals, sometimes described as 'ultra-Protestants', in the upper ranks of the Irish Society, including Lord Farnham of Cavan and Lord Roden of Tollymore, Co. Down. Bowen wrote, 'The Irish Society was greatly favoured by the ultra-Protestants', although its agents 'generally resisted suggestions that they should proselytise directly.'[52]

This resistance did not last, and by 1834 the Irish Society had evolved into an openly missionary or proselytising movement. Rev. Thomas Moriarty described this change, 'Its operations were at first confined to what has been called the mechanical work of teaching the Irish-speaking people to read in their own tongue the wonderful works of God. For sixteen years it was engaged in this simple but effective preparation for what followed.'[53] This change coincided with the arrival in Dingle of Rev. Charles Gayer, who soon became a leading figure of the Protestant mission in west Kerry.

Kingscourt district

Kingscourt, Co. Cavan, was the centre of one of the earliest successes for the Irish Society, and the Kingscourt district of the Irish Society included parts of Cavan, Louth, Meath, Monaghan and Tyrone. Kingscourt became 'the mecca of the Reformation movement',[54] and evangelical activity reached a peak around 1827, 'the *annus mirabilis* of the Protestant Reformation in Ireland'.[55] The term 'Second Reformation' was first used almost exclusively in connection with the Kingscourt district; it was later applied to general evangelical activities.[56] Rev. Robert Winning was the main instigator of evangelical activity in the area, with James Reilly employed as an agent of the society. Reilly was a Catholic and, like many Irish speakers, he believed that the Irish language was incapable of being a medium of heresy.[57] When asked what remuneration he would require, Reilly suggested £12 a year, and he never asked for more. He was 'cheerful, zealous, faithful and indefatigable; he worked incessantly but solely from his devotion to his mother tongue.'[58] However, in reality Reilly was seen as something of a dupe, because 'he would speak of religion with all the bigotry of Romanism, and then enthusiastically and unsuspectingly read, from the Irish Testament, texts the most opposed to its errors.'[59]

One incident in Kingscourt district is worthy of particular notice, as it had reverberations in Kerry. On 28 December 1825, a group of 375 teachers working with the Irish Society in Cavan attested on behalf of five thousand people that their involvement in reading the scriptures in the Irish language was beneficial to them and fully compatible with their Catholic faith. They stated that they were overjoyed by 'the inestimable gift and noblest boon' of 'reading the Scriptures in our own beloved and venerated tongue'. The document ended, 'We consider that the reading of the holy scriptures is our right as men, our duty as Christians and our privilege as Roman Catholics.'[60]

At a meeting in the Rotunda in Dublin in March 1826, this Kingscourt declaration was described as influencing faraway Kerry:

> The spirit of the Kingscourt resolutions soon extended to the part of Ireland most removed from that place and the mountains of Kerry returned the sentiments which the inhabitants of the former had declared. Whoever is acquainted with the enchanting echoes of those celebrated hills is aware that the first return of sound is comparatively faint and single but that after a pause it revives and spreads and increases and circulates until the entire welkin undulates with its harmony. Thus it was with the first response from Kerry [...] We shall presently perceive how the echo spread and swelled.[61]

The Irish Society in Kerry

The records of the Irish Society give some glimpses into its early work in west Kerry, as reported by its local agents. In evaluating these reports, it must be remembered that it was in the interests of local agents to present a positive and optimistic account of their progress to headquarters in Dublin. Likewise, agents of the society would want to record progress in the areas in which they operated in order to sustain their income, which largely came from the donations of supporters in Ireland and in Britain.

Rev. J.B. McCrea was the agent who first reported from the Kerry area, beginning in the year 1825, when, as well as representing the Irish Evangelical Society, he acted informally as agent of the Irish Society. He reported that he supervised four hundred students of the schools of the Irish Society, of whom 220 were taught to read the scriptures in Irish.[62] McCrea accepted that his personal approach differed from that of the Irish Society, saying that its rules prevented any 'dogmatical interference' from him, but he clearly approved of the emphasis on the Bible. The Irish Society supplied him with one thousand copies of Irish Bibles and Irish spelling books, and he found that these had 'an irresistible attraction' to Irish speakers because they believed that 'nothing of the devil's can be in Irish'.[63]

The first account of the Irish Society's activities in Kerry is dated 3 September 1824, written by 'Rev. J.B. M'C', who was undoubtedly John

McCrea. Without mentioning precise locations in Kerry, this early report gave information about its scripture readers, 'Good, it would appear, is doing. The poor people receive them kindly and listen to them patiently.'[64] Six months later a report showed that family Bible-readings were taking place:

> How pleasant that some old unlettered creatures who probably have never understood a word of English and therefore had no practicable mode of obtaining even an imperfect idea of the wonderful works of God, should now have their own children reading to them at their evening firesides those things which the prophets and apostles wrote and spoke.[65]

In April 1825, it was reported that there were sixteen teachers and the 'circulating master' had 878 pupils on his books after only six months working in Kerry, 'the accounts from these quarters have been exceedingly encouraging.'[66] The circulating master gave a sense of the momentum, and even excitement, perceived by the Irish Society members, reporting that 'remote corners of Kerry [...] resound with the inquiry for "Irish books!" Never could I have expected that such a thirst for knowledge, and scriptural knowledge in particular, would so quickly be produced by any natural means.'[67]

The novelty of listening to readings in their own language was an important factor in attracting people, and an added incentive was that they themselves could learn to read also. One correspondent wrote graphically about 'the grey hairs and wrinkled foreheads of seventy, bending over the Irish primer to be enabled to consult the oracles for themselves in the language they understand, in the language which they love the dearest'.[68]

The Irish Society in Dingle

The first specific mention of the Dingle area is in a report of June 1825, written by 'K. D.':

> From what I observed in my short visit to Dingle, I am more convinced that in this and similarly circumstanced districts the objects of the Society are more likely to be attained than in the interior of the country, Irish being almost universally spoken in them, and the people feeling in consequence a prejudice in its favour

[...] Those who have got the scriptures in their hands look upon them with great respect and reverence.[69]

The author then advised scripture readers of the Irish Society to avoid controversies and

simply to get the scriptures into the hands of the people as quickly as possible, leaving the event to him who has promised that his word shall not return to him void. As far as I have opportunities of observing, those who have got the scriptures into their hands look upon them with great reverence and all seem anxious to obtain a whole New Testament in Irish, upon which they set such a high value.[70]

A. Jagoe was another representative of the Irish Society in Kerry, and he reported in April 1826 that 'the anxiety of the people to learn the Irish at all the places I have visited is really astonishing.' Jagoe found that 'the language of the people (at least two thirds of them) from Macroom to Killarney, Listowel and Liscarroll seems to be universally Irish.'[71] Jagoe mentioned experiences that he had in Kerry, 'Old men of 40, 50 and 66 years of age have come running across the country to meet me (as they told me) "to say their lessons".'[72] The people were willing to buy Irish books when they could afford to, rather than accept them as gifts, telling Jagoe, 'It is a pity to spur a free horse to death, sir.'[73] Jagoe specifically mentioned Dingle in relation to an experience that left him very impressed by the respect shown towards the scriptures:

One man (with four children of his) I examined on the roadside beyond Dingle; he took off his hat on beginning to read, which I desired him to put on again, it blew so hard, but he answered: 'Sir, I beg your pardon, it is the word of God'. As you may suppose, I was pleased with his answer and to show him that I was, I took off mine too.[74]

In April 1826, there were two inspectors of the Irish Society in Kerry, and sixteen schools with 450 scholars, of whom 199 were adults.[75] Confirmation of mounting interest in the Irish Bibles was given in the autumn of 1826 when J.B. McCrea wrote from Tralee, 'The anxiety of the people for Scriptural education is every day increasing in every part of the country;

and in one direction (the western or Dingle line) they are said to be "all on a blaze for the Irish scriptures."'[76]

Describing himself as superintendent of the Kerry district of the Irish Society, McCrea reported on 21 October 1826 that he had received a letter signed by thirty-three Irish teachers. McCrea sent the original of the letter to the Irish Society, apologising that it was 'rather stained, I suppose from being passed from hand to hand'.[77] The letter expressed approval and gratitude for the society's structured approach to the teaching of the Irish language. Its contents show that there was an increasing sense of goodwill and harmony, and of optimism for the future.[78] On 16 November 1826, McCrea referred in positive terms to progress in west Kerry, noting that curiosity was a factor:

> In the western part of the county, the circulating masters report, a very uncommon thirst for the circulation of the scriptures prevails. And persons not yet able to read with facility have earnestly solicited to be supplied with the Testament. Nor is it merely for the gratification of reading in their own language that this desire has been expressed, but in order to be satisfied 'what kind of book the scripture is' and 'to see what difference there is between the Roman Scriptures and the Protestant.'[79]

McCrea reported in autumn 1827 on 'a very growing attachment to the principles and operations of the Irish Society in the places where Irish schools have been for any length of time established'.[80] In May 1828, 'R.D.F.' reported that the opposition of the Roman Catholic clergy was the chief obstacle to further advancement, 'Were it not for that, your Society would have a school in every parish in the county.' He also said that there were two women competent to instruct others in the Irish scriptures.[81] As a sign of how keen the people were to read the Irish scriptures, a later report indicated how one man was willing to commit chapters of the Bible to memory and to pay £1 2s for an Irish dictionary.[82] This unattributed report noted that 'females have been very much neglected, very few indeed in the lower ranks can read.'[83] In October 1831, 'the great hindrance' again was the combined opposition by Roman Catholic clergy and that 'female education is miserably neglected, few are able to read or write.'[84]

Statistical returns for the whole of Kerry were listed in reports, but from October 1834 Kerry North and Kerry South appeared separately, and it was noted that the latter was 'only lately established'.[85] By 1835, Kerry

North had seventeen schools and Kerry South had three.[86] In July 1836, the area of Kerry West appeared in the records for the first time, and unlike the slow start by Kerry South, it was immediately listed as having ten schools and 435 pupils. Kerry North had twenty-four schools and Kerry South nine schools.[87] This coincides with the beginning of Charles Gayer's involvement with the Irish Society, as detailed in a later chapter. On the list of officers of the Irish Society heading the report of October 1834, Mr Thomas Moriarty also appears for the first time as an agent of the society.[88]

By 1837, the work of the Irish Society in Kerry was already drawing attention from supporters and observers of its progress. One prominent writer told her readers that 'the hitherto wild, lawless and discouraging region of Kerry is the scene of a work that will ere long astonish and shame such faint-hearted doubters as the boldest of us yet are.'[89]

The Irish language

The agents of the Irish Society were not committed to the Irish language itself; they taught it as a necessary means to their own ends, to win over learners to the truths of Protestantism. Neither were they interested in providing a broad general education. Most of those in the upper levels of the society's administration spoke no Irish, unlike the local teachers and readers. The founding members did not necessarily have a love for the Irish language or any interest in its preservation, and yet their society did help to preserve and promote it as a written language. In the long run, the society expected that students would be weaned off Irish and would adopt English. The preface to *An Irish and English Spelling Book* emphasised the benefit of the book as a means of learning English. It stated that the reader may:

> *through the means of translation*, acquire a knowledge of English with the greatest facility and to as great an extent as he pleases, nay, by the time he goes back a second time o'er this little book and treasures up in his mind the English words and phrases as explained in his native Irish, he will have a considerable stock of English words, a much greater number than he could possibly acquire in a long life, living in the midst of a family and a neighbourhood who speak nothing or little but Irish.[90]

Monck Mason admired and valued the Irish language, and he was instrumental in founding the chair of Irish in Trinity College Dublin in 1844. He believed that the experience of hearing Irish spoken by 'the Saxon and Protestant' was a welcome novelty and had 'a most signal and cheering' effect on relationships with the people, 'Nothing in fact has hitherto brought the conflicting sentiments of the different creeds and races into real communion and amity than the use of the Irish Bible.'[91] He dismissed objections from those who saw the Irish Society as promoting a worthless, dying language:

> It is not a fact that the Irish is a barbarous tongue; it has been, it is true, for a long time the vernacular idiom of a very uncivilised people, but it is an original language, the purest dialect of the Celtic [...] It is better suited to convey abstract truths to the minds of the unlearned than the English or any compounded tongue.[92]

In a shrewd observation, Monck Mason was pleased to note that in the places where the Irish Society had established itself, the English language had become more prevalent, 'This use of the Irish tongue, so far from tending to promote its continuance, has the direct contrary effect.'[93] He cited a story about a bishop on the Isle of Man who found a sure way of bringing the Manx language into disuse – by having it generally taught.[94] Monck Mason responded to the claim that Irish was already a dying language by arguing that the population was steadily growing and that the language would linger on in remote areas, and so the work of the Irish Society was still necessary.[95]

In an anonymous pamphlet written for distribution in England in 1842, the policy of the Irish Society was made explicit for the benefit of its English supporters. A branch of the society was being set up in Cambridge, and in an appeal for support, it was explained that in areas where the society was working, 'the English tongue is only half understood, when at all, and leaves the heart untouched.' One objection was anticipated:

> But perhaps some will say: 'You are striving to keep up a barbarous language, a badge of independence and enmity to England'. Not so – the educated are more likely to turn to the English tongue as being the only channel of further knowledge, than those utterly untaught. Many a generation may yet pass ere the language of the Irish is extinct; meanwhile it is the key to their hearts and they can be easily induced to read the Book of Books in that language when they would reject it with inveterate enmity if presented in the language of the Sassenach.[96]

Some scholars are emphatic in stating that the use of Irish by the Irish Society and other evangelical agencies 'was not meant to strengthen the language'.[97] However, others argue that it did strengthen it. Muiris Mac Conghail wrote that 'the Bible reading activity and the basic teaching of reading and writing from the primers which were distributed throughout Corca Dhuibhne must account for some of the literacy skills which the community acquired.'[98]

Tomás Ó Criomhthain was the first and most influential Blasket Island author; his books were published in the early twentieth century. He was born on the Great Blasket around 1854, and his parents would certainly have been aware of the Protestant mission school there and the Irish primers that were in use. Copies of primers and scripture extracts would probably have remained in the homes of the island even after the mission school had closed. Whelan stated that it was believed locally that Ó Criomhthain, 'the greatest of the Blasket writers, learned to read in Irish from the primers issued by the Irish Society'.[99] Seán Ó Criomhthain, son of Tomás, said that his father had learned to read and write Irish from relatives with whom he often stayed in Dunquin. They had learned to read Irish from the scripture readers, referred to as *léitheoirí an chait bhric* – literally, the speckled-cat readers.[100]

The enrichment that the Irish Bible brought to the lives of new readers is illustrated in a story from a northern district. A priest there was violently opposed to the Irish Society's work, particularly after learning that in Clontibret, Co. Monaghan, eight of thirteen Bible readers had become Protestants. He called to the house of the Irish Society teacher and, finding the man absent, berated his wife, telling her that she was living with two devils, her husband and the Irish Bible. He then picked up the Bible and some tracts and threw them into the fire. The teacher's mother, long accustomed to listening to her son reading from the Bible, was distraught at the priest's action:

> and in an agony of grief, uttered in Irish (in which they were much stronger and more expressive that they are in the translation) the following exclamations: 'Oh God! Oh God! Now is burned the book of books, and father of all good stories; there were stories in it from heaven, stories from angels; oh, yes! and stories of Jesus, stories of his apostles and saints; and amidst all was the dreadful – but oh, the joyful for sinners – the story of the crucifying Friday! Oh, it's burnt, it's burnt – the book of my soul, the book of my heart, the book of my saviour!'[101]

As a gloss on the phrase 'father of all good stories', the unknown author commented, 'The oriental turn of expression is here plainly observable.' In a concluding remark meant to assure evangelical readers that divine retribution followed, the author added that the priest went swimming in the sea two days after this incident and was drowned.

The use of Irish in church services

As a fluent Irish speaker, Rev. Thomas Moriarty was certain that a knowledge of the Irish language was very advantageous in his work. 'Speak little or much of Irish,' he told a meeting of the Kerry Auxiliary of the Irish Society in 1844, 'the people have a reverence for anyone addressing them in that language.' He referred to 'a mid-wall of partition' that could be 'broken down by the music of the Irish tongue'.[102] In Moriarty's view, Protestants should oppose English prayers for Irish-speaking people as strongly as they opposed Latin prayers.[103] At a fund-raising meeting in Winchester in 1857, he outlined how the Irish language had been neglected by Protestants and told his audience, 'The Irish tongue is no patois, no brogue of the English, but a pure language, whereas the English is a conglomeration.'[104] In an address to members of the Irish Society in Cork, Moriarty was proud to declare that 'their church, and their church alone, produced for Ireland a Bible in the native tongue, for which it deserved the name of the National Church'. While many Catholic priests and bishops were fluent in Irish, Moriarty believed that they had 'some hidden reason for not giving the word of God in the national language'. He claimed that a priest in Ventry had thrown part of an Irish Bible into a fire and told his audience:

> It was therefore important to have it known that the Protestant church alone circulated the scriptures in the Irish tongue and spent money and labour in enabling the peasantry to read them, that they spent money on inspectors and gave their own time and talent in the midst of all persecution, shame and reproach, peril and danger, because they loved their country and the people [...] It should be known that though they knew English well, the Roman Catholics could not be reached by it, for obstacles sprung up in their minds against the Protestant religion when explained in English, but the Irish language removed all the prejudices felt to their religion in the sassenagh [English] garb.[105]

Just as the poetry of the Bible worked its power on those who were enabled to read it in their own language, the richness of the Irish language also had an enchanting effect on some of those who encountered it for the first time. In 1880, Canon Samuel Hayman, who is best known as a historian of Youghal, Co. Cork, and who first learned Irish when he was in Glanworth, wrote admiringly of the language, 'Irish is older by centuries than the Greek of Homer and it is yet a living, spoken language – so pathetic, so copious that the proverb runs: "If you plead for your life, plead in Irish".'[106] Hayman also quoted Charlotte Elizabeth Tonna as 'enthusiastically exclaiming', 'If aught could bring me grief in heaven, it would be, when standing alone among those redeemed out of every kindred and tongue and people and nation, to listen and share in their glad acclaim, *if the Irish language was unspoken there*.'[107] Charlotte Elizabeth marvelled at the survival of the Irish language over centuries and advised her fellow evangelicals, 'Destroy it not, for a blessing is in it.'[108] At a meeting of the Irish Society of London in 1843, Rev. Edward Nixon of Castletown, Co. Meath, countered the charge that the Irish language was 'barbarous'. He said, to cheers from the audience, that 'if there was only to be one language in Ireland, he would say let it be the tongue which was the most pure and that was the native language of the country.'[109]

Elizabeth Colthurst, a Cork-born poet and evangelical who lived for a time in Danesfort, Killarney, also appreciated the Irish language. She wrote for English readers in order to elicit financial support for the mission in west Kerry. Colthurst published several short books of morality tales and sentimental verses intended to instruct and inspire older children. Two of these were entitled *Tales of Erin* and *The Little Ones of Innisfail, or The Children of God*, published in the 1840s.

This is Colthurst's description of a religious ceremony conducted through Irish in west Kerry:

> My readers in all probability have never heard the Irish language and perhaps only heard of it as a combination of barbarous sounds. They can then have very little idea of the deep heart-touching pathos with which these poor people, men women and children, made their responses in our beautiful liturgy.[110]

3. Thomas Dowling, inspector of the Irish Society

Thomas P. Dowling was one of the key figures working in Kerry on behalf of the Irish Society. His surname was sometimes rendered as Dooling, a spelling reflecting the Anglicised form of the Irish name Ó Dúlaing or Ó Dúnlaing. Thomas Dowling was a native of the Abbeydorney area in north Kerry, possibly the Fortwilliam townland. He was born around 1787 and emigrated to London, where he worked on the docks. He was raised a Catholic, and he was an Irish speaker but could not read the language. He also spoke and read English. Dowling was a friend of the poet Seán Ó Braonáin, who was born near Ardfert. The poet was greatly dismayed when his friend converted to Protestantism; he addressed several poems to him, appealing to him to return to the faith of his forefathers. One began, 'A dhuine gan chéill do mhaisligh an chléir' (O foolish man, who insulted the clergy), and another began, 'A dhuine tug aithis is masla dot shinsear' (You who disgraced and insulted your forebears).[1]

While in London, Dowling came under the influence of Thaddeus (Thady) Connellan, a Sligo writer and scholar who was fluent in Irish. Connellan converted to Protestantism and worked on behalf of the Irish Society. A religious periodical of 1844 stated that Dowling was employed as a teacher of Irish in London by Lord Teignmouth, who then transferred him to Bristol as master of the Irish school for labourers on the docks there. This source stated that while Dowling was instructing others, 'it pleased God to open his heart and mind to the truths of scripture, and forsaking the errors of Rome, he embraced with joy the gospel of salvation.'[2]

Another account of Dowling's experience in London was given at an Irish Society meeting in Chelmsford in England, which was 'very thinly attended and the greater number of those present were ladies'.[3] Rev. D'Arcy Sirr, a visiting speaker from Ireland, told his audience that Dowling learned to read Irish in London, 'where a party of Irishmen were assembled in the back premises of a physician in Percy Street'. When the group had achieved some proficiency, Lord Teignmouth, William Wilberforce and others visited the room, 'and seeing what was going on applied themselves diligently to the promotion of the work.'[4]

Innisfail

Dowling's personal history is available in a book entitled *Innisfail; or the Irish Scripture Reader*, edited by Joseph Wilson and published in 1841. This is one of the earliest accounts of the progress of the conversion campaign in Dingle and west Kerry. In the preface, Wilson gave his home address as Clapham Common, London, and stated that 'the manuscript of the following tales was placed in my hands by the author', with a request for Wilson's advice on how it might help English readers to understand the work of a scripture reader in Ireland. The author was not named. The manuscript had already been circulated among friends of the Irish Society in Ireland. Wilson had visited Ireland and supported 'the blessed work of scriptural instruction'. He vouched for the truth of all that was in the book, which was clearly written to elicit funding for the conversion campaign. The opening words of the introduction are meant to convey a sense of the exhilaration felt by people who learned to read the Bible in their own language, '"Why were these things kept so long from us?" said a poor Irishman when he had learned to read in his native tongue the glad tidings of redeeming love.'[5]

As the subtitle of the book indicates, most of the experiences recounted in the book are those of a scripture reader who is undoubtedly Thomas Dowling. He is referred to as 'D', and he is praised in a reference to 'the independent yet humble demeanour, the unobtrusive yet self-collected bearing of D, though but a poor Irish inspector'.[6] Dowling was a charismatic figure who drew admiration and respect, and this undoubtedly helped in his missionary work. The author of *Innisfail* captured something of his personality, 'There was a simple earnestness in the manner of [Dowling], a kindling up of countenance as he spoke, a smile on the lip when his theme was one of joy, and a sadness in the eye when he dwelt upon any darker shade of his people's character.'[7]

One chapter of *Innisfail* is entitled 'The Kerryman's welcome to the First Irish Testament'. It describes Dowling's early experiences in England, written as a dialogue:

It is now twenty years since I brought the first Irish Testament to Kerry, said D, all the way from England; and to be sure, the reception which it met with in my own dear native country seemed a fair promise of the blessing which has since attended it by night and by day.

And what took you to England, D?

Oh, I was dwelling for some years in that noble country, next to our own the finest in the world, and dear it should be to my heart, for I went there in darkness and returned in light. It would be too long now to say how the change came about, but it was through meeting a countryman of my own and reading the Irish scriptures, our hearts struck close together in the strange land, and closer still as the chains fell off. Yes! I may well bless my visit to England, though I could not stay there.

And why not, D?

The thoughts of my own poor country would not leave me on my bed at night and at my work by day, its picture was before me, in tears and want and ignorance, wounded and having none to heal, and I knowing the cure, I couldn't stand it. So I gave up all – my good situation, my prospects of worldly advancement, and landed once more in Kerry with the first Irish Bibles that were ever seen there.[8]

Another account by Miss Mahon, 'the much respected secretary of the Ladies Auxiliary Irish Society', said that Dowling was in London when he saw a small notice in a window that read, 'Persons are taught here to read the Irish language'.[9] Mahon explained to readers that the Irish language was 'that tongue which has such a talismanic effect on the Irish heart'.[10] She also mentions that Dowling was influenced by Thady Connellan, and that he was acquainted also with Mr Wilberforce and 'Lord T', most likely Lord Teignmouth. This account says that Dowling was in London 'about 35 years ago', which would place him there in 1814. Miss Mahon wrote that Dowling returned to Kerry after two years, and later became associated with the Irish Society.

Rev. Edward Norman wrote an account of Thomas Dowling's experience in England and locates his first involvement with Thady Connellan in the St Giles district of London 'in or about the year 1818', when Dowling saw a notice inviting people to learn to read Irish. The notice had been placed by Connellan, who told Dowling that no payment was required for the classes but added, 'If I teach you to read, you must promise me that you will teach ten others and teach none that will not give you the same promise.'[11] Dowling answered that nothing could be fairer or cheaper than that and accepted the terms. Norman wrote that, as well as teaching Dowling to read Irish, Connellan introduced him to the Bible, leading to Dowling's conversion. He then returned to Kerry to bring the truths he had discovered to 'his brethren, his kinsmen according to the flesh'.[12]

Dowling's return to Kerry

As a witness in a court case in 1843, Dowling stated that his activity as an itinerant preacher predated his role with the Irish Society. He said he had been 'a long time connected with the Irish Society, but went about the country reading the scriptures before the Society was established'.[13] In the course of sixteen years of this 'wandering life, reading to and instructing any who would listen to him', Dowling is reported as visiting the great Catholic institutions, Clongowes Wood College and Maynooth College. Students gathered around to listen, and Dowling sold four Bibles in one college but was turned out of the other one. All this work was done without remuneration, except for the award of a golden guinea by the Hebrew Society.[14]

At some point, Dowling came to the attention of the Knight of Kerry, Right Honourable Maurice Fitzgerald, who was impressed by him and wrote in November 1819, 'I intend him to be my permanent schoolmaster.'[15] The Knight's main residence was on Valentia Island, and he was a supporter of the evangelical movement. He wrote that 'nothing can exceed the *rage* of the people for reading their own language.'[16] In 1820, Dowling was described as an employee of the Irish Society under the patronage of the Knight of Kerry. By then Dowling was back in Kerry as an itinerant teacher distributing books for people to read. The Knight continued to think highly of him and his work, and he observed that 'the old people take great delight in hearing these books read by their children [...] They want dictionaries much and anxiously look for a grammar.'[17] There are records of various books of the Bible being granted to Dowling from 1821. For example, in December 1822 he was granted one hundred copies of Proverbs, one hundred Pentateuchs and two hundred New Testaments.[18] In September 1821, Dowling was in his home area of Fortwilliam, acting as master of an Irish Society school that met daily from 7.00 p.m. to 9.00 p.m. Between 1823 and 1826, he was 'circulating master' for Cork and Kerry, starting with a salary of £12 per annum, rising to £20 per annum in 1826. In 1827 he became an inspector for the Kerry district, and in 1837 he received £12 in recognition of his long service to the Irish Society. This may have been on the occasion of his departure from west

Kerry to the Brosna and Feale Bridge area of north Kerry, where he worked in association with Rev. Edward Norman in establishing a community of converts.

First responses in Kerry were disappointing for Dowling but he persisted, no doubt keeping the motto of the Irish Society in his mind, 'prayer, perseverance, patience and punctuality'.[19] He travelled around the south-west and was a boatman in Killarney, where 'after spending a day rowing parties on the lake, he used to have his school about him in the evening, teaching the Bible.'[20] Dowling found that while Irish was 'almost universally spoken' in Kerry, only about 200 people could read the language. These included five diocesan priests and Daniel O'Connell, who, according to Dowling, was 'the best Irish scholar he had ever met with'.[21] Edward Norman vouched for the fact that O'Connell 'always had a kindly greeting' for Dowling.[22]

Dowling gave an evocative description of his conversion experience and how his first encounter with the Irish Bible affected him, 'I was in the depths of ignorance when I first of all took in hand the Irish Testament. It was then that the blessed Word which I was endeavouring to make out caught hold of my heart and never let it go, until one by one I was fairly beaten out of all my entrenchments, for I was, as it were, barricaded up, and fought hard before I would let myself be freed.'[23] His experience was not unique, he claimed, and he wrote with enthusiasm about the experience of other scripture readers and teachers:

> They begin with no wish but just to earn something by instructing others to read the Irish Bible. By and by, the word of God rubs off the scales and they see the light, at first dimly, then clearer and clearer, till the perfect day breaks in and they go on their way jumping for joy. Let only the word of God have free scope and it will work on; and why not?[24]

Other sources agree that although Dowling's conversion was gradual, it was unequivocal. Miss Mahon wrote that 'he had "set his face as a flint" against all the abominations of that corrupt [Roman Catholic] church', and in later years, there was scarcely any letter from Dowling that was not headed with the slogan 'No peace with popery'.[25] The *Christian's Monthly Magazine* said, 'While instructing others, it pleased God to open his heart and mind to the truth of scripture; and forsaking the errors of Rome he embraced with joy the gospel of salvation.'[26] Although most sources claim that Dowling was converted while he was in England, Monck Mason suggests that his conversion occurred in Ireland, after twelve years of work with the Irish Society:

> Thomas Dowling, like old Reilly of Kingscourt, commenced about 20 years ago, with the same indifference to anything but the language, to carry about and vend or distribute portions of the Irish scriptures in Kerry; he was paid an equally small salary and was similarly commissioned to raise up native teachers. For upwards of 12 years, he laboured without any result, except in a few individual, detached and not very promising cases; at length the word of God spoke through his spirit to Dowling's own heart and his usefulness, now multiplied and improved, was rewarded with the unexampled results in which he was at length privileged to participate.[27]

Thomas Dowling in west Kerry

Dowling was unquestionably a key figure in the early years of Bible reading in west Kerry, and particularly in Ventry. Norman wrote of him, 'I believe that in the formation of the various new congregations in the west of Kerry, there is not one in which he did not bear a part.'[28] Miss Mahon believed that 'much of the work of reformation now going on so prosperously in that county may be traced to his exertions [...] ere Mr. Gayer was raised up to labour in Dingle or Mr. Moriarty returned to preach in his native vales and mountains.'[29] She wrote that following his initial success, Dowling 'was not much engaged afterwards' in west Kerry but had served 'as the pioneer for more highly qualified labourers'.[30]

At first, there appears to have been an amicable relationship between Bible readers and at least some clergy of west Kerry. Dowling once read the Bible in a corner of a Catholic church while, in another corner, the priest heard confessions.[31] This relationship was not to last, however.

Rev. Charles Gayer arrived in Dingle in 1833 as chaplain to Lord Ventry. It was some years before Gayer learned of the activity of the Irish Society there, and perhaps it is a tribute to the discretion of the Bible readers that it took so long for their work to come to his notice. When Gayer did become aware of it, he offered his services as an agent of the society. He later became independent of it and led the missionary campaign in west Kerry, while Dowling left the district and concentrated his work in the north of the county, in association with Rev. Edward Norman.

Dowling described one of his interactions with Charles Gayer, during which he encouraged the latter's efforts. Dowling had been working with success in the Ventry area, and he assured Gayer that further progress could be made there:

And so I told our dear precious minister it would be at Ventry, though twelve months ago not one convert that is openly avowed could be found, I knew how many spent the long winter evenings over the Irish Bible; aye, and many an hour of night too; and when our other noble friend began to be disheartened, didn't I tell him to wait a little longer and he should see great things. And haven't my words more than come to pass? Look at Ventry![32]

Dowling's simple, infectious enthusiasm for his work and its gratifying, if slow, progress is perceptible in his writing:

It would have done your heart good to have been at the last meeting of the Irish teachers at Ventry. The schoolroom was full from top to bottom with teachers and scholars. At the upper end stood Mr. G[aye]r, myself at the lower, and the curate of Dingle on one side. When we had sang a hymn and prayed, Mr. G—r gave out the questions in English, my business being to translate them into Irish for the teachers, and to receive their answers again, giving the sense of them to Mr. G—r. It was fine to hear the scriptural replies of these poor unlearned men, many of them having contended for the truth and suffered for it too! And one (I mention his name with honour) Sullivan was the first who had the courage in the face of day, of the people and of the priest (for himself was walking down the road with the horsewhip in his hand) to bring his infant into the schoolhouse to be publicly baptised by Mr G—r.

These are the freemen of Kerry, the unshrinking hearts to whom she is to owe her true liberty; and to see them giving an answer for the hope that was in them, with the word of God in their hands, and his love in their hearts, standing in that very schoolroom which the Lord had prepared to shelter them, was enough to melt a heart of stone; and when the examination was over the curate says to Mr G—r: 'Never till this day did I feel the great value of the Irish Society. I had the advantage of you, for knowing Irish well, I understood the teachers' answers, and all I can say is that from this hour, you have me bound to the cause, heart and hand, forever.'

Was not that a nice hearing for Mr G—r and myself?[33]

Dowling looked forward to the time when Ventry would have its own Irish-speaking minister – something that happened in 1838, when Rev. Thomas Moriarty was appointed. In his account of the origins of the mission at Ventry, Moriarty stated that 'the first spark was kindled by the Irish teacher'. He was almost certainly referring to Dowling, but he added that 'it would soon have died away if Mr. Gayer had not taken it up.'[34]

When a new school was being built in Ventry, Dowling expressed his joy, and 'his honest countenance glowed with pleasure':

> I challenge the County Kerry [...] to match that schoolhouse in all respects; for size, it will hold two hundred and fifty of us, and as to situation it may defy the world. 'Oh, boys', said I when they began to tell me how the priest wished that his curse might be down upon the head of any one that aided in building that same schoolhouse, 'Boys', said I, 'don't you remember how, when the temple was rebuilding under Nehemiah, everyone with one of his hands wrought in the work and the other held a weapon? Now yours is God's own work.' And the saying pleased them greatly.[35]

Miss Mahon was told that during long winter evenings, candle-light in a cottage signified a group reading the Bible. She considered the progress remarkable, because a short time before, prejudice was so strong that the coffin of a Protestant child was taken out of a local graveyard and thrown on the roadside.[36] However, Thomas Dowling was not always welcomed in the villages of west Kerry. He was once attacked by an angry crowd in a place identified only as being near Sybil Head (Ceann Sibéal). Dowling's work had been condemned by a priest on the previous Sunday, and when he arrived in the area, he was met by a large, hostile crowd. When Dowling asked how he had offended them, one man replied, 'We are resolved to have your blood because we know you to be a spy and a turncoat and our priest told us last Sunday you have a hundred pounds from the government for everyone you can get to leave the true church.' A melee followed but Dowling was fortunate to escape without injury, finding a refuge in the home of Rev. George Gubbins at Ferriter's Cove.[37]

The author of *Innisfail* was a warm admirer of Dowling and his work:

Often we have seen him weary but never dispirited. The district over which the Irish Society has made him inspector, though extensive, is not as wide as the charity which impelled him to undertake fatiguing journeys beyond its limits, into the remoter parts of this most interesting country to speak a word of counsel or of comfort to those who knew not to express their wants and wishes by a syllable of English and most he delighted to tell of the love with which the converts to the truth in these solitary villages received him.[38]

Thomas Dowling's sincere faith and disarming naivety come across in his account of an annual meeting of the Irish Society, which he attended. The cadences of the Irish language and Dowling's pride in his native county are clear:

In Dublin city itself where I was called up lately to attend a meeting of the Irish Society in a grand room called the Rotunda, a noble lord (I believe his name was Lord Roden) addressed his discourse entirely to the Irish teachers, and if the tears did not come into our eyes and our hearts not burn within us at all the kind things he said and the way in which he said them [...] As to myself I don't know how I felt; my very heart was melted within me to see so many of the Lord's people assembled and Kerry cutting such a figure [...] There's no use in talking but it got the better of me entirely. The grand room and all the company began to swim before my eyes until I fairly wished myself back again in Dingle. But some way or other I was cheered and strength put into me by the wonderful things the Lord was doing for poor Ireland – the hundreds and the thousands that were reading the Bible in the native tongue at Kingscourt and elsewhere – but nothing to be compared to the great work at Ventry.[39]

Dowling was further encouraged when a Dublin lady invited him to her home after the meeting, where he was 'genteely treated and well examined and had a power of questions to answer about Ventry'.[40]

Thomas Dowling's fame as a teacher was acknowledged by leading members of the Irish Society and the wider evangelical movement, and among his many admirers was Rev. John Alcock, whose daughter described Dowling as 'a valued friend' of her father. To her, Dowling was

> a real hero in humble life, whose story, if faithfully told (as we hope it will one day) would abound in genuine romantic interest. Many an anecdote used Mr. Alcock to tell with a kindling eye and animated gesture of Tom Dowling's hair-breadth escapes, of the persecutions he suffered and the encouragements and successes that crowned his labours.[41]

One woman in west Kerry was grateful to Dowling for transforming her husband's behaviour by introducing him to the scriptures:

> Till Mr. D. came to this place I was the broken-hearted woman, striving to please Denis and could not; he was a most dreadful curser. The day he would be from home was always the happiest for me. Oh! What a glorious change to see my husband now, like a child in the house, reading God's books, teaching his children and advising me to live in peace with my neighbours.[42]

Dowling's encounter with Sir Hugh Gough

Rev. Edward Norman recounts one dramatic incident in Dowling's early career, which occurred near Buttevant, Co. Cork, in 1822. Because of illegal agitation by the secret agrarian society known as the Whiteboys, martial law was in force and a curfew was in operation, prohibiting night gatherings. One night, a party of soldiers saw a cottage lit up, and when they raided the house, they found a group of men sitting around a fire with a leader who read from a book in a strange language. This was Thomas Dowling conducting a Bible class. However, the soldiers believed the gathering was political, and that the men were plotting an outrage. The participants were taken into custody and appeared the next day before Sir Hugh Gough, the military commander, with the strong possibility that they would be found guilty of sedition and transported to Botany Bay. However, when Dowling met Gough, he asked, 'Has your honour a Bible? Will you please to get it?' Dowling then read and translated from his book while Gough read the same passage in his English Bible. As they conversed amicably, Dowling told Gough, 'If there was more Bible reading in Ireland, men would learn to be loyal to their king as well as to their God and there would be less need of you and the likes of you in the country.' Gough agreed.[43]

Gough promptly gave Dowling a pass, which read, 'Thomas Dowling is to pass and re-pass through my district at any hour of the day or night without let or hindrance. Hugh Gough, Commandant.'[44] Dowling proudly kept this pass with him, and Norman wrote that he had seen it. Dowling's own account of this incident does not mention the written pass, but he said that Gough sent him on his way with half-a-crown, advising him to have a good breakfast. Dowling continued, 'And whenever I happened to meet him after, no matter where it was or who was by, he would put out his hand to shake hands with me, and very useful I found the respect that he showed me in these times of rebuke and trouble.'[45]

Despite all these tributes, and the clear recognition of Dowling's role in the early years of the Bible campaign, A.M. Thompson's history of the Protestant mission in west Kerry has only one brief reference to him as 'Dolan, the Irish school inspector'.[46] Her intention appears to have been to play down his role and to give primacy to the work of her friend and associate, Rev. Charles Gayer, in bringing the Protestant message to west Kerry.

The death of Thomas Dowling

Thomas Dowling died on 8 June 1849 at his home in Strand Street, Tralee.[47] He was aged 62. The *Kerry Evening Post* wrote of his untiring zeal and energy in the cause of his adopted faith, in spite of all manner of persecution. His last illness 'was contracted in attending the dying bed of another true convert; it was not of long duration.' He remained true to Protestantism, and 'his mind was peaceful and rejoicing' in the face of death.[48]

A detailed account of the gruesome circumstances of Thomas Dowling's sudden death is available. During the cholera epidemic of 1849, he was at the bedside of a man who was dying of the disease in Tralee. The dying man was John Connell, a convert of fourteen years standing; a nailor by trade who lived in a forge with his pregnant wife and four children. It seems a rumour spread that Connell wished to return to the Catholic Church, and a priest was brought to the house. On learning that he was not welcome, the priest withdrew, but later 'a tumultuous mob assembled before the door of the dying man.'[49] Two Protestant ministers, Rev. Anthony Denny and Rev. William Scott, came to the house, and were hooted and abused. Thomas Dowling also came to the bedside. One person from the mob was invited inside to hear the assertion of the dying man, 'I will have no priest but the Lord Jesus Christ – Jesus is my great High Priest.' He repeated that he did not want to see a priest, and wished to have Rev. Scott attend to him. This still did not appease the crowd outside, which dispersed only when magistrates ordered the police to clear the street. The report in the *Post* was headed, 'Revolting conduct of the mob towards a poor convert dying of cholera', and it expressed horror and indignation at acts undertaken in the name of religion, especially in the middle of a raging cholera epidemic:

> Shame, black and eternal shame, upon those who give to such acts, the name or sanction of religion. Shame too be to all who cannot discern between the true spirit of Christianity and the furious bigotry of such doings as these, and shall we not cry shame also upon the teachers who have given no better instruction to their flocks than what is evidenced by such fruits.[50]

Inside the house of John Connell, another horrific drama with tragic consequences was being played out at his bedside. William Scott gave a graphic account of what occurred:

> As I bent over the dying man to breathe a word of gospel comfort into his ear, a rush of sickness came upon him so suddenly and with so great violence that before I could step aside, my hat which I held in my hand and some of my clothes were covered in an instant. Poor Dowling who stood by me immediately snatched away the hat and proceeded with affectionate solicitude to remove all traces of the accident from my person. On my forcing him to desist, he went to my house to fetch another.
>
> Through God's great mercy I experienced neither alarm nor injury, but with poor Dowling the case was different, for immediately on returning with my hat he complained of illness, and at my urgent entreaty retired to what proved to be his own deathbed.[51]

Thomas Dowling died of cholera three days later. Although at first he seemed to make a recovery under the care of a physician, 'the favourable change was transitory and illusory' and Dowling succumbed to a 'consecutive fever'.[52]

Scott had conversations with Dowling in his last hours and assured his readers that he died faithful to his beliefs. He asked Dowling about the state of his soul and received the reply, 'Happy, sir, happy'. It was always significant when a dying convert remained steadfast in his new faith, as priests always predicted death-bed reversals. When Scott asked Dowling if he had any regrets about his conversion, he replied, 'Sorry, sir! Why should I be sorry? Is it for leaving darkness and finding light? For leaving error and finding truth? For quitting man and coming to God himself? [...] Oh, sir, how could I be sorry?' These replies were exactly what supporters of the Irish Society would have wished to read, but there is no reason to doubt Scott's account or Dowling's sincerity.[53]

Rev. William Scott paid a final tribute to Thomas Dowling, 'He has done his work, he has finished his testimony and has entered into his rest, leaving behind him a bright example of faith and love and of great usefulness.'[54] The burial service of 'Thomas Dooling, Irish scripture reader', in St Anna's, Blennerville, on 9 June 1849 was conducted by Rev. A.B. Rowan.[55] There is little information about Dowling's wife and family, but forty years after the encounter with Lord Gough, his widow was living in poor circumstances in an almshouse in Tralee. Rev. Edward Norman wished to help her by giving her 'a few shillings a week'.[56] Sir Hugh Gough was by then a very prominent military figure, hailed as 'the hero of the Punjab' after his victory over the Sikhs in India in 1848. Norman wrote to Gough, reminding him of his encounter with Dowling in 1822 and asking him for some assistance for Dowling's widow. Hugh Gough responded generously on that occasion and whenever Norman made the same request in subsequent years.[57]

4. D.P. Thompson and the Ventry estate

The 1st Baron Ventry was Thomas Mullins (1736–1824), who received the title in 1800 as a reward for the family's support for the Act of Union. Although various members of the Mullins family were very prominent at local and county level throughout the nineteenth century, there are few records of them. The longest account of the family has been published by Mícheál Ó Dubhshláine, who wrote that shadows and echoes of the Mullins family endured into modern times in Corca Duibhne, '[Tá] scáth agus macalla leo fós ann.'[1]

William Mullins, 2nd Lord Ventry

Thomas Mullins, 1st Baron Ventry, died in 1824. His son William succeeded him. Little is known about William, and he does not appear to have spent much time in Dingle, living mainly in France. In 1824, he unsuccessfully petitioned the Viceroy for permission to change his title from Baron Ventry to Baron Burnham. The reason he gave was that the name Ventry 'is obnoxious to a disagreeable and unpleasant interpretation in the continental languages and would expose memorialist to ridicule and contempt, rather than confer that degree of honour and respect which would otherwise attach to a nobleman of the United Kingdom while travelling abroad'. The Viceroy's response was that it would 'not be proper' to recommend this change.[2] (It is likely that Mullins was motivated by the fact that the French word 'vent' means 'wind'.)

In 1827, just three years after succeeding to the title, the 2nd Baron Ventry died at his residence, Chateau de la Cocherie, near Boulogne. He was greatly lamented there, as he was known to spend lavishly. The *Freeman's Journal* reported:

> Boulogne-sur-Mer has experienced a serious loss by the death of the lamented Lord Ventry, who has resided in that town for more than eight years, entertaining his countrymen in the most liberal, hospitable and kind manner and contributing greatly to the

prosperity of the place by the regularity of his payments and the expenditure of three or four thousand pounds per annum.[3]

Lord Ventry left £3,000 per annum to his widow, a legacy of £5,000 to a friend named R. Fenwick, and £1,500 to Miss Harding, described as a protégé of Lady Ventry. The rents of approximately 2,000 tenants in west Kerry no doubt financed this lifestyle, and it appears that his estate was mismanaged and effectively bankrupt by 1827. Encumbrances on the estate were referred to in a court case nine years later.[4]

Thomas Townsend Aremberg Mullins, 3rd Lord Ventry

The 2nd Lord Ventry had no male heir; the title and lands fell to his nephew, Thomas Townsend Aremberg Mullins (1786–1868), who became 3rd Baron Ventry in 1827. Thomas T.A. Mullins was a career soldier who had fought against Napoleon in the Peninsular War in the battles of Busaco (1810) and Albuera (1811). He was severely wounded in Albuera and walked with a limp as a result. He is remembered in Corca Dhuibhne as 'an tiarna bacach' – the lame lord. It seems that he was wounded and lay overnight on the field of battle, until he was carried to safety by a Portuguese man named Jose, who spent the rest of his life in the service of Lord Ventry. Thomas Mullins held sway over the tenants and lands of Corca Dhuibhne until his death, spanning many turbulent and tragic years. However, it appears that he never actually came into complete possession of the whole estate. The Master of the Rolls (Sir Michael O'Loghlen, a senior judge) said in 1839 that according to 'a singular provision in the will of the late Lord Ventry', the current Lord 'does not possess the estate, yet he does represent the interest of his son'. The estate was held in chancery and was managed by a receiver.[5]

The residence of Lord Ventry was Burnham House, which Charles Smith, in 1756, described as 'situated very pleasantly on the south-west side of Dingle harbour, of which it commands an agreeable prospect'.[6] The building is now part of a second-level school named Coláiste Íde and still retains its view across the bay. Thomas T.A. Mullins and his wife Eliza gave their strong support to the evangelical cause in west Kerry. In 1833, he appointed an English clergyman named Charles Gayer as his chaplain, a decision which led to the intensification of the campaign of proselytising that had a profound impact on the area.

The original family name, Mullins, was formally changed to de Moleyns by the 3rd Lord in 1841, in a stratagem to enhance the family's prestige. Writing about the land conflict of the 1880s, Michael Davitt scoffed at how 'the plebeian name of Mullins was changed to "de Moleyns" by royal licence.[7] (In a satirical work published in 1852, William Makepeace Thackeray wrote about a Welsh family named Muggins, one of whom discovered in 'a genealogy found out for him by *Fluke's Peerage*' that the original family name was de Mogyns, 'one of the most ancient families of Wales'. Thackeray may have been inspired by the Mullins/de Moleyns family.[8])

Kerry newspapers

The *Tralee Mercury*, the *Kerry Evening Post* and the *Western Herald* were the main Kerry newspapers during the 1830s. The *Post* was a venerable institution by this time, having been founded around 1775. The *Mercury* was established in 1829 and survived for ten years. The first edition named the printer as John Flynn of Castle Street, Tralee; he was also the owner and editor. The first editorial announced that the paper was meeting the need for 'a liberal and independent local journal' and said that its aim was to 'represent the people and advocate their rights'. It promised that the paper would be 'independent in every sense of the word – undaunted, unpurchaseable and unpurchased'.[9] The *Mercury* was clearly setting itself in opposition to the *Post*, which was unionist, Protestant and Tory. In 1830, the editor of the *Mercury* reaffirmed its role as 'vindicator of popular rights'.[10] *Chute's Western Herald* was also published in Tralee from 1791, and in October 1828, its title was changed to *The Western Herald or Tralee and Killarney Advertiser*. The editor was Thomas Day.

Poverty in west Kerry

The *Tralee Mercury* applied the spotlight of public exposure to landlords' actions during conflicts over rent and tithes. In the summer of 1831, it ran a strong editorial condemning 'the grinding tyranny of many, alas, *very* many landed proprietors'.[11] Two instances of extreme poverty in the Dingle area were cited. One account was of young women who were so poor that they used to join together in order to buy one cloak or shawl between them, which they would then wear in turn on Sundays. The second account was more shocking. Three families were reported to have been exempted by priests from the obligation of attending Mass on Sunday because 'they are not in a position to appear in public – they are naked.' The *Mercury* made a provocative contrast:

> Thus, while the land is covered with plenty, when the landlords and their wives, the parsons and their concubines, appear clothed 'in

purple and fine linen and fare sumptuously every day', the people who administer to their luxuries – the aborigines, as they are sneeringly called by the descendants of Cromwell's troopers – are *naked*, absolutely stark naked. The land is not naked – no, quite the reverse – but the people who cultivate that fair land and who were once its rightful owners are in a state of nudity which shuts them out from all intercourse with their kind, debases and brutalises their minds and feelings and forcibly reminds us of that primeval vesture worn by the mother of all mankind when guilt, and its consequence shame, became the inmates of her bosom.[12]

Support for the *Mercury* came from a correspondent who wrote scornfully of the Mullins family, 'We are yet to learn the vast advantages this country has acquired by their residence among us, the works of public utility they have encouraged, the institutions they have fostered.' The correspondent claimed that Lord Ventry had refused to support a plan by a priest to build a school, saying he could not support popery. The writer also shed light on the estate management:

The first Lord Ventry created amongst his tenantry a vast competition for land, for which, provided he was promised double the value, he was not over particular as to his inquiries about the solvency of a tenant, his darling ambition being through a long life to exhibit a large ideal rent roll. Sometime previous to his demise, he ordered some arrears to be forgiven which he knew could never be collected, and in the depression of the times, some abatements were made by his successors on the purchase property. These however were afterwards ably recovered.[13]

By way of contrast, the writer praised another landowner of Corca Dhuibhne, Lord Cork, 'whose tenantry are very comfortable where they hold under him'. The Earl of Cork held the Blasket Islands and other areas west of Dingle. The agent of Lord Cork was Miss Clarissa Hussey, a devout Catholic.

Lord Ventry spent much of his time abroad, but 'Lord and Lady Ventry and suite' travelled to Burnham in 1832.[14] He then became more directly involved in the management of his estates. In an apparent action to impose the tithe more stringently, Lord Ventry was reported as having been near Dunquin with a detachment of the 32nd Reserves 'protecting the valuators of the tithes'.[15] During 1833 there were several public controversies and

Lord Ventry's evangelical interests were referred to in some newspaper accounts of incidents, particularly in the *Mercury*. The month of May 1833 saw more intense criticism of Lord Ventry himself, when a military force was drafted into Dingle to help collect the tithes. The *Western Herald* reported, 'A detachment of the 77th has marched hence for Dingle to assist the persecuted clergy of the Established Church in the collection of tithes, so long withheld.'[16]

Fr Thomas Healy's letter on Lord Ventry

In 1834, the parish priest of Cloghane, Fr Thomas Healy, wrote to the *Mercury* to complain that Lord Ventry did not contribute to a fund for the support of poor people who had suffered during a cholera epidemic. The outbreak had recently made 'its wonted mischief' in Cloghane parish, the greater part of which was in the estate of Lord Ventry.[17] Of twenty-six victims, nineteen had died, three had recovered and the others were still sick. Fr Healy called to see Lord Ventry, relying on his 'reputed religious character' for generous support such as other landlords in Kerry had offered to their tenants. Healy described the condition of some of his parishioners as a result of the epidemic: a widow had no income after the deaths of her husband, her father-in-law, her mother-in-law and two of her children; another widow had no food and no night covering for her or her children except for one blanket, which had covered her husband until his death.

Healy gave a vivid report of his meeting with Lord Ventry and the 'ungraciousness' of his response to the request for aid:

> When pressed for an answer you said you could give no relief. When reasoned with, your Lordship then said you could not and would not give relief, giving reason that your property was withheld from you by the people, and did not leave you the means of giving charity, as also that your residing in the country and spending your income there, ought to excuse you from demands of this kind. Now, my Lord, I say that your tenants of Cloghane have not withheld any property from you, as they pay their rent punctually […]

> As to your residence in this country, I call on your Lordship to say what benefit did your Cloghane tenants derive from it. Did you give them employment? No. Did you encourage them to bring into cultivation the coarse (and now waste) lands in your Lordship's estate? No. Did you make them any allowance in order to render

their present miserable habitations decent or comfortable? No. Did you give any sum whatsoever for any charitable purpose within the parish of Cloghane? No.

I am at a loss then to know what benefit your Lordship conferred on them by your residence. I now conclude, my Lord, by leaving the public to judge of your Lordship's charitable and benevolent disposition.[18]

It took courage for the priest to challenge the landlord so directly, and to publish an account of a conversation that Lord Ventry might well have expected to be private. Priests generally were discouraged by their bishops from open defiance of landlords, and the publication of this letter must surely have ensured that there could be no future co-operation between the two men. The *Post* responded to Fr Healy's charge by pointing out that Lord Ventry had already given the sum of £5 for poor relief to the Church of Ireland rector of Cloghane, Rev. Richard Legge Tyner. It commented, 'No landed proprietor in this county acts more conscientiously, with more kindness of heart, or with more scrupulous and honourable rectitude towards his tenantry, towards the poor in his vicinity and on his estates, than the nobleman who has been thus wantonly and innocently assailed.'[19]

In 1834, Lord and Lady Ventry left Dingle for England, where they proposed to stay 'for some years'.[20] They had taken a house at Lymington in Hampshire, 'within view of the charming Isle of Wight'. According to a fawning report in the *Post*, their 'well-known benevolence, charity and affability have rendered their departure, even for a season, a source of deep regret to the poor in the neighbourhood of Burnham House and on his extensive estates in this county'.[21] The Ventry couple were in Ryde in 1836.[22] In 1839, Lord Ventry was reported as residing in Boulogne-sur-Mer, but a later report retracted this.[23] The couple did not return to Dingle until 1841, when there were celebrations to welcome them back.

David Peter Thompson, agent of the Ventry estate
According to an affidavit sworn by David Peter Thompson in 1840, his connection with Dingle began in 1830 when he was appointed by the Court of Chancery as receiver of the estate of the Mullins family of Burnham House.[24] He was then living in Tralee, and his father held the office of Treasurer of County Kerry. Anna Maria Thompson, wife of David Peter, was his first cousin; her maiden name was also Thompson. They married in 1828,

when the groom's address was given as Stonestown and Park, King's County (Co. Offaly). Anna Maria's father George lived in Clonskeagh Castle in south Dublin. Her forenames are mentioned twice in Burke's *Irish Family Records*, once as Anne Mary and once as Anna Maria.[25]

During a severe food crisis in Tralee, a relief committee decided to set up 'a public soup kitchen, to be placed under the direction of some benevolent ladies of this town'. The 'ladies of Tralee' duly formed a committee and set up a rota for making and distributing soup in areas of the town. One of the members was listed as 'Mrs. D. Thompson'.[26] Anna Maria had established an orphanage in Tralee, and she transferred this to Dingle when she and her husband moved there.

The Ventry estate was reported as having an annual income of £16,000, and D. P. Thompson was obliged to provide securities of £90,000 in order to be appointed receiver, promising to perform his duties 'with fidelity and impartiality'. This was a huge amount of money.[27] After the death of the 2nd Lord Ventry in 1827, the estate was in a state of neglect and mismanagement; Thompson's role from 1830 was to rescue it.

In March 1832, Thomas T.A. Mullins appointed Thompson as agent 'over his own property, amounting to £9,000 a year'.[28] This appears to have been separate from Thompson's role as receiver of the whole estate. There were approximately 2,000 tenants on Lord Ventry's property, and rents generated an income of £9,000 a year.[29] Thompson was involved in civil and religious affairs in Dingle for the following fourteen years. He collaborated with Rev. Charles Gayer in the evangelical mission, with Thompson's expertise in financial affairs and property management proving useful. Thompson and his wife and family lived at Burnham House until Lord and Lady Ventry returned in 1841; at this point, they moved to Ballintaggart House on the other side of the town.[30] They remained there until tragedy struck in January 1845, when Thompson died suddenly.

The *Kerry Examiner*

During 1839, the *Tralee Mercury* regularly advertised that it was for sale.[31] Edward Lynch, its owner and editor, had died; ownership had passed to his brother John. In the final issue of 20 June 1839, a notice from James Eagar stated that he had just bought the *Mercury* and that it would cease publication temporarily because he had been 'seized with a debilitating illness'.[32] Eagar was a member of the family that owned the *Post*, and since the *Mercury* never again appeared, it seems that it was bought only in order to close it down and silence its voice. If so, the tactic did not work, because within a year, a more strident and more effective newspaper representing popular causes was established in Tralee. This was the *Kerry Examiner and Munster General Observer*, first published on 11 August 1840.

The *Kerry Examiner* was founded by Patrick Robert O'Loughlin Byrne as proprietor, with William Raymond as printer. Byrne was from Hawthorn, Co. Wicklow, and apparently had no connection with Kerry until he founded the newspaper. He married Margaret O'Halloran in Tralee in December 1841; she was the daughter of James of Coolnaleen House, Co. Kerry.[33]

P.R. Byrne was a remarkable man: a controversialist, a nationalist and a fervent supporter of the Catholic Church and its clergy. He was also an able journalist and businessman, and his newspaper later played a central role in recording the sufferings of the people during the Famine years. In his first editorial, headed 'Our Principles and Opinions', Byrne wrote that he was conscious of 'the mighty moral agency of the public press', and that 'an honest and unshackled press is the source of incalculable good to mankind.' He outlined the policies of his paper, among which were the extension of the right to vote to all householders (until 'a real, a true and safe system of universal suffrage is established') and the total abolition of tithes in name and nature. Byrne also expressed 'loyalty to the current government and to our interesting and illustrious Queen', but stated that 'in politics, we take our stand with the progressive reformers.'[34] He promised to address readers in language that would be 'bold, without violence, unsparing of the delinquencies of public men and public measures', adding, 'on no occasion will it descend to low abuse or personal scurrility.' As owner and editor, Byrne promised that he would never 'give vent to any language which he believes inconsistent with his own character and dignity as a gentleman':

> Low, vulgar, coarse and scurrilous personality he repudiates and utterly condemns [...] We are for truth and for the establishment of the utmost purity of principle and practice [...] But let us not be misunderstood: we shall call crimes by their proper names and no matter what garb of concealment they assume, we shall tear off the guise and expose them in all their naked deformity [...] To the open, the determined enemies of Ireland and the unblushing calumniators of her people, we hold out no hopes of mercy from us so long as they and we co-exist on this side of the grave.[35]

The tone of the paper would allow it to be read without offence, said Byrne, 'Nothing, however interesting, shall be raked into the columns of the

Examiner of an offensive, indelicate or immoral tendency, and while its advantages may be felt in the study, care shall be taken that it may with safety be laid on the table of the drawing room.' The paper would be beholden to nobody:

> It shall be, in the full and true sense of the word, the faithful organ of the people and the independent champion of their rights – no searching after patronage at the expense of principle, no smoothening down the asperities of truth for the paltry object of winning individual favour; unseduced by smiles, unawed by frowns, by the PEOPLE we shall stand or fall.[36]

The *Kerry Evening Post* described this manifesto as 'ultra-radical' and expressed its complete opposition to the extension of the ballot and 'the spirit of democracy', describing it as 'the greatest evil which could be inflicted on our land and its people'.[37]

Evictions of 1840

The actions of D.P. Thompson featured in the first edition of the *Examiner*, as they would in so many more in the few years of life remaining to him. This first report was about irregularities in the election of members of the board of guardians of the newly established Tralee Poor Law Union, of which Dingle was part. In the Kilgobbin electoral division, Thompson and Fr George O'Sullivan, parish priest of Castlegregory, charged each other with exercising undue influence on voters in favour of their respective candidates.

Another more serious conflict was reported in the *Examiner* on 25 August 1840, and it eventually reached the columns of the London *Times*. This concerned the eviction by D.P. Thompson of 230 tenants in the Ventry area. This issue of the *Examiner* has not survived, but fortunately, the relevant article was republished in full in the *Connaught Telegraph*.[38]

Under the heading 'The Exterminating System', the article described the evictions as 'a barbarous ejectment' and condemned 'the cruel and despotic conduct of a Mr. David Peter Thompson'. Fourteen heads of evicted families were named in the report, two widows and twelve men, all of whom were said to be willing and able to pay all the rent due. The families included a total of fifty-six children. After eviction, these families were 'lodged in the chapel at Ventry and no other prospect before them than beggary'. Another list of thirty-two heads of families who owed some part of their rents was also published, and these had a total of 130 children. The names of all the forty-six heads of family were followed by the number of children in the household, in parentheses, but remarkably, the mothers were not mentioned at all. Five widows are mentioned by name, but there could have been as many as forty-one other women who seem to have been omitted in calculating numbers evicted. The *Examiner* calculated that a total of 233 individuals had been 'tossed out on the high road under an inclement sky', but the number could have been as high as 274 if the wives had been included.

The night of the evictions, 16 August 1840, was very wet and cold, and the sub-sheriff who was involved was described as being moved to tears at the scenes he witnessed. He gave money to some of those evicted. One hundred people found shelter in the chapel of Ventry; 'the rest stowed themselves into two or three little mud cabins, not much larger nor more habitable than a pig sty.' The *Connaught Telegraph* judged the *Examiner's* report to be 'one of the most barbarous we have read'. It demanded that parliament should enact a law to prevent such evictions, and referred to similar occurrences in Connaught. It ended with a warning to named landlords:

> Hear this, ye Courtowns, Beresfords, Lortons, Charlevilles, Ventries, Thompsons, and all ye who act dishonourably and disgracefully towards your tenantry, and weep! A day of retribution – a fearful day – will yet arrive, when the oppressor and extortioner, against whom the curse of God is recorded, shall have to account before the throne of Him 'who watcheth the poor and consoleth the distressed'.[39]

Thompson's response to these claims appeared in the *Post*. He said that he had treated the defaulting tenants with 'unreasonable indulgence', to the point where he might even have left himself open to the charge of not performing his duty to his employer, Lord Ventry. If tenants could reduce arrears to one year, or even just promise to pay, he was prepared to allow them to stay on. Sixty farmers in Ventry alone were reinstated by virtue of these concessions, he wrote. It seems that the evictions were intended to show Thompson's determination to pursue legal proceedings against rent defaulters and tenants who refused to engage with him, thereby forcing them to face up to their debts. The total amount due in arrears was between £700 and £800.[40]

Thompson further stated that he had postponed the evictions three times. He said that he had to act in August 1840 or otherwise he would become personally responsible for the loss to the Ventry estate. He used 'no undue harshness', and the quiet and even good-natured demeanour of the people showed how well he was regarded by them, he claimed. He allowed tenants a fortnight in which to offer some payment and arranged for them to dig their potatoes during that time. He accused the *Examiner* of trying 'to excite the feelings and goad the prejudices of the peasantry to hostility towards me'.[41] Thompson further stated that it was his intention to restore every tenant who made an effort to pay even 'a moderate proportion of arrears', and he believed that tenants were being manipulated into thinking that he had not the power to evict them.[42]

This case was cited in *The Times* of London, which decided not to publish the name of the *Kerry Examiner*, so as not to give it any notoriety, and referred to it only as 'an obscure journal'. *The Times* declared, 'Many a land agent, especially of Protestant politics, has been murdered in Ireland on lighter charges of oppression than this libellous paper has forged against the Kerry manager.' The *Post* was pleased that 'the leading journal of Europe' should have taken note of the matter and was flattered by *The Times* reference to 'the more respectable columns of the *Kerry Evening Post*'.[43] P.R. Byrne's response was to castigate *The Times* as 'the leading journal of all baseness' and 'the notorious receptacle and sink of all that is black, foul, disgusting and atrocious'.[44] Byrne repeated that 'wholesale ejectments took place' on foot of 'rack-rent arrears' and insisted that Thompson, 'in a spirit of the grossest dishonesty', had furnished *The Times* with a one-sided account.

D.P. Thompson's libel action against *Kerry Examiner*

In the winter of 1840, Thompson initiated a libel case against the *Kerry Examiner*, claiming that its reports were written 'with the intention to hold him up to public contempt and ridicule'.[45] Six months later, the protracted libel case finally concluded with the judge approving Thompson's actions in issuing eviction notices. 'He had no alternative to adopt', said the judge; 'if persons do not pay their rent, were they to be suffered to remain in their holdings? On the contrary, was it not just and reasonable to remove them?' He ruled that Thompson did not act with 'malignant feelings', since he was simply carrying out his duty, 'which was to redeem the estate from the burden under which it was placed'. The judge added that this should be done 'without any unnecessary severity' and concluded that Thompson did try 'to mitigate the sufferings of the poor people as much as possible, consistently with the due discharge of his duty as an officer under the court of Chancery'.[46]

Patrick Robert Byrne was found guilty of libel and was sentenced to six months in jail, but he escaped a fine; Mr Raymond, the printer, was sentenced to one month in jail. The *Examiner* continued to publish and, in time-honoured fashion, a defiant Byrne depicted the result as a victory for him, provocatively repeating the headline 'The Exterminating System':

> An attempt has been made to victimise us, to compel us to surrender principle, honesty, honour and integrity, as if *we* were capable of quailing before the terrors of the law, when we knew we were invulnerable, encased in the impenetrable armour of truth and justice, with a righteous cause for our shield, our lance and buckler. Oppression has done its worst and the oppressors have been foiled.

> Six months imprisonment we may suffer, but it is a poor atonement to our oppressors and the oppressors of those in whose cause we have battled and for whom we are now doomed to imprisonment, that while we suffer six months incarceration, they have been obliged to pay something to the tune of *three hundred pounds* to accomplish an end in which they failed to the extent they sought. They thirsted for money to indemnify them for their costs – they failed and the voracious vultures know no bounds to their rage at being disappointed of their prey [...] We are, after all, the triumphant party, our enemies have been defeated in their greedy hopes.[47]

Byrne duly served time in Tralee jail, and he took a journalistic delight in writing at least two columns from his cell, again under the headline 'The Exterminating System'. The first began, 'As we gaze through the bars of our prison window, contemplating the lofty walls that terminate our view over the little area in front.' Byrne went on to declare 'his stern resolve to battle in the cause of justice and humanity, regardless of personal consequences to himself.'[48] He regretted the imprisonment of the unfortunate Mr Raymond but had no regrets about his own stance; he declared that he would have faced death rather than reveal the names of his sources. Byrne relished his role as a martyr for the cause of tenants' rights and the freedom of the press. The *Examiner*'s role as defender of the people was secure.

5. 'The Rev. Gospellers': George Gubbins and Charles Gayer

In January 1833, a Kerry newspaper published an account of an ascent of Mount Brandon from Faha, near Cloghane. In lyrical prose, one of the intrepid group of climbers described how they set out in the morning, 'ere the lark had sung his matin carol or the mountain eagle had shaken the dew-drops from his wings; the monarch of the day had not yet dawned upon our hemisphere, but the ruddy glow which suffused the eastern skies announced his approach.' A solitary eagle hovered above them as they walked along 'an extensive glen, encompassed with bold, craggy precipices, down which the winter torrents tumbled down into the little lakes which sparkled at the bottom'. The spectacular views from the summit were described in vivid detail. In the foreground, they saw a pile of stones and 'a rude altar' that was covered 'with scraps of dirty rags, rusty pins, old nails etc., the tokens of those who came to do penance under the auspices of St. Brandon, who gives his name to the mountain'.

The group was guided by a local Catholic woman who was described as being motivated by pleasure and by devotion, and the climb provided an insight for the group into the religious practice of what was often termed 'popery'. At the summit, the woman began to pace around 'muttering prayers with her bead in her hand' – saying the rosary. The writer believed that the listless expression on her face showed that she was performing mere lip service. 'How repugnant', he reflected, 'must such mockery be to him who must be worshipped "in spirit and in truth".' The writer's delight in the magnificent vistas evaporated as he launched into a diatribe against priests and their instruction to Catholics that 'the Bible is a dangerous book for every private person to peruse':

> The dark clouds of ignorance which are gathered on the minds of the deluded people cannot always remain, the Gospel light shall not always lie obscured, and may the time speedily approach when it shall dawn with unclouded brightness and disperse before its rays every vestige of Popish corruption.[1]

These observations convey the tone and spirit of the evangelical campaign that enveloped west Kerry during the 1830s and 1840s. It was driven by the conviction that a deluded and ignorant people must be rescued from popery and saved by the light of the gospel.

This was not how the campaign was perceived by the Catholic and nationalist writer Patrick Foley in 1907. His perspective is captured in this sentence, 'Then came the "Gospellers" with their soup and Bibles to feed the starving peasant into Protestantism.'[2] Foley expressed the traditional Catholic view of the evangelical campaign as a sophisticated, manipulative, devious and ignoble system of proselytising, funded by money from Britain, which succeeded only because people were so desperately poor and demoralised that they were willing to sell their souls for food, material reward and comfort. This view of the work of the evangelicals is closely bound with the belief that conversions were linked to the distribution of food relief during the tragic years of the Great Famine.

Anna Maria Thompson began her account of the Protestant mission in west Kerry with a lyrical description of Dingle bay:

> On its northern side, a very narrow passage between two bold rocky headlands opens into a small inner harbour, in which nestles the little town of Dingle, which, rising up the southern slope, enjoys a splendid view across the wide bay to the mountain range of the rugged barony of Iveragh. In this place there is now going on a remarkable work of reformation.[3]

At the beginning of the nineteenth century, she wrote, Protestant worshippers met in a room in the town and 'they were few and careless'. They were subjected to what she termed 'popish enmity', with cabbage stalks and other filth thrown at them as they went to church. Around 1807, a church was built in an ancient churchyard; this is the present St James's church. Thompson's first visit to Dingle was as a tourist around 1830, when 'the majestic scenery of this neighbourhood attracted some adventurous spirits even then, to explore its wilds.'[4]

A.M. Thompson referred to 'a very general belief' that the large numbers of converts in Corca Dhuibhne was 'owing chiefly if not entirely to the work of the Irish Society'.[5] She wished to emphasise that clergymen played a crucial role, and that the society was 'simply the ready handmaid of the faithful pastor'.[6] The book *Innisfail*, with Thomas Dowling's account of his work, had been published in 1841, and it is likely that Thompson had this account in mind when she made these comments. She clearly wished to have ministers such as George Gubbins, Charles Gayer and Thomas Moriarty credited with the great progress of 'the new reformation', and she refers to Thomas Dowling only once, simply describing him as 'one of these Irish readers' and naming him 'Dolan'.[7] Thompson was also keen to stress that 'no *single* agency has produced the outbreak from popery in this district'.[8] She did acknowledge the involvement of the Ladies Auxiliary Society, writing that once the teachers of the Irish Society had broken up the fallow ground, the scripture readers, supported by the Ladies Auxiliary Society, 'cast in the principal wheat by reading and expounding the word of life'.[9] The schools then continued the work.

The number of Protestants in west Kerry in the 1820s is difficult to establish, but it was a small community, and many of the original sixteenth century plantation settlers had become Catholics. After St James's church was built, more regular worship took place. The congregation at Sunday service in Dingle in 1830 could be as small as thirty people; by 1835 it had risen to about seventy. By the early 1840s, as a result of the evangelical campaign, approximately 250 converts were added to the congregation. St James's church was enlarged several times, and a new gallery was built to accommodate the numbers.[10]

Fr John Casey was parish priest of the extensive parish of Dunquin, Dunurlin, Kilmalkedar, Kilquane and Marhin. In 1835, he gave details of the names and numbers of Protestants in these areas. Pádraig de Brún has collated these figures to show that in 1826, there were 18 Protestants living there; in 1831, 122; in 1834, 107; in 1835, 85; and in 1851, 451.[11]

Rev. Arthur Blennerhassett Rowan was a Protestant minister from Tralee who became curate of Blennerville in 1824. It was he who invited Denis Browne and John Gregg to visit Kerry in 1829, and they received a 'singularly enthusiastic overture' from Rev. Goodman of Dingle.[12] Placards posted around Dingle advertised 'Sermon in Irish', and the visitors spoke in a room over the Market Hall. This visit from the two well-known preachers was a significant one for the Protestant community in west Kerry; it became part of the 'foundation story' of the evangelical movement there.

Rev. John Jebb

West Kerry was a remote, isolated part of the Church of Ireland diocese of Limerick, Ardfert and Aghadoe, where little pastoral work was being done and church regulations were only loosely followed. Rev. John Jebb, a newly ordained minister, was appointed as curate to the parish of Dunurlin

(Ballyferriter) in November 1830, and he visited the area immediately. His appointment was something of a formality, as he does not seem to have lived in the area. This first visit to Dunurlin was possibly his only one, but his observations and decisions – recorded in a letter now in the archives of Trinity College – were significant.[13] Rev. John Jebb later went to England and had a distinguished career as canon of Hereford cathedral.

John Jebb recorded the names of the Protestant clergymen attached to the west Kerry area in 1830 as Mr Hurly in Kildrum, Mr Franklin in Kilquane, Mr Keating in Ventry and Mr Tyner in Cloghane; Tyner was the only one who was resident in the area. Jebb had no criticism of any of these men and had a high regard for Tyner, describing him as 'a real blessing to this diocese'. Another minister named Barton had been appointed as chaplain to Lord Ventry, but he resigned the position in November 1830 on account of a dispute with his employer. Lord Ventry had made some unspecified, improper request of Rev. Barton; the latter resigned as a matter of principle. Jebb had no complaint against Barton and believed that he was 'a sincere and conscientious high churchman' and that Lord Ventry was 'fickle as the wind' – perhaps a play on the word 'vent'.

The elderly parson of Dingle was John Goodman, who was English-born and aged 75 in 1830. John Goodman had been curate of Dingle since 1780, vicar of Marhin and Dunquin from 1787 to 1817, vicar of Garfinagh (Garfinny) from 1787 to 1824, and rector of Kemerton in Gloucestershire from 1824 until his death in 1839.[14] Jebb was highly critical of Rev. John Goodman, 'His advanced years and total want of education render him quite inefficient, even had he any zeal for his profession, of which I am afraid he is wholly destitute.' Jebb made it clear that there was no suggestion of any impropriety on Goodman's part – it was simply that 'he has done as little as he could with any decency.'

Jebb made practical proposals for improving the provision of Protestant religious services in west Kerry and generously offered to give financial support out of his own means. A.M. Thompson lauded his 'praiseworthy zeal' in seeking a remedy for the abuses that were prevalent in west Kerry.[15] His proposals did not include any role for John Goodman because, as he wrote, 'one cannot make a silk purse out of a sow's ear'; nevertheless, he believed that 'it would be cruel to turn him adrift [as] he is very poor and thriftless.' He made a personal financial contribution to ensure John Goodman had an appropriate salary. The ultimate objective of Jebb's proposals was 'the nourishing and diffusing of the seed of Protestantism in a remote and extensive district'. He hoped that 'a nucleus might be formed, around which the scattered and lapsed Protestants (of which there are several in that part of the country from the neglect of former and distant generations) might rally.' There was no suggestion in Jebb's letter of any interest in the conversion of Catholics, although he noted that Catholics sometimes attended Protestant services and was amused that some 'have expressed themselves surprised <u>to find so much religion among Protestants</u>'.[16]

The Goodman family
Rev. John Goodman was descended from a family that had provided a bishop and several rectors to Kemerton parish in Gloucestershire since 1738. In 1832, he had the good fortune of inheriting a benefice from Kemerton, described as 'a perpetual advowson' valued at £700 a year 'to be continued in the family in perpetuity'.[17] This was a very substantial inheritance, especially considering how straitened his circumstances were when John Jebb first visited. In a plaque in St Nicholas's church, Kemerton, a list of rectors has several Goodman names, including John in 1832. He is the last Goodman to be listed, so the privilege must not have been inherited by his son. John Goodman died in 1839, having spent sixty years as curate of Dingle. An obituary described him as 'a gentleman of the utmost probity, a good husband and father, kind and charitable in disposition and a hospitable and sincere friend'. He was seen as a magistrate of 'long residence and knowledge of the country, [who] from the confidence reposed in his integrity by the country people, was often successful in reconciling their differences, and preventing ruinous litigation'.[18]

In 1830, John Goodman's son, Thomas Chute Goodman, was a young minister who had responsibility for the parishes of Dingle, Marhin and Dunquin. In Jebb's view, this was sufficient for one man. However, Jebb was scathing about Thomas Goodman's abilities. He saw him as 'far more respectable than his father', but, 'from his defective education and aboriginal habits, incompetent to act without assistance'. Neither of the Goodman ministers was particularly evangelical; they were content to serve the small numbers of existing Protestants without any proselytising or attempts to convert their Catholic neighbours and friends. The Goodman family were intimately connected with the heritage of Corca Dhuibhne and held in high regard among the people. Thomas was a fluent Irish speaker, and Irish was most likely the language of the household in the 1830s. The family had a great interest in traditional music; 'local memories recall evenings of music, song and dance at the Goodman's house in Ballyameen.'[19] These were probably the 'aboriginal habits' that offended John Jebb.

In January 1845, in the midst of bitter sectarian conflict in Dingle, an anonymous threat was issued to Protestant ministers; however, Thomas Goodman was excepted, 'Parson Goodman is a good man, he interfares with no man's religion.' (See Chapter 15.) Thomas Goodman's keen interest in Gaelic culture was passed on to his son James (1828–1896), who also became a clergyman and a renowned collector of traditional Irish music. James became Professor of Irish in Trinity College, where his manuscript collection of 2,300 Irish tunes is held. A statue to his memory stands in Skibbereen, Co. Cork, and a commemorative plaque was unveiled near the Goodman home in Baile Áimín (Ballyameen) in recent years. John Goodman, another son of Thomas, also became a clergyman; he was curate in Ventry for some time.[20]

Coast Guard service

Among the Protestants of Dingle and west Kerry were many officers and men of the Coast Guard service, based in six locations: Minard, Dingle, Ventry, Ferriter's Cove, Ballydavid and Brandon. The inspecting commander of the area was Captain John Bowie.[21] The service was known as the Water Guard or Preventative Boat Service until 1822, when it became the Coast Guard. It was an important arm of the state, comparable to the army, navy and police. It was the sea-based arm of revenue enforcement, responsible for maritime matters and customs and excise. Most Coast Guards were English and about two-thirds were Protestant. Many were retired from the naval service; when vessels ran into difficulties near the coast, their training and expertise helped in rescue operations.

John Jebb wrote that each of the Coast Guard stations west of Dingle had between thirty and forty occupants, including wives and families. They were involved with the local community and had 'gained the good will of the Popish priests by their various little acts of kindness'. Captain Bowie requested religious services for the men and their families; during his visit, Jebb conducted a service in the watchtower of the Coast Guard station at Dunurlin that was attended by forty-two people, among them two or three Catholics.

Rev. George Gubbins (1806–1891): the first evangelical minister

The first of the evangelical ministers to work in west Kerry was Rev. George Gough Gubbins, a native of County Limerick, who was appointed curate of the four parishes of Dunurlin, Kilmalkedar, Ventry and Kilquane in late 1831.[22] This may have been as a result of John Jebb's report. These areas had been served occasionally by Thomas Goodman before Gubbins's arrival. Gubbins was instructed to live in the locality, visit all four parishes once a week (summer and winter), minister specifically to the members of the Coast Guard and generally make his parishes 'exemplary to that portion of the diocese'. A.M. Thompson commented that 'this excellent man' set about his work 'with all the zeal of an ardent mind', but she acknowledged that he had a difficult task, considering that there was no church, no house, no school and no sign that Protestantism had ever before been preached there. Gubbins set himself up in a cabin at one shilling a week, 'deprived of all the comforts of a refined life', and began his work.[23] He lived at Ferriter's Cove (sometimes called Ferriter's Creek) near Ballyferriter.

Whelan described George Gubbins as 'an exemplary evangelical in every way'.[24] He conducted services in each area assigned to him, set up Sunday schools and eventually found five families of lapsed Protestants in the district. He adopted a simple lifestyle and was involved in practical support work as well as missionary work. He became involved in the welfare of the Catholic majority by providing basic medical assistance to people. According to Thompson, Gubbins 'took a leaf out of the Jesuits' book [...] hoping, by manifesting a care for their bodies, ultimately to benefit their souls'.[25]

George Gubbins also took a keen interest in the archaeological remains of Corca Dhuibhne – as did Fr John Casey, parish priest of Ballyferriter. Gubbins was taken to task in 1838 for claiming to have discovered seven ogham stones at Ballinrannig. One writer challenged this claim, stating that several others, including Fr Casey, had first discovered these stones; he claimed that Gubbins was guilty of 'a wilful injustice, by endeavouring to avail himself of the labours of others, and thus deck himself with borrowed plumes'.[26]

Cholera in west Kerry

A cholera epidemic broke out in west Kerry in September 1832 when twenty-six cases were recorded in Dingle town. In a population of five thousand, this was not regarded as too alarming at first, but when twenty-one people died of the disease, panic set in and it was reported that 'nearly half the population have taken fright and removed with everything belonging to them to the neighbouring country places.'[27] In Ferriter's Cove, sixteen deaths from cholera were reported in October 1832.[28] Rev. Gubbins became 'physician-general to the poor' and earned the trust of the people by working tirelessly in providing support, even assisting to bury the dead.[29]

Priests of the area were hard-pressed during the cholera epidemic of

1832. In a diary written in 1850 about his experiences as a curate in Dingle, John O'Sullivan recorded:

> Dingle was the Haceldama of Kerry that year. The cholera raged there with greater fury than in any other part of the diocese. It was not an unusual thing for one of us to go out at night and not return until nine or ten the following morning, moving from house to house preparing the dying. I was myself taken out of bed on thirteen successive nights to prepare cholera patients.[30]

O'Sullivan described a visit to a dying man in Minard, about 11 kilometres from Dingle. He walked across the mountain, and when he arrived, all the people of the village kept their distance from him. He gave the man some laudanum – 'the most effective cure for the complaint at the time', he wrote. He was offered tea and bread by the woman of the house, and 'with the greatest disregard for contagion, sat down and eat [sic] my breakfast alongside the cholera patient in his cabin, for it was a mere cabin, from the very bowl which he had been using ten minutes before, such is habit!!!'[31]

Fr John Casey, who lived in Murreagh, was also active in assisting the people in the Ferriter's Cove area in 1832. A group of officials from Dingle Board of Health accompanied by three policemen went to 'Ferriter's Creek, where the fatal malady rages at present' to find a location in which to set up a cholera hospital. They were opposed by a large crowd of local people and were obliged to return to Dingle. No reason is given for the opposition, but it was likely to have been because of fear of the dangers involved.[32] Fr Casey supported the initiative and accompanied the officials. 'Too much praise cannot be given to the Rev. Mr. Casey', went a subsequent report, 'for his humane and truly Christian exertions on that and every other occasion where his benevolent interposition was necessary for the preservation of peace and good order. The Rev. gentleman had a narrow escape and was hooted and hissed by his own flock.'[33] The chief constable of Dingle, Robert Coote, wrote a report on this incident and on the panic caused by cholera in the area.[34]

In praising the work of George Gubbins, A.M. Thompson made the claim that during the cholera epidemic, 'the Popish priests, terrified of contagion, actually fled the scene and left to the minister of a pure faith the privilege of administering medical aid and kindness to the sufferers.'[35] However, there is no evidence to support this damning charge, and the information on Fr Casey and Fr O'Sullivan indicates that she was in error.

There was a great shortage of Catholic priests in the pre-Famine period, and the steep increase in population in the early nineteenth century meant that people in remote areas particularly were not well instructed or catechised. Church-based devotions were not as conspicuous a feature as they later became. David W. Miller has established, from an analysis provided by the Catholic clergy to the Commissioners of Public Instruction in 1834, that only 43 per cent of Catholics nationwide fulfilled the canonical obligation of attending Sunday Mass. In parts of the south-east, attendance was over 80 per cent, but in parts of Mayo, Galway and south Kerry, it was under 20 per cent.[36]

In west Kerry, attendance ranged from 20 per cent in Ventry to 29 per cent in Kilmalkedar (Ballyferriter) parish.[37]

Table 1: Average attendance at Sunday Mass, 1834.

Parish	No of Catholics	Average attendance	Percentage attendance
Dingle	6,550	1,600	24
Ventry	2,748	550	20
Dunurlin	2,098	500	24
Kilmalkedar	2,387	700	29

The figures in Table 1 indicate that many people were only marginally involved in a fundamental sacrament of the Catholic church. While important life-cycle events such as baptism, marriage and last rites were important occasions requiring a priest, it is likely that the majority of Catholics in west Kerry had little instruction in the doctrines of their faith. Though there was a Catholic chapel in Ventry, there was no resident priest, with Fr John Casey and his two curates being responsible for an extensive district west of Dingle, including Kilmalkedar and Ballyferriter. Historian Oliver Rafferty states that when David Moriarty became bishop of Kerry in 1854, he was shocked to find that 'the general level of practice and knowledge of the Catholic faith was [...] at a low ebb.' Moriarty 'was often appalled at how ignorant adults as well as children were of the catechism'. He found that some priests had an inadequate grasp of theology, and he threatened to suspend two priests unless they improved.[38]

Proselytising

In February 1836, George Gubbins became rector of Dunurlin, replacing Rev. Archibald Macintosh.[39] Gubbins was also described as curate of Ventry, and he set up what he called 'ambulatory assemblies' in the villages of the area as a discrete and unobtrusive means of imparting information to interested Catholics.[40] The *Kerry Evening Post* wrote that Rev. Gubbins's 'kind and benevolent disposition has endeared himself to his parishioners'.[41] There were twenty-eight Protestants in Ventry in 1835 and thirty-seven in Dunurlin.[42]

According to Samuel Lewis's *A Topographical Dictionary of Ireland* (1837), there were two schools in the Dunurlin area. One of them was public, with about forty pupils; the other was private, with about twenty-five pupils. Gubbins was likely to have been responsible for one or both of these. This source states that there was no church or glebe house in Dunurlin; nevertheless, by 1839 George Gubbins had raised enough money to start building a church there. In a private initiative, he went to England to raise money and spoke at Pendleton near Manchester in October 1838, appealing for funds for a church 'in the wild and secluded parish of Dunurlin'.[43] A suitable one-acre site was donated by Lord Ventry, and a donation of £30 was received from the Earl of Cork. At the same time, Rev. Charles Gayer was receiving donations towards a church in Ventry. He acknowledged a total of £165, including £50 from the Earl of Dunraven and £20 from Walter Long, MP.[44]

It seems that in 1839 there were tensions between the three men who were by then the dominant clerical evangelicals in west Kerry – George Gubbins, Charles Gayer and Thomas Moriarty. Moriarty wrote that Gubbins had collected £400 towards Dunurlin church, and would receive a further £400 from the Ecclesiastical Commissioners, but that 'some friends remonstrated' with Gubbins and advised him against building a church in Dunurlin. Instead, they wanted him to build 'a good schoolhouse' there and apply the remaining funds to building the church at Ventry. But Gubbins stood his ground and rejected this proposal. It could be inferred from Moriarty's letter that Gubbins was being pushed aside, as he stated that Gubbins 'has resigned the curacy of Ventry and we have now separate fields of labour'. Gubbins's title for the short time remaining to him in Kerry was rector of Dunurlin.[45] There are hints that he was chafing at being confined to Dunurlin, which he referred to as 'my more contracted sphere of duty'.[46] He claimed that twenty families in the area had, as he expressed it, 'returned to the bosom of the Catholic Church', by which he meant the Church of

Ireland. The term 'catholic', meaning universal, was often used by Protestants for their church – it was *Roman* Catholicism to which they objected.

By this time, public conflicts over religion had begun in Dunurlin. Gubbins claimed that a priest, fearing that he would lose some of the money paid to him in dues, had uttered 'coarse invective' from the altar against him, his scripture reader and all who had converted. In January 1839, the service conducted by Gubbins at Kilmalkedar had been disrupted 'for at least the twentieth time, by a mob of about thirty persons'. Charges were brought against the ringleaders, who included the clerk of the parish priest, and they were convicted. An unnamed priest was accused by Gubbins of forcing a parishioner to turn his son out of his house because he became a Protestant. Citing these examples of what he saw as 'the persecution and starvation inflicted by priestly tyranny', Gubbins scorned one anonymous *Post* correspondent's talk of 'liberty of conscience' and 'freedom of religion' on behalf of Catholics.[47]

George Gubbins wrote to the *Post* describing matters in Dunurlin in May 1839, 'Any person who will speak to the converts is *ipso facto* placed under a curse; cursed is any person who will set them score ground, cursed is anyone who will sell them potatoes, cursed is anyone who will buy of their goods, cursed is anyone who will shelter them in his house.' Because of these sanctions, Gubbins had quietly acquired some ground for the converts' use; he had also provided a boat for them at Ferriter's Cove, so that they could collect seaweed for manure. When this became known, the boat was maliciously released from its moorings in the expectation that it would be wrecked on the rocky coast. However, the little boat drifted towards the Blasket Islands, where it was brought ashore intact. One of the converts was quick to draw a lesson, 'He who led the children of Israel safely through the Red Sea, can as easily steer through the Atlantic our little boat.'[48]

Transfer of George Gubbins

In 1840, Gubbins was transferred to Ballingarry, Co. Limerick, to establish a similar mission there. Looking back at his time in west Kerry, Gubbins later stated, 'When I first became curate of the district in 1831, it contained only five Protestants, four of whom went sometimes to Mass.' There was no church, glebe house or school in any of the four parishes of the district when Gubbins first arrived; when he left, there were four places of worship, four scriptural schools, two churches in progress of erection, and two residences for clergymen. Gubbins stated:

Since my departure, four Irish speaking clergymen have occupied
those parishes where I first worked alone [...] I believe I am below
the calculation if I say over one thousand persons throughout that
and the adjoining district have been added to the church. Persecution
and want of sympathy have forced numbers of the converts to
emigrate, and it is no sufficient test of the extent of the missionary
work to count merely the number that are there at present.[49]

Gubbins was disappointed at not being allowed to finish his work in Corca
Dhuibhne. He wrote that 'circumstances over which I had no control have
withdrawn me from that interesting field of labour', and although he dearly
wished to finish the church at Dunurlin, he was obliged to accept that 'the
Lord has ordered otherwise'.[50] In a parting address to friends and
parishioners, he made his feelings clear, 'I leave you with sorrow; my future
path is untried.' In a response, parishioners testified to his work as a 'good
Samaritan and faithful shepherd' during the cholera epidemic, 'when the
pestilence walked among us in the noonday'. The signatures attached to this
tribute suggest that they were most likely members of the Coast Guard
station at Ferriter's Cove rather than local people: A.H. Thompson, Daniel
McFall, Henry Jane, James Grenfell, William Williams, S. Chinoweth,
Richard Foot.[51]

Dunurlin church

When the foundation stone of Dunurlin church was laid on 21 July 1841,
it was a significant milestone for all those involved in evangelical work in
west Kerry. Rev. Anthony Denny noted that there were about 800 present
at the ceremony and that the Hon. Dayrolles Blakeney Mullins, the eldest
son of Lord Ventry, laid the stone. Denny 'could not but feel gratified at the
perfect tranquillity and good feeling evinced by the Roman Catholic
peasantry'. He hoped that it was a sign that 'prejudices against our Protestant
cause is giving way amongst them.'[52] The author of *The Little Ones of Innisfail*
conveyed her sense of awe at the surroundings:

Scenes upon which the wonder-working hand of the divine
architect was so legibly impressed that few could look from Dunurlin
on the grand combination of mountain cliff and island and above all
on the ocean's wide expanse without feeling that it was a spot
consecrated by nature for the worship of nature's God.

Lord Ventry and his family were present at the event, along with ten clergymen. Two hundred boys and girls from the schools attended, the girls wearing new frocks and white bibs – gifts from Lady Ventry. About two hundred Catholics stood watching with interest, and they were differentiated only by the fact that they kept their hats on during the singing. 'Never had the great Mount Eagle reverberated with such sounds as awakened the echoes of its solitary caves when nearly a thousand voices blending in harmonious union with sweet music wafted the hundredth psalm to heaven.' Among the Irish hymns sung was the popular 'There is a fountain filled with blood'. One man was heard to exclaim in ecstasy, 'Surely paradise is here!'

Speakers included ministers Anthony Denny of Tralee, Charles Gayer and Thomas Moriarty. After the ceremony, the adults adjourned for a meal provided by the curate of Dunurlin and the children received penny loaves from the rector of Ventry.[53] Rev. George Gough Gubbins returned for the celebrations, and 'almost overcome by the intensity of his feelings', he was pleased to see that the parsonage had already been built and the schoolhouse would soon be completed. Gubbins was proud of what he had achieved and again expressed regret at leaving Corca Dhuibhne, observing that 'he had been removed from them but not in heart.' He said that hands which had once been raised to stone him had welcomed him that morning with sincerity and warmth. He loved the area and had a particular reason for wishing to remain there: his first-born child was buried in Dunurlin graveyard, so 'that parish was endeared to him by the tenderest and most sacred ties.'[54] The headstone marking the infant's resting place is still to be seen in Dunurlin graveyard today. It reads, 'Eva, Daughter of the Rev G G Gubbins. Died Feb. 13 1837. Aged 6 months.'

The Protestant church at Dunurlin has long been levelled, but the large house that was the parsonage still stands as a private residence, Granville House. In the late nineteenth century it was extended and became the barracks of the Royal Irish Constabulary; in the mid-twentieth century it was a hotel. A modern house stands on the site of Dunurlin mission school.

Rev. George Gubbins served as vicar of Ballingarry from 1840 to 1865, prebend of Kilpeacon, Co. Limerick, from 1865 to 1881 and chancellor of Limerick diocese from 1881 to 1891. He died in 1891 and is buried in Kilpeacon cemetery. His son, Sir Charles Decimus O'Grady Gubbins, became a prominent doctor and political figure in South Africa.[55]

Rev. Charles Gayer (1804–1848)

Charles Robert Gayer was born in Somerset in England in 1804, the second son of Edward Echlin Gayer, a major in the 67th Regiment of Foot. His mother was Frances Christina Dobbs, only daughter of Conway Richard Dobbs, MP, of Castle Dobbs, near Carrickfergus, Co. Antrim. Charles Gayer graduated from Trinity College with a BA in 1826 and with an MA in 1832. He was ordained by the bishop of Meath and served in parishes in Cloyne, Co. Cork; Inishmacsaint, Co. Fermanagh; and Kinnegad, Co. Westmeath. After this, he moved to Kerry, having been appointed to Dingle. He was married to Catherine King. Rev. Gayer came to Dingle in 1833 as private chaplain to Lord Ventry and assistant curate to Thomas Goodman. Recent genealogical research has established that Gayer and Lord Ventry were seventh cousins once removed, but it is unlikely that they were aware of this.[56]

A.M. Thompson's account of the 'change in religious opinion' in west Kerry paid a grudging tribute to the work of the Irish Society. 'None who love the truth', she wrote, 'can fail to bid the Irish Society "God Speed".' But she emphasised that the ministers of the church had a more significant role in evangelisation.[57] She emphasised that the first evangelical work undertaken in Dingle was by Rev. Gayer. 'I distinctly state,' she wrote, 'and I request that it may be particularly observed, that religious inquiry here first began in the town of Dingle, *where the people speak English*.'[58] This was to counter any claim that the Irish Society was responsible for conversions in Dingle, since its mission was primarily directed at Irish speakers. However, people in Dingle did undoubtedly speak Irish at this time, even if many also spoke English.

As already noted, Thompson gave only passing recognition to the work of Thomas Dowling. She attributed the expansion of the Dingle congregation to the work of Charles Gayer – a result of 'the excitement and novelty of evening service being performed in the church, which attracted the curious and intelligent youths of the town to go and hear the new parson under cover of the dusk of evening'. It was a novelty, because Parson Goodman had not conducted regular services in the town. Thompson wrote that after Rev. Gayer's service, people met in his house 'to ask questions concerning the scriptures and the way of salvation'. According to her, the first conversions followed these activities, and by the end of 1835, before Gayer had even heard of the activities of the Irish Society, there were seventy converts in Dingle town. She claimed that some converts 'from the lower orders' were motivated by a realisation of the errors of Catholicism and some by 'their contempt for the avarice and tyranny of the priests.'[59]

J.G. MacWalter, who in 1852 described Dingle as 'this now widely famed and interesting missionary station', also stressed the curiosity factor in Charles Gayer's early success. Gayer's 'evening lectures on controversy [...] attracted all the "curious" to go see "just what was going on". The first visits were productive of such good, that soon, instead of a stealthy "curiosity seeing", many, in open defiance of priestly authority, showed an earnest desire to procure information.'[60]

Speaking in Cork in 1845, Charles Gayer gave his perspective on his early experiences in Dingle and said that he became aware of the Irish Society's work about eighteen months after his arrival. He was visited by an inspector of the society, whom he does not name but who was most likely Thomas Dowling. The inspector told Gayer that he had just come from a chapel where he had examined an Irish school and read the Irish scriptures in one corner while a priest heard confessions in another. 'At that time there was little excitement on the subject,' said Gayer, contrasting that harmonious relationship with the polarised situation in west Kerry in 1845. Gayer offered his services to the Irish Society in 1836, and within a year twelve schools in the area were affiliated to the society. When conversions followed, the priests began to denounce the work. Gayer stated that some Catholics had very inaccurate impressions of Protestants, believing that they prayed to an evil spirit or to the devil. He quoted one woman as asking, 'I wonder if they ever speak of God at all?' Gayer acknowledged that the publicity generated by the priests' condemnations actually helped his cause, 'The agitation was, however, very useful, for the people began to inquire what was in the Bible and what it was the Protestants believed.'[61]

In her determination to give primacy to the work of Rev. Gayer, A.M. Thompson wrote that 'when tidings of the conversions from Romanism in Dingle' reached the Irish Society, an inspector was sent to visit Gayer and it was then that he realised how the society could be 'an effectual instrument' in expanding his labours. Gayer became a superintendent of the society, and by the end of 1836 he was overseeing the work of twenty Irish teachers and there were 120 men reading the Irish scriptures in Dingle schoolhouse. They were not converts, but 'their prejudices against Protestant contact [were] being overcome by their love for their own language.'[62]

Charles Gayer worked zealously to bring what he believed was the light of true belief to the benighted people of west Kerry. Although the scripture readers of the Irish Society began work in west Kerry in around 1824–25 and the evangelical work of George Gubbins began in 1831, it was the year 1836 that saw the intensification of the campaign for the 'Second Reformation' in this part of the country. The aggressive evangelical efforts to win converts from Roman Catholicism would dominate public life and newspaper debate in west Kerry for the next three decades.

There were some initial indications that priests in west Kerry were not uniformly hostile to the Irish Society's activities. One inspector reported that a priest met him on the road and asked how many students he had; he replied that he had forty. The priest responded, 'Yarra, Paddy, it was as easy for you to have forty more.' Three years earlier, the same priest had 'strenuously opposed the activities of the Irish Society' and had 'got on his horse and literally chased the inspector out of his parish'. The report concluded, 'This shows at least that times are altered.' The same report stated that 'out of eleven schools in this district, only one has been closed because of the influence of the priest.'[63]

Nevertheless, in July 1837 it was reported that eight schools had closed because the scholars had stopped attending 'through terror of the priests' curses' and on account of 'systematic warfare' by priests, 'A tremendous effort was being made during the last quarter by the priests to put down the society's labours.' One priest was said to have dramatically held a lighted candle upside down and intoned, 'As this candle melts in my hand, so may God melt every man who does not give up the Irish books!'[64] Agents of the Irish Society were attacked by mobs and prevented from doing their work, 'In west Kerry the excitement and inquiry after truth is great [...] It is now come to open warfare and persecution, so I think it better to show how we are working and that our enemies need not think that they shall be able to crush us. Babylon is falling.'[65]

Open conflict between Rev. Charles Gayer and Fr John O'Sullivan
One of the earliest examples of a direct confrontation in the press between a priest and a Protestant minister began in January 1837 when Rev. Charles Gayer addressed a long letter directly to Fr John O'Sullivan, a curate in Dingle. This important letter is the first open declaration of Charles Gayer's grievances. Beginning with a quotation from Shakespeare's *Othello*, 'Nothing extenuate nor set down aught in malice', Gayer continued:

> After much deliberation I have resolved to address you on a subject which has lately engaged the attention of many, both of your congregation and of mine, viz. the language you have used in the

chapel respecting some of those persons who have left your communion and others who send their children to be instructed at our school. But before I proceed I would disclaim having any unkind feelings whatsoever either towards you or any members of your church, although reports have been circulated to that effect. God forbid that I should harbour any such feelings towards any who differ from me in religious sentiments. Whatever dislike I have towards the *doctrines* of your church, (and on this point I will not hide my opinions because I think they dishonour that Saviour who is all my hope for time and eternity), I have none whatsoever to the individual who holds them.[66]

Gayer asked O'Sullivan to consider whether his conduct had been in accordance with the example of Christ. He asked if it was love of Christ that made O'Sullivan threaten the parents who sent their children to his school – if love of Christ made him tell his congregation not to buy from or sell to them. He also accused O'Sullivan of refusing to baptise children whose parents could not afford the fee he demanded. In some cases, claimed Gayer, these parents then came to him to have their children baptised. Gayer also accused the priest of refusing to conduct funerals when people did not pay him the mandatory one-shilling fee, thereby consigning their souls to eternal misery, according to Gayer. Citing several passages from the Gospels, Gayer asked, 'Oh, Sir, was this the example our Saviour left you?' Gayer then referred to the language used by O'Sullivan from the altar, claiming that it was one reason why people turned away from the Catholic Church in abhorrence. For example, he condemned O'Sullivan's use of the phrase 'one-handed miscreant' to describe a disabled retired soldier. Gayer's letter went on:

Doubtless, Sir, you feel elated by the cheers and tokens of applause with which you are greeted when you hold up to ridicule persons of a different persuasion from yourself [...] But Sir, notwithstanding the seemingly universal applause you receive on such occasions, I would take the liberty of telling you that some of the respectable part of your hearers are dissatisfied that the house dedicated to the worship of God should be used for such purposes. Hath not God said: 'My house shall be called a house of prayer'? Oh! Sir, consider how far at times your chapel deserves the appellation of the house of God.

Gayer warned O'Sullivan that people went to church to 'have their souls fed with something more solid than abusive language against their neighbours' and told him that he would lose members if he continued with his condemnatory style of preaching. Gayer then advised the priest about how he should preach, ending his powerful letter by describing himself as 'your well-wisher for eternity'.[67]

Fr John O'Sullivan chose to reply in the columns of a national paper, the *Freeman's Journal*. O'Sullivan asked why Gayer had not sought a private interview with him instead of going to the press, and he quoted scripture in his support, 'When thy brother has sinned against thee, go and correct him between thyself and himself.' He then indignantly asked Gayer, 'What right have you to bring me to an account for what I preach or for what I practise? Pray, Sir, by what authority do you take me to task for the manner in which I deport myself towards my congregation?' O'Sullivan defended his right to ask for fees for his services, saying that, as curate of Dingle, he had an income of £7 10s a year, whereas Gayer had £150 a year from Lord Ventry. O'Sullivan felt justified in asking parishioners for 'occasional shillings well earned by many a laborious ride in the inclemency of the night and the pelting of the storm'. (A priest's income came mainly from the various dues levied on parishioners and charges for services provided. Parish priests generally controlled finances; curates were poorly recompensed, often depending on the generosity of the parish priest for a share of the income.)

Describing Gayer's letter as cant, written out of 'feelings of disappointment and defeat', O'Sullivan went as far as associating Gayer with the devil, 'You protrude the cloven foot from under the mask of sanctity and from behind the cloak of religion you fling the mire of disappointed vanity and mortified ambition.' Throughout his reply, O'Sullivan quoted liberally from the Bible, demonstrating that he was as familiar with it as any of the evangelicals (who always cited scripture to support their arguments).[68] But Gayer was not impressed by O'Sullivan's first scripture reference. In a letter that followed, he told O'Sullivan that they were not brothers and that the text he quoted was 'totally inapplicable', as they belonged to churches that were as different 'as east from west or day from night'. He listed some of the doctrinal differences – the core beliefs at the source of all the religious conflict that was engulfing west Kerry:

Every doctrine of your church tends to give glory to man – every doctrine of ours to God. Salvation in yours is set forth to be by works – ours of grace. Yours sets forth many saviours for sinners – ours but one, Jesus Christ. Yours makes the sufferings of man an atonement for sin – ours sets forth the sufferings of Jesus Christ alone as a 'finished' atonement. Yours proclaims that after death there is a fire which can cleanse from sins – ours that the 'blood of Jesus Christ cleanses from all sin'. Yours teaches that the priest can forgive sin – ours that Jesus Christ our great high priest is exalted to give remission of sins. Yours sets forth more mediators than one – ours that the 'one mediator between God and man is the man Christ Jesus'.[69]

O'Sullivan's letter had said that Gayer's 'wanton attack' was not caused by any provocation on his part. Gayer scoffed at this, reminding O'Sullivan of how often he had used offensive language about him in church – so much so that Gayer was warned by a friend not to go out at night for fear that he would be attacked. Gayer said that apart from some insults called out by children, he had received only 'uniform civility and respect' from every class of person since he had come to Kerry, 'You, and you alone, Sir, are the only person who showed any kind of wish to insult me.'

Gayer accused O'Sullivan of vilifying the charitable work of Protestant ladies – of preventing the starving poor from receiving food and clothing from the women by telling them it was 'a trap for their souls'. Gayer also accused O'Sullivan of telling his congregation that converts were being offered a leg of mutton and a weekly stipend, and that Gayer received £100 for every convert recorded. Gayer denied ever bribing anyone:

No, Sir, religion is, in my mind, too solemn a thing to be thus lightly dealt with – it is the work of God the Holy Ghost alone […] I would not give one shilling to bring over every one of your flock, were I assured at the same time that they would merely change from the forms and ceremonies of one church to the forms and ceremonies of another.

Gayer ended this letter by saying that if Fr O'Sullivan wished to continue the debate, he would have to use 'language which one gentleman should use to another', otherwise Gayer would not partake in discussion.[70] The *Tralee Mercury* believed that 'polemical newspaper warfare' on religious topics was futile and unseemly, and that the Gospels should not be 'ransacked in a super-serviceable zeal for the purposes of reviling a priest or taunting popery with its errors'.[71] But the *Post* responded that it was a far greater scandal that the Catholic church in Dingle had been turned into 'a theatre for turbulent and acrimonious discussion' on Sundays by 'unprovoked and false aspersions' against a minister of religion.[72]

Ventry conversions

While this newspaper controversy was underway, a significant event took place in Ventry when four scripture readers of the Irish Society decided to convert to Protestantism. According to an evangelical source, the four 'had become convinced of the errors of popery, [and] declared their intention of publicly coming to church in Dingle as there was no church nor a Protestant at that time residing in the parish of Ventry'. Their example led to 'a flood' of conversions in the Ventry area, which 'created great excitement and immediately directed the anathemas of the priests against the Irish schools'. By the end of 1837, seventy people in Ventry, young and old, had converted. The Catholic priests reacted by issuing curses, claiming that bribery was used and accusing the converts of 'selling their Saviour for money, as Judas did of old'.[73]

A.M. Thompson also gave an account of the four Ventry conversions, writing that they created 'immense excitement [...] and a fresh flood of priestly wrath', because this was clear evidence of success spreading beyond Dingle town. She wrote that 'the altars rang with curses' and Gayer was accused of using British money to bribe people to convert. Among the wild rumours that were in circulation was one which said that converts were bled and then infused with 'Protestant blood'.[74]

On 1 January 1838, another significant milestone was passed when a school was opened in Ventry for the converts' children, 'then amounting to about forty, and only one of whom could speak a word of English'.[75] From these beginnings, Ventry became a notable example of the success of the Protestant mission in west Kerry, especially after Rev. Thomas Moriarty was appointed as minister there in 1839.

The events of the year 1837 could be seen as the opening shots of a bitter, personalised propaganda war between clergymen of the two Christian denominations, marking a definite change of tone and style. For several decades to follow, this antipathy between Catholics and Protestants would frequently erupt in unseemly newspaper controversies, some of which gained national and even international attention.

6. Bell, book and candle: the excommunication of Ellen Waters, 1837

20th Report of the Irish Society

Twenty years after the foundation of the Irish Society, its progress in west Kerry was a source of great satisfaction to its members. The twentieth annual report, published in March 1838, declared, 'Never since the formation of the Society have we had to present from any part of Ireland a more exhilarating account than we are now enabled from this wild country.'[1] Those who attended the annual general meeting heard that the society was spreading 'with a rapidity and blessing surprising to its friends and in the same degree alarming to its enemies'. The hostility of Catholic clergy was acknowledged, 'At Ferriter's Cove, Ventry, Dingle and Tralee-ward, their activity and persecution against the disciples of truth is kindling considerable excitement.' However, the society reported a change among the people: one inspector said that in 1837 there was hardly any house in Dingle where he would be welcome to stay, but in 1838 there were thirty houses open to him.

By 1838, the Irish Society's policy had evolved to include the establishment of formal schools; it had forty-six schools in County Kerry with 1,644 pupils, of whom 1,370 were adults. The adults included 131 women and 11 people aged over fifty. In west Kerry there were ten schools with 256 pupils, of whom 203 were adults, including 6 people over fifty and 10 women. At a meeting in Tralee, sixty-three Catholics attended for examination, each person with a Bible. In Dingle, eighty-four people attended a similar meeting, and the correspondent added, 'In fact, I may safely say that the parish is our own – this is the Lord's doing.'[2]

The national accounts for the year show that the Irish Society brought forward £587 from the previous year, and received £2,880 from the London Irish Society. The society had a total income of £5,157 for the year, including contributions of £342 from England, £101 from Scotland, £162 from auxiliary associations in Ireland and £1,038 from other sources. The highest expenditure was £2,981, spent on inspectors' salaries and gratuities to teachers. Other expenses included travel, stationery, printing, rents, postage and book-binding. Cash grants were given to various districts, with Kerry receiving £120.[3]

Schools in west Kerry

Alongside the schools of the Irish Society, other formal schools were being established in west Kerry around this time by the Kildare Place Society. This institution was formally known as 'The Society for the Promotion of the Education of the Poor in Ireland', but was usually referred to as the Kildare Place Society (KPS) because of the location of its head office in Dublin. Founded in 1811 by a group of philanthropists, it provided funding, teacher training, school textbooks and other supports for schools all over Ireland. Its founding has been described as 'a landmark development in Irish education' because it 'pioneered a number of distinctive features in education in Ireland'.[4] KPS aimed to be non-denominational in character, and the Bible was to be read in schools without note or comment. Although the society initially had support from Catholics, its policy in relation to the Bible was in due course regarded as unacceptable and the schools faced Catholic opposition in most places. KPS received government funding up to 1831, when the National School system was established; it then went into decline, but it continued its work as a Protestant education system. Many KPS procedures and practices were incorporated into the National School system.[5]

Under the initiative of Revs Gubbins, Goodman and Gayer, Kildare Place schools were set up in Dingle, Dunquin, Dunurlin, Kilmalkedar and Kilquane. These were some of the ten schools that were absorbed into the Irish Society structures when the region of West Kerry first appeared in their records.[6]

Catholic schools

Other schools in Dingle were set up under Catholic auspices. In 1829, it was announced that the Sisters of the Presentation order would establish a convent and school in the town, and details of its funding were carried in the press. Dr Cornelius Egan, bishop of Kerry, gave £1,000, and the parish priest, Fr Foley, donated £100 and a building that he had refurbished at a cost of £300. The *Post* welcomed the initiative, 'We trust the female poor of Dingle will derive from this establishment the same solid advantages of education and moral instruction which the poor of this town [Tralee] have so long experienced from the unremitted and praiseworthy exertions of the ladies of Tralee convent.'[7] The *Mercury* gave an enthusiastic welcome to the new institution, 'which is so admirably fitted to diffuse the best blessings of heaven, religion and education [...] in the most western part of Europe.' It highlighted the fact that the school had the support of all classes, including 'the noble house of Burnham'.[8] A committee was formed to secure more funding, and 'the ladies of the town' collected £30, with a further £15 coming 'from the poor of Dingle'.[9] A total of £150 was collected; the largest individual donations were from Miss Hussey and Fr John Casey, who contributed £10 each. P. Hussey gave £5, Patrick McKenna £4 and Fr Patrick Foley and John Foran each gave £3. Eighty-five others were named as giving contributions of £2 or under.[10]

An editorial comment in the *Mercury* suggested that the building of a new school by the Presentation Sisters was a reaction to the opening of Bible schools. In 1829, none of the controversial clerical evangelicals had yet arrived in the area, but it is clear from the *Mercury* that the issue of proselytising had already become a matter of debate:

We trust that we shall have an end of the disguised efforts at fanaticism in that parish. They now cannot allege the want of opportunity to instruct and enlighten the children of Dingle; no pretext then for forwarding a plan of proselytism. Let them desist their puny efforts. They will, they must, prove abortive in the end; and for ourselves we promise that, should they be persevered in, no consideration of rank, no regard for village despotism, shall prevent our exposing to public indignation any attempt that may be made to disturb the quiet of the place or molest the religious feelings of the inhabitants.[11]

This is the first specific reference to proselytism in Dingle seen in the records, and it seems to be directed at the teachers and readers of the Irish Society, rather than clergymen.

At this time, in advance of the founding of the National School system in 1831, hedge schools or pay schools, known as *scoileanna scairte* or *scoileanna gearra*, provided elementary education in most localities.[12] According to Patrick Foley, the first National School for boys was founded in Bleach Green, Dingle, in 1834. It was under the patronage of Fr Foley, PP, cost £300 and had accommodation for five hundred boys. This building was in ruins when Patrick Foley wrote in 1907.[13]

By the late 1830s, it was clear that the scripture readers and teachers of the Irish Society were working in close association with the evangelising mission of the Protestant ministers of west Kerry. In its annual report for the year ending 17 March 1840, this was acknowledged in a positive account of the progress of the Irish Society's work there, with conversion explicitly cited as its aim:

> The open and violent opposition which raged last year is now at an end in this branch. When the work of conversion began, the priests were up in arms and waged a regular crusade [...] The priests are now, strange to say, preaching peace and goodwill towards us, to the great surprise of their flocks who have not forgotten their former conduct [...] The people in general are now friendly to the converts [...] Our Irish teachers and readers, as well as the Irish minister, have free access in every village [...] We begin the work everywhere by the Irish operations; we first get up the Irish teacher, then the scripture reader and then the minister has an open door to preach, the field is prepared to receive the seed.[14]

A meeting of the Irish Society was held in the new schoolroom at Ventry on 5 September 1839 with about 250 present, young and old. An unnamed priest was induced to enter the room and was amazed to see many who were formerly in his own flock in attendance. The report simply said, 'He retired, as may be conceived, in great confusion.'[15]

The excommunication of Ellen Waters

Ellen Waters (also known as O'Connell) lived in Dingle town, where she worked as a washerwoman. She was a Catholic and a mother of several children; she decided to send some of them to the KPS school run by Rev. Charles Gayer. As a result, she found herself condemned publicly by Fr John O'Sullivan in a dramatic ritual of excommunication carried out in the Dingle Catholic church on 18 May 1837. The first newspaper reports did not name the priest or the woman, but a month later the *Post* named her as Ellen O'Connell, better known as Ellen Waters. It also identified the priest as Fr O'Sullivan.[16]

A.M. Thompson wrote that Ellen Waters, who was pregnant, was 'anathematised and excommunicated' by the dramatic ritual of bell, book and candle performed by the priest at the end of Mass. Thompson described this solemn ritual conducted by the priest dressed in black robes as 'terrific to superstitious persons':

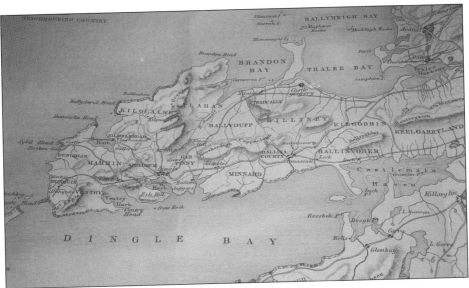

001 West Kerry in the 1840s. AMT

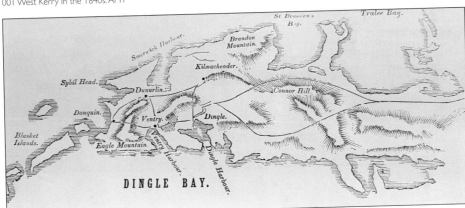

002 West Kerry in the 1840s. *Persecution of Protestants*

003 View of Dingle, showing Conor Pass road. *Irish Intelligence*

004 Irish class at Brosna, Co. Kerry. *Irish Intelligence*

005 Reading Irish books by candlelight, with man at the door who is not fully committed. *Irish Intelligence.*

006 The Irish teacher's cabin. *Irish Intelligence*

007 West face of Burnham House today, seat of Lord Ventry.

008 West face of Burnham House today, part of Coláiste Íde.

010 Mrs Catherine Gayer. Courtesy of Anthea Kennedy Gayer Mitchell

009 Rev. Charles Gayer. Courtesy of Anthea Kennedy Gayer Mitchell

Right—011 Archdeacon John O'Sullivan as parish priest of Kenmare.

Below—012 A View of Ventry, from a fund-raising circular issued by Rev. Charles Gayer, 26 September 1839. The buildings are 1) rectory, 2) school, 3) church, 4) mission cottages. The boat *Crusader*, which sailed to the Great Blasket, is marked 5. Also included are clusters of villages, the small Catholic church between 2 and 3, and the ruined Rahinnane Castle on right. Archives of St Columba's College, Dublin

Above—013 Another view of Ventry. *Irish Intelligence*

Left—014 Ventry mission buildings. From left to right: parsonage, school, church. *Persecution of Protestants*

015 A sketch of the class of converts as they were being examined at Ventry on Monday, 8 August 1842. From left: James Gloster, teacher at Dunquin; John Sullivan, Irish reader on the Blasket Island; Dan Sullivan, Irish reader at Ventry; Tom Connor, Irish reader at Ventry; Tom Kennedy, Irish reader at Ventry and the parish piper; James Jordan, schoolmaster at Ventry. These six men were employed by the Ladies Auxiliary or Readers' Branch of the Irish Society. The other man was described as 'an interesting old man whose script. knowledge, tho' lately acquired, surprised us very much'. National Gallery of Ireland, Catalogue No. 7808. Unknown artist, nineteenth century. Ink on paper. 18x22cm. © National Gallery of Ireland

Above—016 Ventry church in the 1960s.
RCB Library Photography Collection.
RCB LIB Ms. 139/3/22

Left—017 Ventry church interior before
demolition. RCB Library Photography
Collection. RCB LIB Ms. 139/3/22

Below—018 Ventry today, showing the
buildings of the Ventry Collegiate School.

Above—019 Ventry Colony cottages today.

AN

BIOBLA NAOMHTHA;

ANN A BHFUILID AN

TSEAN TIOMNADH;

AR NA THARRUING GO FIRINNEACH AS

A NEABHRA UGHDARACH.

RIS AN TATHAIR RO ONORACH A NDIA

UILLIAM BHEDEL,

EASPUG CHILLE MOIRE;

AGUS AN

TIOMNA NUADH;

AR NA THARRUING GO FIRINNEACH AS

A NGREIGIS UGHDARACH.

RIS AN TATHAIR IS ONORUIGHTHE A NDIA

UILLIAM O DOMHNUILL,

ARDEASPUG THUAIM.

LONDON:

Printed by J. Moyes, Greville Street,

FOR THE BRITISH AND FOREIGN BIBLE SOCIETY;

And sold, to Subscribers only, at the Society's House, 10, Earl Street, Blackfriars.

M.DCCC.XVII.

Left—020 Irish Bible, published by the British and Foreign Bible Society in 1817. School of Theology, Boston University.

Below—021 Advertisement for headmaster of Ventry Collegiate School in *Dublin Evening Mail*, 10 January 1855.

VENTRY COLLEGIATE SCHOOL,

FOR THE

EDUCATION OF IRISH SPEAKING YOUTHS,

With a view to their becoming Ministers of the Gospel.

WASTED, by the Trustees of the above Institution, a HEAD MASTER, whose acquirements and competency as a Teacher must be of the highest order.

A Married Clergyman would be preferred.

Salary £150 per annum, with Board and Apartments.

Application to be made to the Rev. D. A. Browne, 17, Upper Sackville-street, Dublin, on or before the 20th inst.

IN CHANCERY.
COUNTY DUBLIN.

In the Matter of Mary) TO BE LET, pur-

022 St James's church, Dingle, built c. 1807, is still a place of worship as well as the venue for Other Voices

023 Dunquin school/church in the 1960s. Sunday services were held here up to the 1950s. RCB Library Photography Collection. RCB LIB Ms. 139/3/22

024 Mission school/church in Dunquin. *Persecution of Protestants*

The priest is to commence by ringing a bell to summon all to hear, then close the book of life on the refractory individuals and, calling their names aloud, extinguish the candle on the altar, by which is meant the light of heaven is extinguished unto them and that they are given over unto Satan and the powers of darkness.[17]

Thompson included a verbatim account of the questioning under oath of a witness to the excommunication ritual. Neither the questioner nor the witness was named, but both were male. Thompson wrote that this interrogation was carried out in order to present it as evidence to a committee of the House of Lords, but this does not appear to have transpired. This is the text of the interview, with Thompson's observations in parentheses and her emphasis in italics and upper case:

What did the priest say?
—I'll be bound, he cursed her well.
What did he say? Did he give a reason for cursing her?
—He said it was for going *here and there*.
What did he mean by that?
—Because, he said, she was going to-and-fro, sometimes to Mass and sometimes to church.
What did he say?
—Enough, I'll be bound.
But what did he say?
—*He cursed every inch of her carcase!*
Did he bid the people not speak to her?
—He desired them not *speak to her, or deal with her or have anything to do with her.*
Did he curse her child?
—He cursed everything that would spring from her.
Did he say anything of the child she was carrying? Did he curse the fruit of her womb? (The poor creature was pregnant at the time.)
—I did not hear him say THAT: he cursed everything that would spring from her.
How was he dressed?
—He threw off the clothes he had on and put on a *black dress*. 'Tis the way the clerk quenched all the candles but one, and himself put out that one, and said 'so the light of heaven was quenched upon her soul', he shut the book and said 'the gates of heaven were shut upon her that day'.

What do you mean by stating that he cursed every inch of her carcase?
—He cursed her eyes, and her ears, and her legs and so on, every bit of her.
What did you think of such doings?
—I wished myself at Carminole. (A proverbial expression.)
What did you mean by that?
—I wished myself a thousand miles off.
Did the rest of the people seem to like it?
—How could they like it? They all disliked it, some were crying, some women fainted.
Did anyone speak to the priest about it?
—I'll be bound they did not, they left him to himself, they would be in dread of their lives to stir.

The witness appealed to his questioner not to expose him by name because 'it would be better for me to be dead a thousand times than to have my name brought in question about this business.' He said that there were five hundred people who could give the same account – the congregation in the church. A.M. Thompson was personally involved in gathering information on this incident; another witness told her that the priest cursed the fruits of the woman's womb, 'and that it should become *rottenness* in her bones – that it should be the untimely fruit that should never *see light*'.[18] One reason why the matter did not proceed as far as the House of Lords was that witnesses such as these two may not have been willing to repeat these private statements in public.

Thompson wrote that Ellen Waters was indeed shunned by neighbours and shopkeepers – was thrown out of her lodging and deserted by her husband, who was a shoemaker. She was refused food, even bread for her family. When her children once heedlessly ran into a neighbour's house, hot water was thrown at them. One of Ellen's sons was exempted from the curse because he was 'in the service of a Roman Catholic lady', but he was forbidden to speak to his mother. Ellen Waters was sheltered in a Protestant house; when she was close to giving birth, Mrs Gayer warned Fr O'Sullivan that if Ellen or her child died, he would be held responsible and would be prosecuted. According to Thompson, it was only then that the priest gave permission for a midwife to attend her. After the birth, a reconciliation of sorts took place between the priest and Ellen Waters, with Ellen doing penance and withdrawing her children from the Protestant school. Thompson thought that Ellen might have been influenced by a desire to have her child baptised as a Catholic. Ellen was pardoned, publicly received back to the Catholic congregation and 'made much of by the Roman Catholic ladies of the convent', and Fr O'Sullivan became sponsor to the child. However, in handwritten notes on his copy of A.M. Thompson's book, Fr O'Sullivan wrote 'a lie' about many of her claims, including that hot water had been thrown at one of Ellen's children.[19]

According to Thompson, once Ellen saw that she and her newborn child were not affected by the priest's curse, she abandoned the Catholic Church, warning Fr O'Sullivan that she would prosecute him if he should speak ill of her again. She joined the Protestants of Dingle, apparently without any further reaction from the priest. However, because of his curse on her and the land she walked on, people in the town still shunned her and 'crossed the street to avoid walking in the same path that she trod'.[20]

Thompson's account of the incident is substantially supported by newspaper reports. The *Post* claimed that it had a reliable source of information and gave details similar to Thompson; for example, in describing the reaction of the congregation, it stated, 'Some began to cry, others to faint and some ran out of the chapel.'

The *Post* ended with this comment:

> Great is the sensation produced by it amongst all classes and it is generally reported that two others for the same crime are to be cut off from the Kingdom of Heaven on the following Sunday. Oh! when will our poor benighted Catholic countrymen be permitted to read for themselves the following passages of God's holy word which breathe a spirit so different from that put forth by His professed minister against an unoffending woman: John 3:17: 'God sent not His son into the world to *condemn* the world but that the world through him might be *saved*.'[21]

The *Post* then published an anonymous letter, signed 'Alpha', addressed directly to 'the Roman Catholic Priest, Dingle'. It condemned the priest's action:

> Your bell rang to summon all the devils in hell to take her; you closed the book of life against her, and by the blowing out of your candles you gave the people to understand that the light of heaven to her was forever extinguished. She is a washerwoman and hence you cursed the very clothes that might pass through her hands. You cursed

everyone in the community who might speak to her, sell her goods, buy from her or employ her. You had no mercy on her or her children – you doomed all to starvation in this world with one 'fell swoop' and to damnation in that which is to come. This was a severe and dreadful punishment.

How did you feel in pronouncing such a curse? Did you not tremble? Some people say you were in a violent passion. I hope for your own sake this is true – that it was a mere temporary fit of phrensy. If you did it coolly and deliberately, there is no apology for you. It discovers a hardihood and wickedness truly indescribable. You cut the poor woman off not only from bread but from the mercy of God; you damned her even before the time […] Truly it was a heavy, bitter, burning, terrible and eternal curse.[22]

The writer then weighed the punishment against the crime, noting that the washerwoman's offence (at this time, Ellen had yet to be named in the papers) was not of the order of atheism, idolatry, murder, adultery or perjury, but was simply a defiance of the priest's authority by sending her children to a Bible school. Ellen had not, at that stage, converted.

On foot of a request from a sceptical reader for more details, the *Post* named Ellen Waters and Fr O'Sullivan, 'lest the veracity of our information should be doubted'. Ellen was described as 'a quiet, well-conducted woman whose character is unimpeachable' and who was in long-term employment in a respectable family. The school to which she had sent her children was 'conducted on the Kildare Street [KPS] plan and superintended by the Rev. Thomas Goodman and the Rev. Charles Gayer'.[23]

On first hearing of the excommunication ritual, the *Tralee Mercury* referred to the horrifying detail in the *Post*'s report, acknowledging that 'a proceeding such as our cotemporary describes would give pain to any well-regulated mind'. However, it was convinced that the account was 'extravagantly exaggerated' and invited 'some Dingle friend of ours' to submit an account of 'the real facts of the case'. The *Mercury* believed that 'a serious charge is made, nor ought it to be passed over in silence.'[24] Silence, however, was exactly what followed in the *Mercury*; there appears to have been no further coverage of the incident in its pages.

Many of the details from A.M. Thompson's account are confirmed in the *Post*. It stated that people followed the priest's instructions and refused to deal with Ellen and her children – and that her daughter was threatened with scalding water in one shop. A Catholic woman who was asked to attend at the birth of Ellen's child refused, saying that 'she could not possibly think of attending an excommunicated woman', and Ellen depended on Protestants for food and for support.[25]

The editor of the *Post* compared the incident to the days of the Inquisition, and solemnly informed readers that the Latin title *Vicarius Filii Dei* (Vicar of the Son of God, which was similar to the Pope's title of Christ's Vicar on Earth) could be shown to reveal the number 666, the so-called 'mark of the beast' in the Book of Revelations. This feat was achieved by adding the numerical values of the Roman letters of the Latin title. The letters A, R, F, E and S have no numerical value and the remaining letters are: D (500), C (100), L (50), V and U (5), and six instances of the letter I (1). The sum of these values gives the total 666.[26]

Fr O'Sullivan's journal

Fr John O'Sullivan, who was described as 'the rampant priest' in the *Post* of 10 June 1837, was a native of Tralee. In the course of a conflict between him and D.P. Thompson in 1838, the editor of the *Post* remembered him as 'a gawky schoolboy' now transformed by 'the power of the vestments [...] into the arbiter of the management of a great estate'.[27] O'Sullivan was ordained in 1830 and was appointed as curate in Dingle. In 1839 he was promoted to the position of parish priest of Kenmare.

O'Sullivan's private journal, describing visitations to parishes of the diocese in the early 1850s, is a source of much interesting information on the diocese and on its priests. The journal has a reference to the excommunication incident, and to the attempt by Protestant ministers to prosecute him. In 1850, O'Sullivan met a woman named Peggy Pierce, a friend of Ellen Waters, and this prompted him to write as follows:

> When souperism first began to spread in Dingle the whole burden of its opposition fell upon me. I was continually pelting and pounding them. A woman named Ellen Connell, better known as Ellen Waters, sent her children to church tho' professing to be a staunch Catholic herself, and I got leave from the bishop to excommunicate her, which I did in due form with bell, book and candlelight, leaving no tailoring on the business. Ellen was, in consequence, shunned and avoided by the whole community and the parsons thought they had a fine ground for prosecution. Parsons Rowan and Denny came from Tralee to arrange the matter and their

principal witness was Peggy Pierce, the poor woman who came to renew her acquaintance with me today. She was then waiting maid to Mrs. Hussey, had been giving her a full account of the excommunication and told the whole details of it so freely, and besides was so beholden to Mrs. Hussey, that they thought Peggy would not have the slightest hesitation coming forward to give evidence, but when the thing was plainly put before her, and when she understood what they wanted her to do – to swear against the priest Father John!! Horrible!! Peggy was thunderstruck and took very little trouble in concealing her feelings on the subject, and the whole affair fell to the ground. Ellen Waters too, unfortunate woman, gave birth soon after to a monstrous distorted child, and tho' she seemed at first to acquiesce in the prosecution, in the end wavered and faltered, 'et sic servatus est Father John'.[28]

The journal contains further information about Fr John O'Sullivan's time in Dingle. He wrote, 'I had the onus of the parish on my shoulders for a long time, and was fairly harassed from the rascally soupers who were just then beginning to make head.'[29] He wrote that, because he was born in Tralee, he 'had no Irish in my jaw' when appointed to Dingle.[30] Nonetheless, he went on to learn the language. Bishop Egan was keen to promote the Irish language among his clergy; in fact, he had delayed John O'Sullivan's ordination for a year to ensure that he became more proficient in the language. O'Sullivan disagreed with the bishop's policy of promoting Irish, believing that he was 'going against the tide, in fact, in seeking to keep up the Irish language, and yet he will fain do so'.

O'Sullivan saw his parish priest Fr Divine as 'a very disinterested, zealous and indefatigable man, and entirely given to the duties of his calling'. But he regarded him as a failure in terms of meeting the challenge presented by the evangelicals, because

his forte was the confessional and when he should have been animating and exiting [sic] the people and rousing their feelings in favour of religion, he was buried in the confessional hearing the scruples of some old hag who had confessed them over twenty times, perhaps even to somebody else before himself.

O'Sullivan believed that Fr Divine was unwilling to upset the bishop and so 'kept back from him the real extent to which apostacy was extending' in the Dingle area. When O'Sullivan tried to inform the bishop, the latter was not disposed to believe him, saying he had heard otherwise from Divine.[31]

The tragic and shocking case of Ellen Waters became notorious in the propaganda war between the evangelicals and Catholics; it was often cited as an example of priestly inhumanity. Two years after Waters's excommunication, another Dingle curate, Fr John Halpin, wrote a letter attacking 'the shameful system of proselytism' prevailing in Dingle; he blamed Rev. Gayer for it, saying that 'the poor of Dingle never brought their souls to market till he opened an emporium for spiritual commerce.'[32] This was in the context of a dispute over a poverty-stricken woman, Mrs Fitzgerald, who accepted material support offered by Charles Gayer and finally opted to become a Protestant. Halpin also referred to the case of Ellen Waters. He admitted that he did not have complete knowledge of her case but referred sarcastically to 'the victory which this "maid" of Dingle, this modern Joan of Arc, gained at least over the church of Rome'.[33]

A.M. Thompson did not have a high opinion of Ellen Waters, describing her as 'a stubborn character [...] neither a convert nor a Christian', who ultimately 'did not show herself to be a respectable person and has left Dingle, but continues to be a Protestant in profession'.[34] Nothing more is known of the subsequent life of Ellen Waters.

Fr John O'Sullivan served as parish priest of Kenmare for thirty-five years and became archdeacon and vicar-general of the diocese. He was indefatigable in his work among the poor during the Famine and corresponded directly with Charles Trevelyan, who was responsible for government policy during those tragic years. He travelled to London on two occasions in 1847 to highlight the state of the starving poor of Kenmare Poor Law Union. He had good relationships with Protestant clergymen in and around Kenmare, helped by the fact that they were not involved in proselytism.[35]

At Archdeacon O'Sullivan's funeral Mass in 1874, Bishop David Moriarty acknowledged his remarkable achievements in founding the Poor Clare convent in Kenmare and building Holy Cross church 'at his own sole cost'. He praised O'Sullivan's great exertions in the cause of education, religion and charity; he noted that he was manager of thirteen schools, 'fed and clothed one hundred and fifty children in the Kenmare schools for over twelve years' and 'made provision for continuing his charity forever in the parish'.[36]

7. Ventry, 'the centre and citadel' of the mission

In 1849, a visitor to Ventry recorded that 'there was not a single individual resident in the village who is not a Protestant, save one old woman.' The writer contrasted this with the year 1836, when there was not one Protestant living there. He celebrated the fact that the village had been transformed, with 'cleanly cottages and well-fenced gardens and whited walls' which announced to visitors that 'Protestantism has there taken up her abode and expelled the superstition and filth and misery and demoralisation of popery from the locality.'[1] The writer was Rev. Daniel Foley, a Tralee-born convert who was professor of Irish in Trinity College from 1849 to 1861. He was not an impartial observer, as he was an ardent supporter of the evangelical movement; nonetheless, his statement about the number of Protestants in Ventry was probably accurate. One author stated that it was the evangelicals who first gave the English name 'Ventry' to Ceann Trá, or Cantra.[2]

By 1849, Ventry was hailed in the evangelical press in Britain and Ireland as an outstanding example of the success of the conversion campaign. By then, Rev. Thomas Moriarty had been ministering in Ventry for ten years; nevertheless, before his return, there was already a strong community of Protestants in Ventry, almost all of them converts. As already noted, it was Thomas Dowling who initially built up this community and encouraged Gayer when he was disheartened about slow progress there. Because of the remarkable number of conversions in Ventry, it attracted great attention from evangelical commentators. Wilson gave this description of the 'beautifully situated' village:

> Its humble village runs chiefly along the seashore, commanding one of the best and safest harbours in Ireland, and never did the ocean waves flow in upon a smoother fairer strand. To the rear of the village the great Mount Eagle towers in lofty pride, and far to the right, seen amid the waters of the great Atlantic, the Skellig rocks lift their red marble pyramids like the ancient ruins of some giant fortress of the sea.[3]

He went on to quote from a letter of December 1837 confirming that the Ventry mission started with the Irish Society's work and had surged ahead:

> In that village the Lord has been pleased to do great things. And we have there a little colony of fifty-six Protestants; although the [Catholic] chapel is in the centre of the village, and from its altar, Sabbath after Sabbath, curses have been denounced upon the Irish masters and scholars. Six months ago we tried to establish a school at Ventry but we were obliged to give it up as the priest then had sufficient influence to take away every child. But now we have forty-two children whose attendance can be relied on and the expectation of more.[4]

The writer then learned that there were many adults in Ventry who had 'thrown off the Popish yoke' and wished to have a divine service. 'This was so clearly an opening for the Lord that I immediately inquired if a house could be got,' he wrote, and he was successful in this. The villagers rallied to help adapt it to a schoolhouse, which opened in early 1838:

> We now have the whole village on our side. It would have delighted your heart to see about forty of us working away (to use their own expression) for the bare life, in the best humour with one another possible. Surely we have great reason to bless the Lord for having given us such favour in the sight of the people. Twelve months ago, had we been engaged in the same work in Ventry, we would have been torn in pieces by the very people who were working with us today [...] It has caused great joy among our people, and I already have a congregation of about sixty persons young and old.[5]

It is interesting that this account uses the term 'congregation' rather than 'class'. The transformation of Bible-reading groups or classes into congregations was already taking place. The letter writer gave one indication of why Ventry was strategically significant to the work of the mission:

> Of all the villages in the barony, Ventry is the most important to have on our side for it is the one through which every person coming to Dingle from the west must pass, and which was dreaded before; but now (if necessary) our masters and our scholars would seek for and find refuge there.[6]

A letter of 10 January 1838 (probably written by Charles Gayer) stated that a school had opened in Ventry with an attendance of thirty-two children; the numbers were lower than expected on account of bad weather and lack of clothing. Adults came too, including three elderly women who laughed together as they read a spelling book. In another sign of great change in Ventry, the heads of six families sent a letter to the priest telling him that they were no longer part of his church – they warned him not to curse them from the altar or they would sue him. 'This was a great blow to popery, for the whole parish heard of it and as he [the priest] did not turn these bold converts into goats, they are sure that he has not the power to work miracles.'[7]

Until a new church could be erected in Ventry, service was held in the schoolhouse. It is difficult to accurately chart the progress of the mission at Ventry in terms of numbers, but Rev. Gayer wrote about a 'glorious meeting' there on New Year's Day 1838, with

upwards of one hundred and twenty present, all from all parts of the country. Our converts came forward boldly before four hundred people, who had just come out of the [Catholic] chapel. The priest remained in a neighbouring house, I suppose to look on. Eight Roman Catholics came into the schoolhouse; the day was beautiful, the only fine one for the last three weeks [...] Our prospects are most cheering and if we are all spared another year, I trust that our schoolhouse will not hold all that will attend. I understand that the eight Roman Catholics who heard the word preached on New Year's day intend to leave popery, which I expected would be the case as the courage with which they faced such a multitude proved their sincerity. We have great cause to bless the Lord for the first fruits of our labours at Ventry.[8]

In May 1838, there were fifty-six pupils in the school at Ventry, and seven convert families from Dunquin attended services there.[9] The first baptism of a child, named Sullivan, took place on 6 May, to the indignation of the parish priest. The Catholic bishop of Kerry, Cornelius Egan, visited Ventry to celebrate High Mass and to investigate the reasons for so many defections from his flock. He was reported as rebuking the priest as follows, 'I cannot impute to you want of zeal; on the contrary, your zeal seems to have been too fiery. You should not be always cursing the people. Curse them at the high festivals – curse them four times a year, but do not be always cursing them.'[10] One man from Dunquin, Paddy Connor, defied the parish priest by refusing to attend confession or to pay the dues required by the priest. 'Let him turn me into a hare or a goat if he can', declared Paddy, 'for this blessed day, before you all, I defy him.'[11] When he later spoke about his conversion to a crowd of over a hundred people in Dingle, he was praised for having the courage to 'boldly proclaim the gospel before a whole town'.[12]

Charles Gayer wrote about his hopes for the future of the mission, 'I should like to have a battery in every parish to the west of Dingle and the walls of Babylon would soon have a good breach in them.'[13] There was great interest around Dublin in what was occurring in Kerry, he wrote, and he looked forward to the day when the Protestants in Ventry would have their own church.[14] He did not speak Irish, but he understood the advantage conferred by having a fluency in it, and he saw the need for teachers and preachers from among the people. When two local men asked to be trained as scripture readers, he said they were worth six regular readers because of their local influence.[15]

According to Gayer, Thomas Moriarty offered to come to work in his native area, 'to preach about the country, hold controversial lectures and invite the priests to discuss their doctrines'.[16] The offer was taken up, and Moriarty became the resident minister in Ventry, where his influence was of enormous significance for over two decades.

A.M. Thompson's account of Ventry

Anna Maria Thompson's account of Ventry stressed its poverty:

> Ventry, lying in the centre of the district, became a gathering place and many converts from other parishes collected for strength and mutual support into this poor village which had been nearly depopulated by the cholera; even in this wretchedly poor part of the country, where there is not so much as one resident gentleman, Ventry was superlatively wretched and squalid. Misery marked every countenance, the untenanted houses were falling into ruin or become the haunt of lawless men, the place had what we call in Ireland 'a bad name'. It is situate[d] at the head of a stretch of shore, called therefore *coun tra*, 'the head of the strand'. Yet here in this despised spot had the Lord a people to bring from darkness to light, and from the power of Satan unto God.[17]

Thompson witnessed with delight the growing numbers attending the school, but in contrast to the attitude of the writer of *Innisfail*, constantly remarked on the abject state of the 'creatures who for uncivilised aspect and poverty of garb might bear competition with the most savage nations'. She conveyed the atmosphere at the Sunday service, where the minister's words were translated for the congregation while 'the women squatted on the floor nursing their infants – elder infants were supplied with a potato or perhaps a live bird to keep them quiet – but all thirsting for the word of life.'[18]

In a circular letter to potential donors, Gayer gave a lyrical description of Ventry, stressing its beauty and its lore:

> In the background is Mount Marhyn, to the left of it appears a shoulder of Mount Eagle, a stupendous mountain which overlooks the Blasket Islands. Behind the church are the ruins of Rahannan Castle, an old fortress belonging to the Knight of Kerry and destroyed during the wars of the Commonwealth. The church on the rising ground, the school house to the left, the missionary's residence at the extreme point, and the cottages connected with the mission on the right (for the erection of which a kind Christian lady in England has liberally contributed) are all situated on a small promontory jutting into the harbour of Ventry. In the creek underneath the house is the mission boat, employed in carrying the glad tidings of salvation along the coast and to the neighbouring islands. The place has also been the scene of romance and history. The legendary tales of the country people refer to the wonderful achievements of Finn McCoul (the Fingal of Ossian) on the strand of Ventry; in this same spot the last stand was made by the Danes before their expulsion from Ireland, when we read that Ventry, formerly Fintry i.e. the White Strand, was reddened with the blood of the slain and the silent loneliness and wild grandeur of the scenery was disturbed by the clash of arms and the din of battle.[19]

Gayer wrote of the unique features of the Ventry congregation – the fact that it consisted entirely of converts from the church of Rome, 'knowing no other tongue but the Irish and ministered to exclusively in that tongue; and secondly, the fact of this very place and congregation being the centre and citadel of an open and extensive field of missionary labours extending even to the remote Blasket islands.'

In ending his 'appeal to Christian friends in Ireland and England', Gayer wrote:

> The country around is losing the horror with which they hitherto regarded Protestantism and is imperceptibly stealing into the same light. And I have no doubt that hundreds would be glad to make an open profession of it, if the step did not involve them in the loss of subsistence and consequent starvation. Many heads of families have come to us saying that they had work and subsistence as Roman Catholics but that if we could secure them the same in any way they would be glad to join us; we cannot but regret our inability to do so.[20]

According to Thompson, in the summer of 1838 there were 170 converts in Ventry; they had a service in the schoolhouse every Sunday, taken alternately by Rev. Goodman and Rev. Gayer, with Rev. Gubbins visiting on another day.[21] In August, Gayer proposed to the Irish Society that Thomas Moriarty be sent to take charge in Ventry. Gubbins offered to surrender the salary he had in respect of Ventry to Moriarty, but the Irish Society agreed to pay his salary and the salaries of three Irish readers, a schoolmaster and a schoolmistress. This was a great boost to the Ventry mission. The ambitious plan for the mission at Ventry was shown by Gayer's decision to travel to England to raise funds for a church, a clergyman's house and a new school house. The editor of *The Warder* compared the mission in Ventry to that of Achill, 'Like the missionary settlement at Achill, Ventry is "stretching out her hands to God" in the attitude of a pure worship', leading 'every sincere lover of divine truth to exclaim "What hath God wrought."'[22]

Because Catholic congregations had been told by priests to have no dealings with those who left their congregation, it was difficult for converts to buy food in the market place in Dingle. D.P. Thompson intervened, using his authority as magistrate and land agent of the Ventry estate to compel dealers to engage with the converts. Lord Ventry also played his part by leasing some land in Ventry so that converts could grow their own potatoes and become more self-sufficient. This convert farm was administered by five trustees: D.P. Thompson and ministers Gayer, Goodman, A.B. Rowan of Blennerville and Anthony Denny of Tralee. Similar farms were acquired in other areas of Corca Dhuibhne around this time, and eventually clusters of houses for the converts would be built.

Foundation stone of Ventry church

A significant event took place in Ventry in early 1839: the laying of the foundation stone of a new church; an important occasion for the Protestant community there.[23] The stone was laid on 13 March by Major Mullins. An eye-witness recorded that he had begun by doubting claims about the number of converts in the area, but was genuinely astonished at the numbers attending the event. He expected to see forty or fifty people but instead saw 'four hundred men and women, poor indeed in circumstances but rich [...] in grace, who had fled from the abominations of the scarlet lady.' Among these were four men who had been parish clerks to priests in the area. Sixty children were present.

Rev. Thomas Moriarty conducted the proceedings in Irish. Two hundred Catholics were said to have observed the event, and Moriarty spoke 'in a strain of impressive, pious and soul-cheering Irish eloquence'. Rev. John Alcock, 'in his usual pious, impressive and overpowering manner', translated for the benefit of non-Irish speakers. For seventy minutes, people listened intently as Moriarty spoke of the importance of the Bible and told them that Christ wanted 'no advocate or mediator, no Virgin Mary, saints or angels between him and the true believer'. He told them of 'the errors of popery, particularly transubstantiation, saint and angel worship'. The crowd had by then swelled to seven hundred, according to this account, and the ceremony concluded with the laying of the stone. At the end, refreshments of bread and porter were provided for all.[24]

Another visitor's account, quoted by J.G. MacWalter, stated that the foundation stone was laid in November 1838, on a day on which 'everyone and everything wore a cheerful aspect'. The visitor was highly impressed, 'Our attention was attracted by a number of children advancing towards us, about sixty in number, two by two, with Mr. Moriarty at their head, who was conducting the little ones from the old schoolhouse to the new and more commodious one.' This account estimated that four hundred people were present, and Thomas Moriarty opened proceedings with the hymn 'Guide us, O thou great Jehovah!' and a prayer, both in Irish.[25] Monck Mason quoted an eye-witness account that described Moriarty as speaking in Irish 'at considerable length':

> The English part of the congregation were spectators more than auditors. All this time however, even as spectators, they were far from feeling uninterested, they read in the countenances of their Iresian brethren the drift of Mr. M.'s discourse; and as they observed intense

anxiety, riveted attention and deep interest, sparkling animation and sometimes an inexpressible burst of lively approval, they could easily judge how the arguments and appeals of the speaker told on the minds of his more intelligent audience.[26]

It took several years for Ventry church to be completed. When an English visitor named Clark visited Ventry and the Great Blasket with Charles Gayer, he observed with regret that Ventry church stood half-finished.[27] 'But why was not Ventry church finished?' he asked. 'Why did it stand a mark for the scoffer, while the increasing congregation crowded into a schoolhouse, looked sorrowfully at its walls?' As he gathered samples of 'some of the beautiful mosses from the sparry cliff' on the Blasket Island, Clark formulated a plan to raise funds in England for the completion of Ventry church by publishing an account of the missionaries' work. He printed a thousand copies and, in a shrewd marketing ploy, included 'a specimen of the moss or seaweed from the Blasquet isle' with each copy.[28] The result was that he returned the following year with £140 to donate towards the completion of Ventry church.

These verses described the church in its unfinished state, and were written to elicit donations towards its completion:

> The congregation wait the church to fill,
> Christians! The house of God is roofless still.
> Unfinished it stands upon Ventry's shore
> So fam'd in the page of our country of yore,
> Where the spirit of liberty anciently trod,
> And now where the poor are converted to God.
> It stands all unfinished and shall it remain,
> On the truth of our Christian profession a stain?

When Ventry church was finally completed, these lines were added:

> Unfinished, unhonour'd no longer it stands;
> The fisherman rests on his oar
> And raising in silent thanksgiving his hands,
> Or points to his comrades as joyful he lands,
> The church upon Ventry's shore.[29]

Thomas Moriarty was very proud of the church in Ventry and the fact that it was the only church anywhere in Ireland in which all services were conducted in the Irish language. The building survived until 1963, when it was demolished.[30]

Sketch of Ventry converts

A pencil drawing depicting seven men who were scripture readers and converts in Ventry is held in the National Gallery of Ireland.[31] The inscription on the back reads, 'A Sketch of a class of the converts as they were being examined at Ventry on Monday 8th Aug. 1842.' Six of the men are identified as James Gloster (schoolmaster at Dunquin), John Sullivan (Irish reader on the Blasket Island), Dan Sullivan, Tom Connor, Tom Kennedy (Irish readers at Ventry) and James Jordan (schoolmaster at Ventry). These men were employed by the Ladies Auxiliary or Readers' Branch of the Irish Society. The seventh man is described as 'an interesting old man whose script. knowledge tho' lately acquired impressed us very much'. Tom Kennedy was a piper who lost his source of income when he converted; he passed on hundreds of traditional tunes to Canon James Goodman. James Jordan later went to the Blasket Island as a teacher in the mission school and lived there for thirteen years.[32]

8. Rev. Thomas Moriarty and Ventry Collegiate School

Thomas Moriarty was born into a well-known Dingle family in 1813. His father Denis ('Denis the Mill') has been described as both a miller and a farmer; his mother Margaret was daughter of Dr Thomas Griffin.[1] The family was Catholic, and Moriarty was educated at a school run by Thomas Dee and Mr Finnerty.[2] This was one of the best schools in the south of Ireland, according to Moriarty, 'and was attended by sons of the local gentry and middle-class people'.[3] Various accounts of Moriarty's first encounter with a Protestant preacher were later published. In 1829, the meeting held in Dingle by Rev. Denis Browne and Rev. John Gregg was interrupted by noise, which stopped when Gregg spoke in fluent Irish. The disturbance was caused by Thomas Moriarty and other schoolboys, who were concealed under chairs. Some writers date Moriarty's conversion to this incident. For example, Rev. James B. Leslie recorded:

> The story of his conversion from Roman Catholicism has been romantically told. One version is that he in early life went to a meeting in Dingle at which a clerical missionary of the Irish Society was speaking, and tried to drown his voice by hammering an anvil; another that he pounded the floor with a cabbage-stalk. [4]

Many years later, Moriarty gave his account of this incident, explaining that it was merely a schoolboy prank and not related to his conversion. Young Moriarty and his friends had seen placards in the town announcing the lecture and 'thought to have a bit of fun in connection with it':

> The Assembly Room was large and at the time fitted for amateur theatricals. There were raised seats at one end for the audience, and under these we were concealed. When the preaching began, we made noises in various ways. The preacher had to stop, when another stood up and spoke in Irish. Such was the effect of this on us that we ceased making a noise and the service went on without any further

interruption [...] This was all the effect it had on any of us, to my knowledge, and the memory of it was lost to me until revived by my own conversion.[5]

It was under the influence of Rev. John Alcock that Thomas Moriarty converted to Protestantism; this took place in around 1831, when he was 18 years old. Details of his conversion experience are vague. It seems likely that it occurred in his hometown, although one account says that it happened while he was in Kilkenny. In this account, he was said to have gone to Kilkenny as a Catholic, and 'as bare as a crow', in the late 1820s; while there, he came under the influence of a Mr Cole, who introduced him to Kilkenny library. 'In gratitude to his patron,' went this report, 'nothing else would serve him than to renounce the religion of his fathers.'[6] Moriarty subsequently attended Trinity College, Dublin, and was ordained deacon on 9 September 1837 and minister on 15 June 1838, at the age of 25.

Kilkenny certainly was the location of some of Thomas Moriarty's formative experiences. While he was a student, he was also a tutor to the sons of Rev. Benjamin Morris of Desart, Co. Kilkenny. Moriarty married Matilda Bailey, the daughter of a church organist in Kilkenny, and the couple had four sons and six daughters.[7] In 1835, Rev. Simon Foote, curate of Knocktopher, Co. Kilkenny, learned that Moriarty was 'a thorough native Iresian'. Foote held regular meetings in the glebe house at Knocktopher, where he read and discussed the scriptures with 'intelligent Roman Catholics'.[8] Foote invited Moriarty to attend a meeting and address the group in Irish. Moriarty was inspired by the experience and marvelled that 'when the Irish scriptures were read, prejudice was removed.'[9] The participants read the opening verse of John's gospel, and Moriarty asked them what they had learned from it. Many decades later Moriarty recalled that 'one of the men, with much feeling, gave me an answer that I have never since forgotten: "I learn, Sir, that my saviour is man to feel for me and God to help me."'[10]

Moriarty was expecting to be appointed as a curate in Kilkenny after ordination, but when Henry Monck Mason heard about his talents from Rev. Foote, he invited Moriarty to become an agent of the Irish Society. Monck Mason wrote that while the society had 'for a long time been most anxious to obtain an agent who should be at once a gentleman, intelligent, pious, anxious on the particular subject and a vernacular Irish scholar, they scarcely expected to meet with such at least for a long time'. There was a pressing need for 'an agent, or rather missionary, among the poor native Irish-speaking people' of the Kingscourt district of the Irish Society, where there were 'hundreds of individuals [...] as sheep without a shepherd'.[11] Moriarty agreed to the proposal, and Rev. Morris facilitated the Irish Society by releasing Moriarty from his obligation as tutor to his sons.

Thomas Moriarty began working with the Irish Society on 15 May 1834 and went on to become one of its leading figures, held in high esteem for his piety, oratory and fluency in Irish. His ordination was described as a seminal event in the history of the Irish Society:

> The date of Mr. Moriarty's ordination we therefore fix as the third and most momentous era in the history of this Society, not only because of the divine blessing that has followed it, but because then – not before – did the Society fulfil the Saviour's whole behest, which requires us to *preach* the Gospel as well as to *teach* it to every creature.[12]

This writer continued with a rallying cry:

> Is it true that the Reformation in Ireland has failed? Is it true that popery is inevitable there and that Ireland must be Popish forever? No – a thousand voices from Kerry cry and a thousand voices more re-echo it throughout the land: we are witnesses, living monuments and proofs that popery is not indestructible.[13]

Moriarty began his ministry by working with the Irish Society in the Kingscourt district. When twenty-five converts were received into the Protestant church in Kingscourt in 1837 by Rev. J.W. Charlton, 'an appropriate sermon' was preached by Thomas Moriarty, then a deacon, assistant curate and agent of the Irish Society.[14]

In 1838, Thomas Moriarty returned as a minister to his home area, by which time the expansion of the convert community around Dingle had generated a growing sense of alarm among the Catholic priests and people. The return of this charismatic preacher and organiser added to the concerns of the local priests, who knew that he and his family were held in esteem by the people. A Dingle historian wrote that Moriarty was a brilliant scholar and 'in manners and conversation, he was mild, social and homely'.[15] Moriarty was to spend twenty-four years as a minister in Corca Dhuibhne, during which time he earned a reputation as an influential speaker at evangelical meetings in Ireland and England, and as a writer in the Protestant press. He later served as rector of Tralee from 1862 to 1869 and was appointed Dean of Ardfert in 1879.

In the reports of the Irish Society, 'Mr. Thomas Moriarty' is listed as an agent at the head of each report from October 1834 until July 1837. His starting salary was forty guineas per annum as well as expenses, later rising to £100 per annum plus expenses.[16] Moriarty visited his home area to help with the work there during the summer of 1838, and because of his family connections, he found that he was readily accepted. Two of his brothers, Matthew and Denis, converted and became Church of Ireland ministers in the post-Famine period; in 1844, their sister (whose name is not known) also converted. Matthew was ordained in 1853 and spent most of his ministry in the diocese of Raphoe, in counties Derry and Donegal; Denis was ordained in 1859 and ministered in the diocese of Limerick, Ardfert and Aghadoe.

In late 1838, there was a concerted effort to ensure that Thomas Moriarty would remain in west Kerry on a permanent basis. On 30 October, some of the converts in Ventry and Dunquin sent a petition to the headquarters of the Irish Society stating, 'we are going to loss for a minister to preach the Gospel to us and to build us up in the true faith', and requesting that the society 'leave us Mr. Moriarty entirely'.[17] The petition went on, 'We cannot keep together without a shepherd, and if we had one, many more would be brought into the fold; we all know and understand Mr. Moriarty and have already got great comfort from his preaching and we don't know what to do if he don't be left with us.'[18] The petition represented forty-seven adults and ninety-three children, but had only eight signatures because 'no more of us can sign our names'. Leaving out children, this meant that only 17 per cent of the adults could write. Their request was granted, and Moriarty began his formal ministry in west Kerry, where he was known as 'Parson M'rarity'.[19] He was immediately subjected to intense vilification by local priests, and portrayed as a turncoat and a man who had betrayed the religion of his forefathers.

In due course, three of Matthew's sons became clergymen, as did Thomas's eldest son. For these reasons alone, the Moriarty name was prominent in Church of Ireland circles for many years; nevertheless, they have been largely forgotten in Kerry. They deserve to be remembered, not least for the significant roles played by Thomas and Matthew during the Great Famine, when they regularly sent reports to the local press on the shocking conditions in the Ventry area and worked diligently on various relief efforts. Thomas is remembered in folklore as Tomás an Éithigh, 'Thomas of the lie' or 'Lying Tom'. This nickname was an unjustified and partisan characterisation of the man and his principles.

Adare Narrative in St Columba's College

In the archives of St Columba's College in Whitechurch, Co. Dublin, there is an account of the origins of the college written by Viscount Adare, MP, son of the Earl of Dunraven and an active supporter of the evangelical crusade, who had a special interest in the education of Irish-speaking ministers. The account includes transcriptions of letters written by Charles Gayer and Thomas Moriarty in the years 1838 to 1840. This bound volume, headed 'Narrative by Viscount Adare', is the source of the following information. This is an early entry:

> In October 1838 Wm. Monsell and I went to Ventry to form some idea of the work of conversion which had extended considerably in that neighbourhood. We here first saw Mr. Moriarty, he was then doing duty for Mr. Gubbins of Dunurlin Parish. We met a body of the converts who were examined by Moriarty: the scene was very striking and after he had concluded, several of the converts, wild-looking, half-clad fishermen, came up to us and entreated us with tears in their eyes that we would use our influence to enable Mr. Moriarty to remain among them for, said they, if once he goes, what can we do: scarcely one of us can speak English and no other minister in these parts understands Irish. This most interesting and important fact made a strong impression on us and from this time we took an active interest in the affairs of Ventry. In this same autumn Mr. Moriarty came to the resolution of residing in this district and subscriptions were begun to build a church, clergyman's house and school house, the buildings to be invested in five trustees, viz.: Thompson, Denny, Goodman, Rowan & Gayer.[20]

The Adare Narrative includes a printed circular from 10 November 1838 written by Charles Gayer to potential donors in which he describes the situation in Ventry. Gayer wrote that within the previous two years, 170 individuals, fifty of whom were adults, had renounced the church of Rome. Gayer was amazed that the converts happily attended services in English although few understood the language. When he asked one man why he travelled 3 miles to listen to a service in an unknown language, the reply was, 'I am not worse off than when I went to Mass, for that was all in Latin, and I believe that the blessing of God is here, and therefore it is that I attend.'[21] Gayer was pleased to inform his readers that Thomas Moriarty had been providing a service in Irish since September 1838, and that he was to remain in Ventry. Since Moriarty's arrival, several families had joined the congregation as converts.

There were two schools in Ventry 'in connection with the mission', one with sixty pupils and the other with thirty-three – and a third school was being set up. Work had already begun on building a clergyman's residence at a cost of £350 and a schoolhouse at a cost of £150, and there were also plans for building a church at a cost of £650. 'Friends in England' had already contributed the sum of £350; that left £850 outstanding. Converts would be employed in the building work; this, according to Gayer, would help them to support their families, as they had lost their regular employment by converting.[22]

The Adare Narrative includes transcriptions of several letters from Thomas Moriarty written to Viscount Adare and William Monsell. In the first such letter, dated 10 December 1838, it is clear that Moriarty had moved beyond the mild approach of the Irish Society, of which he continued to be an agent and itinerant preacher. He wrote that he wished to see a church and minister established in every parish 'on the aggressive principle' and believed that the Church of Ireland had 'fallen short of her duty and privilege' in not having done this already.

Death of Thomas Moriarty's father

It seems that there may have been some initial tensions between Moriarty and the other ministers, as he wrote cryptically, 'Mr. Gayer, Mr. Gubbins and myself are very good friends – we now understand each other.'[23] In January 1839, Moriarty's father Denis died. Although Denis Moriarty had not formally converted, he had expressed a wish to be buried under Protestant rites; his widow and immediate family agreed.[24] Other relatives opposed this, and as the funeral procession made its way to the graveyard, the atmosphere was tense. When the coffin was set down at the first crossroads, according to local custom, for prayers to be said, 'several men with sticks stationed themselves in the road' to stop the funeral. Thomas Moriarty, assisted by his mother, 'who rushed into the crowd', managed to keep the peace. Also present was Thomas Moriarty's 96-year-old grandfather. Gayer was impressed at the authority that Moriarty held over his own people, 'The influence Mr. Moriarty possesses over his relations was wonderfully seen, in as much as they bore to be struck by him with his whip without in the least resenting it; indeed some of them told him he was welcome to do it.'[25]

The exact location of the graveyard is not given, but this description by Gayer suggests that it may have been in Dunquin:

> The churchyard is situated in the centre of an amphitheatre of mountains in front of the Blasket islands against whose precipitous cliffs the waves of the Atlantic were breaking furiously and dashing the foam to a great height and the ruins of a beautiful old church which had stood for centuries defying the ravages of time added not a little to the interest of the scene. [26]

This was the first burial under Protestant rites in the graveyard. Gayer wrote that one mourner (probably a sister of the deceased) was so deeply disturbed by this that when the bones of relatives were exposed in the grave-digging, she gathered them up in her apron and took them to another part of the graveyard, 'lest they be contaminated by Protestant prayers'. A.M. Thompson also wrote of this incident, saying that the woman moved her parents' bones so that 'they might not be polluted by the neighbourhood of heretic's bones.'[27]

The death of 'Mr. Matthew Moriarty' of Dingle was reported in the *Post* of 12 January 1839. He was described as a respectable inhabitant, 'whose probity and intelligence through life had gained him the respect of all classes in the community'. Although his forename is incorrect in this report, it undoubtedly refers to Denis, father of Thomas.

The night of the big wind

An event of national significance took place on the night of 6 January 1839 – 'the night of the big wind' or *oíche na gaoithe móire*. A letter by Gayer on 12 January suggests that the gale had a more severe impact on Catholics than Protestants. He could not resist a sideswipe at Catholic rituals:

> We had a tremendous hurricane here on Sunday night which has done a great deal of damage; the gable end of our new schoolhouse was partly thrown down, but without doing any serious injury. The [Catholic] chapel was well stripped of its slates, and the chancel window was carried out into the field, and the stable was thrown down upon the priest's horse, and his hay was blown away. The house

that suffered most at Ventry was the one belonging to the priest's clerk – it was nearly blown away although he sprinkled several quarts of <u>holy water</u> about it during the storm; but little the hurricane cared for the holy water. The converts' house escaped pretty well.[28]

The *Post* used the storm to poke fun at the powers attributed to the clergy by superstitious people. It claimed that converts had been emboldened by the fact that the priests' curses on them seemed ineffectual – 'they were neither turned into hares or goats as had been confidently expected' and there were murmurs that 'there was no good at all in a priest's curse nowadays'. If the hurricane was a sign of the wrath of God and was evoked by the curses of the priests, the *Post* said it was surprising that it was Catholics who suffered most from its effects.[29]

Thomas Moriarty's preaching

The following brief extracts from the early letters of Thomas Moriarty in the Adare Narrative reveal more about Moriarty's beliefs and how he conducted his proselytising mission. Affirming that his motto was 'no peace with popery', he described how he and George Gubbins visited the villages west of Ventry over several days, and how each evening he would arrive home quite hoarse from speaking:

> In one village we began to converse and soon to discuss with a man at a gable end of one of the houses; very soon the people in the village at the time were attracted by this and stood listening at the ends of the rows of houses. A river divided the village and the women were beetling in it. They listened. A man comes up with 'a cliav' or basket on his back and stops to listen; another with a ladder and a smith with a hammer; some thatching ceased their work to listen. I exposed every error of their church, sketched how the Lord brought myself out of it and invited them into the true holy catholic church of which Christ alone is the head. We parted in peace and with a blessing.[30]

Moriarty continued, 'I have no doubt but that we are only in the infancy of a great work.' He knew that he had an advantage over other ministers in working among his own people, 'The people are very clannish and I am more or less connected with them all.' He also expressed his pleasure at discovering the powerful effects of his fluency in the Irish language, 'I seemed never till now to value the great privilege of speaking my native tongue.' He later wrote, 'My heart throbs with delight at the thought of providing for my country the only balm for its wounds – the gospel preached by the church in their own tongue.'

In 1840, Moriarty explained why members of the Irish Society devoted 'our labours, our anxieties and our prayers' to preaching the scriptures to Irish speakers in their own language – the language in which he was 'cradled and reared':

> Why, it may be asked, are they the object of our care? Why trouble ourselves, why not let them alone? We cannot do this. As neighbours, countrymen, patriots, then Christians, we cannot do this. Shall we see our neighbour's house on fire and not hasten to extinguish it? Can we witness danger without hastening to the rescue? Shall we not then be concerned for our beloved people? With the Bible before us, we must be convinced that their minds and lives are wrong. If light is in the Bible, darkness is in their system.[31]

Sectarian conflict

Whatever about Moriarty's pleasure at being among his own once more, public controversy erupted in an exchange of letters to the press in the early months of 1839. A Dingle correspondent who signed himself 'Peter Ferriter Redivivus' wrote:

> It is a melancholy consideration that this moral and once extremely social town has been torn asunder by religious discord and converted into a bear garden by a few public 'hirelings' who to evidence their zeal are always coming into collision with the inhabitants.[32]

He lamented the fact that the local gentry, magistrates and men of property had aligned themselves with 'a few foreign fanatics' against the native Catholics with whom they had previously been on good terms. He particularly resented the fact that a meeting of 'conservatives and parsons' was held to discuss the provision of relief for Catholics in distress, but that no Catholics were allowed attend. Previously another anonymous writer had condemned the evangelicals as 'ravenous wolves' who prowled around Dingle, where people suffered 'from the infestation of these itinerants who are daily flocking to this rotten borough in crowds'.[33]

A dispute arose over an appeal to help those affected by the failure of the potato crop and an acute shortage of turf in the early months of 1839. It was at this point that Thomas Moriarty entered the fray. Potatoes were selling at sixpence a stone in the market – 'starving prices', according to Moriarty. 'The poor in general', he wrote, 'depend for their very existence on these articles, and their distress at present is quite melancholy.'[34] A formal appeal to the Lord Lieutenant was drawn up by Captain Hickson of The Grove; when Fr John O'Sullivan was asked to sign it, he reacted by tearing up the paper, declaring that it was part of the proselytising campaign. Moriarty said this was an insult to the people whom the priest knew to be suffering hardship, and that the appeal had 'no more to do with proselytising than the man in the moon, as we say here'. Moriarty said of O'Sullivan's action that 'every respectable and sensible Roman Catholic must feel ashamed of it, and the poor of this place have little reason to be pleased at it.' He said that O'Sullivan was hampering the relief of the poor, 'by whose hard earnings he is supported'. In response to the petition, the Lord Lieutenant, Lord Normanby, sent a personal donation of ten guineas for the relief of distress in Dingle and described Fr O'Sullivan's action as 'unwarranted and unbecoming'.[35]

Moriarty also made public the text of a private letter he wrote to Fr O'Sullivan in which he challenged the priest's denunciation of the converts from 'the church of Rome':

> You know that I also came out from the same church, and you must be aware and doubtless won't deny, that you include in the same charge all the members of that branch of Christ's holy catholic church to which we now belong. Our cause is one, our creed is the same.

> Now, Sir, I, as a minister of that church, say of the church of Rome that she has apostasised, or fallen away from the faith once delivered to the saints and that consequently both cannot be right and that one or other teaches a way, the end of which must be death, though it seem to be right.

> The people of Dingle are my relations, friends and acquaintances, and will, I hope, feel assured that I wish them no hurt and that my heart's desire and prayer to God for them is that they might be saved. I now earnestly invite you to come with me before them publicly and examine this most important question fairly and charitably that the truth of God may be established.[36]

Moriarty summarised the progress of the conversion campaign and, like A.M. Thompson, credited Charles Gayer with introducing the Irish Society into the area. Moriarty strongly denied that there was any bribery involved in the conversions, 'But our trade, thank God, is not making merchandise of men's souls. We have no bribes to offer them but Christ and his truth and we trust they seek no other.'[37] Subscriptions were being raised in England and Ireland, and the work on building a church, school and clergyman's house was providing employment for some labourers during a time of hardship. Converts were abused and cursed, he said, and people refused even to sell potatoes to them. Moriarty told of how one convert, the father of a starving family, appealed to a close relative for food; he offered his shoes as a pledge of future payment, but he was refused and told to leave the house. The father came in despair to Moriarty, who bought potatoes for the family using money donated by a woman in Dublin. 'Such is our bribery,' wrote Moriarty, 'here is a specimen of it. Let the public judge and call it bribery if they please.'[38]

Moriarty's invitation to Fr O'Sullivan to engage in public debate received no response. He then invited the Roman Catholics of Dingle to come hear him speak at 7.00 p.m. every Monday evening during Lent in Rev. Gayer's school in the town. 'I hope you won't refuse me fair play or condemn me without a hearing,' he wrote. He assured people that they would not hear him 'abusing you or belieing [sic] your church, but stating your case fairly and showing my reasons for what I have done'.[39] In public notices around the town of Dingle, Moriarty repeated the invitation to engage in a public debate, but it was still declined. This poster then appeared on the door of the schoolhouse in the town:

> Tommy Moriarty, Take Notice. And we are given you particular notice, you — breed, you murderly breed, that it would be fiter for you to be a miller in the mill than to be disturbing the parish of Dingle, at the first opportunity we will get of you, as sure as God is in heaven, we will have some of your hart's blood, and the same notice to the reformer Keevan who posted up the bills that he is sure of the same before it long, for imposing the Rev. John Sullivan and the clergy, you infernal rascal. March 5, 1839. The Men of Dingle.[40]

According to the anonymous letter writer who recorded this notice in the *Post*, the convert named Keevan was attacked and severely beaten after this. The *Post* condemned the use of violence against the evangelicals and converts,

'Shame, shame upon those who can call out at one moment for a "clear stage and no favour" and at the very next have recourse to the *lawlaider* or the argument of the bludgeon.'[41]

Thomas Moriarty's public speeches and letters

Because he was a central figure in the Bible campaign, and one of only a small number of well-educated converts, Thomas Moriarty's declarations of his beliefs are of crucial significance in attempting to understand the motivation of both the converts and the evangelical preachers. Moriarty wrote regularly in newspapers and religious journals, and he spoke at numerous meetings. He was a master of the art of public speaking, and his many speeches were forceful expressions of his credo.

One speech was delivered in 1840 at a meeting of the Tralee branch of the Irish Society – at which the attendance was reported to be over 400.[42] The branch had an income of £482 for the previous year and had charge of fifty-three schools and 1,725 teachers. Moriarty began by saying that the Irish Society's work was not to impart religious instruction directly but to teach 'the ABC of ordinary knowledge [...] To teach the words of scripture is the simple object of the Irish Society.' The society simply prepared the way for church teaching to follow, 'The Irish teacher goes forward like the pioneer before the army, with his axe on his shoulder, to cut down opposing forests. This Society levels obstructions and makes a highway for the entrance of the gospel of peace.' Moriarty spoke passionately of his love for his native language and its significance:

> The Irish language comes home to the Irish heart. The Irish language will find its way into the bosoms of the Irish people. The Irish language is the key which will open the lock, though that lock be bolted by the Pope of Rome himself [...] Even if the people spoke English equally well, still the heart warmed to their native tongue [...] The Irish Society, by teaching the people to read the scriptures in their own language, breaks down the middle wall of partition between them, and like the levelling of the middle wall of partition between Jews and Gentiles, it is our heart's desire and prayer that we may all be one in Christ Jesus.

It is interesting to read the views of 'Tomás an Éithigh' on truth, what he saw as 'the moral degradation' of his countrymen and the obligation he felt to convert them:

The truth may give pain, truth may provoke irritation, but still faithfulness forbids us to forbear. We are not men of art but of honesty. We must speak what we know and testify what we see. We are not skilful in paying French compliments. If a man is drowning we catch him by the hair and care not that it spoil his curls. It is painful to be subjected to the construction of appearing, as it were, in arms against any of our fellow men, but we are constrained by the love of Christ.

Accepting that there were doctrinal differences between his church and the Roman church, Moriarty said that these were magnified by superstitious elements of religious observance. So while a priest would claim that the Mass was a sacrifice, he would disagree and say that there was only one sacrifice – that of Christ on the cross.

The representative of a foreign priestly despot might tell me here that the Mass is a sacrifice offered for the living and the dead [...] But what do I find when I go out to Ventry and Dingle? I find this Mass, consisting as is taught, of the body and blood, soul and divinity of Jesus Christ, offered for *sick pigs*!! Nay, laugh not. It is a thing over which to weep. Yes, this pretended sacrifice of the body and blood, soul and divinity of Jesus Christ is offered for sick pigs and sick cows and sick everything. It is not enough that Romanism should have corrupted Christianity, the corruptions of Romanism are re-corrupted in accommodation to the superstitions of the people. It is monstrous, it is an abomination, this prostitution of even the pretended sacrifice of the Mass, a sacrifice which implies a supposed transubstantiation of the wafer into Christ's body and blood, soul and divinity, into a sacrifice offered for a pig to litter. Ten days ago a priest offered the sacrifice of the Mass for the success of a fishing boat!!

Moriarty told his audience that the congregation in Ventry was between 260 and 270. He related a story about an old man who wished to be buried under Protestant rites, although he had been unable to attend their services. He asked the old man if he had received the sacrament before; the man replied, 'Yes – *vee shen boccough*!' (*Bhí sin bacach*, 'That was lame'.) Moriarty commented, 'A lame sacrament indeed it is. It is only of one kind and stands as it were on one leg.'[43]

In May 1840, Thomas Moriarty wrote to a fellow clergyman giving an account of his progress. He said that there were three men from Kerry in Trinity College training for the ministry: his brother, Mr Foley and Mr Hamilton, who was Foley's uncle. 'Are not these, dear friend, tokens of good for poor Ireland?' he asked.[44] He described how he was working 'to build up and cement my congregation', seeing himself more 'like a missionary among the heathen than an ordinary minister of the church' since the people were 'grossly ignorant, not knowing a word of English'. Moriarty had developed a particular strategy that worked well:

> I am in the habit of *holding stations*, as I call them, at the houses of my congregation in turn. I give notice that I will, D.V. [*Deo volente*, or God willing], be in such a village on a certain night in the week at such a person's house. All belonging to the congregation will be there and some of the neighbours, the Romans, never fail to come in by way of no harm. My plan is on such occasions to catechise and explain the church services, seasons, festivals etc., pointing out as we proceed the additions and corruptions of Rome.[45]

Moriarty wished that his friend could see the congregation on the Sabbath, 'all now understanding the different parts of the service and audibly uniting and responding'. He was pleased that so many adults had converted, but believed that 'our fine school of children is in fact the most important part of all; this is what will give perpetuity to the work. We have about 100 children fast growing in sound scriptural and church knowledge. You would be most delighted to examine many of them. They are most promising.'[46]

Writing later in 1840, Moriarty described his progress, 'I returned to my kindred and people, had the ministration of the church in their native tongue and preached the gospel in the same and after two years we have a congregation of nearly 300 souls.'[47] Moriarty did not refer to any persecution in this letter, only to the 'superstitions and delusions' of the Catholic population. He understood the challenge that his message presented to a people whom he believed had never been allowed individual choice before, 'All this is alarming, for heretofore the Irish mind has been attached to Pope and popery – but how? By not daring to doubt, by not daring to think, by keeping the mind enslaved, by having it in bondage, so that if they dared to think, it was damnation.'[48]

Moriarty addressed a meeting of the Kerry Auxiliary of the Irish Society in Tralee in 1844, when once again over four hundred people were present. By this time, the 'old Protestants' of Kerry were fully supportive of the work of the evangelicals. In an introductory speech, Rev. Anthony Denny, from a family long established in the town, gave the seal of approval to the conversion campaign, 'When we see our fellow countrymen bowing down to a system of superstition [...] is it not an act of mercy to bring them before the truth which will carry them (the Roman Catholics) to salvation?'[49]

In his address, Moriarty emphasised the Irish language:

> It is not the English speaking but the *Irish speaking* population of this country that are the objects of our interest. Three millions of people in Ireland speak Irish as well as English and half a million speak nothing but Irish – these are our objects, we wish to bring all who speak or love the Irish language to read in their own tongue of the wonderful works of God. This is a true and Protestant principle [...] We are the national, patriotic and Irish church for we are the only church that provided the word of God in the language of the people.[50]

For Moriarty, 'the music of the Irish tongue' was like 'the harp of David that drove the evil spirit out of Saul'. He was aware that 'it is no easy task for a man in this country to hear the word of God and afterwards to become a convert', and he cited several instances of persecution with which he was familiar. Even if some converts were hypocritical and motivated by material aims, Moriarty believed that they were under extreme social pressure and deserved support:

> I trust that every Protestant, till he has good and palpable reason for suspecting a poor man of hypocrisy, will not throw a bucket of cold water on him and drive him back to apostasy but give him protection and secure him liberty of conscience against this pressure from without. I say, let what will be said, we are determined to stick by these poor people.[51]

Moriarty keenly felt the alienation that followed his own change of religion, and in powerful words he declared:

> Some men claim exclusive patriotism. If they are Irish, so are we.

Am I not Irish, heart and soul and tongue? Have we not Irish hearts and love of country and as much Irish blood as they? And shall we not take as our motto to make Ireland 'great, glorious and free' as well as they? I do admire the natural sentiments of honest religion amongst the people but I pity their ignorance; and because I have true charity, I am determined to persevere so long as God gives me strength in the work of their enlightenment.[52]

The Hibernian Bible Society was another evangelical organisation of which Moriarty was loud in his praise. 'All their societies, Christian, benevolent or charitable,' he told a meeting of the Kerry Auxiliary Bible Society, 'are but a skeleton without the Bible Society.' He was grateful to the Bible Society, which had sent him a hundred copies of the English Bible for distribution in his area, but 'it was not for the English Bible that his heart was so grateful as for the Irish Bible.' The Irish Society had given the people of Ireland 'an edition of God's word in the language of the people [...] they, as Protestants, ought to feel proud that their church had been the first to give birth to an Irish Bible.'[53]

Moriarty spoke about the first Irish Bible that had come to Dunquin. It was given by Lord Ventry to 'poor Shamus Bawn' about fifteen years earlier, 'long before the labours of the Irish Society manifested themselves'. Speaking movingly of this particular book, Moriarty evoked laughter when he said 'he loved it not less because it had the smack of cabin smoke upon it and the potato skin stuck to the cover of it.' Moriarty kept this Bible on the pulpit in Dunquin and 'he looked on it with more pleasure than if it was bound in gold, as being the first messenger of heaven.'[54] Séamus Bán O'Connor has been described as the first convert in Dunquin; he was a poet and man of learning.[55] Thompson described him as 'a village sage' who read the Bible to local gatherings on winter evenings, with the result that 'when the Reformation began in Ventry, many from Dunquin joined company with them.'[56]

Monck Mason recorded a telling incident that confirmed the efficacy of Thomas Moriarty as a communicator. Moriarty agreed to provide a Sunday service in the schoolhouse in Dunquin in order to spare parishioners the hardship of travelling to Ventry. One of the 'most zealous opposers' of the Protestant mission came to observe what was happening. While the service was being conducted in Irish, 'he stood for some time opposite to Mr. Moriarty, listening attentively with his arms crossed. At length he exclaimed: "If you go on praying as you do and if the priests go on opposing you as they do, it's not one church (meaning the schoolhouse) but twenty you will have to build.'"[57]

Satires

A meeting of the Protestant Operative Association was held in Cork in July 1843. It was addressed by two Moriarty brothers, Thomas and his younger brother – who wasn't named in the newspaper report, but was 23 years old and a student at Trinity College at that time. Those attending were derided in the nationalist *Cork Examiner* as 'the lowest and most truculent class of Orangemen' and 'a heterogeneous congregation of hideous humanity'.[58] The younger Moriarty, described as 'a hulking, broad-featured illiterate person with a tongue redolent of turf and potatoes', gave an impassioned twenty-minute speech that involved 'stamping, vociferating, menacing and attitudinising, like one determined to tear a passion to tatters'. The young man directed his attack on 'the old wretch who sits in the Vatican', but also criticised Irish Protestant leaders for not exerting themselves in opposing 'the cloven foot of popery [that] was stalking all over the land from Cape Clear to the Giant's Causeway and from the Blaskets to Donaghdee'.

Thomas Moriarty was then introduced as 'the great gun of the evening [...] the hero of Dingle, the beloved of the saints, the pioneer of Protestantism amid the crags and bogs of the Blaskets'. He was described as speaking with 'an affectation of gentility, a show of moderation, a soothing silveriness of brogue'. He explained that 'he would not use abusive language towards popery' and that his brother was inexperienced and more hot-blooded than he was. But when the audience made it clear that they preferred his brother's declamatory style, Thomas was reported as having become more passionate in his condemnations of popery.[59]

Thomas Moriarty was also mocked in the *Freeman's Journal* after a meeting of the Irish Society held in the Rotunda in Dublin under chairman Lord Roden. The paper declared that the society's annual report was, 'of course, full of wonderful statements relative to thousands of nameless converts in remote rural districts' and went on:

> A letter was read from the Rev. Thomas Moriarty which was one of the funniest things ever listened to. A whole congregation had, it asserted, sprung up in some faraway district in consequence of the exertions of the society; converts were as thick as midges in a sunny land, and one old man died in the true faith notwithstanding that his various relatives surrounded him like demons at his last hour.[60]

Moriarty's accent was mocked in a satirical article by 'Will o' the Wisp' in the *Kilkenny Journal* after he had spoken in Knocktopher, Co. Kilkenny, appealing for contributions for the converts of west Kerry. The report described the converts as 'poor, ignorant, naked, half-starved wretches who get provisions and money from Tommy and Gayer for joining their Irish Bible Reformation'. Moriarty's lecture, which elicited £30 in donations, was described as a 'sarmint' (sermon) in which 'the wants of the neophytes were painted for the ladies in the most "iligant" style.' The report concluded with heavy irony:

> Posterity will stand amazed at the light that now dawns over the kingdom of Kerry. Some ages hence when Rome shall be no more [...] the church of the saints will always look back in rapture at the bright era at which the gospel light beamed with such glory upon Ventry and Dingle.[61]

Plans for a college in Ventry

Soon after he was settled in Ventry, Thomas Moriarty started to implement a long-cherished plan for the training of young men as teachers and ministers. He wrote to Viscount Adare about his scheme. Always conscious of 'the deplorable want of good teachers in this country', he had resolved, 'if ever I should be permanently fixed in a parish, to train persons for that office'. He envisaged an institution for the education of young men 'for the office of scripture readers and schoolmasters and anyone of peculiar promise for the university with the view of raising up Irish ministers also'.[62] Students would become fluent Irish speakers, and scriptural education would be central to their training. Moriarty preferred young converts from Roman Catholicism, as they would be more effective among the people. The college would also serve as a kind of 'refuge' for these young converts, who would find themselves cast out from their own people. The students would be instructed in English reading, writing and grammar, arithmetic, elements of science, history and geography. Moriarty saw the institution as being 'under my own special care' and envisioned that the students would have 'a real practical education in school and out of doors'.[63]

On 5 June 1840, Moriarty explained that his plan was to build a large house for the schoolmaster; that it would include accommodation for about twelve young men, who would be trained by him and by another schoolmaster. Moriarty subsequently suggested a good house for a gentleman, or perhaps a clergyman and his wife; a good schoolroom to accommodate fifty boys; and a dormitory.[64] The total cost would be £1,000, along with a salary of £100 a year for a teacher. Students would be asked to pay £30 or £40 a year, and there would be exhibitions or scholarships for those unable to pay. 'The situation you know is good', wrote Moriarty, 'the purest air, the ordinary education should be good and above all there would be a <u>full Irish service</u> every Sabbath.' Moriarty stressed that the college would provide 'not only Irish speakers able to preach but able to minister in Irish [...] and nowhere in Ireland can this be had but at Ventry.'[65]

Viscount Adare pondered over Moriarty's ideas and discussed them with a friend in London, Dr Boynton. The two men agreed to promote the college envisaged by Moriarty, who expressed his appreciation of their support in a letter of 30 July 1840 in which he again spelled out his philosophy. He condemned the way the established church had neglected areas like Ventry, which, he explained, was 'not manifestly like an ordinary parish throughout Ireland', because it had no glebe house, no church, no school. Moriarty declined to play a prominent role in publicly promoting the college; he deferred to Charles Gayer and D.P. Thompson as persons who were more important than he was.[66] Perhaps he was conscious of his position as curate, or the fact that he was a recent arrival — although he undoubtedly carried much more influence among the people of west Kerry than Gayer or Thompson did.

The plans for a training college for potential ministers were discussed by Moriarty and three visitors as they sat on a cliffside in Corca Dhuibhne in the summer of 1840, admiring the magnificent vista of the Blasket Islands. The visitors were Viscount Adare, William Monsell and Dr William Sewell, an English clergyman, theologian and author. Monsell was a landowner in Tervoe, Clarina, Co. Limerick. He later had a political career, served in several ministerial posts and became 1st Baron Emly in 1874. The four men went as far as identifying a site in Ventry for the college and approving a plan for Moriarty to begin the education of a small number of students. Three young men named Morris, Murphy and Collins were the first students. Adare sent a list of instructions to Moriarty setting out, in detail, how they should be taught. However, when Viscount Adare, Monsell and a Dr James Henthorn Todd of Trinity College visited Ventry in October 1841, they were most disappointed to find that 'Mr. Moriarty, by his numerous avocations, had been prevented from paying to [the students] the attention they required.' He had seldom inquired into their studies and had not enforced the regulations as set down for him. Adare and his companions concluded, 'His manner towards [the students] was not that of a master towards his scholars. The evil effects of this want of supervision were very evident.'[67]

Viscount Adare, along with Todd, Monsell and Sewell, went on to establish a training college for future ministers without any further involvement from Thomas Moriarty. In 1843, St Columba's College was established in Stackallan, Co. Meath; it moved to Whitechurch, Co. Dublin, in 1849. Sewell gave a speech on the opening day and generously acknowledged that Moriarty was 'the first person into whose heart God put the thought' of such a college. He recalled the day spent 'on one of the wild Atlantic cliffs of that desolate but interesting coast' in west Kerry, and said that 'it was on that spot, with that clergyman for its chief director, that it was first intended to establish the present institution, though on a far humbler scale.'[68]

Ventry Collegiate School

Thomas Moriarty realised his personal ambition by establishing Ventry Collegiate School, and it was on a humbler scale than St Columba's. Information on the college is limited, but some brief references to it are found in newspaper sources. In 1844, the college in Ventry received official approval from the Irish Society for the instruction of Irish-speaking youths, and in 1845 four exhibitions, or scholarships, were established in Trinity College as a further encouragement for students of the Irish language.[69] The Irish Society was pleased to report that 'its Irish school at Ventry has already sent out many pupils who are now employed as clerical missionaries.'[70] In 1846, Monck Mason recorded that two young men from the 'seminary' called 'Ventry Irish School' had already entered Trinity College to train for the ministry.[71] In 1850 there were twelve students in Ventry Collegiate School.[72] In 1853 the Irish Society advertised for a headmaster. A married clergyman was preferred, and he was required to have gained honours in his undergraduate course and to be 'thoroughly qualified to prepare young men for sizarships and honours in the university'. Applications were to be made to the secretary of the Irish Society or to Rev. Daniel Foley of Trinity College.[73]

In 1854, a Mr Hackett spoke at an Irish Society meeting in Tralee and stated that Dr Salmon, 'a scholar of European fame', was astonished at the high standards of Ventry Collegiate School. Hackett claimed that 'no school in Ireland [...] presented such advantages' to young students. Eleven converts from the west Kerry district had become ordained ministers, according to

Hackett. Other graduates included a man named Long, who was a teacher in a ragged school in London, and another who was a missionary in the Himalayas.[74] The obituary of a Lt James Charlton, who died as a result of injuries received at the siege of Lucknow in India, stated that he was a former pupil of the college. He was the son of a church minister in London.[75] Another former student was Canon Charles Jordan, vicar of Tauranga, Bay of Plenty, New Zealand, who died in 1912. He was also mayor of Tauranga for many years. He was the son of James Jordan, one of the first converts in Ventry and a teacher in the mission school on the Great Blasket.

When Rev. George Scott of Banagher visited 'Ventry Collegiate Institution' in 1854, he found 'teaching such as the richest parent in our land might desire for his children'. The teacher was Mr Heazle, a graduate of Trinity College, who was examining the class in a text by Euripides and who 'required nice and accurate translation and gave the lads a great sifting in the moods and tenses of the Greek verbs'. The school was described as a cottage with a neat flower garden in front, and there were eighteen students, one of whom had previously studied in the Catholic seminary in Louvain, Belgium. Scott explained that 'it is required of every pupil received into this seminary [Ventry] that he should be able to speak Irish and destined by himself and friends for the office of the ministry'. Ventry college had already 'produced good fruit', he wrote, 'for it has furnished four ordained clergymen to our church and eight students to our university, all of whom have Irish tongues'.[76]

An advertisement for Ventry Collegiate School in 1855 listed the archbishops of Armagh and of Dublin as its patrons, and seven other bishops as vice-patrons. Thomas Moriarty was one of the trustees, along with Rev. William Salmon, fellow of Trinity College, and Revs Daniel Foley and W.D. Sadleir, doctors of divinity.[77] The headmaster was Rev. Garrett Nugent, and the Irish master was James O'Sullivan, Bedell Scholar of Trinity College. Fees were £20 per annum for boarders, along with an additional £3 entrance fee; it was six guineas per annum for day pupils. The students were promised that 'the utmost attention' would be paid to their moral and religious training under the 'constant superintendence' of Rev. Thomas Moriarty. No other such advertisements have been found, suggesting perhaps that the college had resorted to advertising because it was having difficulty in attracting candidates. It is not clear when the college closed down, but the building still stands, now divided into separate houses.[78]

9. War of words, 1839–41

Famine conditions

The summer months were the hungry months, before the potato harvest came in. For three years in a row, 1839, 1840 and 1841, Corca Dhuibhne suffered extreme food shortages and consequent hardship, and the evangelical ministers and Catholic priests were actively involved in providing relief to the poor. In the early summer of 1839, potatoes were selling at high prices and the need for food and clothing was acute among a hard-pressed and hungry population. The *Mercury* feared that 'destitution in its worst form is likely to be general in this county.' There were 'four months of ordeal' remaining before the harvest, and 'starvation is threatening to stalk abroad.'[1] Meetings were convened around the county to plan for the relief of the suffering poor, and a relief committee in Tralee had already raised £409. An anguished letter from 'the dilapidated and sinking town of Dingle' began with descriptions that are hauntingly similar to press reports of conditions early in the Famine year of 1847:

> The famine which at the present moment rages in this town is really frightful. Potatoes are 9d per stone and no employment for the poor, nor is a single effort yet made to provide any. Two or three individuals have died here lately for want of food. These harassing cases of misery present to the mind the melancholy contrast of a country teeming with abundance while the labouring classes are walking spectres – the single anomaly of vessels freighted with corn daily leaving our shores while the poor are actually starving! The apathy evinced (in this trying crisis) by the representatives of the landed interest is truly extraordinary [...]

> There are four months of famine still before us – and gracious God! What are the poor to do in the interim? Are they to starve and perish in detail?[2]

The letter was signed 'Beta'. It berated Lord Ventry and Col Townsend (landlord of Dingle town) for not contributing a shilling to relief, and implied that the Earl of Cork, another landlord, had not contributed either. The *Mercury* editorial supported the letter writer, 'The soil ought to feed its poor and the lords of this soil, whether absent or resident, are morally bound, above all others, to relieve the wants of their perishing fellow creatures throughout their respective patrimonies.'[3]

The *Mercury* cited another letter from Beta on 13 July 1839, stating that seventy tons of potatoes had been ordered by the Lord Lieutenant but twenty tons of that amount were found to be rotten. Fr Divine, Major Mullins and John Hickson set up an effective relief operation for the poor, but it was reported that D.P. Thompson, Charles Gayer and Captain Forbes of the Coast Guard service refused to help in distributing the aid because of 'sectarian jealousy'.[4] In response, D.P. Thompson explained that Lord Ventry had received £100 from the Master of the Rolls for relief. Of this, £40 went to Castlemaine, Castleisland and Killorglin, where there was great distress, and the remainder to Dingle. Thompson claimed that, at his own expense, he had bought a cargo of oatmeal and potatoes to the value of £400; he stated that this was sold indiscriminately at reduced prices in Dingle. Thompson arranged for potatoes to be given on special credit terms to the poor who had walked long distances into Dingle so that they would not have to return home empty-handed. This helped to relieve the pressure on Dingle market, he said, and as a result, prices had been kept low. On learning the full facts, the *Mercury* corrected the earlier claims and acknowledged that Thompson's actions reflected 'high credit' on his humanity.[5] The *Post* also praised Lord Ventry and D.P. Thompson for 'the active readiness which they have shown through this season of distress in assisting to relieve the wants of the poor'.[6]

The distress of 1839 was repeated in 1840. A letter writer named Michael O'Halloran wrote of 'the unparalleled misery and destitute condition of the poor of Dingle' after successive seasons of hardship. The poor were pawning their clothes, potatoes were selling at high prices and labourers' wages were scarcely enough to buy one meal in twenty-four hours, 'They are emaciated objects, with just enough food to make them feel unceasingly the yearnings of hunger [...] These harrowing objects of misery present to the mind the unnatural contrast of a country teeming with abundance and the strange anomaly of vessels laden with corn daily leaving our shores while the people are falling victim to the dire consequences of famine.'[7]

The Poor Law Act of 1838 established Poor Law Unions throughout the country. The barony of Corca Dhuibhne, with its fifty thousand inhabitants, was part of Tralee Poor Law Union. The union workhouse was built in Tralee and finally opened its doors in February 1844. The barony of Corca Dhuibhne was 'the poorest and most populous in Kerry', and places like Dunquin and Dunurlin were 40 miles from Tralee. O'Halloran blamed the local gentry for not procuring a separate workhouse for the barony of Corca Dhuibhne, 'We have two or three months of famine still before us and how are the poor to live in the interim?' He urged civil and religious authorities to heed 'the practice of that part of pure and undefiled religion, which is to feed the hungry, seeing that a few months of famine and disease would utterly sweep away whole bodies of human beings'.[8] A month later, a report from Dingle stated that Mr Gayer was 'straining every nerve to raise subscriptions in Dublin and in England' to alleviate the distress:

> The poor are literally dropping in the street from the exhaustion induced by want of food. This is a fearful state of things in a Christian country and blame of no ordinary degree is attributable somewhere; but in what quarter we are not prepared to say.[9]

In 1841, when the hardship continued, Charles Gayer and his wife were reported as 'constantly engaged throughout the summer in the importation of potatoes for the relief of all without distinction of profession or creed'. In Gayer's absence from home, his wife Catherine sold potatoes to 120 Catholic families at a reduced price. The missionary boat named *Brothers*, with a cargo of potatoes worth £120, was driven onto the rocks of Kerry Head in a storm. Responding to a claim that this was a judgment of God on the evangelicals, Rev. Edward Spring, curate of Dunurlin, wrote that, on the contrary, the survival of the crew – three men and a boy – was miraculous. Spring wrote that they were greeted warmly by their Catholic neighbours on their return to Dingle.[10]

Propaganda war

In the three years of hardship, 1839 to 1841, a war of words was carried out in newspaper columns and in pulpits, with the tenor of exchanges being extremely sectarian and vitriolic. Some letters were published under pseudonyms, although it is likely that the identities of the writers were known to newspaper editors, and perhaps to many readers. One such letter, signed 'Veridicus', appeared in the *Mercury* on 2 March 1839. The writer condemned the 'shameless system of proselytising' and the 'traffic in souls' that was taking place in Dingle. As examples of inducements offered in Ventry, he stated that some prospective converts were allowed abatements of two or three gales (instalments) of rent; he claimed a boat worth £10 was given to some, and turf and potatoes were sent to others. One poor man was reported to have been offered clothing for his three children if he attended Protestant services and sent the children to the school. Another man was offered £5 as a scripture reader, and he wondered if the priest would allow him to 'take the money from the rogues' if he remained 'a staunch Papist in his heart'. Veridicus claimed that servants who worked in evangelical households were obliged to become Protestants. He was convinced that bribery was rampant and that most of the converts were insincere. He cited instances of people returning to the Catholic Church and doing public penance when their expectations of rewards for conversion were not met. He claimed that some who purported to be converts recited the 'Hail Mary' prayer silently while attending Protestant services.[11]

Veridicus also referred to the provision of soup, indicating that it was not only the distribution of soup that was perceived as offensive but also the fact that it was given out specifically on Fridays, a day when Catholics were forbidden to eat meat, 'When their honest neighbours are provoked by the blasphemies of the "perverts" they naturally return the compliment and cry out "soup", which is the beverage distributed on Friday to these poor creatures and for the avowed purpose of "expelling the Pope from their stomachs".'[12]

The *Post* described Veridicus as 'a skulking libeller' and published a response from Rev. George Gubbins in which he condemned the 'persecution and starvation of priestly tyranny'.[13] He related how he had set up home at Ferriter's Cove in November 1831 – how he had preached and gone from house to house during his eight years there. 'The result has been, through divine grace, most glorious,' he stated. He had recently appealed to friends in England to support the building of a church in Dunurlin, and the response had been very generous.

Rev. Gayer also responded to Veridicus's letter by denying that either of his two Catholic servants was obliged to attend Protestant services. His cook had asked to be excused from family prayers and this was permitted. He stated that tenants in Ventry were not granted rent reductions or remissions in return for attending Protestant services. Neither were converts in Ventry

given a boat worth £10; rather, he allowed them to use his own boat to
fish, as and when he permitted, 'on account of their being excluded from
the boats of their Roman Catholic neighbours'. He claimed that support
in the form of turf was never given to people, and potatoes were given only
to families 'who would otherwise go to bed supperless'. Gayer stated that
support was provided regardless of religion, and that the great majority of
those in receipt of relief from the evangelicals were Catholic families,
because 'Our Lord's command is that even if an enemy hunger, we should
feed them.'[14] Gayer stated that misguided Catholics may have mistakenly
believed that souls could be purchased by offers of clothing or money, but
he emphatically denied that it ever happened. He concluded by stating that
'no soup whatever [was] given out on Friday, or any day of the week, to
converts.' The editor of the *Mercury* decided that he could not adjudicate
between the contradictory claims made, but he placed the sectarian conflict
in a national context, stating that 'a spirit of proselytism, by no means of
the purest character, prevails almost through the whole length and breadth
of this island.'[15]

Fr John Halpin, curate of Dingle, joined in the press attacks on the
evangelicals. He was prepared to sign his name to letters, regretting that
other correspondents had not the courage to do likewise. He had no doubt
that people were being bribed and wrote that 'the naked and famishing
poor of Dingle' who went to the church on one or two Sundays and who
sent their children to the Protestant school could be seen later with 'warm
plush doublets' on their backs and plenty of 'black bulls' (potatoes) in their
cabins:

> Is it not a notorious fact that one woman who was first a Catholic
> went to church, then did penance for her crime and returned to
> Mass, and that now, pinched with famine she goes again to church?
> What could induce her thus to 'wheel about' like a weathercock, but
> to receive the premium [laid out] to perversion?[16]

In reference to the numbers of converts, Halpin challenged the claim that
there were two hundred Ventry converts at the laying of the foundation
stone of the church there; nevertheless, he accepted that there could have
been that number of converts in the whole barony. He declined to engage
in a public debate with Protestant ministers, but ended with a practical
proposal for a kind of truce between them:

Let them mind their own congregations and I will give them the 'turncoats' into the bargain. Let them interfere no further with the creed of poor Catholics, and we priests will continue to discharge our humble labours towards our own flocks, which are not the worse of being purged of the infected sheep.[17]

Rev. Charles Gayer welcomed the openness of Fr Halpin, but he defended his own actions. He wrote that when people converted, they 'expose themselves to reproach and persecution and insult of every kind from their neighbours'. In such circumstances, Gayer saw it as a privilege and a duty to assist them and relieve their distress:

Common humanity, independent of Christian feeling, would oblige us to do so in any case but especially when we see them persecuted for righteousness sake. Now here again, I solemnly declare that I never held out a bribe of any sort, directly or indirectly, by myself or others, to any individuals to leave the church of Rome.[18]

Gayer wrote that it would be foolish to offer inducements to people to convert. He told of a man who came to him saying that he was willing to convert on Gayer's terms. 'What terms?' asked Gayer. 'Oh,' he said, 'the leg of mutton and three shillings a week.' On being asked where he had heard of such an offer, the man said that Fr O'Sullivan had told his congregation of it in church. A woman who came to Gayer on the pretext of selling eggs told him that her real motive was to obtain the blanket and clothes given to anyone who converted. Gayer asked her if she would really sell her religion for a blanket and she replied, 'Oh, no, not for a blanket without the clothes.'

Gayer claimed that Fr O'Sullivan was himself not above giving financial inducements to individuals to return to the Catholic Church, naming four as examples: Ellen Waters, Mrs Fitzgerald, Mr Quinn and Catherine Fitzgerald. Gayer also refuted the claim that there were only fifty or so converts in Ventry, saying that over three hundred converts from the general area attended the laying of the foundation stone, and that two hundred of these were from Ventry itself. They were a congregation 'once perverted, now converted, once infected with the poison of popery, now under the influence of the balm of Gilead'. The letter ended with Gayer challenging the Dingle priests to debate the issues, 'We are ready and willing to meet him and his brethren in Dingle, Ventry, the Blaskets, or anywhere they please, for our motto is "No peace with Rome".'[19]

In reply, Fr Halpin conceded that the priests gave relief to some members of their congregations to prevent them being lured away from the faith because of their poverty. Nonetheless, he said that this would not be necessary if Gayer and his confreres had not actively campaigned to convert people, 'The poor of Dingle never brought their souls to market till he opened an emporium for such spiritual commerce.'[20] Gayer was 'the highest bidder' in the contest. Halpin described Ellen Waters as 'pawning her children' and said that all of the fourteen thousand Catholics in 'these parishes' believed that 'the 200 turncoats in Ventry, whom the Rev. Mr. Gayer toasts of as the "glory and crown of his apostleship" are confirmed hypocrites.' Halpin predicted that, in time, without financial support from England, the church, schoolhouse and glebe of Ventry 'will become like the ruins of Babylon, "the haunt of owls and foxes"'.[21]

Rev. Charles Gayer was a formidable, tireless propagandist, and his writings and lectures were designed to boost the morale of the converts, to inspire reverence and awe, to influence the wavering and to encourage readers and listeners to contribute financially to his work. One of his letters, published in *The Warder*, deserves particular attention. Introducing Gayer's letter under the heading 'Progress of Pure Christianity in the County of Kerry', the editor stated that it 'cannot fail to awaken the liveliest emotions of gratitude and to lead every sincere lover of divine truth to exclaim: "What hath God wrought!"'

Gayer's letter described the building of a church, a schoolhouse, a house for the clergyman and several cottages in Ventry, where there was a congregation of 220. Gayer was optimistic 'that the spirit of inquiry is still unabated' and that the people 'were losing the horror with which they hitherto regarded Protestantism'. Six converts had died without reverting to their old faith; Gayer believed this had a deep effect on the people, who had been assured by priests that converts would return to Catholicism on their death-beds. While Ventry church was being built, a wall fell on one of the workers and crushed him. He lay there close to death for some hours, and people thought that he would ask for a priest to attend him. He firmly declined, saying that 'his trust was not in man but in the Lord Jesus alone.' In Gayer's words, 'he was tried and found faithful' and then made a full recovery.[22]

Gayer said that many people who wished to convert pointed out that they had 'work and subsistence' as Catholics which they would lose by changing allegiance. Gayer told of an elderly convert who was beaten close to death by a mob. Several of those involved were taken to court and convicted, but according to Gayer, the converts magnanimously chose not to enforce the penalties.[23] These incidents of hardship and opposition were interpreted as tests of the faith for the converts, and they were also used to elicit sympathy and financial supports for them.

Charles Gayer in Chester

Rev. Charles Gayer made several visits to Britain to speak at evangelical meetings and raise funds for his building projects. He was generally well received, but in Chester in December 1839 he raised hackles. The *Chester Chronicle* reported that 'a clerical gentleman calling himself the Rev. Mr. Gayer' spoke at a meeting in the city; that 'he was charged to the bung with some monstrous tales about the Dingle Roman Catholics', accusing them of 'horrible immoralities and idolatry'. The editor 'shrewdly suspected the fellow was an arrant impostor', since 'his statements bore the impress of self-evident falsehood.' Gayer's speech was not reported in detail in any newspaper, but the *Chester Chronicle* published a response from Fr Divine, parish priest of Dingle. He had succeeded Fr Thomas Foley, who died in April 1839. Fr Divine rejected Gayer's statements as unfounded and malicious, and he challenged his assertion about the numbers of Protestants in Dingle. He wrote that relics were very rare items – that he knew nothing of 'holy stones and saints' teeth', and that images and scapulars were used for their proper purpose and were not adored. After reading Gayer's 'monstrous falsehoods', Divine responded that 'it would not be to me a matter of surprise that the Rev. Mr. Gayer said the people of Dingle had tails.' According to the priest, the evangelicals' work consisted of 'bribing a few sheep-stealers and seducing a few starving families'. Fr Divine referred to the converts as 'our turncoat Paddys', and claimed they were motivated by a harsh summer, the decline of trade and the fear of eviction. It was these economic hardships that caused 'the temporary conversion of a few creatures', and not 'the Protestant Bible or the Irish preaching of an unprincipled apostate'. This was a reference to Rev. Thomas Moriarty.[24]

The *Chester Chronicle* accepted Divine's rebuttal, which it saw as confirmation of its own suspicions about Gayer, and it condemned attempts to arouse ill-will towards Catholics, 'Their errors are great enough, but to charge them with the worship of images and relics and to assert that they give adoration or divine homage except where it is only due, is most wantonly wicked.' As regards the scriptures, the paper said that Catholics did not reject the Bible, but only the authorised version of the Bible – and only because they had their own approved version. It stated that a Protestant clergyman would not allow the Catholic Douai Bible to be promoted among his flock, and that it should be no surprise to anyone that priests were opposed to the authorised version of the Bible being promoted among their parishioners.[25]

The controversy was immediately taken up in the *Post*, the only Kerry newspaper being published at the time. An editorial condemned the words 'liar' and 'impostor', which the Dingle curate, Fr John Halpin, was said to have used in church to describe Rev. Gayer. In a restrained letter, Thomas Moriarty tried to calm the debate by appealing to the Catholic people of Dingle not to form a judgment until they had heard from Gayer himself, 'All I want is to have what Mr. Gayer said clearly ascertained from his own lips, and not from liars and slanderers.'[26] The *Post* continued to fan the flames by claiming that the Pope had called the Bible 'the devil's book', and that there were many superstitious practices among Catholics, 'practices which our poor credulous peasantry are taught to rely upon as passports to heaven'. As examples, it cited the practice of having Mass offered in a fishing boat and unspecified rituals around St John's Day.[27] In reference to the charge that it was only those who were starving who converted, the *Post* claimed that the most recent converts in Ventry were a family with whom a priest had shared breakfast every morning after Mass – that they were certainly not starving. The *Post* commended Thomas Moriarty, saying that everybody knew that he had given up 'very flattering prospects elsewhere' in order to return to his own county to work.[28]

Thomas Moriarty wrote again, posing this question about Fr Divine, 'Can this be our new priest, who was reported so different from the rest, as all meekness and charity?'[29] Moriarty said that he was content to leave the spirit and language of Fr Divine's letter to the judgment of those who read it. He conceded that the converts were bribed – but quickly explained that the only bribe was 'the unsearchable riches of Christ'. As regards Divine's description of him as 'an unprincipled apostate', Moriarty said that he was willing to justify his principles before the public, and he appealed to Divine to show 'some of the charity which thinketh no evil'.[30]

Fr Halpin also wrote to *The Pilot*, referring to 'the extraordinary gambols of bigotry and intolerance' displayed by 'a reverend tourist (a Mr. Gayer) who is at present paying off his antics at Chester'. He did not mince words, accusing Gayer of 'enormous lying', of speaking 'with all the narrow-minded virulence of a bigot' and of being 'steeped in the very mire of fanaticism'. He blamed Gayer and his patron, Lord Ventry, for spreading a spirit of religious intolerance in the area. Halpin wrote that Gayer first established a soup shop, then 'a mart for the vending of coarse remnants of cloth and blankets' and finally a temperance movement – all in order to entice the poor into changing their religion. All these efforts failed, according to Halpin. He challenged Gayer's claim that a priest had threatened to turn a parishioner into a jackass, saying that it was a tale which would 'throw Gulliver himself into the shade'. Halpin also directed his fire at Thomas Moriarty, stating that he 'had not the remotest claim to any property or respectability or consanguinity with any respectable branch of the Moriarty family'.[31]

News reports of the controversy that his Chester lecture had stirred up in Kerry eventually reached Gayer, and he responded from Manchester in late December. He denied many of the charges made against him. Nevertheless, he acknowledged that he did believe relics were worshipped in Dingle, citing the case of a crucifix being carried in a procession after a woman named Kate Cronan claimed that blood was emanating from it. He denied saying that the clergy believed the Bible to be the devil's book, but he did assert that ignorant Catholics believed that. Finally, he confirmed that when he was reported as saying that there were no Protestants in Dingle until recently, he actually meant Ventry.[32] Gayer accepted that Divine did not wilfully misrepresent his words, but he demanded a retraction of the claims of 'monstrous falsehoods' and 'knavery', which Gayer regarded as very injurious to his character as a clergyman and a gentleman. Gayer demanded that this retraction should appear in the press. By January 1840, no retraction had been published and Gayer challenged the two priests, Halpin and Divine, to a public meeting to either substantiate or withdraw their charges. If they failed to take up that offer, he said that he would have to take other steps to vindicate himself.[33]

Continuing his tour in England, Charles Gayer gave a two-hour lecture in Duke Street, Leicester to an audience that was comprised mainly of women. He stated that there had been four hundred conversions in the Dingle area, where priests were telling their congregations that Protestants promised to give three shillings and a leg of mutton to each convert. Priests also stated that new converts were bled in order to prevent them returning to Catholicism. Gayer spoke of the favours granted to Protestants by providence: they caught more fish in their nets, and when a section of a cliff fell, it did no damage to boats owned by Protestants. Gayer also exhibited Catholic relics, and he spoke of superstitions, the greed of the priests, and Catholic beliefs about St Joseph and the Virgin Mary to which he objected. Gayer's lecture concluded with a pronouncement that popery was 'a mass of damnable idolatry'. He was challenged by one member of the audience, a Catholic man, who told him his stories were 'incredible and ridiculous'.[34]

Swizzle

Bitter as the exchanges over religion had become, there still were occasions for humour. In bidding farewell to the year 1839, the *Post* entertained its readers with a satirical piece by 'Swizzle' describing the condition of Dingle, once 'famous for her pigs, dried seal and black pollock', and 'good fellowship, simplicity of manners and peaceful life', but now 'hot in theology'. Swizzle issued a warning in verse, 'Zeal's a dreadful termagant / That teaches saints to rail and rant, / Turns meek and sneaking secret ones / To raw heads fierce and bloody bones.' Instead of traditional greetings being exchanged on the streets of Dingle, 'you are now accosted with the queries of whether you believe in the "apostolic succession" and "acknowledge the authority of the fathers".' Letter-writing was the order of the day, the priests were up in arms and 'liar, apostate, ruffian etc. are the genteelest terms in their vocabulary.' On the other side, 'the Protestants accuse the Roman Catholics of believing in holy bones, holy stones, holy bushes, holy rags, holy heads, holy saints' teeth, holy scapulars, holy rings and sundry other Papistical emblems of sanctity too numerous to mention, of being idolators, of worshipping "the Beast".' Swizzle feared that if matters remained as they were, 'the visages of the combatants will assume a fixed unchangeable scarlet hue, with such zeal are they animated against each other.'[35]

Visit of the bishop of Limerick, Ardfert and Aghadoe, 1840

Dr Edmond Knox became bishop of Limerick, Ardfert and Aghadoe in 1834. When he visited Dingle in September 1840, it was seen as a sign of official approval of the conversion campaign. Bishop Knox attended a service at Ventry, where he addressed a congregation of approximately 250. He advised the converts to 'stand fast in the truth of the gospel' and expressed himself 'highly gratified with the evident reality of this important work'. He later preached in Dingle, where the congregation included a hundred converts. The *Post* welcomed the bishop's endorsement of the evangelical campaign, 'The countenance thus afforded by his Lordship to this valuable work, while proving it to be in strict accordance with the Established Church, is calculated to strengthen the hands of those engaged in it and to produce confidence in the minds of the converts themselves.'

One of the converts was reported as saying, 'we have now got a father and we hope to prove ourselves obedient children.'[36]

The foundation of the the *Kerry Examiner*

The *Kerry Examiner* was first published in August 1840 under its combative editor, Patrick Robert O'Loughlin Byrne, and it quickly announced its confrontational approach towards landlords, land agents and the leaders of the conversion campaign. It vigorously opposed the long-established *Kerry Evening Post*; the tenor of the exchanges between the two papers was rancorous from the outset. In November 1840, while the *Examiner* was engaged in its campaign against the activities of D.P. Thompson, it published a strongly worded letter by 'Villicus'.[37]

Villicus referred to the 'the pseudo-pastor' Thomas Moriarty and scorned accounts of 'the Ventry perverts' as 'productions low and grovelling in their composition, mean and pharisaical in their objects, false and absurd in their general tendency'. He described Gayer and Moriarty as 'arch-hypocrites, traffickers in the souls of men' and 'promoters of this farcical reformation', which was based 'on hypocrisy and fraud'. Ventry 'owed its only celebrity to being an asylum for the most profligate and abandoned characters' and 'a den of the most notorious sheep-stealers'. Referring to the conversion of Thomas Kennedy, the piper of Dunquin, the letter described him as 'an old Irish bag-piper' who had experienced 'a strange conversion from the horrors of popery'.

According to Villicus, Kennedy converted because he had been condemned as a public nuisance by Fr John Casey, who saw him as a desecrator of the Sabbath and 'a seducer of youth in his parish' by means of his 'midnight orgies'. Villicus wrote that the piper was 'a wandering minstrel' who had been 'enticed by the savoury odour of the soup-pots of Ventry' and, 'after laying aside his drones', was soon 'metamorphosed into a teacher of the gospel'. Villicus went on to blacken the reputations of the converts by asserting that one of them had been convicted of 'violating a woman' and others were convicted of sheep-stealing. Finally, Villicus condemned the so-called reformation, 'which tends to light the torch of religious discord in all the rancour of ancient barbarity in a country where peace and Christian concord has before dwelt'.[38]

Elizabeth Colthurst gave a different account of the conversion of Tom Kennedy, who had previously played the pipes at rural festivities, weddings and Pattern days, and made a living from the pennies on the plate that he passed around. She stated that it was the word of God that induced him to give up his pipes, declaring, 'Never again should his pipes excite his thoughtless neighbours amid scenes of unhallowed mirth, where God was not honoured nor his laws obeyed.' He voluntarily gave up his source of income, the means of supporting his family, but he was at peace with God. For her young readers, Colthurst highlighted the sacrifice of Tom Kennedy, saying that it was proof of the power of the word of God.[39]

The views of Villicus were echoed by editorial comment in the *Examiner*. Patrick Robert Byrne relished conflict and being a champion of the people and Catholic values. He reported provocatively on a meeting of the Irish Society in Tralee, claiming that the speeches contained 'diabolical falsehoods, gross slander and vile misrepresentation'. The speakers were dubbed 'these reverend vagabonds', and Byrne declared, 'Heavens! That such a pack of canting knaves and hypocritical rogues should be found in these realms in this boasted age of civilization and enlightenment.'[40]

The *Post* responded by referring to P.R. Byrne as 'the bully-boy of the *Examiner*' who published 'the most ferocious vulgar abuse, unmixed with one attempt at argument, but the most absurd outrageous assertions and assumptions abundantly introduced everywhere'.[41] The *Post* and several of its readers were particularly incensed by this statement by Byrne, 'We deny that the church of Rome ever persecuted.'[42] This was scorned by the *Post* in subsequent articles, and the Spanish Inquisition was invoked as one example of Catholic persecution.[43] One critic denounced Byrne for a display of 'feelings of which a demon might be proud'. He could not understand how Byrne could justify 'so grossly monstrous and shamelessly impudent an attack on reason and religion'.[44] An editorial in the *Post* referred to Thomas Moriarty's account of Mass being offered 'for a SICK PIG!!! or for a HERRING BOAT!!!' and stated succinctly, 'We have no language to describe our abhorrence of such desecration of solemnities.'[45] Byrne defended such practices, saying that prayer and sacrifice had at all times been offered for temporal blessings, even in the Protestant church, and that Christ had looked with particular favour on fishermen.[46]

P.R. Byrne derided 'a certain "Reverend" in the neighbourhood of Dingle who rejoices in the name of Moriarty':

It comes well from the Rev. Apostate to ridicule and misrepresent the church within whose pale he was baptised and with whose spiritual milk he was nourished until, seduced by the mammon of the world, he renounced her authority, derided the lessons of truth she had earlier taught him and now treacherously and ungratefully defames her character and stabs at the bosom that nurtured him in the days of his youth.[47]

When letters in the *Post* used strong language to condemn Byrne, he responded in like manner. He characterised the letter writers as 'mongrels' and 'a set of vulgar ignorant fanatics', and claimed that 'their scurrility and vituperation' would have no effect on him. He wrote:

> An entire pack of yelping curs have been set loose upon us in the columns of the last *Post* taking up their position on the ground on which the editor in the exercise of his remarkable prudence thought better to abandon. Column after column is packed with the virulent outpourings of their bastard nature and while pretending to bark in support of the sayings and doings of a gang of pharasaical mountebanks, three-fourths of all that proceeds from their foul mouths is a species of bitter snarling against ourselves personally, betraying many a symptom of a rabid disposition to bite, if they only could dare.[48]

The owners of the *Kerry Evening Post* were John and Charles Eagar. They acknowledged with regret that the editorial tone of their paper had become more strident, but they were equally defiant in laying the blame for this development elsewhere:

> We shall say once for all that we are sensible how much of late our articles have taken a polemical turn. We regret it much but there's no help for it. The fault lies with the party and the men who complain of 'hostile array' against him. The Romish priests of Kerry have set up a journal and imported a disputant from Galway to open, as he terms it a (popgun) 'cannonade' on Protestantism [...] If in the course of such a discussion as this we are obliged to observe on documents or hair-brained statements of this self-constituted and aggressive champion of popery, in a manner unpleasant to the feelings of Roman Catholics, we do not feel that we are to blame.[49]

Fr Mathew in Dingle

There was one brief interlude of harmony in Dingle when Fr Theobald Mathew, 'the apostle of temperance', visited before Christmas 1840, promoting his crusade against alcohol. The occasion brought some Catholics and Protestants together. Byrne wrote that 'every difference arising out of creed or politics was merged in one feeling which actuated every mind and exalted it above all grosser considerations.' Captain John Hickson of The Grove gave permission for the assembly to take place on his demesne, and 'the Protestant gentry gave all the assistance they could give, individually and collectively, in the hallowed cause.'[50] Twenty-five thousand people were reported as taking a pledge to abstain from alcohol. There was no mention of Protestant clergy being present, but they would certainly have had no objection to the promotion of the cause of temperance. Fr Mathew was probably aware of the controversies that raged in west Kerry, as he reminded his listeners of

the necessity of that brotherly love and affection which should invariably subsist between Christians of every denomination, entreating on them by all means to abstain from all bickerings or arguments on those abstruse texts of scripture, while they may at the same time be forgetful of that plain and obvious passage of Saint Paul which inculcates the love of one another.[51]

Dunurlin church foundation stone

The context in which vituperative exchanges took place perhaps explains their intensity. It was abundantly clear that the conversion campaign, aided by generous donations from Britain, was making steady progress in west Kerry. This was evident in the new buildings being erected. Before George Gubbins left Corca Dhuibhne, he had raised funds for a glebe house, church and schoolhouse for Dunurlin. On a fund-raising mission to England, Gubbins had raised £500. This was passed on to D.P. Thompson, who then organised the building of houses in Ventry and Dunurlin, postponing Dunurlin church until a further sum of £500 was provided by church authorities.

A.M. Thompson graphically described a special occasion for all the converts – the day, in August 1841, on which the foundation stone of the church at Dunurlin was laid. The stone was laid by Hon. Dayrolles Blakeney Mullins, the 12-year-old son and heir of Lord Ventry. It was an impressive spectacle, a public affirmation of the success of the mission. The children of all the convert schools marched in procession, two by two: one hundred and twenty from Dingle, eighty from Ventry, thirty from Dunurlin and forty from Dunquin. A.M. Thompson was present and estimated that a thousand people attended, of whom seven hundred were converts:

It was a beautiful and novel sight for many who, with the writer, stood on an eminence to watch the long line of these babes in the faith winding its way among the hills; now visible, now for a moment hidden by some impeding crag or jutting hill, the sun shining on their clean white aprons and tippets, while every vehicle within twenty miles was to be seen coming carrying those who wished to assist at the interesting ceremony. Large groups of the adult converts were gradually assembling on the ground and the summits of the neighbouring heights were crowned by Roman Catholic peasants come to see the strange sight. To many it was doubtless a galling sight, but the generality seemed to enter into the gladsomeness of the scene and no mark of incivility or enmity was evinced throughout the day, though the converts, going and returning, walked miles in every direction through a numerous population of Romanists.[52]

A band provided music, psalms were sung and speeches were delivered in Irish by Revs Goodman, Moriarty and Gubbins, who had returned specially for the occasion. 'When the sound of the Irish reached the ears of the Roman Catholics standing far off, on the tops of all the banks near, they closed in and gave earnest attention to the things which they heard that day for the first time, and many were seen to speak thoughtfully to one another.' Finally, 'a plentiful supply of bread, apples and beer' was served out by the pastors to the people.[53] The laying of the foundation stone was highly symbolic for the Protestant community, and the spectacle must have had a significant impact on the Catholics of the area.

Rev. Anthony Denny wrote an account of the day, claiming that eight hundred persons of all classes attended, 'of whom 230 were children of the parish and neighbouring schools, principally composed of converts from the church of Rome'. Denny concluded, 'I could not but feel gratified at the perfect tranquillity and good feeling evinced by the Roman Catholic peasantry, especially at such a moment when the county has been so fearfully convulsed by the elections, an evidence I trust that prejudices against our Protestant cause are giving way amongst them.' Denny hoped that the new church would in time be a place where people could worship God 'according to the sound form of our scriptural Church'.[54]

The death of the convert Denis Dunlevy

One of the first converts in Ventry was Denis Dunlevy, known as 'a man of naturally ungovernable temper' until his behaviour altered for the better on his conversion. A.M. Thompson devoted six pages of her book to the story of Dunlevy's transformation and tragic death.[55] He was a prominent figure, the father of eight children, described as 'the once turbulent Dunlevy, the boldest and the proudest of his clan'.[56] Colthurst, in *Tales of Erin*, devotes twelve pages to Dunlevy, stating that with his conversion, 'the lion [was] transformed into the lamb, the untamed and fiery spirit into the meekness of a little child.'[57]

Dunlevy was involved in a dramatic shipwreck in 1841; he was captain of the missionary boat, a hooker called *Brothers*. This was 'laden with potatoes for the relief of the poor' of Dingle, and sheltered overnight in the Maharees in April 1841. During a fierce storm, the hooker broke its moorings, with Denis and three others still on board. The boat was eventually broken up on rocks at Kerry Head, near Ballyheigue. It was feared that the four men had perished. However, they were rescued and returned safely to Dingle, 'to the great joy of their friends who had given them up for lost'.[58] Colthurst wrote that an old man rescued the ship's Bible, dried it out, read it and declared, 'I never read so fine a book before.'[59]

The shipwreck affected Dunlevy's health and spirits; in December 1841, he contracted influenza and died. In A.M. Thompson's sensitive account of his last hours with his family, she regularly used his first name, 'Poor Denis! He never seemed to recover his spirits after the loss of his boat; the shock and anxiety of the night (he being the responsible person) lay on him perpetually.'[60] While on his death-bed, he resisted the sustained efforts of his family to persuade him to return to his Catholic faith. He told them, 'I want no priest. I have Jesus Christ as my high priest.'[61] Accounts of his wake show how familial and community bonds were severed, to the great distress of family members. Colthurst wrote that Denis's two sisters (who were known as 'the mastiffs of the Quay' on account of their 'awful temper') were very agitated at the prospect of his burial under Protestant rites and wanted him to have a Catholic burial. Thompson described the scene:

> His sisters caused much disturbance and excitement at his funeral, being resolved to have him buried as a Romanist, which Mr. Moriarty and Mr. Gayer would of course not permit; the poor women then acted more like *fiends* than human beings, and did everything in their power to interrupt the solemn service.[62]

The family gathered round for what was described as 'the coronach, or death song composed in extemporaneous Irish verse and sang alternately by his sisters'.[63] Thompson wrote that the sisters sang 'in the wildest manner the following recitative to the "Irish cry"'.[64] Colthurst recorded that a scripture reader was present at the wake, sitting 'in a corner of the house and unnoticed by the nearer relatives', and that he wrote down the dirge. The following translation was then made of the *ex tempore* lament sung by the sisters:

First sister:

In the deep mighty ocean, the dark night it found thee,
The tides and the billows were foaming around thee,
When doubling the headlands, oh! here's the sad token,
Thy heart and thy vessel together were broken.

Chorus:

Oh, Donagh, Oh, Donagh, can it be
And hast thou left us so,
The gentle flower of all thy race
With heretics to go.

Second sister:

My sorrow, my sorrow, it drives me to madness –
Oh, never again shall my sad heart know gladness –
Oh, sorely it grieves me to think that those dangers
And troubles came o'er thee while toiling for strangers.

Chorus:

We lay thee in thy father's grave
Beneath thy mother's head
No parson e'er shall o'er thee pray
No Bible e'er be read.

First sister:

Oh! Would that thy grave were made under the billow,
And would that the wild shark himself were thy pillow,

Than thus on thy bed, in thy senses to die –
And our church and her priesthood so boldly deny!
Chorus: (pointing to his children)
No children of Dunlevy's line
Are ye, nor of his race.
Beneath him ye shall never lie,
Nor in his grave find place.[65]

A.M. Thompson's version differs slightly from the above, and has this additional verse addressed by Dunlevy's sisters to his widow:

His gatherings and his earnings all,
They may belong to thee,
But we his kindred flesh and blood,
Deep, deep *in him are we.*[66]

The burial of Denis Dunlevy passed off peacefully. In the morning, Thomas Moriarty arrived at the Dunlevy house and waited there for Rev. Gayer. When the funeral procession reached a crossroads, the coffin was laid down for a short while, according to custom. At the graveside the coffin was carried three times around the graveyard. Rev. Moriarty then read the service in Irish, and 'won over the crowd'.[67] Ventry burial records for this period have survived, and among eleven burials listed, one is that of 'Denis Donleavy' of Ceantra, aged 50, on 24 December 1841.[68]

John Murphy, a convert who lived in Dingle for a period, knew Denis Dunlevy and his background, and he added a little to the story of his death. Murphy afterwards returned to his Catholic faith. He wrote that it was 'a high ambition' of the reformers to ensure that converts died as Protestants, as this would be a certain proof of their sincerity. In this respect, wrote Murphy, they saw the death of Denis Dunlevy as a 'windfall' that they were 'gifted with'. Murphy himself was aghast at the adulation shown to Dunlevy as 'one the first converts of Ventry and a witness for the truth'. To him, Dunlevy was 'by profession an Irish teacher and by practice a drunkard, aye, and a very noisy one to boot'. Murphy claimed that Dunlevy's wife had often come to him to complain that she had no money for food, as her husband spent it all on drink.[69]

10. The charge of souperism

'Soup kitchens' are usually associated with the Quakers, or Society of Friends, who set up these food centres to provide emergency relief to the starving during the Great Famine. The government adopted the same policy when the system of public works proved inadequate to meet the crisis. However, long before the Famine, the distribution of soup as relief to the poor in times of hardship was not unusual in Kerry. In Tralee in June 1840, 'the very humane and liberal conduct' of Mr Moore of Castle Street Hotel was commended. He had been 'for the last four or five days, dealing out on an extensive scale very excellent and nourishing soup to the poor of this town'.[1] As already noted, taunts about soup and conversion appeared in the columns of the *Tralee Mercury* in March 1839. In December 1839, the satirical writer Swizzle noted that the Dingle priests had accused the Protestants of supplying the converts, 'or turncoats as they call them', with soup. Swizzle observed that the fashionable new cant phrases in London included 'Is Murphy right?' and 'Does your mother know you're out?' In his opinion, none of these expressions was

> so laconic or half so expressive as the cant lately got up in Dingle of the solitary word 'soup' – you hear 'soup', 'soup' wherever you go. The converts are aroused in their peaceful homes by the cry of 'soup' borne on the western blast. But now they are getting so hardened as not to take much notice of the exclamation and it is to be hoped the uncomfortable feeling will wear off.[2]

Making fun of the fact that a pot containing a leg of mutton was stolen from a priest by some of his parishioners around this time, Swizzle wrote that the converts responded to taunts by saying that even if they did take the soup, at least they had not stolen the priest's pot to cook it in. In another account of this incident, the priest was outraged at the theft of his pot, calling it 'an offence of the blackest die' and condemning the culprits as 'thieving, shameless cormorants'. He added, 'I do not believe that Parson

G. and his turncoats, bad as they are, would have committed a crime of such enormity.'[3]

A.M. Thompson gave this explanation of the origin of the derogatory term 'souper', as applied to converts, 'This term of reproach grew out of the circumstance of a soup-shop having been opened by a benevolent lady of the town in a time of great scarcity and distress, and soup offered for sale to the poor. The Roman Catholics might have purchased but were forbidden by the priest; all who did avail themselves of it were henceforth termed "soupers".'[4] In his copy of Thompson's book, Fr John O'Sullivan wrote a note emphatically contradicting this, 'No. I was the first that ever baptised them soupers, long before Gayer ever came to Dingle.'[5] This comment suggests that the term was used before 1833.

The first use of the specific term 'souper' in print occurred in 1841. This was in the *Kerry Examiner* of 30 March, in a letter in which the term was used four times. A correspondent signed 'JEH' wrote about the grandiose claims made by members of the Irish Society at its twenty-third annual meeting in Dublin, where people were 'piously enthusiastic' about all the 'signs and wonders' achieved by them in various districts. He mocked the reported statement of Rev. Thomas Moriarty that he and his colleagues were 'tearing popery into rags' in west Kerry. JEH wrote that 'no sooner does this unflinching champion of the Bible open his mouth before his assembled brethren than out flies victory after victory from his veracious lips.' He went on:

> When speaking of his Ventry congregation, one would naturally infer from the would-be biblical importance he throws about it that this society of the *elect* is composed of honest truth-seeking men who were converted from the errors of popery by the happy instrumentality of the 'Word of God in their native tongue', by the magic of the *Irish Bible*. But what is the fact? Come forward, you Ventry *Soupers*, and answer this question.[6]

The reality, according to JEH, was that 'scarce a single man of character is to be found among [...] such a motley crew of worthless renegades.' The Ventry converts were in fact 'a singular congregation of the most worthless characters, vagabonds and sheep-stealers', who were converted 'not by the beauties of the Irish Bible but by the dint of the most shameless, barefaced bribery'. Among the charges levelled by JEH against the converts were the violation of a woman by one man and 'unconcealed fornication even beneath the eye of their Rev. pastor'. They were also cattle stealers, he wrote; hoof-prints of stolen cattle could be 'traced by their wary neighbours to the fold of the soupers, as they are appropriately called'.[7]

A few months later, at an election meeting in Abbeydorney in north Kerry, John O'Connell of Grena, Killarney, brother of Daniel, used the term souper as a rallying cry when he referred to William Talbot Crosbie of Ardfert Abbey, a prominent landlord and a supporter of the evangelical movement, 'And there is another phrase you know the meaning of, you can say meow, and I am sure you will be delighted to see the soupers (groans) and you must have great respect for the gentlemen of Ardfert who give soup on a Friday.'[8] O'Connell ended his speech by asking the assembly to 'give a groan for the soupers and a cheer for old Ireland.' Another speaker wished that he could put Mr Crosbie, 'the soup manufacturer', and other Kerry landlords 'in the same stew-pan – and very bad soup they'd make!'[9]

When the American evangelical Asenath Nicholson visited Dingle in April 1845, she observed that the converts were known as soupers and implied that it was a local term.[10] The word appeared in publications outside of Kerry in 1845, but not in any significant way. In February 1845, the *Dublin Weekly Register* copied an item from the *Kerry Examiner* that referred to 'the Soupers, with the Gayers and Moriartys at their head'.[11] The term first appeared in the *Freeman's Journal* on 26 April 1845, but only as part of an advertisement for the *Dublin Weekly Register*. David W. Miller has established that the word souper did not appear again in the *Freeman's Journal* until 25 September 1849, and 'from that time forward "souper" ceased to be mere local jargon in Dingle and became a term continually used throughout Ireland to describe and humiliate converts from Catholicism to Protestantism.'[12]

Bribery controversy

The question of whether the west Kerry conversions were genuine or not, whether the converts were dupes or hypocrites, whether they were lured by material gain or motivated by faith, continued to bedevil all debate about religious developments in west Kerry. Newspapers reported on accusations of bribery directed at the leaders of the conversion campaign. In a case taken against Charles Gayer, Michael Power stated that he was induced to convert by 'good feeding and generous promises', but later reverted to Catholicism. He had worked for Gayer and was claiming wages of £4 not paid to him. Kate Power, Michael's sister, gave evidence that Gayer had offered her 'plenty of victuals [...] plenty of potatoes' and money if she 'turned', or converted. The *Examiner* described her as 'a miserable looking creature' who was barely clothed and spoke no English. Kate told the court that Gayer had plenty of money, 'Sure wasn't he getting it in hatfuls from abroad.' The *Examiner* explained that she was referring to 'the "contributions" of "the faithful" to enlighten the benighted Irishers!' The judge ruled that Gayer should pay £3 in wages due to Power.[13]

Charles Gayer denied promising any inducements to Kate Power, but he accepted that he had helped poor people during times of hardship and had personally been 'instrumental in preserving during the last two severe summers' the lives of poor Catholics. He stated that there was not a single instance in which he had ever offered a bribe, 'or even spoken to them a word about changing their religion when relieving their temporal wants'.[14] Gayer published a statement signed by thirty-six Dingle converts affirming that he had not offered them any bribes. The signatories were heads of families, and the document is an important record of the names of some convert families in 1841.

Those who signed were: T. Cramer, John Leahy, John Connor, Susan Handlon, Ellen Murphy, Agnes Fitzgerald, John Shea, John Slattery, William Sealy, Joseph Markham, James Fitzgerald, Patrick Scanlon, Daniel Connell, Richard Thomas, B. Moriarty, Ellen Connell, Edward Hickson. Nineteen people could not sign their names and made their mark. They were: Bryan Foley, Alice Fitzgerald, James Carney, Mary Day, Margaret McCarthy, Mary Finn, Mary Stack, David Moriarty, Nicholas Bruce, Timothy Looby [?], John Moriarty, John Breen, Jane Moore, Thomas Fitzgerald, Pat Harnet, Jeremiah Leahy, James Murphy, Catherine Thomas, John Moore.[15]

Rev. Edward Spring of Dunurlin was incensed at an insult that he believed was directed at him. He asserted that Fr Patrick Foley, curate of Ballyferriter, had told his congregation that some of the money subscribed to the evangelical campaign was spent by unmarried clergymen on their concubines. Spring was the only unmarried clergyman in the area, and he vehemently rejected what he saw as 'a most serious imputation against my moral character'. Spring gave some examples of what he saw as Foley's intolerant treatment of converts. He expressed how he deplored those who exercised their 'sacerdotal authority to starve a fellow creature out of the world because he dares in matters of religion to think for himself'.[16]

Some controversies were centred on Thomas Moriarty. In one instance, the *Examiner* reprinted an article from the *Kilkenny Journal* that belittled him. The *Post* responded, stating that the editor of the *Examiner* 'haberdashes popery just as well as he does pronouns', and that his attack on the man who represented 'the first fruits of the harvest of souls' of west Kerry was ineffectual, as Moriarty could afford to 'smile at the harmless darts of the enemy'.[17] The *Post* saw Moriarty as a 'zealous Christian pastor [...] rooted in the affection of his Irish-reading, Irish-praying, Irish-hymning and Irish-lectured little flock'.[18] When Moriarty was on a fund-raising tour in Limerick in early 1842, the *Examiner* described him as 'a self-dubbed missioner [...] pouring out his fanatical rhodomontade in the presence of a stultified audience of Limerick saints'. Byrne told his readers that Moriarty and his colleagues were spreading 'senseless cant', with 'the whites of their eyes lifted towards heaven and their hands at the same time industriously occupied in the pockets of their dupes'.[19]

In November 1841, Charles Gayer wrote to the *Post* referring to an article in the *Examiner* that described him and his colleagues as 'hireling missionaries', 'wolves in sheep's clothing', 'an unscrupulous gang of pious hypocrites' and 'reverend gospellers whom the Church of England has spawned'. Gayer accepted that the writer was very angry but reminded P.R. Byrne that anger and malice were mortal sins in his faith. He again denied specific cases of bribery and cited two prominent gentlemen in Dingle that had converted: Mr Hussey and Mr Robert C. Hickson. They certainly did not do so in order to get 1s 6d a week, wrote Gayer. Gayer estimated the number of converts in west Kerry as between six hundred and seven hundred; he understood that this fact might have provoked the writer's anger. Gayer claimed that one sure sign that converts were sincere in their new faith was the fact that out of sixteen converts who had died, not one had reverted to Catholicism.[20]

T. Cramer, who described himself as a 'classical teacher', wrote to the *Post* defending Charles Gayer against 'a gross and unmerited calumny'. Cramer quoted scripture to support his claim that Gayer was 'a fisher of men' whose 'bait was a spiritual and not a carnal one'. He argued that 'when famine stared them in the face and threatened havock' among the poor, Gayer 'in the true spirit of a Christian and philanthropist procured them and served them with potatoes, meal and bread etc. without distinction of sect or creed'. One convert told Cramer that Gayer was effective because 'he preaches nought but what he practices.' Cramer compared Gayer to the village parson in Oliver Goldsmith's poem 'The Deserted Village':

> At church, with meek and unaffected grace,
> His looks adorn'd the venerable place;
> Truth from his lips prevail'd with double sway,
> And fools, who came to scoff, remain'd to pray.[21]

One visitor to west Kerry at this time wrote that he had been sceptical about the scale of conversions there, but after the visit he concluded, 'All you have heard of the Lord's work here falls very far short of the reality.' He estimated the total number of converts as over 600; he acknowledged that they were not all perfect but argued that it was unrealistic to expect them to be so, 'We are so unreasonable as to expect that they must all at once make a change from error, superstition and crime into truth, real devotion and lasting virtue.' He described the conditions endured by converts, 'Poor converts! How much they have to endure! Persecuted by all, cast off by their nearest and dearest friends and relatives, thrown as pitiless wrecks upon the world's wide waste!'

When he asked one convert why he had abandoned the Catholic faith, the writer received the answer, 'Because that church is false and leads people astray and its priests are wicked and bad men.' When the visitor raised the question of bribery, he received a forceful response:

> 'Bribed! Bribed!' he repeated with becoming indignation. I looked with pleasure on his manly features. There was in his eye a sparkling fire that replied to and drove back the unworthy insinuation. 'Bribed, sir,' added he, 'and for what? That for some time past, my wife, my child and myself should not be able to provide even the common necessaries of life?' His face was quite pale [and] I felt the truth of his statement. 'Bribed!' he said again, 'is it the effect of bribery to have my wife and child in want and I myself to have to wear these rags!' He pointed to his tattered garments. I looked at him again: his face, his look, his dress, his entire manners and appearance added to, or rather should I say confirmed, his testimony and the truth of his melancholy expressions broke painfully upon my soul.[22]

One observer believed that only one in ten of the conversions in west Kerry was genuine, but still conceded that the real truth 'can only be known to the highest power'.[23] Sometimes the sincerity of the converts was questioned by fellow Protestants. At a meeting of the Kerry Auxiliary of the Irish Society in Tralee in 1844, Thomas Moriarty said that he was not surprised that Catholics would describe a convert as a hypocrite, but the fact 'that Protestants should throw cold water on him and freeze him down and thus make excuses for their own neglect of the poor man is the greatest trial the poor convert has to endure'.[24] Moriarty urged fellow Protestants not to be too judgmental, citing the case of a man who freely admitted that he had converted for the wrong reason but was later 'awakened to the truth of Christ'. He asked his audience to hold out the hand of friendship to all converts:

> If the converts be hypocrites, what is the best cure for hypocrisy? I would rather be deceived by ninety-nine hypocrites than that one just man should be driven to perdition by my neglect. Was there not hypocrisy even among the twelve apostles? [...] Pause before you throw a bucket of cold water on him and drive him back to apostasy.[25]

Catherine Hartland Mahon acknowledged, in 1843, that 'many blame us for giving temporal relief and accuse us of bribery.' She cited precedents from scripture to justify providing people with food and clothing, and she believed that it was unfair to expect converts to endure starvation as a test of their sincerity. She also pointed out that the supports provided to converts were provisional, with colony cottages being rented only from week to week.[26]

If it was difficult at the time to know the inner motivation of individual converts, it is more difficult to judge now. There is evidence that converts' lives were greatly transformed by the decision to change from the religion into which they had been born, and in which their families, their communities, their history and culture were steeped. The decision involved a personal uprooting, and it did not always bring material or spiritual comfort. One determined convert was unmoved by her relatives' opposition to her choice and, after some months, made an attempt at reconciliation with them. She was received amicably at first, but then discussion turned bitter and she was accused of being a devil and a turncoat, and finally was driven out of the house. 'Don't be calling me turncoat,' she told her cousins, 'it little matters which side of the coat is out – call me *turned-heart* and pray that my heart may be turned back from all evil ways and bad words.'[27]

Most of the converts were from the poorer classes, and undoubtedly some were motivated by the prospect of material reward. There were just a few converts from the more affluent levels of society whose motivation was unlikely to have been material gain. Among these were Peter Bodkin Hussey of Farranakilla, a prominent barrister; the Moriarty brothers and their sister; and Mr Hickson. Also among the influential converts were those who went on to become ordained ministers of the church. Timothy Hamilton was one; as was Daniel Foley, who later became a prominent preacher and writer of religious tracts, and professor of Irish in Trinity College.

The converts of west Kerry were despised for what loyal Catholics saw as a betrayal of their faith, their forebears and even their country. The stigma and shame associated with conversion lasted until well into the twentieth century in many parts of the country. Writing in the early 1900s, Patrick Foley attempted to explain to his readers that in using the term 'souper', he did not wish to cause offence, and that the word had 'the sanction of general usage' as a term for Roman Catholics 'who while still believing in their former religion, went over to the Protestant church under the colour and pretence of converts'. He accepted that nobody should be censured for believing that he or she had 'truth and justice on his side'; nevertheless, he stated, 'what should be condemned are the *means* which were adopted to force the people to reject the Catholic religion and adopt Protestantism.'[28]

'The souper's lamentation'

Ballads were a popular form of entertainment, and it is certain that the religious conflict in west Kerry was often the subject of ballad makers. The *Kerry Examiner* published these verses, entitled 'The souper's lamentation', to be sung to the air of 'The girl I left behind me'.

As oft I rove on Ventry's shore,
Where manhood's years came on me,
Ere I left my parents' blissful home
And friends who loved me dearly;
I think upon those mirthful hours
Ere Satan's sons allured me –
The dupe of Mammon's sordid powers
Which cast some spell around me.

The tears fast trickle down my cheek
When I meet my former pastor,
Whose holy prayers I heard each week
From our ancient chapel altar –
Oh! he it was whose Christian care
Cheered my poor afflicted father
When the landlord stript him, left him bare,
Till death relieved him after.

My mother too is now laid low
Her heart by me was broken.
Methinks her spirit parted slow,
As she glanced at me forlorn.
Since then I bear the outcast's brand,
The tool of venal teachers,
I swell their lists, support a band
Of speculating preachers.

Alas! my creed I have disgraced!
Alas! that I've been faithless!
Alas! my soul by vice debased!
Alas! how [illegible] ensnares us.
My adopted creed, what has it brought,
But mental aberration.
In my dreams at night, hell is my thought,
A hypocrite I waken!

Shall I continue in this course,
On Friday drink their gravy?
Deceived by bigots and what's worse,
Lieutenants in the navy.
Are there the saints to preach the word
When other prospects fail them,
Does Gospel truth require the sword
Of a well-paid pampered alien?

Curse the day I joined those knaves,
Like more deluded creatures.
Oh! could our grandsires leave their graves,
What a lesson they could teach us.
Look back and weep o'er hallowed names,
Oh! could death's bolts be riven
Nor cast disgrace on their remains
Nor forfeit hope in heaven!

Disgraced we are, a hopeless few!
Despised by all as 'soupers',
Dependent on a scheming crew,

The breed of Cromwell's troopers.
No longer then I'll bear the darts
Of a pervert mind in patience,
Midst those who pounce on rotten hearts
Like carrion-loving ravens.

Then adieu! you flesh-pots, soup-tureens,
Tho' worldly trials await me,
I ne'er shall look for *gayer* scenes
Than those once left behind me.
Adieu! you bribes, you preachers false,
Whose breath brings desolation,
I now can raise my head in peace
And hope to gain salvation.[29]

11. Establishing the colonies

In the mid-1830s, Rev. Edward Nangle had established what was termed a Protestant colony on Achill Island in County Mayo. He was a native of County Meath who dedicated himself to converting the people of Achill to Protestantism. He established the Achill Mission Colony in 1834 and published a journal, the *Achill Missionary Herald*, to report on and promote his activities.[1] In the early 1840s, colonies were also established in west Kerry.

A.M. Thompson credited Captain Forbes of the Dingle Coast Guard with the initiative that led to the formation of the Kerry colonies. Forbes spoke to a group of people in London, promoting the idea of a shelter for converts, which would act as an encouragement and support to people who had apprehensions about declaring their conversion openly.[2] Thompson said that Forbes spoke at a dinner party in London in 1839, but the *Christian Examiner*, an evangelical journal, stated that the event took place on 8 December 1840.[3] According to the latter account, Forbes explained to the other guests that when people in Dingle converted, they lost the means of earning a living, as the priests had instructed their congregations not to have any dealings with them. Tradesmen lost customers, and labourers lost employment. Forbes told the London group that all those who converted were turned out of their employment – even out of their houses – and were forsaken by family and friends. 'If we do not help them, they are left to starve,' he said.[4]

According to Thompson, 'a Christian lady' who was at that table in London was inspired by Forbes's idea and initiated an appeal for subscriptions to provide the type of protection advocated by him. The woman was Catherine Hartland Mahon, a native of Cavetown, Co. Roscommon, who later married Col Archibald Inglis and lived in Castle Douglas in Dumfriesshire, Scotland. She promptly composed a circular letter appealing for funds for the establishment of colonies in Dingle. This led to an organisation being set up to further the plan, with Lady Lorton – who was married to Robert King, 1st Viscount Lorton, of Boyle, Co.

Roscommon – as patron. Catherine Mahon's initial letter to her associates stated that the converts in Dingle were 'destitute, afflicted and forsaken', and she explained her proposal to establish 'a colony where those converts can have refuge, protection, support and instruction'. She appealed, 'Can it be then that through the supineness of Protestant or coldness of Christian hearts these poor creatures will be left to perish?'[5] Forbes commended Catherine Mahon for taking the first practical steps towards 'a great and important undertaking', saying that he had often asked friends 'to help me in establishing what you have commenced'. At the time, Catherine Mahon had no personal connection with Kerry; she visited Dingle for the first time in the autumn of 1841.[6]

Charles Gayer responded positively to her initiative and confirmed that there was widespread 'social persecution' of converts, of whom there were '180 individuals in about thirty families' in Dingle alone. The site for the colony and the adjoining farm was donated by Lord Ventry, and the plan was to establish similar colonies in other parts of the peninsula. Gayer said that a cottage and an acre of ground would support a family for a year.[7] By the end of 1840, sufficient funds to build fifteen cottages were in hand. Three men agreed to act as trustees: Rev. Gayer and two Coast Guard officers, Captain Forbes and Lt Clifford.

The building of colony houses in Dingle was commenced in the spring of 1841 – 'the day before yesterday', according to a letter from Dingle published on 25 March 1841.[8] The site was off John Street, which is a slope. There is a reference in *The Little Ones of Innisfail* to 'the little town of Dingle, where on the gentle ascent of a sunny hill, fifteen neat cottages have been recently erected, and are at this moment inhabited by ninety individuals, all converts from the Church of Rome'.[9] Another site, chosen later, was off Quay Lane; the houses built there were known as the lower colony.[10] Although there were two locations with colony houses in Dingle, they are often referred to in the singular as the Dingle Colony.

The buildings of the lower colony off Strand Street, as Quay Lane is now known, have survived; they are commercial premises and private houses. The John Street colony was known as the upper colony; it seems that none of its buildings survive today. Ordnance survey maps show the upper colony located off John Street to the north, and a late nineteenth century photograph shows eight small cottages, six of them in ruins, projecting north from John Street.[11] There is no sign of this row of cottages today.

Monck Mason and Gayer on the Dingle Colony

In late 1841, opposition to the Dingle Colony came from an unexpected source. Henry Monck Mason, one of the founders of the Irish Society, wrote to the *Christian Examiner* objecting to the whole concept of colonies. It is clear that he saw the Protestant mission in Dingle as a move away from the objectives of the society. He advised Catherine Mahon that instead of forming colonies and duplicating missionary activities, it would be better to work with the Ladies Auxiliary of the Irish Society and combine her zeal with their experience. He disagreed with a policy of removing converts from their own homes and pointed to the additional expense involved in building colonies. He also believed that it would be confusing for British donors to be subjected to multiple appeals for the same objectives – donors were already 'exceedingly puzzled by the variety of claims which are presented to their bounty'. Above all, Monck Mason said that there was no scriptural basis for colonies; that converts should never 'hide under a bushel' or flee from danger, but should be 'in the midst of things'.[12]

Charles Gayer's reply to Monck Mason was forceful. He objected to the timing of the criticism, saying that it could have been made earlier rather than when fifteen houses had already been built and ten more planned. He also considered that Monck Mason's criticism should have been conveyed privately to him or to the trustees instead of in public. Gayer told Monck Mason that he had 'an entire misapprehension of the locality, nature and internal management of the Dingle colony'. Addressing Monck Mason's point that there were no colonies in Kingscourt district, Gayer responded that the converts there were not poor and starving like those in Dingle. In Gayer's view, the converts in the Dingle colony were not fleeing persecution but exposing themselves to it. The colony was not in a remote area 'on top of one of our mountains'; it was in the heart of the town, opposite the residence of three priests. Gayer also claimed that the provision of housing could not be described as bribery or as conducive to creating hypocrites, because they were only available to those who had proven themselves true believers – not to recent initiates. Of the eighty-six colony residents, most were converts of six or seven years' standing, and only a few were of two years' standing.[13]

Gayer had no doubt that the colony would bring about an improvement in the conditions of the converts, and he stated that his expectations were not grandiose, 'Just here and there a little band will be collected out of the apostasy of Rome.' He instanced the fact that the people living there were employed and rented an acre of ground at a charge of £1, as compared to

£6 or £8 outside. They were protected from interfering priests, and their 'morals and conversation' had already improved. The people in the colony were much better off than before, when 'during the last four dear summers, owing to the failure of the potato crop, it was no uncommon thing for a family to be fasting for twenty four hours or to be depending on one meal of dry potatoes.' Gayer's view was that the whole purpose of the colony was to promote the moral, social and spiritual welfare of the converts, to raise their standards of living, to promote 'more cleanly habits than when living in a smoky filthy cabin', and to promote Bible reading.

In a parting shot to his letter of 1 December 1841, Gayer had a polite but curt message for the Ladies Auxiliary and for what he called Monck Mason's 'favourite child', the Irish Society, 'We wish you good luck in the name of the Lord.'[14] It appears that a coolness was developing between the Dingle mission and the Irish Society as the former moved towards establishing a separate, independent organisation.

St James's church in Dingle was enlarged in 1839; it was expanded again in 1841, when a gallery was built at a cost of £60. This was referred to as 'the converts' gallery'. The congregation was between four and five hundred, four-fifths of them converts, according to A.M. Thompson, 'brought from the lowest state of ignorance and of moral and social habits into decent order and intelligence'.[15] Thompson proudly compared these numbers to the congregation of thirty that attended there in 1830, before the evangelical campaign began. A new parish school in Dingle was also established to accommodate six adult classes, with twenty-two people in each class, and eight child classes. In 1845, Thompson was one of the teachers there. She regretted that there was a shortage of teachers, which meant that some classes were not being taught or had to double up with others.[16]

In the dispute with Monck Mason, Charles Gayer found an ally in Rev. Edward Nangle, who regretted that someone like Monck Mason, whom Gayer 'esteems as a brother', should be 'among the hinderers of a work in which God has so signally blessed him'.[17] The animosity between the Dingle evangelicals and Monck Mason did not last long. By the time he published his book in 1846, Monck Mason had lavish praise for the work of Gayer and Moriarty. He wrote that Gayer was 'ardent in the love of souls and zealous for the promotion of scriptural religion', and Moriarty was a man of 'personal piety and orthodox views [...] not only perfect in the language but in every provincialism of the place'.[18]

Report of the Colony at Dingle (1842)

The organisation first known as the Dingle Colony Association, or just Dingle Colony, was established in 1841; it was later known as the Dingle and Ventry Mission. This organisation marked a kind of declaration of independence by the Dingle evangelicals, who were reliant on their own fund-raising from then on. A short publication, published in 1842 and entitled *Report of the Colony at Dingle*, provides information on the first year of the colony.[19] Lady Lorton, the first patroness, had died; the two new patronesses were the Countess of Bandon and Lady Ventry. The trustees were Rev. Charles Gayer, Captain Forbes and Lt Clifford. Gayer was also treasurer; Catherine Mahon was secretary. The ten members of the all-female committee were: Lady Adelaide Webber, Mrs John Hare, Mrs Irwin, Mrs Hunter, Mrs T. Delacour Carrol, Mrs Ludlow, Elizabeth Colthurst, Mrs Gayer, Mrs Morgan, Miss Maginnis.

Gayer reported on 25 November 1841 that there were fifteen houses in the colony; eighty-six individuals were living there, including seven widows and their children. 'We hope to erect ten more in Dingle and some at Ventry,' Gayer wrote. The 'ten more' appears to refer to the lower colony. The rent of each house was twelve shillings a year. The colony farm, consisting of 27 acres, was half a mile distant and was rented at £25 per annum. Three houses on the farm could be made into comfortable residences, wrote Gayer. The farm would be let to people in amounts of a half-acre or one acre at a rent of thirty shillings (£1 10s) an acre. Anticipating objections to this low rent, Gayer explained that the converts were unable to get work anywhere in the area, that they were tested for a long period before being given a house in the colony, and that the tenancies were week to week only. The tenants would work on the farm and keep a pig to pay the rent.

The colony would be a refuge and would prevent any priestly interference with converts, as happened when they lived in isolation. Gayer wrote of how a convert not living in the colony had been forcibly taken out of her house and the priest was brought to her to persuade her to return. That could not happen to anyone living in the colony. Gayer also proposed a widows' and orphans' fund, training for apprenticeships, and 'a refuge for pious young men who have renounced popery and have been cast off by their friends'. This refuge – an 'appendage' to the colony – would act as a college to teach the young men Irish and prepare some of them for the ministry. There were already two young men in training for the ministry, according to Gayer. It seems that he was planning a second college in Dingle town, like the one established in Ventry, but this did not come to pass.[20]

Catherine Hartland Mahon, writing from 12 Mountjoy Square East, Dublin, on 2 December 1841, described how she was overwhelmed by her first visit to Corca Dhuibhne, 'where nature wears her grandest, loveliest dress [...] My heart has been awed into silent wonder as I beheld its varied and stupendous mountains round which the wild waves foam. I have stood upon its cliffs, the awful and sublime grandeur of which thrilled my spirit.' She was moved by the sincerity of the converts, whom she visited in their colony houses. She wrote that while her heart was gladdened by this,

> it has been grieved at finding so many thousands still walking in darkness. Five thousand immortals who worship they know not what! Creatures, who though in such a fallen degraded state retain much kindness and nobleness of heart, notwithstanding that they are by nature enemies to God and to good works!

She stated that there were funds to build ten more houses, and that work on them would start immediately. She concluded the report by giving the names and addresses of people in Dublin and London to whom donations could be sent.[21]

The *Achill Missionary Herald* acknowledged Mahon's success with the Dingle colony, saying that all the funds were raised 'by the unsolicited exertions of one young lady who is neither connected to the place nor had ever seen it before the last month'. [22] The report stated that the colonies were built with funding provided by 'the liberality of strangers', including a £10 donation from Lord Morpeth, the departing Chief Secretary for Ireland. It also stated that 'the building of another lot is to commence immediately.'[23]

The experience of a group of visitors who went on a day's outing from Dingle with Rev. Gayer and his family is related in an idealised account dated 19 July 1841, 'Every peasant smiled upon us as we passed, and the fisherman mending his nets or repairing his boat looked up with a blessing on the family of his beloved minister.' The group consisted of nineteen people. When they reached Dunquin, a poem in Irish written by Thomas Kennedy, the piper of Dunquin, was read by his son Tom. 'Mr. M.' (probably Thomas Moriarty) pointed out the graves of Tom Kennedy's brother Michael, who had died young, and an elderly convert named Paddy Connor, whose son was a Bible reader.[24]

The second year of Dingle Colony

A brief account of the second year of the Dingle Colony has also survived. In it, a letter from Charles Gayer, dated 31 December 1842, stated that a total of 750 people had converted in the west Kerry area in the previous seven years, including 250 in Dingle town, 200 in Ventry, 110 in Dunquin and the Blasket Island, 65 in Dunurlin and 45 in Kilmalkedar. About fifty other converts were scattered in other areas. In Ventry, ten houses were being built, in addition to the church and schoolhouse. A church and school had been erected in Dunurlin, and 'a commodious building' was nearing completion in Dunquin; the latter was to be used as a schoolhouse during the week and for church service on Sunday. A schoolhouse and a residence for the teacher had been erected on the Great Blasket Island. Gayer was particularly gratified that out of nineteen converts who had died, none had abandoned their commitment. To him, that was a certain proof that their conversions had been sincere.[25]

Gayer stated that by the end of 1842, a total of twenty-five houses had been completed in Dingle; five had been completed in Ventry, while five more were in progress there. In Dingle, 176 children attended Sunday school, the adult Sunday class had increased from 70 to 130, and 150 people were living in the colonies. The original plan to provide an acre to each cottage in the Dingle Colony had been altered, and the trustees now managed the farm and employed the converts on it. They worked on reclaiming the land and cultivating potatoes, which they could then buy with their earnings. 'Thus, habits of industry are produced amongst them,' wrote Gayer. A letter of support from Rev. Denis Browne stated that on a visit to west Kerry he had 'found the reality to far exceed my most sanguine expectations [...] As great a work of revival is likely to be produced in that district as in any other I ever visited.'[26]

Report of the Dingle Colony (1844)

The annual report for 1843 was headed *Report of the Dingle Colony* and it was published in 1844. The patron was the Duke of Manchester (formerly Lord Mandeville of County Armagh) and the patronesses were the Duchess of Manchester, the Countess of Bandon and Lady Ventry.[27] The president was Col the honourable Edward Wingfield, of County Wicklow. The two trustees were Charles Gayer, who was also treasurer, and Lt Clifford R.N.; the secretary was Catherine Hartland Mahon. The committee of ten women included Mrs Gayer. Details in this report indicate that there were eight houses in the lower colony and fifteen in the upper colony. Catherine

Mahon reported that they were anxious to build nine or ten more houses but funds did not allow this. There was £190 in hand, but this was required to pay readers and teachers, and to cover spring work on the farm. She expressed sorrow at the death of Captain Forbes of the Coast Guard service, 'a name beloved by every Dingle convert'. In Gayer's report, dated 2 December 1843, he noted that Daniel O'Connell's campaign to repeal the Act of Union had stirred up passions in the area, with converts being warned that when Repeal was won, they would be the first to suffer.

Two farms of about 20 acres each, at Dunurlin and at Kilmalkedar, had been acquired for the converts. Gayer explained, 'It is quite impossible that the converts could exist at all without ground to cultivate potatoes, as their enemies would gladly starve them out of the country. This was the system resorted to when it was found that curses and excommunications were disregarded.' To donors who might object to their money being spent on renting farms, Gayer gave a long explanation of how isolated and vulnerable converts were, and of the dilemma they faced. If hunger drove a convert back to Catholicism, he was branded as a hypocrite; if he remained and starved as a Protestant, he would prove his sincerity. The end result was that he either suffered the loss of his good name or loss of his life. The converts could not survive without work or gratuitous relief, and the only people who could provide these were the missionaries; therefore, Gayer asked his supporters not to expect rigid adherence to principles of political economy. He assured them that gratuitous relief was only given to widows and orphans, and to those who were unable to work due to illness. Catherine Mahon also addressed this issue, acknowledging that 'many blame us for giving temporal relief and accuse us of bribery.' She responded by posing this question, 'Is it wise to drive these poor creatures back to popery by starving them as a test of their sincerity?'

The missions at Ventry and Dunquin, including some salaries, were supported by the Ladies Auxiliary of the Irish Society. The expenses of the Dingle mission were supported by Mahon's fund, and the expenses of the mission to the Blasket Island were solely in the hands of A.M. Thompson.

The following information is drawn from the complete 1843 colony report held in the National Library.[28] Long lists of donors of small amounts were given, and the total income for the year 1843 was £1,018. This would be the equivalent of approximately €110,000 today. There were thirty-four life members, who either paid £10 or arranged a collection of £20 or more. These life members included Her Majesty, the Queen Dowager and many titled persons. Donors' addresses were generally not given, but collections had taken place in Donaghdee, Bath, Kensington, Ware, Dartmouth and Gainsborough. The following were among the many donations listed: 'a few poor people' in Great Cressingham, Norfolk (3s 7d), Marquis of Cholmondeley (£3), Lady Gore-Booth (£1 10s), Miss Nicholson's school, Leominster (5s), Cressingham Rectory children (6s). Some donations were specifically intended for Rev. Edward Norman's mission activities at Brosna, and he was duly sent £60.

The Dingle Colony's expenditure in 1843 included funeral expenses (£3 5s), seed potatoes for three farms (£26 in total), support of widows and orphans (£102), maps (£19), clothing for Dingle schoolchildren (£17), clothing for Dunurlin schoolchildren (£5 14s 7d), clothing for Kilmalkedar schoolchildren (£5) and apprenticing two children (£10). Printing costs were £11 8s 6d, and postage was £16 4s 6d. Ground rent and poor rates for thirty months for the fifteen houses and ground at the upper colony in Dingle amounted to £23 9d. The rent for eighteen months for the eight houses and land of the lower colony was £37 17s 11d. Rent of the Dingle farm for eighteen months cost £41, and rent of farms at Kilmalkedar and Dunurlin for six months cost £9 3s 11d and £7 10s respectively.

A sum of £203 was spent on labourers, car hire and manure for the Dingle farm. Salaries of scripture readers and teachers amounted to £121. Expenses of ten houses at Ventry amounted to £40, and a large house for two families on John Street cost £50. (This suggests that the upper colony may have included houses on John Street itself, as well as the row of cottages off the street.) Expenses of £4 were allowed for a deputation to Bath; this was presumably a fund-raising trip. Mrs Gayer received £8 for training young men as scripture readers. A balance of £191 14s 4d was in hand at the end of the year.

There were substantial sums of money circulating in west Kerry, which would have been the envy of Catholics priests. Although direct bribery was always denied by the leading evangelicals, there is no doubt that people would have been influenced by the economic power they wielded and the visible signs of progress and improvement that accompanied their work. Indulging in wishful thinking in 1843, the editor of the *Kerry Examiner*, P.R. Byrne, suggested that the conversion campaign was losing momentum; he was pleased to report that 'matters in Dingle are beginning to wear a gloomy appearance – while the funds rose no doubt they looked *Gayer and Gayer* every day, but the funds have fallen and so alas has the "pious cause".'[29] The *Examiner* continued its attacks on the evangelical work in Dingle, describing those involved as 'finished foxes in their way, accomplished and dextrous at a game of biblical thimble-rig and in the division of a good round lump of prize-money supplied by the weakness and credulity of some English saintly simpletons'. It added perceptively, 'In the west of Kerry, is it no bribery to build snug houses with a snug plot of ground attached for the Catholics who have gone over to parsons Gayer and Moriarty? There are direct and indirect means of bribing and the bribery, we maintain, is resorted to in both ways.'[30]

Other colonies

Colonies with associated farms were also established in Ventry, in Kilmalkedar and in Cloonties near Ballyferriter, all receiving financial support from the newly formed Dingle Colony Association. Ó Mainín wrote, 'Is gearr go raibh colonies dá leithéid chéanna i gCeann Trá, ar an gCill agus ar na Cluainte. Bhí tithe agus feirmeacha ag gabháil leo seo agus coistí chun iad a riaradh agus chun airgead a bhailiú.'[31] (Before long, colonies of the same kind were established in Ventry, Kilmalkedar and Cloonties. They were comprised of houses and farms, with committees to manage them and to raise funds.) Thomas F. O'Sullivan recorded that there were thirty families of converts in Cloonties, and that the farm, which was acquired in 1843, was first managed by Mr Anderson and then by Mr Whittaker. He also stated that there were colony farms at Ballineanig, at Ballintaggart and on the Great Blasket.[32]

Dunquin

A.M. Thompson described Dunquin as 'a spot as desolate and lonely as any in the kingdom [...] the most western parish in Ireland, and the headland perhaps the most western point in Europe, exposed to the mighty blast which rolls over the vast Atlantic, and like Dunurlin, having only the wild waves between it and the American shores'.[33] A small group of Dunquin converts travelled to Ventry for Sunday service, but this changed after they sent a petition to Rev. Thomas Moriarty. The petition read:

> We beg leave to state to your reverence the manner in which we are situated here in the parish of Dunquin and the Blasquetts. Your reverence has been aware that we have to travel five miles to Ventry and back again over a steep lonesome mountain to go to prayers every Sunday. As for ourselves, we would not murmur at it had we to go farther, as the Lord was pleased to call us out of darkness to the light of the gospel. But we regret our children to be growing up

without regularly attending public worship and also your reverence knows the women and old people cannot go to Ventry every Sabbath day; the length of the way and the inclemency of the weather prevent them, whereas if they had service in this parish they would all be glad to avail themselves of the opportunity. We are doing our best to instruct them in the word of God but what we can do does not avail much: they wish to attend public worship and to hear the gospel preached to them in their own tongue. Moreover we beg leave to state to your reverence that there are many in this parish anxious to hear the word of God if the opportunity offered and the people are always glad to see you come amongst them. Therefore we feel it is our bounden duty to address you in this manner and humbly request that you will come to us on Sundays if you can at all. And also if your reverence could get a schoolhouse built, it would do for Sundays. And we hope we won't die till we see a church in our parish.[34]

A schoolhouse was duly built in Dunquin, with Thomas Moriarty rejoicing in the event:

We opened our house at Donquin, which is used for school on weekdays and divine service on Sundays. There were present on the occasion 80 converts from that remote and beautifully wild little parish, including two families from the great Blasquet Island opposite; of these it is remarkable that only one man knew a word of English. I had the great satisfaction of preaching to them from the first Irish Bible that was read there many years ago. Its place shall be the pulpit there, while the Lord spares me to preach from it.[35]

Dunquin schoolhouse was in Baile na Rátha Thuaidh. In 1931, Thomas F. O'Sullivan recorded that before it was built, services were held in the Coast Guard station in the adjoining townland of Ballyickeen (Baile Ícín). He wrote that Dunquin school closed 'about thirty years ago' and that the last schoolmaster was named Fallon. The building was still in use for services for the small number of Protestants remaining in 1931.[36] A recent publication gives more information on the school, and on some of the Protestants who lived nearby.[37]

Kilmalkedar

A remarkable event took place in Kilmalkedar in 1842: eleven families suddenly asked to become Protestants, apparently even taking Charles Gayer by surprise.[38] The Irish Society had a presence in Kilmalkedar when George Gubbins was rector, but this sudden group conversion seems to have been effected by one influential individual named Laurence Sullivan. At one time he had been a clerk of the parish priest Fr John Casey, but as soon as he began to read the Irish Bible, he was transformed. As he expressed it, 'I couldn't be easy going to Mass and I couldn't be easy going away from Mass.' Sullivan pondered long over his dilemma and did not convert immediately; instead, with a troubled spirit, he left for America. He told A.M. Thompson, 'Before I was a year there I found the Lord in earnest and never had rest or peace in my mind till I came back to tell the neighbours what I found out to be the truth.' Sullivan seems to have undergone a sincere conversion and test of faith. He ultimately concluded, 'There's no power in man as will let him run from the Lord.'[39]

On his return he was at first rejected by his community and feared for his life:

> Sure enough I thought they'd murder me and cruel enough they did look on me surely, even my own wife. I couldn't bear it by any means; so one day says I to them, 'Well, boys, you needn't be so black and turning away from me as if I didn't belong to you. Sure here I am, you may kill me if you like, and maybe it's to kill me you will; but I don't care, I am ready to die for the Lord Jesus, and the sooner the better, but I'll not hold my tongue while I have breath to speak'.[40]

Gradually, relationships were restored and Laurence Sullivan's neighbours 'took to hearing a chapter now and then out of my book, till it pleased the Lord that they should see the truth and we kept quiet till we all came out of Babylon together, and by the blessing of the Lord we shall never be caught in the devil's net again'.[41] This was another example of the influence of one passionate, charismatic convert on his community. Very soon, Laurence Sullivan was teaching forty-seven converts in an Irish school in Kilmalkedar, for which Mrs Gayer had secured funds. The Ladies Auxiliary of the Irish Society paid for a scripture reader.

According to Thompson, Fr John Casey, parish priest of Ballyferriter and Kilmalkedar, was 'less fiery in his sentiments against Protestants, so much so he had acquired the name of the Protestant priest'.[42] John Casey, a native of Ballyheigue, was a venerable old man and a well-known antiquarian with a deep scholarly knowledge of the archaeological sites of Corca Dhuibhne. For this reason, visiting scholars always called to him, and he received them warmly and undertook to be their guide.

The colonies in 1844

A letter written in early 1845 by Catherine Hartland Mahon, under her married name of Inglis, confirmed that the missionaries in Dingle had become independent in 1841 and operated under the name Dingle Colony Association.[43] She wrote that this was distinct from all other societies and did not receive help from any of them. Its purpose was 'to protect, employ, shelter and instruct these poor sufferers for the truth of the gospel by schools and scripture readers which it supports'. In January 1843, the converts of Dingle numbered 310; in March 1844, they numbered 330, comprised of seventy-three families. Schoolchildren numbered 180, and 130 adults attended classes on Sunday.

In Kilmalkedar there were eighty converts, with forty-one children attending school. At Dunurlin there were fifty converts, with twenty-eight children at school. The Dingle Colony paid salaries of scripture readers and teachers in Dingle, Kilmalkedar and Dunurlin, while Ventry and Dunquin were still under the auspices of the Irish Society, and the Blasket Island mission was funded by A.M. Thompson. Gayer was quoted as saying that he had to turn away some converts, as he could not provide them with work and they could not survive in the colony without it. If only he could provide work for converts, he believed that the numbers of converts could be doubled. The *Post* endorsed Mrs Inglis's appeal for more financial support for the Dingle mission.[44]

The Little Ones of Innisfail gave an idyllic picture of the men of Dingle Colony working on the farm and the women doing needlework at home while the children attended school. It concluded, 'The peace of God [...] seems to dwell in these cottages.'[45] This kind of report was exactly what supporters of the Dingle Colony would have wished to hear, and they would have been gratified at the results of their generosity. However, when Patrick Foley later wrote about the establishment of the lower colony, it was with a sense of grievance. According to him, to make way for the colony, 'The sick poor then residing along Strand St. were flung out of their dying beds to perish on the roadside.'[46]

Even though the colonies were an apparent success, the problem of providing sufficient employment for converts persisted, since there were so few Protestant employers in the area. A.M. Thompson wrote regretfully that young converts were being sent far away from Dingle: females to go into service with Protestant families and males to become apprentices to Protestant tradesmen, and some of the better-educated young men and women to become teachers all over Ireland. Assisted emigration also began; Thompson wrote, 'some whole families have been shipped off to America.' She saw the implications of this loss of talent, 'This not only prevents the apparent growth of the body, but withdraws from it perpetually its best members.' [47] These departures may have been a significant factor in the eventual decline of the Protestant community of west Kerry after the Famine.

Graveyard conflicts

Confrontations continued to take place, with two incidents occurring in graveyards at times of burial. In 1843, Mary Breen was being buried under Protestant rites at Dunurlin, and Rev. Edward Lee Sandiford, a curate, was asked by Mary's husband and sister to officiate. But when the funeral cortege of about forty or fifty converts arrived from Dingle, they were confronted by a group of over a hundred Catholics, including other relatives of Mary Breen, who were there to prevent the burial service. [48] The larger group was led by William Forhan, a visitor to the area. When Rev. Sandiford asked him who he was, Forhan replied, 'I am myself and who are you?' [49] The police arrived and advised Sandiford that violence would follow if he proceeded with the service, and so he decided to leave. Forhan was indicted 'for a riot and exciting the people'; at his trial in August, he conducted his own defence. He said that he had no objection to 'hereditary Protestants' like Sandiford; his issue was with converts or soupers, 'the very scum of Dingle' and 'rascals of turncoats', whom Sandiford had brought to the service. They were 'the scruff of the place, people who had sold their God'. Forhan apologised for his insolence in replying to Sandiford in the graveyard, but he told the court that that was his only offence. [50]

Forhan was sentenced to three months in jail, but he was released on the grounds that he had already spent time in custody. The judge, Baron Richards, said that he recognised that Forhan was a young man of 'ardour and steadfastness' but that his action was 'uncharitable, unjust and illegal'. The judge made some general observations on conversions:

If people do change their religion for mercenary motives, they certainly do what is wrong; they make a traffic of their salvation and deserve the utmost contempt that can be showered on them. I hope such instances

TO THE IRISH-SPEAKING PEOPLE
OF
DERBY.

THE GOSPEL WILL BE PREACHED (GOD WILLING)

In the Irish Tongue,

IN

ST. MICHAEL'S CHURCH, DERBY,

On Wednesday Evening, March 23rd,

At Eight o'clock,

BY

THE REV. THOMAS MORIARTY,

Rector of Ventry, Co. Kerry, Ireland.

You are most affectionately invited to attend, and hear the story of the Cross in your own much-loved tongue.

All the seats in the church are free; come early, in order to get a good one.

THERE WILL BE NO COLLECTION.

Cum na nÉireannać a nDerbi.

Beiż Seanmóin a nÁaoiłże (le toil Dé) a dteampoll naoṁ Mićíl,

tratnóna Diacéadaoine ro éúżain, an 23 lá Márta, aṅ oćt do ćloż,

le

Tomáṡ Mac Muirceartaiġ,

Ministir an tSoirżéil a bParáiste Fiúntráż a ĵContaé Ciarraiże a nÉirinn.

Atá cuireaḋ ćartanać aĵ Éiġniż uile teaćt ćum ĵéil na Croiże aĵus na ṫiotćána ḋéirteaċt anairże.

Tá na ṡuiḋeaċáin raon do ćaċ, má tiżiṡ an tam.

"Ó cad é breáżtaċt cor na muintire rorirżculan an driocáin, aĵus do rorirżculan neiże maża."

Pól ćum na Róṁánaċ, caib x. 15.

025 Bilingual notice of lecture by Rev. Thomas Moriarty in Derby. Date not known. *Tomás an Bhlascaoid*

026 Dunurlin (Ballyferriter) church, school and parsonage. *Persecution of Protestants*

027 Granville House today. The section on the left is the former parsonage.

Above—028 View of the Blaskets. *Irish Intelligence*

Left—029 Scoil an Mhisiúin, the mission school, on the Great Blasket. *Persecution of Protestants*

Below—030 Ruins of mission school on the Great Blasket today.

031 Lower colony cottages, Dingle. *Irish Intelligence*

032 Lower colony cottages, Dingle. *Persecution of Protestants*

033 View of Dingle with John Street in foreground. St James's church is on right and St Mary's church is in centre. AMT

034 Dingle town with upper colony cottages projecting right from John Street. National Library of Ireland, Lawrence Collection, Call No: L_CAB_061665

035 Lower colony cottages today.

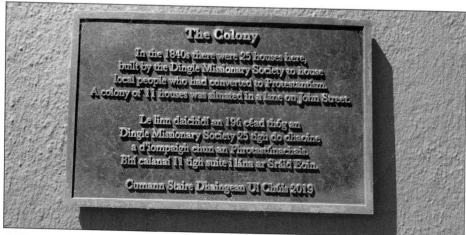

036 Plaque on lower colony today.

037 Title page of *Report of the Colony at Dingle 1841*.
NLI Ms 24,445

038 Title page of *Report of the Dingle Colony 1843*.
NLI Ms 24,445

039 Mission church at Cloghaneduff, near Kilmalkedar, now refurbished as a modern home.

040 Former Dingle Parochial School, now the office of Sacred Heart University, Dingle Campus. Courtesy of Gary Delaney

041 Beacon towers erected by Rev. Charles Gayer, 1847, Entrance to Dingle Harbour. National Library of Ireland. JOLY ET A475. Drawn on stone by Samuel Watson, 17 Richmond Cottages, Dublin

042 Eask Tower, the only remaining beacon tower.

043 Plaque commemorating Rev. Charles Gayer and his wife Catherine in St James's church.

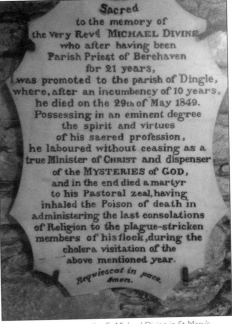

Sacred
to the memory of
the Very Revᵈ MICHAEL DIVINE
who after having been
Parish Priest of Berehaven
for 21 years,
was promoted to the parish of Dingle,
where, after an incumbency of 10 years,
he died on the 29th of May 1849.
Possessing in an eminent degree
the spirit and virtues
of his sacred profession,
he laboured without ceasing as a
true Minister of CHRIST and dispenser
of the MYSTERIES of GOD,
and in the end died a martyr
to his Pastoral zeal, having
inhaled the Poison of death in
administering the last consolations
of Religion to the plague-stricken
members of his flock, during the
cholera visitation of the
above mentioned year.
Requiescat in pace.
Amen.

044 Plaque commemorating Fr Michael Divine in St Mary's church.

The strangest reports were circulated; nothing was too absurd for bigotry or credulity to swallow: it was said that any one willing to become 'A man of Mr. Gayer's,' 'a souper,'* 'a turncoat,' the various appellations the convert bears, was immediately BLED by Mr. Gayer, and PROTESTANT BLOOD infused into his veins. This caused a panic amongst the relations of the converts, which would have been ludicrous, had not the occasion been so solemn; others were absolutely believed to have been turned by priestly power, as a punishment for their heresy,

* This term of reproach grew out of the circumstance of a soup-shop having been opened by a benevolent lady of the town, in a time of great scarcity and distress, and soup offered for sale to the poor. The Roman Catholics might have purchased, but were forbidden by the Priest; all who did avail themselves of it were henceforth termed 'soupers.'

No. I was the first that ever baptise them soupers. Long before Gayer came to Dingle. JOS

045 Note written by Fr John O'Sullivan, on his copy of A.M. Thompson's book. It reads, 'No. I was the first that ever baptised them soupers, long before Gayer came to Dingle. JOS.' Kerry County Archives

046 Satirical cartoon from *Kerry Evening Post*, 1845.

are few but we are all bound as Christians to put the best construction on men's motives and it is certainly improper and uncharitable for persons to presume that because a person in high or low life changes his religious beliefs he does so from base or sordid influence.[51]

The *Post* approved of the words of Judge Richards and hoped that 'the over-zealous western friends of Fr. Divine and co.' would heed them.[52]

Another graveyard incident took place in Kilquane at the burial of John Kevane, who had died by drowning. Revs Gayer and Goodman were in attendance, and they were confronted by a hostile crowd. They could proceed only because of the support of the Coast Guards and policemen who happened to be nearby.[53] The *Post* condemned 'the spirit of popery' in 'this priest-ridden, benighted land' and compared 'the intolerant, persecuting spirit' of 1843 to the religious conflicts of 1641.[54] The *Chronicle* named the dead man as Sylvester Moriarty rather than John Kevane; it claimed that the coroner had been prevented from viewing the body and had to rely on assistance from Lt Clifford of the Coast Guard. This report said that there was a crowd of four to five hundred people at the graveyard, and it named Sub-inspector Gillman, along with Constables Carpenter and Moroney, as being present to ensure the burial could take place. Francis Twiss and Lt Collett of the Coast Guard were also present.[55]

In May 1843, the twenty-first annual meeting of the Irish Society of London was held under the chairmanship of the Earl of Galloway, its president. The *Post* was delighted to record that 'almost every gentleman who addressed the meeting alluded to the signal success of the Society in this county.' The paper devoted almost a whole page to the proceedings; it also quoted Archdeacon A.B. Rowan as saying that priests told their people that 'if they die in communion with the Ventry church, they will be buried with the burial of a dog.'[56]

The social isolation that followed the decision to convert was a constant theme of evangelicals when they appealed for financial assistance from sympathisers in Britain. These verses were published in an evangelical journal under the title 'Lines written by a convert on being excommunicated by the Church of Rome':

An exile at home I must dwell
None dare to converse or make free,
From the reach of all men I'm expelled
No share with the elect for me!

The priest all his power has exerted
His craft o'er the world prevails;
All men from my face are deserted
Not one to accost me remains.

My cabin is lonesome at night
No foot sound I hear at the door.
My friends who were once my delight
Will visit my cottage no more.

My spouse who was tender and kind,
Her affections were faithful and free,
She's gone and has left me behind,
For in death she is severed from me.

Two orphans of mother bereft,
Yet tender in years to condole,
Are all the companions that's left,
Their forlorn sire to console.

But yet through the gospel of glory
I search for the truth there foretold,
And read to my babies a story
Once wrote by the prophets of old.

I'm nourished by Christ's invitation
Who calls on the weak and oppressed,
And says to a world of nations:
'Approach me, I *will* give you rest.'[57]

The Churchman

In August 1842, a correspondent of an evangelical publication named *The Churchman* visited Dingle and surrounding areas. He published an account of the visit in the issues of February and March 1843.[58] (For convenience, the anonymous author is referred to here as 'Churchman'.) The writer was a supporter of the mission, and he spent some weeks in west Kerry. The well-written report gives valuable insights into the state of the missionary work just after the colonies had been established. The account began with this description:

The south-western part of Ireland is singularly indented by deep bays, which running far inland are separated by narrow peninsular tracts of wild mountainous country. Of these bays, that of Castlemaine or Dingle, for it is indifferently called by either name, is one of the largest. On its northern side a very narrow passage between two bold rocky headlands opens into the small inner harbour of Dingle, surrounded by high bare and often rocky hills; bosomed in which nestles the little town of Dingle-i-couch, which rising up their southern slope, enjoys a splendid view beyond the harbour mouth, across the wide bay, to the mountain range of the rugged barony of Iveragh. This range though not very lofty presents an outline of uncommon beauty and of such varied tints as could not fail to engage and charm a painter's eye [...]

All the headlands along this part of the coast are, towards the sea bold, lofty and perpendicular but decline rapidly on the land side, thus forming a succession of very steep eminences with lower cliffs or small bays between. At these lower parts sands (too frequently driving sands) prevail and are encroaching sadly upon the land, increasing the poverty of the neighbouring people. But, on the other hand, it must be mentioned that many excellent roads having been made through parts of the country where twenty years ago nothing but a mountain pony could have travelled, agriculture has in consequence rapidly increased and little fields of golden oats, niched every here and there between the brown rocks, give proof of the awakening industry of the small farmers and cottiers.[59]

In Dingle, Churchman found that there were between four hundred and five hundred in the Protestant congregation, three hundred of whom were converts. Sunday school had an attendance of one hundred and forty children, and one hundred adult converts attended classes in an upper room of the school. The adults, men and women, were divided into groups according to level of proficiency; they were taught in either Irish or English as appropriate. There was also 'a large and flourishing' parochial school, and two schools for 'old men' and 'old women'. The writer noted that seven young men were being prepared for the ministry, and he named three local men who had become Protestant ministers: Thomas Moriarty, Thomas Jephcote and William Dee, who was described as late headmaster of the school for the sons of clergy at Lucan, Co. Dublin. The names of Rev. Dee and Rev. Jephcote do not appear in other sources.

Churchman described the converts who attended Sunday service in Dingle church as 'filling one deep gallery' and participating 'with every appearance of deep devotion and feeling':

> Some of them very poor, wild-looking barefooted creatures, dressed in the peculiar fashion of this district – a scarlet petticoat; above it either a gown, the skirt pinned up, or a short dress of cinnamon-coloured stuff; on the neck, a scarlet, plaid, worsted handkerchief; one to match tied on the head, the corner hanging down at the back; the hair braided over the forehead. Not a cap did we see except on maid servants in the houses of the gentry or on some of the better-most townspeople and shopkeepers. It had a most striking and touching effect, the seeing so many thus wildly attired going to the table of Our Lord.[60]

Because Ventry church was not yet completed, a Sunday service in Irish took place in the schoolroom, followed by classes for adults and children – two in English and four in Irish. The Ventry congregation was two hundred strong. At 'Dunorling' (Dunurlin), Churchman saw 'a lately built good glebe-house and a remarkably nice new church, while a large school-house is in progress', with thirty-five children attending daily. He also noted numbers of converts at Kilmalkedar, where Patrick Connor had settled as a scripture reader after he left the Blasket Island, and smaller numbers in Kilquane and 'Iniscall' (Annascaul).

Churchman described his journey to Dunquin for 'the opening of the schoolhouse for divine service':

> It was a gay and striking scene along the broad sands of Ventry Bay (which, it being low water, we crossed a part of) and up the long steep rocky road over Marhyn hill, enlivened as it was by jaunting cars, gigs and horses, all hastening to see this interesting event. And when we topped the hill, how glorious was the view of the ocean stretched before us in the silver splendour of the noontide sun, near us the rocky Blasquet Isles, beyond them the boundless Atlantic.[61]

The gathering included between eighty and ninety converts and large numbers of children; they were all praying and singing with gusto, the Irish language 'sounding rich and agreeable even to our unaccustomed ears'.

Churchman walked with friends around 'this very poor nest of cabins' and was welcomed by Roman Catholics, 'who seemed quite as much pleased to see us as did the converts'. He related the story of how old Séamus Bán O'Connor, 'the village sage', was given a copy of the Bible by Lord Ventry and subsequently decided that the Catholic Church was in error.

Churchman noted 'the kindly spirit of clanship' that prevailed in west Kerry. He saw this as a measure of protection for the converts, because although people might not speak or trade with them, 'they neither murdered nor beat nor in any other way injured them.' In his opinion, the priests' denunciations had little effect on people, because 'such violence was so abhorrent to them that no chapel exhortations or anathemas succeeded in exciting them to commit such outrages.' Churchman gave a parable-like account of a dutiful favourite son who became a convert. The young man passed by his mother, brother, sister and the girl he loved as they went to Mass on Christmas Day, and he was dismayed when, 'rather than look at him, they turned away their heads and walked mournfully by.' The convert was disheartened until he read his Bible and took courage from it. His 'steadfastness in the truth and sacrifice of his affections to it' were held up as a bright example of the sincerity of the converts.[62]

Churchman stressed that conversion had brought moral, spiritual and material improvement into the lives of converts. 'There is not one drunkard, not one Sabbath-breaker, not one ill-conducted female among them [and] they are much improved in cleanliness and a desire for the decencies of life.'[63] Of nineteen who had died, not one had reverted to 'former superstitions'. A few who joined in hope of material gain soon fell away, realising there were no advantages to be gained; Churchman was adamant that 'there can be no doubt that these poor people make this momentous change from conviction, for nothing is given, nothing is held out to them as an inducement; on the contrary they suffer the extreme of poverty and deprivation.'

As he walked around Dingle, Churchman visited a woman in the colony:

Being pleased with the open countenance of one of these colonists, I stepped into her tidy little cottage and entered into conversation with her; she seemed cheerful and contented and spoke freely on the state of her mind. After having talked with her for some time, I enquired whether, when she was conscious of having erred or done wrong, she ever felt a desire to return to her former customs and try to atone for it by some penance. 'Oh, no!' (said she, clasping her hands with energy) 'my heart is as light in my breast as a bird, since I learned to place my whole trust and hope in the Lord and saviour and only him, and left off them weary penances and pilgrimages that did me no good and that I never felt the better for or satisfied after'.[64]

Churchman described the effects of 'exclusive dealing':

> The small shopkeeper or huxter had no custom, the weaver can no longer ply his shuttle, nor the spinner her wheel, nor the labourer his spade, for none will hold communication with them or give them any work. Their Romanist neighbours do them no bodily despite; they simply leave them to their own resources, and these resources being absolutely *nought*, the poor creatures are reduced to a state of actual starvation.[65]

He believed that supporting converts with charity would be 'imprudent and dangerous', as it could become a temptation to hypocrisy and a reward for idleness, as well as grounds for charges of bribery. And, he explained, this was why 'twenty small cottages of the plainest description, with a small potato garden attached to each' had been recently built 'in the outskirts of the town of Dingle'. These houses were let at low rents to 'the destitute but very decent converts, who are now always spoken of as the *colony*'. A supervisor was appointed; weavers in the colony were lent some money to buy yarn; flax and wool were bought for spinners, and worsted for knitters. After inspection by a supervisor, the items of clothing were then sold in the market. (There is no suggestion here that exclusive dealing was a barrier in this transaction.) The chief object of all this enterprise was to assist the converts 'through their own exertions, to lead them to industry and independence, to cultivate good habits and to avoid the necessity of charitable donation'. Churchman ended by saying that Dingle 'cannot, of its poverty, supply funds sufficient to support such a business as this. Must it then fall to the ground? Must the people perish in involuntary idleness? Or rather will not the generous public still step forward and of "their silver and their gold" give the means for such a righteous purpose?'[66]

12. The mission to the Great Blasket

'Only for us it is a certain fact that everyone in the island would starve this year.'[1] This stark statement was made by Charles Gayer at a time when hunger was wreaking havoc in Kerry. He was referring to the relief that he and other Protestant missionaries provided to the people of the Great Blasket during the savage winter of 1846–47. Even allowing for exaggeration, this statement alone is a reason to examine the work of the Protestant evangelicals from their first involvement in the lives of the islanders in 1839.

Visitors to the Great Blasket today pass by the ruined Protestant schoolhouse, the first building to the left on the uphill path from the landing place. Protestant missionaries kept records of their experiences, and their accounts provide significant insights into aspects of island life before the Famine. A.M. Thompson devoted a chapter to the Blasket mission, and she had a particular interest in the island. Some letters and journals written by the teachers and readers of the Protestant mission who lived on the island have also survived. Charles Gayer and Thomas Moriarty visited regularly, often accompanied by local followers and guests from elsewhere. Copies of letters written by them and held in the archives of St Columba's College provide invaluable insights into their perspectives on island life. These letters have not previously been accessed by historians of the Blaskets. The names of individual islanders appear in the accounts and some conversations were recorded, adding colour to the narratives.

The Blasket Islands were also known as Ferriter's Islands and the Blasquetts. A.M. Thompson described them as follows:

> The Blasquetts are a group of eight rocky islands of which two only are habitable. They lie about three miles westward from our iron-bound coast which presents cliffs to the stupendous waters of the Atlantic a thousand feet high. The sound that lies between those islands and the mainland is of the most dangerous description; in it one of the largest of the ships of the Spanish Armada sunk with all on board; the currents and tides which rush through it are terrific

and render it impassable except in a long continuance of calm weather.[2]

Thompson estimated that there were approximately 150 inhabitants on the largest island, the Great Blasket, in the early 1840s; she described them as being 'in a state of extreme ignorance – not a single individual in the island could read, write or speak a word of English.' It is telling that an inability to speak or write in English was a mark of ignorance for Thompson. The islanders spoke Irish exclusively but could not read or write the language. Only a handful of people lived on the smaller islands.

Thompson's population estimate tallies with the 1841 population figure of 153 (eighty-five male and sixty-eight female) living in twenty-eight houses.[3] The landlord of the island was the Earl of Cork. He leased it to Clarissa (or Clara) Hussey, a prominent Catholic; her rent collector was also a Catholic. Miss Hussey, who leased other property in Ballyferriter from the Earl of Cork, was described by Patrick Foley as 'very severe upon her tenants'.[4] Although Foley described her as 'among the worst type of landowners in the county', he acknowledged that she was 'a most bountiful benefactress' of the Catholic Church.[5] She was buried in St Mary's church in Dingle, where a plaque records that the church is 'her monument', as it was built 'chiefly at her expense'. There was no resident priest on the Blasket Island, and no regular religious services were held there. Once or twice a year, or even every two years, a priest would come to the island to collect his 'dues' in the form of wool, mutton or eggs. One writer listed these items given to the priest, 'lambs, pigs, geese, ducks, chickens, wool, yarn and whatever else could be obtained from their poverty.'[6] Another partisan source claimed that the priest visited only once a year 'to look after *the fleece – the flock* he appeared to care little about, and he returned to the shore taking his dues, chiefly in wool and eggs.'[7]

When Mass was being celebrated at Dunquin, a white sheet would be hoisted there as a signal; the islanders would then kneel on the cliffside and pray.[8] An English publication described how Fr Casey celebrated Mass 'for the Dunquin people to hear the Latin actually and the Blasquett islanders by telegraph or signal, three miles across the sea – a broom on a pole, with a white handkerchief, conveyed the Mass across a dangerous sound unscathed.'[9]

The first missionary landing on the Blasket
According to A.M. Thompson, there were 'insuperable difficulties' operating against the introduction of the Bible to the Great Blasket. The first attempt by Rev. Gayer to promote his message there was inauspicious. In 1835, he

sent a scripture reader, but that man promptly departed when the islanders threatened to throw him over a cliff if he landed. However, when the news of the schools at Ventry and elsewhere reached the islanders, their attitudes changed; in 1838, 'a deputation' from the island asked Gayer to send a teacher to set up a school there, saying that they felt 'like the cows and horses' as they were.[10]

According to Thompson, during the visit of 'some good men, eminent ministers of the gospel', to Ventry in the summer of 1838, it was decided 'at all hazards' to establish a mission on the Great Blasket.[11] She personally undertook to raise funds for the mission in order not to deplete resources set aside for other projects on the mainland. Thompson wrote that the initial funding for the mission to the Blaskets came from 'a few Irish friends in England' to whom she wrote for support. One woman immediately sent the equivalent of a year's salary for the scripture reader, and she became an annual subscriber. Thompson took a strong personal interest in the island; she donated the profits from the first edition of her book 'to the relief of the starving people of the Blasket island, without distinction as to religion'.[12]

In a description of the beginning of the Blasket mission, the author of *Innisfail* was incredulous at the fact that so many Protestant missionaries travelled far across the world to preach the word of God, while 'these lovely isles that gem our native sea [...] have been left to mourn unpitied and unblessed.'[13] This book is written in a florid style and is propagandist in tone, written by a supporter of the Protestant mission for other supporters. It conveys a clear sense of the significance of the Blasket mission to all those involved. The ultimate objective of accounts such as this was to raise funds in Britain and to assure donors that their money was well spent. Despite this bias, such accounts provide insights into island life. This is how fire-side gatherings of fishermen were described:

> Twenty fires sending up their daily smoke wreaths to the clouds denote as many families residing on the Great Blasket island; and round these fires, when the weather is sufficiently calm to admit of their landing on its dangerous but singularly beautiful shore, more than a hundred fishermen will oft assemble from all the surrounding coasts and, while their simple meal of potatoes is being prepared, beguile the interval of time with tale of shipwreck, strife or superstition dread. Such has been the state of the Great Blasket island, its poor inhabitants for centuries unchanged in manner, mind and language.[14]

Charles Gayer's own account of the beginning of the Blasket mission was told in *Innisfail*. He related how three attempts over three years to gain a foothold on the island came to nought because 'the Lord's time was not yet come.' His description of the first attempt differs slightly from Thompson's. He wrote that the reader succeeded in landing on the island; once landed, he found that people were hostile and threatened to throw him over the cliff. A kind woman made an appeal on his behalf, and he was allowed to stay for a few days, half-starved, before he was sent back to the mainland. 'This was rather discouraging,' wrote Gayer.

On the second occasion, Thomas Dowling planned to go to the Blasket. But when he learned in Dunquin that the priests were making their annual visit, he abandoned his plan. Two other men later set out for the island, but they found two priests there, working with a party of men improving the landing place, and they also withdrew, 'after getting well hooted'. Soon after this came the dramatic change of attitude on the part of the islanders when they saw the benefits of the educational work on the mainland – and saw that the curses of the priests were not having any impact. The turning point came when an islandman offered to rent a house to the crew of the mission boat as a place to stay while they were on fishing expeditions. Gayer readily accepted the offer and prepared for their first visit, initially planning to settle a convert family from Ventry on the island.[15]

And so came the day when Charles Gayer, Thomas Moriarty, Captain Forbes and five other men landed on the Blasket, 'this long-wished-for scene of missionary labour'. Thompson and subsequent writers date this landing as taking place on 1 January 1839, although this was an inauspicious time of the year for the dangerous crossing. The party was welcomed with traditional hospitality – they were given eggs, potatoes and milk – and they were told that if the islanders had had advance notice of their arrival, a sheep would have been killed for them. Some of the visitors went walking to admire the scenery, and others, who spoke Irish, went 'to try and find out the minds of the people'. Gayer recorded, 'The result of our inquiry was that the people seemed anxious to have a school. They said they did not care a farthing for the priests who never came near them except to claim their dues.'[16]

The missionary party returned to Dingle in high spirits. Gayer then reflected that it would be best to settle matters before the priests or Miss Hussey heard of their initiative and interfered. He returned to the island the next day, accompanied by a family of converts whom he intended to settle there. The man who had offered to rent the house (later identified as

Maurice Guiheen or Muiris Ó Guithín) assured Gayer, 'Arrah, man, all the priests and the landlords in the world should not prevent me from letting you my house.' Another man offered Gayer a cabin for a schoolhouse, and Gayer asked about the number who would attend. The man replied, 'Och, I will go to school myself! Never fear, you will get enough of them.' A woman told Gayer, 'Oh, man, the whole island will join ye!' Another man offered Gayer his 'one white quilt […] and plenty of mutton' if he lodged with him.

Gayer described another occasion when he and Moriarty visited the Blasket to find that agents of Clarissa Hussey were there to impound the cattle of those who assisted the missionaries. The two men thought it best to stay away from the village and sat on the cliffside. Gayer wrote:

> In a short time, one or two of the islanders came to us, then a few more, until at last we were surrounded by more than twenty. One old woman looked at Mr. M. for some time and at length exclaimed 'I am sure you must be a M[oriarty].' 'Why do you think so?' said he. 'Because,' she replied, 'you are so like the family.' 'Well,' said he, 'I am a M[oriarty].' 'Oh then,' cried the old woman, jumping up and shaking hands with him, 'your father's son is welcome here, for I am a Moriarty.' This made us all great friends. The poor people seemed to forget the loss of their cattle when Mr. M. set the truth before them in their own dear native tongue. What has God wrought? The wildest most uncultivated people in our land, from being our greatest enemies are become our warmest friends. Surely the Lord has work to be done amongst them yet.[17]

The exhilaration generated by the first visit to the Blasket was captured in verse:

> The ocean shone a mirror bright,
> Hushed was each stormy gale,
> As now the missionary boat
> Spread wide its snowy sail.
> The sunny ray glanced on the sea
> With bright auspicious beam,
> When heralds of the lord of life
> To the Great Blasket came.
> In awful grand magnificence

And beautiful as grand,
The isle appear'd, when safely steer'd,
They drew their boat to land.[18]

Elizabeth Colthurst

The writings of Elizabeth Colthurst reveal how support and funding were elicited in Britain for the missionary work on the Blasket. They also disclose how children were inducted into the project of cultural and spiritual imperialism, which was one of the driving forces of British society in the mid-nineteenth century. Colthurst also shows how the conversion campaign in Ireland was part of a colonial mission, similar to those carried out in parts of the world where Christianity was unknown. British missionaries around the world were depicted as heroically bringing light into darkness, and dispelling ignorance and superstition. Colthurst observed of the Blasket islanders that 'the total ignorance of these poor people may be inferred from the fact of there not being found a needle or a pair of scissors on the island.' She related the story of an island woman who visited Dingle and, looking around in astonishment, declared, 'Oh! If Dingle is such a fine large place what must the world be!'[19]

In *Tales of Erin*, Colthurst published a long verse account of the beginnings of the Blasket mission, with this description of the reception experienced by the first evangelical visitors:

And soon, to hail the welcome sail,
Appeared a busy crowd,
With Irish words of welcome kind,
And gratulation loud.

In cordial greeting, women, men
And little children vied,
And soon a hospitable board
Their frugal stores supplied.

Potatoes new, eggs not a few,
The peasants' simple fare
More grateful to the guests appear'd
Than costly viands rare.[20]

Following his first visit to the Blasket Island, Gayer was overjoyed and declared,

'The Blasket islands I trust are won! Long has Satan reigned, triumphantly sitting on the scarlet-coloured beast, in that wild and desolate region; but his end seems near. The victory will be gained without sword and without spear.'[21] Making arrangements to send a teacher to the island took some time; an impatient islander met Rev. Gayer in Dingle and asked him about the delay. Gayer explained that he was concerned that the priest would prevent the children from attending the school. The man responded, 'Never fear that, for we are determined, the next time that he comes lecturing us, not to keep our tongues in our pockets. And by my word, it is too many children, not too few, you'll be thinking that you have at the Great Blasket – only try it!'[22]

Thomas Moriarty wrote another version of this encounter in which he stated that he and Gayer had met an island couple in Dingle. Moriarty assured them that if they were sure of getting scholars to attend, the school would be set up without delay. The couple promised that there would be nine students immediately, and more would follow. Moriarty's account continued, 'We remarked that the priest would drive them all away on his first visit to the island. The woman at once said that when he came again, they would not have their tongues in their pockets as before.'[23]

Patrick Connor, the first teacher on the Great Blasket

A.M. Thompson was aware that the isolation and dangers of working and living on the island made it an unattractive prospect for a teacher. It was 'a place where sickness and death might be months unknown on the mainland, where the simple food he would require was not always to be had' and where a man 'might be murdered with impunity'.[24] Nevertheless, in early 1839, a young convert named Patrick Connor (O'Connor) agreed to take up the position of teacher on the island; he crossed over some months later, accompanied by Thomas Moriarty, Charles Gayer, Captain Forbes and others. It is possible that Patrick was the son of Séamus Bán O'Connor of Dunquin, the poet and scholar who was well disposed towards the evangelicals.[25] However, Churchman wrote that Patrick Connor's father was 'a very comfortable farmer several miles distant from this part of the country', and that he was strongly opposed to Patrick's conversion.[26]

Thompson described the reception given to the party of visitors, 'The islanders came down in numbers to the rocks and would have carried these gentlemen in their arms up the almost inaccessible path over the cliffs, called, and indeed forming, their only landing place.' Prayers and blessings were said, and Thompson wrote that 'the words were words of wonder to their ears. Never had they heard such – they were amazed!' In the evening, the islanders bade a tearful farewell to their visitors, and 'every house opened its doors to the reader and the wondrous things out of his book were heard with gladness.'[27]

Rev. Daniel Foley was one of those in the party accompanying Patrick Connor to the Blasket. He described this memorable experience:

> We landed on a rock and nine of us put up united prayers to our heavenly father for the success of our mission. It was a solemn scene amid the roar of the Atlantic to hear too the hymn as we changed the verse 'Cry aloud and tell the nations &c.' into 'Cry aloud and tell the Blasquetts, Jesus reigns for evermore.'[28]

An authoritative account of the arrival of Patrick Connor on the Blasket on 28 May 1839 was written by Charles Gayer, who said that Connor had been ill with fever for two months before then:

> The day was very fine and we were accompanied by several Christian friends. We reached the island around 12.00 o'c. and Mr. Moriarty and some of our Irish readers were engaged most of the day in reading the scriptures to the people who had collected in different places and were most attentive.

> It was nearly 8 o'c. before we had all settled to return, but before we did, we all met on the rocks to commit our teacher, and the important work in which he was about to be engaged, to the care of the Good Shepherd who had given us favour in the sight of the poor benighted people. The evening was most lovely and the sun was about to set in the Atlantic ocean which looked like a polished mirror and reflected the mountains and stupendous cliffs which form the barrier to the otherwise irresistible force of the mighty waves which, when the winter storms arrive, roll like hills whose tops are white with snow against them and dash the spray several hundred feet high. The golden tints which the setting sun cast on every object around promised that the day which would succeed would be brighter still and seemed to bode, at least in the minds of those who witnessed it, that a scene far more glorious would yet succeed in that wild, desolate region when the sun of righteousness should arise and shine upon it with healing in his wings and this 'desert should arise and blossom as the rose'.[29]

Connor was 'naturally in very low spirits' as his friends were about to leave the island, but they buoyed him up with hymns, prayers and scripture readings at the little cove. There was already some encouragement for him, as he found 'every house was open to him' and one family had converted. Gayer and others went to visit him some days later; they learned that Fr John Casey had been on the island and 'had cursed the people for admitting Connor amongst them'. Despite this, 'the barbarous people had shown him no little kindness and had treated him like a brother, to use his own words.'[30]

Patrick Connor stayed in the house of Maurice Guiheen for a year before moving to other lodgings. Thomas Moriarty said later that Guiheen, who did not become a convert, was 'a bad man', but because he was the only one to offer accommodation, his offer was accepted.[31]

Fr Casey's visit

According to Gayer, when Fr John Casey next visited the island, he was alarmed that his dues from the islanders would be reduced in the future, and he went around muttering to himself, 'They have set their anchor here, they have set their anchor here, they have set their anchor here.' Maurice Guiheen replied, 'Well then, set about and haul it.' Gayer gave an account of a dramatic encounter between Fr Casey and Maurice Guiheen, and quotes their direct speech:

> Fr. Casey: You must put the man Connor out of the house you set him.

> Maurice Guiheen: Oh, I can't do that for he has a lock and key to it.

> Fr. C: Aye, there's the anchor, there's the anchor. Did not I tell that they had fastened their anchor here?

> MG: Go and turn him out of it yourself.

> Fr. C [angrily, to the people]: Good people, I call you to witness that this man wants to hang or transport me, for you hear how he tells me to break open the door. [To Maurice] I tell you what it is, I will blot out your name from my books.

> MG: Well then, I hope God will write it in his.

> Fr. C [finding he could make no hand of Guiheen, to the people]: You must turn this man Connor out of the island and the way you will do it is by neither speaking to him or selling him anything and then he will have to run away.

Gayer wrote that 'an ignorant old man' responded to the priest, 'We are under the impression that you have the power to drive even the devil anywhere you please, and why not exert it now and drive this man away yourself and give us no further trouble about him?' According to Gayer, the priest pretended not to have heard this question and left the island 'after collecting what wool and fish he could'.[32]

A.M. Thompson also gave an account of a visit by Fr Casey, describing it as part of 'the tug-of-war and trial of faith'. The priest denounced the people 'for letting a Protestant land on the island' and described the scripture reader as the emissary of the devil, if not the devil himself, and his book as the devil's book. Thompson wrote that although the people were affected by the priest's words at first, after his departure they resumed their interaction with Connor. Fr Casey returned a few months later and was furious to find the reader still there:

> His wrath rose and he stormed most vehemently and ended by the usual ceremony of cursing; he cursed them 'by land and by sea', in their 'flocks and in their nets', 'in the winds that blew' and 'the air they breathed'; he excommunicated the man with whom the reader lodged and left the island carrying away more of their property.[33]

Swizzle wrote about the reaction of the priests to the Blasket mission:

> The priests now act on the offensive system, they accuse the Protestants of making converts by bribery and corruption, of going on a cruise to the Blasket islands, carrying by way of an olive branch plenty of long yards of clay, pig-tail tobacco, pigs' crubeens and a jar of the *craythur* to seduce the natives into selling their souls for dirty lucre. A priest declared solemnly that the devil was in the boat they used on the mission, and that it would certainly sink.[34]

As the boat did not sink, Swizzle left it to his readers to decide whether it was a case of the devil taking care of his own or proof that he was not on the vessel. It is likely that the missionaries did bring gifts with them on their visits to the island. Patrick Foley certainly believed so, 'It would appear that some of the "lads" would go to meet a mission party when about landing, and that for a piece of tobacco would listen to a chapter of the Bible read to them for a quarter of an hour.'[35]

The first island converts

Throughout the year 1839, Gayer and Moriarty made several visits to the Blasket. In a circular letter to supporters dated 26 September, Gayer referred to their work on the island. This was published in *The Warder*, and the editor introduced the letter by saying that 'the pleasure is much enhanced when we consider that O'Connell's county is the scene of missionary labours, and that one district of it is gradually approximating to an acknowledgement of the true faith. The work of conversion has begun and nothing can impede its progress.'

Gayer wrote:

> We see the lord's work manifestly with us in these islands. About three years ago I sent a reader there to attempt something but the people there were so wild and ignorant and superstitious that they were going to throw him over a cliff; lately again I made the attempt and the event has been beyond our most sanguine expectations. We have been most kindly received by the people and Mr. Moriarty has in the course of several visits declared the truth to almost everyone in the islands. We have rented a house and sent a most pious and judicious man, one of the converts, to act in the double capacity of schoolmaster to the young and reader to the old and they have received him and treated him as a brother, to use his own words, although their landlady who is a Roman Catholic grievously persecutes them and the priest, who has been there twice lately, has cursed them by land and sea for seven generations. We have truly reason to say that the Lord is over-ruling everything for good as regards the furthering of his work.[36]

A.M. Thompson referred to a setback for the missionaries on the island: when tenants who had welcomed the teacher were threatened with eviction. 'Many in whom worldly motives and old superstitions were stronger than desire for instruction went back, and walked no more with him, nay, closed their doors against him.'[37] According to Patrick Foley, in spite of denunciations by priest and landlord, four families, comprised of sixteen individuals, remained loyal to the reader and eventually became converts. They were named as two

O'Shea families, one Connor and one Sullivan.[38] Thomas Moriarty named three convert families – those of Michael Shea, Tim Connor and Michael Sullivan, who was 'the boat-captain'.[39]

An important source of information on the families of the Blasket Island in the 1830s is a census collated by Fr John Casey in 1835, details of which were published in 1974. There were nineteen families living on the Great Blasket, including four families named Shea and one named Sullivan. However, the name Michael does not appear as head of any of the four Shea families. There was one family named Sullivan, but it was not headed by Michael. There was no family named Connor on the Great Blasket on this list, but a family headed by Timothy Connor lived on the nearby island of Beginnis.[40] It is possible that this family had moved to the main island by the 1840s.

A letter from the Great Blasket

Patrick Connor's living conditions on the Great Blasket were harsh:

> Much did he endure of cold and wet and discomfort. The rain penetrated through the roof, and filth and smoke begrimmed everything round; his bedstead was made solid-roofed to keep his bed dry and for the rest, we trusted that he would count these discomforts of no weight, when endured for his Saviour's sake.[41]

A letter written by Patrick Connor to A.M. Thompson from 'Blasquets' has survived and was published in 1843. This letter confirms that Fr Casey had abandoned his ministry on the island in frustration, and that 'Father Pat' had taken over. This was most likely Fr Patrick Foley, curate of Fr Casey. Connor's letter of 26 August 1842 has significant details and gives a valuable perspective on the progress of his work:

> Since your last visit to this island, the priest has been among us; he delayed some days on the island which is a longer stay than any of the people recollect that a priest ever made with them; this island has been seldom visited by any of them oftener than once a year and then would only stop for one day. I am sure that his object in coming was to oppose the reading of the Irish scriptures to the people and if possible to frighten me out of the island. The parish priest, who always visited this place once a year, when he saw that cursing the people would not keep them from hearing the Bible read, or from sending their children

to school, said he would in future leave them in the hands of Father Pat, who is certainly as clever at cursing as anyone could be.

He prayed that the wrath and vengeance of the Almighty would pursue them until the day of their deaths, as close as their shadows in a summer's day, and not only that, but their seven generations, if they kept company with or talked to me, or if they would receive me into any of their boats, or carry a note for me out of the island or bring a note to me or any one thing. He told them to throw me overboard and drown me if I went into any of their boats and to serve any person who would be accompanying me in the same manner. He said that I would not be allowed to live in the part of the country I belonged to, for those turncoats are tied neck and heels and left until they repent and return to Mass again. But (said he) I am not telling you to tie him, but only telling you what is done in other places and certainly he ought to know that his life is in daily danger in such a place as this island.

Those who have their children at school, he cursed every member of their bodies and every hair of their heads; he said they were guilty of so awful a crime that they could not atone to God for it; he told them what a heinous thing it was to make the devil a present of their children whom the Lord had given them and as sure as they would send them to my school, they would give them by the right hand to the devil, as I was his servant and employed by him to fit any who would listen to me for hell and destruction. He endeavoured to convince the inhabitants that I and the converts were sheep-stealing on the island, which made them think the less of all he said, they knowing the converts to be men of blameless character; and even in three days after he said this, the thieves were detected in the very act of slaughtering a sheep, which made the priest a liar.

I trust that the Lord will bring good out of evil and enable these poor deluded people to form to themselves a just judgment of the character of these priests. As for the converts, the proceedings of the priest, while here, have served to increase their horror of popery. A woman, who I feared was a little favourable to it, said to me that although the priest had spent four days in the island, she could not hear that during that time he said anything to instruct the ignorant or to comfort the afflicted, and as for relieving the distressed *it need not be expected from the like.*

Notwithstanding all these awful threatenings and denunciations the people speak to me as usual and I am as much open to talk to them on the gospel as before. Only two Roman Catholic children have been withdrawn and I think they will shortly attend again.[42]

The mission to the Blasket might well have come to a tragic early end. On their way to celebrate the laying of the foundation stone of Dunurlin church, Patrick Connor and seven men, including island converts and stonemasons working on the school, ran into difficulty as they crossed the treacherous Blasket Sound. In the crisis, 'party feeling and religious dissension were forgotten' and they were rescued by Catholic boatmen, who put their own lives at risk. The convert party regretted that they could muster only one pound to recompense their rescuers, but a donation of £2 15s was later added. It was a very fortunate escape, which would otherwise have turned a day of celebration into a tragedy, and 'the cries of the widow and the orphan [would] have chilled Dunurlin's hymn of praise.'[43]

Food supplies for the Great Blasket, 1842

The people of the Blaskets were affected by the hardship of the early 1840s, when the potato harvest was poor and prices were high. In June 1842, in the Protestant church of Harold's Cross, Dublin, an appeal from Charles Gayer was read to the congregation in which he described the great distress in Dingle and surrounding areas. A fortnight later, Gayer acknowledged receiving £36 8s from the congregation, and his letter of thanks was read out by Rev. Robert McGhee, who introduced it by referencing famines around the world, 'The voice of the Lord crieth upon the land [...] It crieth in the feeble wail of those that are being consumed with famine. Surely its echo from India, from Paris, from Hamburg, from Hayti, has not yet died on our ear!' He then spoke of the suffering of 'our own poor dear afflicted countrymen' and quoted from Gayer's letter, dated 11 July 1842:

I have just returned from the Blasket island where I took some meal and potatoes for the relief of the people, hearing from our scripture reader and schoolmaster there that they were in great distress and I found that all the people, to the number of 160, had been living for the last week on seaweed and limpets picked off the rocks, not having provisions of any kind and they looked the picture of starvation. I felt great pleasure on relieving them. It may be satisfactory to our Christian friends to know that their contributions have been the means under God of saving many from starvation; and I am sure they will not be angry at my extending relief to others besides the converts who were of course our first object; but I could not see them perishing before my eyes. I will thank you to express to those kind friends who have come forward to help us, my best thanks on behalf of our poor people.[44]

Gayer's letter shows that, at a time of great hardship, his charity extended beyond those who had converted. This would be a characteristic of his relief efforts in the more acute crisis to come during the Great Famine.

Sheep-stealing

There is very little about the Protestant mission to the Great Blasket in local newspapers of this period, but Maurice Guiheen appeared as 'a Blasquetteer of the name of Geehan' in the *Kerry Examiner* in 1842. He was one of a number of men who were convicted of sheep-stealing, and the *Examiner* carried the story under the heading 'The Dingle Saints: Theology versus Sheep-ology'. Geehan was depicted as a convert who carried away a sheep on his shoulders during the night (with the Irish Bible tucked under his arm) and enjoyed 'rich soup from the parson's flesh-pot' during the day. Geehan was described as the only person on the Blasket Island to have converted under the influence of Connor, the agent of the Irish Society.[45] The editor mocked those convicted, saying that the case revealed the hypocrisy of the converts, 'To carry home a stolen wether and then read aloud a chapter in an Irish testament is no uncommon practice in the Dingle district, the chosen spots of saints and sinners, where both professions are wonderfully combined.'[46] However, the *Examiner* was later obliged to concede that Geehan was not actually a convert – that he had only rented a house to the evangelicals.[47]

A.M. Thompson's visits to the Blasket

As she had committed herself to raising funds for the Blasket mission, A.M. Thompson took a keen interest in the island; before she departed from Kerry in 1845, she visited at least twice. She gave this account of her first visit, after the completion of the new school house:

I went at this time into the island to inspect our new acquisition. I had not been in it before, landing being difficult for a female, as it is necessary to take advantage of the swell of the waves and leap on to the rocks from the boat which perhaps is the next moment carried several yards back on the retiring wave. I succeeded in landing, however, and was more affected than I have power to describe by witnessing human nature reduced to the savage state it is among these islanders, within almost earshot of religious light and civilisation. When I got into the new schoolroom the women and children in great numbers crowded in and squatted themselves on the floor around me, chewing seaweed incessantly, a large supply of which was in every woman's pocket and lap, and of which they pressed the long strings into their mouths with their thumbs in a most savage manner and spat about unceremoniously at will; they touched my dress, turned me round and round to look at every separate article, laughed with admiration at my shoes and gloves, kissed and stroked my old silk gown, repeating 'Bragh! Bragh!' 'Nice, nice' though the reader may believe I did not wear anything very handsome on such an expedition. After submitting to this inspection for a much longer time than was agreeable, I made the reader my interpreter while I spoke to them of Christ.[48]

Thompson was astonished at how little the women knew about religion – particularly when she asked them what their idea of sin was, and was told it was sheep-stealing. Thompson visited again in May 1843. She was beginning to form the opinion that the mission school had been a waste of money, because there were so few children attending; however, she was encouraged to hear that about seventy fishermen had found shelter in the schoolhouse during a severe storm. She was also heartened by the baptism of a child that took place while she was there, with forty-two islanders in attendance.[49]

Thomas Moriarty's visits

Thomas Moriarty and his wife Matilda visited the island in August 1843, staying there for a week. He was told that children wished to attend the school and their parents wished to send them, but they were fearful of being evicted as a result – afraid 'to be driven on the wide world without a shelter'. Moriarty appreciated their dilemma, 'I felt their case was hard, and while sympathising with them, I endeavoured to urge them to do what their conscience approved, and trusting in the Lord, to obey him rather than man.'[50]

Moriarty taught the schoolchildren and conversed with the islanders in the evenings. He observed that 'they were dissatisfied, or at all events, indifferent to popery, without being at all concerned about their souls – in fact, infidels as regards religion, without knowing what that means or being conscious of it.'[51] He found it painful to note 'their insensibility and indifference to religion', although they listened carefully to what he had to say. He saw the people as open-minded and speculated that this was on account of their isolation, 'without priest, chapel or other machinery of popery'. No doubt, if the priest visited the island twice a year at most, and then primarily to collect his dues, the people may have had very little instruction in the Catholic faith or experience of its liturgy and rituals.

By August 1844, aware of Clarissa Hussey's power over her tenants on the island, Moriarty accepted that a Protestant community could not be sustained there – that all they could hope for was 'to make ready a people, who when instructed, must pass out of the island, and join the Ventry congregation'.[52] Despite his pessimism about the future of the Blasket mission, Moriarty is listed in Griffith's Valuation as leasing several properties on the island. Mícheál de Mórdha's study shows that Rev. Thomas Moriarty was the 'immediate lessor' of seven properties to occupiers named Mary Shea, John Dunleavy, James Dunleavy, Michael Sullivan, James Guiheen, Catherine Kearney and Thomas Guiheen. He was also listed as the occupier of one property – the schoolhouse – acting on behalf of the Dingle and Ventry Mission rather than in a personal capacity.[53]

Despite the inauspicious outlook for the mission on the Blasket, Thomas Moriarty's brother rejoiced at a baptism performed there:

Truly the scene I witnessed there was a happy one: my brother baptising in Irish a child belonging to one of the island converts and thirty-eight of the islanders present, persons who would three years ago, have cast myself and my brother, had we told them the truth as we did this day, over some of the many wild cliffs that surround the island. It was indeed encouraging to us who knew them in their wildest state to find three large families who have completely shaken off popery, and are now anxious to be placed under the teaching of our church, besides a general spirit of inquiry being apparent in the minds of all we conversed with. Since January twelve months they care not for the priest, as he then cursed them for seven generations by land and sea, on account of their receiving us on the island; and he told them that their potato crop would fail and they would catch no fish; but it so happened that they had that season the best crop they had for many years and caught more fish than they had done for the last ten years.[54]

John Sullivan and James Jordan

With the passage of time, Patrick Connor became discouraged by his lack of progress, and he asked to be removed 'to some situation where he would have a freer field of labour'. He said the people expressed 'a great deal of regret' at his departure, particularly Tim Connor.[55] Churchman observed, 'It is no wonder that this poor man's mind should have sunk and that he should wish to quit the island after a residence of two years of such anxiety.'[56] The new teacher was John Sullivan, described as 'another active zealous reader'. However, A.M. Thompson was not so enthusiastic about Sullivan, referring to 'the apparent inefficiency which seemed to attend the effort of our second agent'.[57] In 1844, Rev. Gayer 'thought it advisable to change the reader again' and James Jordan was appointed. Thompson was pleased to report that under Jordan, 'the work is now prospering greatly.'[58] James Jordan spent thirteen years as teacher and scripture reader on the Blasket, from June 1844 to October 1857. He was succeeded by his son John, who stayed until 1863. Tomás Ó Criomhthain wrote that a rock near Pointe an Ghoba, a favourite fishing place of James Jordan, was known as 'stocán Jordain'.[59]

The Blasket school

There was one site on the Great Blasket over which the landlord Clarissa Hussey had no jurisdiction. This site was government property, intended for the building of a Martello tower in the 1800s, but no construction had taken place there. In 1840, the site was rented at £5 per annum by the missionaries for the erection of a schoolhouse and dwelling place for the reader. With this, they sought to 'obtain a solid footing in the island'.[60] This was the first school on the Blasket Island, and the location was Gort Bán, below the village.[61] Clarissa Hussey was extremely annoyed at this development and, through her agent, warned her tenants not to help in any way with the building work. Consequently, tradesmen, labourers and materials had to be brought from the mainland, adding considerably to the cost. The islanders looked on as the school was completed, with a room attached for the reader and another added for a visiting clergyman. One woman was asked by Gayer what she thought about it, and she replied philosophically, 'Oh, then, it's no harm you're about at all events.'[62] According to Patrick Foley, stones from an old church elsewhere on the island were used in the new building.[63]

Colthurst gave an interesting description of the building of the schoolhouse, including some details not found elsewhere.[64] Timber, slates and lime were brought by boat from the mainland for 'the finest and largest building ever erected on the island'. Stonemasons were brought in, as well as a donkey. The islanders were fascinated by the building project, 'Even a hammer, a chisel, a saw were objects of curiosity and the women flocked to look upon the strangers with as much wonder as ever did their sisters of the African desert.' One man who had been watching the work for some time finally took up a spade and was planning to start work to earn some money for his family. However, when an agent of Miss Hussey appeared on the scene, the man withdrew. Colthurst wrote that the 'very plain schoolhouse' appeared like a palace to the islanders when compared with the 'huts half-buried in the sand with which it was surrounded'. Elsewhere, she described the building as 'the finest structure that ever was erected on the Blasket island where they construct huts half-sunk in the earth with long grass or potato stalks'.[65]

However, by the time the building was ready for use, there was only one family of converts on the island, the others having moved to Ventry because of intimidation.[66] Numbers attending the school fell during 1843; A.M. Thompson was discouraged, admitting that she 'felt tempted to repine at having gone to the expense of building the mission house'.[67] The building cost £127, and in 1843, a large part of this sum was outstanding.[68] Fr Casey jubilantly wrote that the Blasket school 'caps the climax of absurdity and fraud', because it had cost £300 to build and had only 'the nominal attendance of five ragged children', while the teacher, 'like the Roman general of old', spent his days collecting shells on the shore.[69]

There is no complete record of numbers attending the school in the early 1840s, but in 1847, there were fifty-six children. Thirty of these were converts and twenty-six were Roman Catholics.[70] The school was used for the distribution of food during the Famine, and this explains the dramatic rise in numbers. The number of convert families on the island increased to ten in 1847 – also probably as a result of food distribution by the missionaries. Nonetheless, the numbers fell again when the worst of the crisis was over. Twelve adults and twenty children attended a Sunday service in 1850, and a visitor in 1854 found seventeen children attending the school, four of whom were Catholics.[71] It was because of the distribution of food through the school during the Famine that it became known as 'Scoil a' tSúip' or 'Mainistir na Súpanna' (the soup school).[72]

The mission school finally closed in 1864, the year in which the first National School was opened on the Great Blasket. The latter opened in

January 1864; by the end of that year, there were sixteen boys and eighteen girls on the roll. On 15 March 1864, the Protestant mission school was described as being 'in connexion with some London Society, but it is attended by only two pupils'.[73]

The Irish language

Muiris Mac Conghail believed that the evangelical mission in west Kerry had a significant influence on the development of the Irish language there:

> Whatever the Protestant school and its bible-readers did for the island, the bible-reading activity and the basic teaching of reading and writing from the primers which were distributed throughout Corca Dhuibhne must account for some of the literacy skills which the community acquired.[74]

He cited expressions still in use today, such as *ar mo leabhar* (on my book), an affirmation referring to the Bible, and *ar mo leabhar breac* (on my speckled book), referring to the Irish primer.

Mac Conghail made a strong case for his belief that Tomás Ó Criomhthain, the renowned author, acquired his ability to read Irish from copies of the Bible used in the mission school on the Blasket Island, and from his contact with those who had been pupils of the school.[75] Mac Conghail stated that because of the stigma of souperism attached to the mission schools in the post-Famine years, people who could read Irish were reluctant to say how they acquired the skill. When asked in the early years of the twentieth century, Tomás Ó Criomhthain said that he had learned to read Irish during the time he spent with his relatives in Ballyickeen, Dunquin. However, Mac Conghail speculated that this was because he wished to conceal any association with the mission school. Although Ó Criomhthain was too young to have attended the school, Mac Conghail believed that he would have met people who had attended it, and he would have been aware of the stigma that later became associated with it:

> Mura ndeachaigh Tomás ar Scoil an Mhisiúin, bhuail sé leis na scoláirí agus bheadh a fhios aige an smál a bhí ag baint le cuimhne na scoile sin [...] Bí cinnte de go bhfaca Tomás Ó Criomhthain Bíobla agus gur oscail sé é de bharr fiosrachta. Creidim gur ón teagmháil a bhí aige leo sin a dhein freastal ar Scoil an Mhisiúin a tháinig léamh na Gaeilge go dtí é agus gur ón léamh a d'eascair an scríobh.

(Even if Tomás did not attend the mission school, he met those who did and he would have been aware of the stigma which was associated with the memory of that school [...] Be assured that Tomás saw a Bible and opened it out of curiosity. I believe that it was as a result of his contact with those who attended the mission school that Tomás learned to read Irish and from that sprang the writing.)

After the mission school on the Great Blasket closed down, memories of it faded. In July 1880, a visiting botanist named Richard Barrington recorded that he had slung his hammock from the rafters of the schoolhouse.[77] Mac Conghail also pointed out that memories of the mission school faded, 'Creidim [...] gur tháinig athinsint ar scéal na chéad scoile ar ball agus de réir a chéile gur glanadh aon chuimhne cheart uirthi.'[78] (I believe that over time accounts of the first school changed and gradually accurate memories of it disappeared.)

In the census of 1901, an island couple – Eugene Connor, aged 55, and his wife Kate, aged 50 – wrote 'Irish Church' as their religious profession. Their four children were described as 'Roman Catholic'.[79] Mac Conghail identifies the couple as Eoghan Bán Ó Conchúir, a weaver, and his wife Cáit Ní Bhriain Uí Chonchúir.[80] They were the last Protestants of the Great Blasket, and it is interesting that, as regards their religious affiliations, it is the distinction between Irish and Roman which was highlighted in their census return. The family lived in the old mission schoolhouse in 1901, but the names of the couple do not appear in the census of 1911.

Appeals to children on behalf of the Blasket mission

These lines on the Blasket were included in *Innisfail*:

Near fair Hibernia's western coast
A lonely island stands;
In summer's smile, on that lone isle,
The hardy fisher lands.
But when the strife of storms is rife,
When the great Atlantic's roar
Is heard from far, not the boldest tar
Would steer for the Blasket shore,
Where the dark basaltic rocks uprear
Their pillar'd forms on high
And wild winds sweep thro' the caverns deep

And the threatening breakers lie.
Dark centuries o'er that lonely isle
Unbless'd appeared to glide,
In ignorance the natives lived,
In ignorance they died.
When on the mainland raised they saw
A white flag waving o'er,
The signal made that Mass was said,
They knelt down to adore;
To supplicate they knew not what –
The angel of the storm –
They looked not to a God of love
In Christ's redeeming form.
But twice a year, when skies were clear,
Two dreaded boats would come
With priestly views for priestly dues
To tax each island home.
No heralds of sweet mercy they,
But messengers of ill;
They bear no embassy of joy,
But evil tidings still.[81]

In her preface to *The Little Ones of Innisfail*, Colthurst wrote of children in England who were saving money to buy a little toy boat. When they were told about the Blasket Island mission, they chose to devote their funds instead to the purchase of a missionary boat, seeing it as 'the ark of promise to the inhabitants of these wild romantic islands':

The children heard of isles remote,
The lovely isles of Erin's nation,
To which a 'missionary boat'
Might waft the tidings of salvation.

With pure self-sacrificing joy
Which an accepted offering made it,
They yielded up the favourite toy
And gave their heart's desire to aid it.[82]

This was 'a link of love' between the children of England and those of 'our less favoured isle'. The children were gratified to hear in due course of the purchase of the missionary boat, which flew a white flag with the emblem of a dove:

> Her snow-white flag, it is floating fair,
> And the dove of peace is pictured there;
> The islander rejoicing sees
> The flag of promise on the breeze;
> The swift oars kiss the glittering spray
> And she steers for the Blasquett Isles away.[83]

The Blasket Island appeared in another religious publication for children – alongside stories, poems and illustrations from Africa, China, India and elsewhere. The tone is Anglo-centric, patronising, sentimental and evangelical. Among tales of missionary experiences in the Sandwich Islands, Bengal and Singapore, there were some from Ireland, including one about the Blasket mission. It began, 'Dear little friends: As it is very likely that many of you have not ever heard of these islands, I must ask you to open the map of Ireland and look at the south-west coast.' The article was written by 'A Mother'; it broadly follows the account of A.M. Thompson but predates her book. The writer told her young readers that 'the people who live on these islands seem almost out of the world, and a short time ago, there was not one of them who could read or write or talk English.' The author ended by encouraging the children to 'send sometimes a thought across to the Blasquett Islands and offer a silent prayer for the poor little children in their schoolhouse on the rock and for the good scripture reader who is trying to point them to the Lord Jesus Christ.'[84]

13. The conversion of Fr Brasbie, Catholic curate, 1844

On 30 May 1844, Bishop Cornelius Egan appointed Fr Denis Leyne Brasbie as curate in Kilmalkedar. Brasbie was a native of Killarney and had served in various Kerry parishes since his ordination in 1834. In his letter of appointment, Bishop Egan wrote:

> As the sea air may be good for you, I will write by this night's post to the Rev. Mr. Walsh to take your place at Boherbee, and you will be with Mr. Casey for the Sunday after next. I shall expect that you will exert yourself in that locality, where zeal and activity are required to check the current of proselytism. Indeed, I may say, it is now pretty well checked in that parish; still, the fire must be kept up. Mr. Casey is comfortably lodged and both his curates live in the house with him.[1]

This letter of appointment was made public by Brasbie after he had endured extreme vilification for his decision to convert to Protestantism. The tone of Bishop Egan's letter is polite and solicitous, and there is nothing to suggest that Brasbie was not in good standing in the diocese. In fact, the bishop appeared to be concerned with what was best for Brasbie's health. The appointment was clearly intended to be a direct response to the activities of the evangelicals in an area where the parish clerk, Laurence Sullivan, had unexpectedly converted and brought eleven families with him in 1842.[2]

The surname Brasbie is unusual, but there was a 'Brasbie's Lane' in Killarney at this time.[3] Denis Brasbie went to Maynooth seminary in 1828 and was ordained in 1834. He served successively in Listowel, Tralee, Lisselton, Lixnaw and Boherbee. As a curate, Brasbie displayed an independence of spirit on several occasions. He once visited another parish to speak in public but did not inform the parish priest; he was subsequently reprimanded by the senior priest for not observing clerical etiquette. Brasbie responded in an open letter to the *Post*, saying that he did not observe the usual etiquette because his 'primary object was to promote the happiness of the poor. This motive induced me to dispense with the courtesy to which you allude.' Brasbie's assertive response to his older colleague ended with these lines, 'Mine honour is my life; both grow in one / Take honour from me and my life is done.'[4]

In 1840, when Fr Brasbie was transferred from Tralee to Lisselton, the *Examiner* paid him this tribute:

> Mr. Brasbie carries with him the warmest wishes and the kindest regards of the inhabitants of this town, without distinction of class or creed, to whom he has endeared himself by his gentlemanly and Christian-like demeanour in all the intercourse of social life, while his loss is feelingly deplored by the poor to whom he was affable in manner and a generous benefactor.[5]

The same newspaper would become his most bitter critic after he converted. In his various postings as curate, Fr Brasbie was involved in fund-raising for the Repeal movement. The *Freeman's Journal* recorded that upwards of £20 had been remitted by 'this excellent gentleman'.[6] He also supported the temperance movement and the promotion of indigenous industry. He wrote from Lixnaw in 1841 that '3,000 persons in this part of the country have (within the last few days) pledged themselves on the altar of their country to use no article in future but Irish manufacture. I had the pleasure of administering the Irish manufacturing pledge in person and am convinced they will adhere to it with firmness and fidelity.'[7] It is clear that by the time of his appointment to west Kerry, Fr Denis Leyne Brasbie was an enterprising and popular priest.

Fr Brasbie's conversion

Within two months of arriving in west Kerry, Denis Brasbie announced that he was converting to Protestantism. According to A.M. Thompson, he 'had been passing through a gradual process of emancipation from the worst excesses of his creed for five years'.[8] She claimed to have had the privilege of a good deal of conversation with him after his conversion, and she wished 'to convey his sentiments as nearly as possible' to her readers. She learned that, like other young priests, he had emerged from Maynooth 'with ardent and blind zeal [...] awed as well as intoxicated with the conception of his new powers'. Then, in the midst of his everyday clerical duties, all sense of the sublime and the solemn departed from his experience, and he found 'little leisure for meditation or necessity for reading'.

He soon found himself mired in the mundane realities of making money: a shilling for a sick call, two shillings and sixpence for communion, marriages at anything from thirty shillings to twenty pounds, and baptisms from two shillings to one pound. Thompson referred to these as 'the tricks of his trade'. While she had her own reasons for highlighting these aspects of a priest's life, it is true that poor curates depended on such stipends for their survival. 'To do these jobs every hour of the day and calculate their earnings in the evening, constitutes the life of a priest,' wrote Thompson, claiming that Brasbie believed many of his priest colleagues were 'dissatisfied with their creed'. Thompson wrote that he had previously expressed his doubts 'in a jocular manner' but then experienced a genuine loss of vocation and agonised for five years until 'the terror of the Lord came upon him and he could brook its warnings no longer.' He then approached Rev. Gayer, saying that he believed 'his soul could not be saved in Rome.'[9]

It is unlikely that Brasbie had any contact with Protestant missionaries in west Kerry while he was a curate in Boherbee – a good distance away – nor did he have any tuition from them before his conversion. His announcement was an astounding development and an unexpected coup for the evangelicals. It came 'like a thunderbolt upon the poor persecuted Catholics', wrote Patrick Foley in 1903.[10] According to a local tradition, Brasbie ended his final Mass by walking down the church aisle, dramatically casting off his vestments one by one, to be met at the gate of the church by Charles Gayer and his daughter. Another folklore account was that Brasbie had left to marry Gayer's daughter or Thomas Moriarty's sister.[11] Thompson wrote that Brasbie was popular among the people, but after his conversion, 'envenomed tongues of slander' were turned against him and 'every vile motive was attributed to him.' These included accusations of 'drunkenness, debt, incontinency, hypocrisy'. He was unable to venture out in public, and he received insulting letters from priest colleagues accusing him of turning traitor and predicting that he would die like Judas.[12] In a note on the margin of his copy of Thompson's book, Fr John O'Sullivan wrote that Brasbie was an 'irreligious scamp'; he also claimed credit for alerting the bishop to him, 'I warned Dr. Egan of Brasbie early [...] I saw thru' him.'[13]

The day of Brasbie's recantation

On Wednesday, 17 July 1844, the *Kerry Evening Post* announced that on the following Sunday, Denis Leyne Brasbie was to be inducted into the Church of Ireland at a service in St James's church in Dingle. The town was abuzz with anticipation, and there were fears of violent disorder. An impressive display of force was mobilised to prevent any incidents:

The fact of a priest abjuring popery caused great excitement and the magistrates having got full notice that the mob were determined to execute lynch law on the priest on his road to the church, they took full precautions to preserve the peace. Before service commenced the townspeople were astonished to see the Hon. Captain Plunkett, of H.M. steamer *Stromboli*, march into town from Ventry with a force of about 100 men, including the marine artillery and marines, with drums and colours. This fine body of men, armed to the teeth, having joined the seamen and marines of H.M. Brigantine, the *Lynx*, under the command of Captain Nott, presented such an imposing appearance that, we need scarcely say, everything passed off very quietly.[14]

In St James's church, Brasbie read 'the tenets of the church of Rome as contained in Pope Pius IV's creed and renounced them one by one'.[15] He then read the Apostles' Creed and the Nicene Creed, and declared his allegiance to their articles. After the service, the Coast Guards of all the surrounding stations, fully armed, accompanied Denis Brasbie to the house of Charles Gayer. 'Dingle, for the last twenty years, never presented such a force,' commented the *Post*. There was a report that seven thousand people were in town that day. One commentator was scathing about the naval presence in Dingle. He referred to a statement delivered in parliament by Lord Aberdeen in which he apologised for not sending a naval force to Morocco because the vessels were on duty on the coast of Ireland. The writer continued:

> We now see the awful nature of the 'duty' which deprived the Mediterranean of the presence of the British flag. The *Stromboli* and the *Lynx* were required to assist the 'Missionary Church' [...] in the acquisition of the Rev. Mr. Brasbie to her fold! [...] The transition from Popish error to Protestant truth is performed by the beat of a drum and with the flourish of military colours [...] The orthodox parade of 'such a force as Dingle had not seen for twenty years' is requisite to give due éclat to the Rev. Mr. Brasbie's exchange of Pope Gregory XVI for Pope Victoria as head of his church.[16]

Catherine Hartland Mahon was present, and she wished that her English friends could have witnessed what she had experienced with Brasbie that day, 'the hideous yells and shouting that accompanied us as we walked home with him, and which I am persuaded would not have ended there, had it not been that an armed force of nearly twenty men had been provided by the magistrates'. She concluded her account, 'Popery is popery still, it hates the light. May the Lord in his great mercy deliver poor unhappy Ireland from its power.'[17]

Records in the National Archives show that Brasbie received further protection in the weeks after his recantation. Rear-admiral Pigot wrote from Cork that the *Volcano* under Lt Edward Miller had been despatched to Dingle. Miller gave this account of his role:

> I landed thirty men armed in obedience to the magistrate's requisition, and in conjunction with the police and Coast Guard escorted Rev. Mr. Gayer and the converted priest to and from church, repeating the same service in the evening; there was a little excitement, some hooting, but little of any moment occurred.[18]

On 12 August, H. Gillman, Sub-inspector of police, wrote that thirty marines and sailors, as well as twenty-five Coast Guard members, were sent to assist the police. Gillman reported that although a great crowd of five thousand people had gathered in the town, showing 'a bad disposition' towards Brasbie by yelling and hooting, there was no breach of the peace, 'owing I think to the strong force which were assembled'.[19]

Attacks on Brasbie's character

The *Kerry Examiner* led the public attacks on Brasbie's character. Comparing him to Lucifer, it stated that he had fallen into 'an abyss of perdition and disgrace', and claimed that such conversions generally were as a result of 'pique, instability of mind, weakness of judgment, presumption arising from a bad education and above all from avarice and PRIDE, or from all these causes put together'. Brasbie's defection, in its view, was 'a deed of damning scandal' and 'a treasonable abandonment of the altar of the Most High'. The *Examiner* saw the conversion as 'a desperate and fatal plunge into the gulph of apostacy'; it referred cryptically to 'pranks and strange doings' by Brasbie over some time.[20] Under the headline 'The Apostate Brasbie', the *Examiner* observed sarcastically that the Protestants were 'in raptures over the invaluable prize they had obtained' but then asserted that he had abandoned the Catholic Church 'at the moment it was about to abandon him', suggesting that he was about to be disciplined by the bishop for some unspecified reason.[21] The *Examiner* mocked the warm Protestant responses to Brasbie's conversion, saying that he was in danger of being smothered by the many compliments he received.[22]

Brasbie's apologia

In public lectures and in pamphlets, Denis Brasbie explained his conversion at length. His statements are important to an understanding of his conversion experience, especially because there is very little information on the motivation of other converts, and because his decision was a matter of conscience rather than a result of hunger or destitution. In a lecture in Dublin in 1845, Brasbie said that his character had been maligned since his conversion. He recalled that as a priest, just before his formal conversion, he was sent to the Blasket Island, and after he had settled into the cabin provided for him, he walked along the strand reading the daily office of priests. The reading of the day related to St Dionysius the Areopagite, who was beheaded and, according to tradition, walked 3 miles with his head under his arm. Brasbie told the audience that he paused on the strand, 'gazing on the western ocean, the red round sun setting at the time in all its splendour, and exclaimed: "Oh, deluded priests and people of the church of Rome to swallow such absurdities!"' He recalled another occasion when he was administering the last rites to an old soldier. Even after he had been anointed, the man remained in distress, without consolation and without hope. Brasbie reflected that if he had given the poor man 'the soothing consolations of the gospel of peace', it would have been more beneficial to him than 'mumbling a few words of unintelligible Latin over him, or by anointing him with oil of olives'.[23] It is clear that Brasbie had experienced a personal crisis of faith and of vocation.

Brasbie concluded his Dublin lecture by declaring that the solution for Ireland was 'Repeal of the Union'. This appeared to be a political reference, but it was in fact a jocose comment, and he quickly clarified that he was speaking not of political union but of the union with Rome, 'the bonds that unite our poor deluded countrymen in spiritual allegiance to the Italian despot.' When 'the pure light of the gospel [was] permitted to spread its refulgent rays over the length and breadth of the land', Ireland would be 'great glorious and free, first flower of the earth and first gem of the sea'. This phrase was a quotation from a popular nationalist anthem often heard at Daniel O'Connell's public meetings, and Brasbie explained that he was once 'an agitator' himself. Brasbie's spiritual conversion necessitated a political one, from nationalist and repealer to unionist.[24]

Brasbie's open letters

Denis Leyne Brasbie wrote three open letters that were first published in newspapers and later as pamphlets. The first was dated 19 July 1844, and it appeared in the *Post* on 24 July under the heading 'To the Roman Catholic parishioners of Kilmalkedar'. The *Examiner* also published this letter, describing it as written in a 'threadbare style of cant, hypocrisy and falsehood'.[25] Brasbie's letter began by thanking his former parishioners for their 'extreme kindness' to him during his short stay with them and asking them to reflect seriously on their 'present dangerous situation'. He explained that he, like them, had been 'a creature of prejudice' for many years. He had begun to search the scriptures over the previous five years, and one text in particular had had a profound effect on him. This was, 'For what shall it profit a man if he gain the whole world and lose his soul' (Mark 8:36). Brasbie came to the conclusion that 'salvation could not be obtained in the church of Rome', which he saw as 'this mighty Babylon, this hideous monster', as described in the Book of the Apocalypse, or Revelations.

Accusing the Roman Catholic Church of idolatry, Brasbie told his former parishioners that when they bowed their heads as the bell rang before the words of consecration during the Mass, they were idolising simple bread and wine. Referring to the words of consecration said by the priest, he then asked the people, 'Now, let me ask you, my dear friends, in the language of sober seriousness, do you imagine that they have such a power? I know it is your belief, but allow me to tell you that they have no such power.' He asked them to imagine a situation where a priest consecrated a gallon of wine and then drank it. He would undoubtedly get drunk, wrote Brasbie, and he asked how then could the wine have been transformed when it was still clearly alcoholic. It could not be the blood of Christ while retaining all the qualities of alcohol. He urged the people to accept that 'transubstantiating or changing the bread and wine into the body and blood of Christ [was] a supposition quite repugnant to common sense and not to be admitted.'

Brasbie continued by questioning how a church that claimed to be based on charity could adopt such an 'intolerant, cruel and persecuting spirit' towards those converts who conscientiously changed their affiliation. He referred to the 'great sacrifice' he had made:

I have severed those sacred ties which bound me to my friends and relatives. I have incurred the displeasure of thousands who are at this moment straining every point to vilify my character, who, when they cannot convict me of any crime, have recourse to the usual plea of 'madness'. Gracious heavens! A man is said to be mad because he endeavours to procure the salvation of his 'immortal soul'. What folly! What infatuation![26]

Despite the furore surrounding his momentous decision, Brasbie had no regrets. He wrote that his conversion had brought him more peace of mind than he had experienced for years, and he was willing to suffer persecution, and even death, rather than return to his former church. In its response, the *Examiner* ridiculed one of Brasbie's assertions by telling him that the reason a bell was rung before the consecration of the Mass was simply to indicate to the congregation that a solemn moment was approaching. 'If Mr. Brasbie did not know this, he must have been a great dunce as a priest – no wonder he packed off with himself.'[27]

In his second letter, published in the *Post* of 31 July 1844, Brasbie reiterated his complete rejection of transubstantiation because of 'the absurdity of that doctrine'. He said that it was 'a monstrous doctrine [...] that a man can make, at his pleasure, his God and then eat him'. Not even in the pagan world was there 'so gross a doctrine', he wrote. He appealed to the people's common sense, 'I ask why do Roman Catholics fasten a literal interpretation on the words "This is my body?"' He asked how Catholics could prove that 'when Christ said "this is my body" he intended to say more than "this represents my body". Do not we ourselves frequently substitute the "is" for "represents"?' He referred to similar expressions of Jesus – 'I am the door', 'I am the true vine' – saying that these were obviously intended to be understood figuratively and not literally.[28]

Brasbie's third letter to his former parishioners appeared on the front page of the *Post* on 20 November 1844. He appealed for the right to 'liberty of conscience' and explained at more length his objections to the doctrines of transubstantiation, purgatory and devotion to the Virgin Mary. He also wrote of his personal experiences and 'the storm of persecution' that had raged over him since his conversion, with 'the basest and most unworthy motives' attributed to him, provocative ballads sung about him and his life being endangered.

On this occasion, Brasbie published the letter of appointment he had received from the bishop and asked how it could be that he was 'most instantaneously and most miraculously transformed into an "angel of darkness"' as soon as he converted. He accused the Catholic clergy of firing 'poisoned arrows' at him from their pulpits, and of being interested only in maintaining their influence and 'preserving their treasury in a flourishing condition'. He was not bitter, he wrote unconvincingly, and not interested in retaliation against his persecutors. Brasbie ended by exhorting the people of Kilmalkedar to 'let no one, therefore, interfere between you and your God; worship him according to the dictates of your conscience, uninfluenced by the threats of selfish men.'[29]

The aftermath of Brasbie's conversion

Denis Brasbie remained in Corca Dhuibhne while he was being trained for the Protestant ministry under the guidance of Charles Gayer. It was an uncomfortable time for him. He claimed that 'during a siege of nearly eight months', he had been 'literally blockaded' and 'deprived of personal liberty'. He stated that he had received a message from the Catholic bishop of Kerry saying that he would give Brasbie £1,000 and the priests of the diocese would give another £1,000 if he would agree to return to the Catholic Church. If he did so, Brasbie would be provided with 'a rich living' in America. Brasbie's own view of the offer was that it was a trap which would result in 'either a watery grave in the wild Atlantic or *a dose of Prussic acid* in Yankee land!!'[30]

The *Post* listed some of the trials that Brasbie endured. His own relatives attempted to lure him into a boat, 'for the purpose of drowning him and his convictions altogether'; he was assaulted by a mob in Dingle as he returned from prayers on a Sunday evening; a mob attacked Gayer's house with the intention of dragging Brasbie out; unfounded criminal charges were brought against him; and finally, 'unjust obloquy and unbounded abuse' had been heaped on him by 'the Romish press, with the *Kerry Examiner* at their head'.[31] The *Achill Missionary Herald* reported on the attempt made to drown Brasbie, claiming that one of those involved said, 'If we could have got the fellow once into the boat, he should never have left it alive.'[32]

Brasbie said that during an eight-week period in which he stayed in the house of Lt Clifford of the Coast Guard, he could not walk in the garden because he was pelted with stones by the boys in the nearby National School. The girls from the convent school also threw stones at him and 'used language to which the boys would be ashamed to give utterance'.[33]

In August 1844, an extraordinary scene took place at Rev. Gayer's house when a bailiff named Quill called to issue a summons against Brasbie over an unpaid debt. Perhaps because he was alert to the danger of an attack on his person, Brasbie challenged Quill with a pistol, but he did not fire at him.[34] Brasbie was subsequently fined £1 for possession on an unlicensed weapon.[35] Brasbie wrote from Dingle on 9 September 1844, 'The spirit of persecution which rages against us is beyond description – it is awful in this part of the country.' He dismissed the charges brought against him over the pistol, saying that he was 'as innocent as one of the angels'. He was grateful for the protection of 'Rev. Gayer and his amiable lady' and ended by affirming, 'I am ready to lay down my life for the faith of my adoption.'[36]

When Rev. Gayer left Dingle in October, Brasbie moved from his house to that of Thomas Moriarty in Ventry. Brasbie wrote to the *Freeman's Journal* that 'every stratagem that human ingenuity could devise or human malice suggest' had been employed against him after his conversion.[37] He was in fear of his life and wrote of 'attempts to remove me not only from Dingle but from the transitory scene'.[38]

The spirit of antagonism that was stirred up by Denis Brasbie's conversion generated considerable ill-will and antagonism around the county in the summer of 1844. A priest in Listowel delivered a harangue from the altar, condemning Brasbie and another convert, a Listowel butcher named Laurence Buckley. According to the *Post*, the priest's language was so strong that several people showed their disgust by walking out of the church.[39] The *Post* also reported on a case of 'unmanly and cowardly ruffianism and outrageous bigotry' shown in an attack on Gayer's children and two young ladies who were staying with the family. The unprovoked attack 'was committed by a demon, in the shape of a young man', who beat and kicked his victims. The *Post* had no hesitation in laying the blame on 'the bigoted and intolerant spirit of popery'.[40]

Rumours of Brasbie's retraction

In early 1845, a false report circulated to the effect that Brasbie had come to regret his conversion, 'Conscience has triumphed in the bosom of the Rev. Mr. Brasbie and he has thrown himself on the mercies of that church he betrayed.'[41] He would be welcomed back like the Prodigal Son, wrote the *Examiner*, but it soon transpired that the report was without foundation. Brasbie claimed that the rumour of his return to Catholicism was spread in an attempt to turn Protestants against him. He described further attempts to intimidate him, one of which was in a letter that gave him twenty-four hours to either make his coffin or return to his original faith.[42] Brasbie was firm in his conviction, 'I have never even once thought of deserting the faith of my adoption, a faith for which I am ready not only to be quartered, but cut up, aye, inch by inch [...] I have suffered much. I am ready and willing to suffer ten thousand times more.' Despite this denial, the *Examiner* insisted that Brasbie had made private overtures to Fr Divine in Dingle about returning to the Catholic faith. It depicted him as a 'desperate, reckless and [...] lost man' who was 'playing the double game'.[43]

Brasbie continued to argue his case robustly and at length. In one letter, he listed and analysed fifteen lies that he detected in the reports of the *Examiner*, and he asserted:

> My separation from the church of Rome was an act purely my own. It was an exercise of that religious liberty which every British subject should enjoy, but of which, unfortunately, Irishmen in this part of the country are altogether deprived owing to the unhallowed and misdirected influence of their priests.[44]

Brasbie as a national figure

Denis Brasbie left his native county in February 1845 and travelled to Dublin on board a steamship named the *Dee*. The *Examiner* noted that the commander was a Lt Luther, adding, 'If that ain't wonderful!'[45] During the year 1845, he became prominent at national level as a propagandist and itinerant lecturer on behalf of the Priests Protection Society.[46] This society was founded in May 1844, and its headquarters were in 23 Upper Sackville Street, Dublin. Its patron was the Earl of Roden, Robert Jocelyn. The aims of the society were to protect priests who converted to Protestantism, to train them as ministers and to secure positions where they could serve. Brasbie wrote and lectured on behalf of the society, speaking, for example, in Dublin and in Manchester.[47] He made a tour of northern towns and addressed meetings in Belfast, Derry, Coleraine and Enniskillen.[48] Pádraig de Brún established that Brasbie earned £454 from the Priests Protection Society over a five-year period from August 1844, most of it to cover travel expenses.[49] Rev. Brasbie also assisted in services at St Audoen's church in Dublin, at which converts were inducted into the Church of Ireland.[50] He wrote to the press opposing the government grant of financial support to Maynooth College.[51]

The *Examiner* continued its personal attacks on Brasbie, referring to him as 'Brass-boy'. Describing his speaking tours on behalf of the Priests Protection Society, the *Examiner* said that he was being paraded like 'the lion or the ouran-outan of the saint-crowded menagerie, dragged about from town to town'.[52] The paper tracked his movements from London to St Audoen's, where 'Rev. D.L. Brass-boy' was reported as 'starring'.[53]

One of Brasbie's lectures included a dramatic performance. He spoke in the headquarters of the Priests Protection Society and began by demonstrating the vestments used at Mass. He then produced several large wafers like those used in the Mass and said the words of consecration over them, 'as he was wont to do in the days of his darkness and superstition (a power which the Roman Catholics believe a priest always retains)'. The report continued, 'He then elevated the host, and smashed it into pieces and thus showed that no transubstantiation takes place in the elements, that the wafer is a wafer still, that the idol of Romans is a bit of paste, and that there is no God made with hands or by man's device.' The report concluded, 'All present listened with almost breathless attention [...] It was certainly the best *practical lecture* we ever attended on the sacrifice of the Mass.'[54] This report was not published in any of the Kerry newspapers, and if it had been, it would have further shocked and outraged Brasbie's former colleagues and parishioners.

Brasbie's letters to priests and people of Ireland

After he became a national figure, Denis Brasbie felt emboldened to address open letters to all the priests of Ireland. In his first letter, he wrote, 'You know that the doctrines which you teach and which secure for you so much human respect are purely of human invention.' He then expounded at length on the doctrines of transubstantiation, private confession and purgatory, and he challenged his former colleagues to show any biblical foundation for them. His wide-ranging references invoked St Patrick, who, he said, never made any allusion to purgatory, 'this imaginary but lucrative place'. He also declared that the Roman Catholic bishops of Ireland were 'the most irresponsible body of men in the world'. The letter ended by appealing to priests to turn away from their old prejudices and shelter in the 'open arms' of the 'asylum at Achill' run by Rev. Nangle or under the Priests Protection Society.[55]

In another letter to priests, Brasbie went into meticulous detail to calculate the amount of time and money spent by priests in agitating for repeal of the Act of Union. He appealed to them to be 'true ministers of Christ and not political agitators', and to join him in the 'great religious revolution' already under way.[56]

Brasbie's next letter broadened his range by appealing to the whole people of Ireland. He began by explaining that although he had sent his previous letters to each of 2,298 secular priests in Ireland, he had not received any response. He was not surprised by this, knowing that 'the magic spell which so strongly binds them to the mammon of this world could not be dissolved by any language of mine.' He then listed twelve questions that Catholics should put to their priests. These questions focussed mainly on the absence of scriptural foundations for Catholic doctrines. One question asked why a Mass offered in Ireland for the release of a soul from purgatory cost five shillings, whereas in France it cost only one franc, the equivalent of tenpence. Brasbie finished this letter with an affirmation that

> it is only the blood of Jesus Christ alone that cleanseth from all sin, *not your good works*, nor your *popes*, nor your *priests*, nor your blessed *hair*, nor your blessed *teeth*, nor your blessed *nails*, nor your blessed *garments*, nor your blessed *buttons*, nor your blessed *bones*, nor your blessed *scapulars*, nor your blessed *cords*, nor your blessed *candles*, nor your blessed *oils*, nor your blessed *ashes*, nor your blessed *earth*, nor your blessed *water*.[57]

Brasbie's letters were reprinted as pamphlets by the Priests Protection Society, and they sold widely. In January 1845, what were described as 'fanatic publications' were distributed to homes in Dublin, emanating from Philip Dixon Hardy of the Sackville Street Tract Depository and containing 'a rabid and unbecoming address by an apostate priest named Denis Leyne Brasbie' to his former parishioners. The *Dublin Weekly Register* mocked the publications and suggested that the paper could be put to use 'in various household requirements'.[58] In a court case in Cork, 'the dissemination of offensive pamphlets' by 'a quondam Catholic' named Brasbie was blamed for 'exciting ill feelings among the people'.[59] Two of Brasbie's letters to his former parishioners were translated into Irish, as was one of his letters to the priests of Ireland.[60] By 1847, the print run for his publications was impressive: five thousand copies each of two letters, and one thousand copies of one letter in Irish.[61]

Later career

In a letter of 1854, Brasbie gave an account of his career after his conversion.[62] The letter was addressed to Vice-admiral Duff and was published under the heading 'Maynooth: Rome's persecution of converts from popery: Letter of the Rev Denis Ligne [*sic*] Brasbie to Admiral Duff'. Duff was a benefactor of Brasbie's and had asked him to give a summary of his experiences since his conversion; Duff could then use this to help him find a permanent position.

Brasbie's letter stated that a complete account of 'all the various losses, distresses, disappointments and privations he had suffered' since his conversion would be too long and so he could only give a general outline. He confirmed that he had been 'anxious for a considerable time' to join the converts, and that after he did so, he became 'the object of most bitter an unrelenting persecution'. He claimed that for three successive Sundays, it was necessary to have the protection of a force of two hundred armed soldiers when he attended service in Dingle. He remained in west Kerry from June 1844 until February 1845, mainly confined to his room, which was guarded by armed police at night after an attempt had been made to kill him. Brasbie told Duff that he had hoped that the excitement would subside and that he could take an active part in ministry in west Kerry, but that this proved impossible. Even though 'there were ships of war anchored in the harbour to protect the converts', persecution continued, 'fanned by those altar harangues by which the priests of Rome so successfully work on the superstitious minds of their poor eluded votaries'. When his new friends became convinced that Brasbie's life was in danger, he was secreted on board the *Dee*, with the consent of the Admiralty, and sailed to Portsmouth. He then travelled to London and eventually on to Dublin. There he was supervised by Rev. Robert Wood Kyle, who duly gave him a certificate of fitness for ministry.

In October 1845, Brasbie was appointed as curate in St Matthew's parish in Birmingham, diocese of Worcester, at a salary of £100 per annum. In order to grant Brasbie a licence to preach, the bishop required a certificate of ordination and wrote to the president of Maynooth College, Dr Laurence Renehan, requesting the document.[63]

Dr Renehan duly sent the certificate, adding this observation:

> My readiness to do so should not be understood as implying any doubt on my part of Mr. Brasbie's having been justly suspended for misconduct by his bishop, or any opinion that he has been for some years past a fit person to be employed as minister of the Established Church or any other.[64]

The bishop of Worcester baulked at this accusation of misconduct. Brasbie understood the bishop's dilemma and decided not to take up any position in the Anglican Church until he could clear his name of a charge that he considered slanderous. There followed two years of delay, during which Brasbie said that he again experienced 'intense anxiety and painful distress' and became penniless.[65] It galled Brasbie that while he had, for the sake of his conscience, given up a promising career as a priest, he now had his reputation 'surreptitiously filched from me' by Dr Renehan, a man who had a secure and very prominent position in a state-aided college. Brasbie charged Dr Renehan with defamation of character and claimed damages of £5,000. He won his case before the Court of Queen's Bench in Dublin in July 1847, but the jury of seven Protestants and five Catholics awarded him an amount that fell far short of his expectations. He wrote to Duff, 'The result of that trial was a verdict in my favour and £25 damages!! A verdict which reflects an indelible disgrace on the men who made it.'[66]

All the publicity had a disastrous effect on Brasbie's career. He wrote to many bishops in England and was shocked when, 'with the exception of one or two, they did not condescend to answer the letters of one who might have been, did not conscience interfere, a bishop himself.'[67] (This gives an indication of Brasbie's early ambition as a priest in Kerry.) From October 1845 to May 1851, Brasbie was unable to secure even a temporary position in the Church of England; he seems to have survived by the kindness of friends. Around 1850, Vice-admiral Duff, his wife and her sister came to the rescue in some way not made explicit in Brasbie's letter.

Denis Brasbie's family

Denis Brasbie married Alicia Kellett in Monkstown Church, Co. Dublin, on 20 June 1848. She was daughter of James Kellett of Annesbrook, Co. Meath, and niece of Rev. John Kellett, rector of Agher, Summerhill, Co. Meath.[68] In the records of Monkstown parish, Brasbie's residence was given as Donnybrook and his wife's as Kingstown (Dún Laoghaire); Brasbie's father Michael was described as 'merchant'.[69]

When Brasbie wrote the letter to Vice-admiral Duff in 1854, there were three children in his family, and they lived in Hopeman, near Elgin in Scotland. Brasbie's letter expressed the hope that 'perhaps a generous public, even now at the eleventh hour, may cooperate with you in making some permanent provision for the family of one who has suffered so much in the cause of truth.'[70] The Brasbie couple eventually had five children, one girl and four boys. The eldest was born on the Isle of Man and the others in Scotland. In 1856 or 1857, the family left for Canada, where a census of 1871 showed them living in Georgetown, Halton, Ontario.[71] By 1885, they had moved to Guelph in Wellington County, Ontario, where the death of 'Denis Leyne Brasby' was recorded on 30 March 1885. He was described as a clergyman born in Ireland, and the cause of death was paralysis. His son James registered the death.[72]

Folklore records

There is little memory of Denis Leyne Brasbie in west Kerry today, but one record refers to him as 'Brasby an tsúip a thug a chúl leis an aifreann' (Souper Brasbie, who turned his back on the Mass).[73] De Brún noted that some of the brief folklore references to him are factually inaccurate, particularly the unsupported claim that Brasbie left the priesthood because of a romantic involvement with a woman. This allegation began to circulate immediately after his decision to convert. It surfaced again during the libel case of 1847, when a Maynooth professor said that he was told by a Kerry student that Brasbie had been dismissed from the priesthood because of 'some impropriety towards females'.[74]

Miss Moriarty's conversion

A second dramatic conversion also took place in 1844: that of Thomas Moriarty's sister, who lived in Ventry with him and another brother, Matthew. Denis Brasbie moved to Ventry in early October to stay with the Moriartys, and three days later, Miss Moriarty (whose first name is not recorded) announced that she was converting to Protestantism.[75] A.M. Thompson wrote that the news came as 'a clap of thunder' and that 'the stunning effect of this conversion on the whole district cannot possibly be described.'[76] It seems that nobody apart from her confessor had any inkling of Miss Moriarty's gradual conversion. Up to this time, she had been 'the idol and pride, the boast of the priesthood', an exemplar of steadfastness in her Catholic beliefs. When a Protestant visitor to Ventry expressed his shock at the condition of the Catholic chapel there, he noted that there was no seating except for one chair placed in the centre in front of the altar. This was 'the seat of honour for a young lady, the only respectable person in the congregation and the only member of her family who had not joined our church'.[77] He was undoubtedly referring to Miss Moriarty, as he went on to state that the young lady had since become a Protestant.

Miss Moriarty had lived with her brother Thomas for seven years, and the priests were wont to tell their congregations, 'See Miss Moriarty – she has had opportunity of judging Protestantism: if there were any truth or superior sanctity in it, she would have found it out and you see, she wavers not.'[78] With the conversion of Miss Moriarty, this argument was undermined and, not surprisingly, Brasbie was blamed, with a story circulating that he had used 'a Satanic charm' on her.[79] However, A.M. Thompson wrote that the young woman 'boldly came out' soon after Brasbie's arrival in the household, 'foreseeing her conversion would be attributed to Mr Brasbie if she delayed'.[80]

A report published in the *Achill Missionary Herald* said that 'the escape of Rev. Mr. Moriarty's sister from the apostate church has set them all mad.'[81] The *Post* likewise wrote that this conversion infuriated the priests and 'caused their rage to boil over in the Dingle district', because Miss Moriarty had been such an exemplary Catholic:

> She was held up in the chapels as a bright example to the faithful and was called a saint and an angel. They never felt anything so much as her leaving them after all the boasting of her constancy, as is evident from the vile and unmanly manner in which she has been so unsparingly abused by their reverences.[82]

On the Sunday after Miss Moriarty's conversion, 'every chapel in the vicinity resounded to opprobrious discourses, of which she was the theme' and the young woman was subjected to 'the vilest epithets, the lowest and most scurrilous language'.[83] John Cavanagh, another convert, claimed that she was disparaged by Fr Scollard in a manner which 'not only proved him to be a stranger to the feelings of a gentleman, but tended to annoy and disgust many of his poor, deluded, though well-inclined hearers'.[84] The *Post* gave one example of the effects of the conversion. Miss Moriarty had an orphan cousin in the care of the nuns in Dingle, and the young girl was knitting stockings for her. After hearing of Miss Moriarty's conversion, the sisters were reported to have instructed the girl to stop the work and return the wool to her cousin. 'Poor spite', commented the *Post*, 'but a nice specimen of popery and nuns.'[85]

Ballads on Denis Leyne Brasbie

Several ballads were written about Brasbie – one by a man who was reportedly brought to Dingle by the priests, from a distance of 70 miles, expressly to write it. The ballad ran to four 'editions', each with a different caricature at its head.[86] This was probably the ballad that was read in court in March 1845 in a libel case taken by Rev. Charles Gayer. It was read by Rev. McIlwaine of Belfast, who said that it was published in a newspaper there:

> You Romans of this nation of every rank and station,
> Attend to my dictation while here I do relate;
> My heart is agitated, my heart is enervated
> Since Brasbie has reformed from the holy Roman faith.
> He now forsook in earnest the holy lamb of patience

That suffered for his creatures all in his bloody gore,
He embraced the reformation of Luther's cursed dictation
To dwell in Pluto's regions now and forever more.

That minister distracted that really has deserted
The holy church and gospel which Christ himself ordained,
Selected as a pastor to that pure and holy altar
Where Jesus Christ a victim forever will remain.
A member of that table where Christ himself was seated
Ten years without cessation there Brasbie did remain.
When he was truly feasted his flesh and blood he tasted
But now he's a member of Gayer's foul cursed train.

Cruel Brasbie worse than Judas our Saviour he abused,
The sacrament and altar he really has disgraced.
Since Gayer is his director he really has neglected
That pure and holy order in which he was ordained.
Them spotless robes so white wherein he should delight
He treated them with slight, the cruel renegade,
For no such rotten member should ever be depended on
Nor in a pew or pulpit be e'er allowed to preach.

Thanks to our dear Saviour! With what humiliation
You allowed that cruel traitor your blood again to flow.
He has renounced your graces that filled the Bible's pages
Us low and humble creatures your holy will to know.
For a small remuneration his Lord he has forsaken
He'll find he was mistaken as Judas was before,
When sunk in consternation in the abyss of d[amnatio]n
Both him and cursed Gayer in sad horror to deplore.

Then with what resignation he read that recantation
And said transubstantiation was nothing but a scheme.
His baptism he degraded, the laws of God violated
And wilfully rejected the Blessed Virgin's name.
I think it no great wonder that flaming fire and thunder
Should rend the skies asunder with anger and with rage,
To see those depredators embrace the reformation
Which was but instigated now in a latter age.

The holy Church and Gospel which Christ himself adopted
And sent his dear disciples the same to celebrate,
They suffered persecution, insult and destitution –
All this they bore with patience for their Redeemer's sake.
Nine hundred years most pleasing and that without sensation
Was the continuation of the true Roman creed,
Until the Greeks revolted from the service of our altar
Which [*sic*] the instigation of barbarous wicked deeds.[87]

14. Winter of rage

After the conversion of Denis Brasbie in August 1844, Fr John Casey resigned and Fr Daniel Healy became parish priest in Ballyferriter. The *Post* saw it as a forced resignation, reporting that the bishop resolved 'to pension off the old rector Casey, who was an easy man and not sufficiently violent for the purposes of persecution'. He was replaced by 'two young firebrands',[1] one of whom was Fr John Scollard. The *Post* explained, 'It was also considered that Devane [Divine] and Halpin were not at this alarming crisis sufficient to stem the torrent of Protestantism that flooded the parish of Dingle. Accordingly they were reinforced by the addition of young Scollard, just fresh from Maynooth and eager to distinguish himself in the cause of his church.'[2] Fr Halpin was known as 'Bully Halpin'.[3] A.M. Thompson's book has a reference to an unnamed priest who was 'a very brutal man'; in Fr John O'Sullivan's copy of the book, he wrote a note identifying the priest as Fr John Halpin.[4]

Fr Scollard soon became known as 'the cursing curate' and 'Fr Scold-hard' on account of his fiery sermons and condemnation of converts. The nickname Scold-hard may have originated with his own flock.[5] While none of his sermons have survived, letters that he sent anonymously to the *Kerry Examiner* give a clear indication of his style. His sentiments were always enthusiastically endorsed by the *Examiner*, and when writers in the *Post* responded in kind, the overall effect was to ratchet up the tensions in west Kerry during the winter of 1844–45. The propaganda wars on the pulpits and in the press were intertwined, with the *Examiner* and the *Post* outdoing each other in insults, and the tone of letters and editorials becoming increasingly vicious and abusive.

There were occasional outbreaks of violence, such as an attack on two priests that the *Examiner* reported as being carried out by 'a gang of those misguided wretches denominated "soupers"'. The two priests escaped injury only because they were on horseback and could get away quickly. The editor of the *Examiner* claimed that the *Post* chose to ignore these violent acts directed at Catholics. He advised those who might be attracted to the evangelicals, 'If such be its fruits, rather resign your Bibles than imbrue your hands in the blood of innocent men.'[6]

John Cavanagh of Ventry Cottage, a convert, publicly denounced the threats and curses of Fr Scollard. He referred to a sermon preached by Fr Scollard in Ventry in which he condemned Miss Moriarty and described Cavanagh as once 'the timber of a priest' but ignorant of Greek or Latin or even Christian doctrine.[7] Cavanagh described a confrontation he had with the priest: Scollard, 'more like a maniac than a minister, looked at me and said: "You scoundrel, you shall not be teaching scripture in this parish." I told him I would do so in spite of him, and that I would never shun to declare to all who would listen, the tendency his teaching had to idolatry.'[8] Two days later, Cavanagh was walking from Caheratrant when he was attacked on the strand by three men with blackened faces who forced him to the ground and discussed whether they would kill him. They agreed to let him go if he promised never again to speak to, or about, a priest. Cavanagh laid the blame for this assault on Scollard's preaching.

Many writers to newspapers were anonymous but identifiable. One letter from Testis Oculatus (Eyewitness) denounced the *Post* as 'the vilest organ of the vilest party that ever disgraced the world'.[9] Latin pseudonyms usually indicated that the writer was a priest; it was later revealed that Testis Oculatus was Fr John Scollard. The letter attacked Lord Ventry and described the converts as

> a group of the most abandoned and profligate wretches throughout the length and breadth of the land, huddled together here under the patronage and protection of a pettifogging lord in leading strings and petticoats on whose imbecile brow chance, or something worse, placed a coronet.

This letter referred to Rev. Thomas Moriarty as 'lying and unprincipled Tom' and to his sister's conversion as 'the apostasy of an unfortunate girl in this locality'. It described the convert John Cavanagh (whom he named Keevan) as 'a crack-brained apostate' who had applied to enter Maynooth to train for the priesthood but had failed the entrance examination, 'on account of his total ignorance of the principal mysteries of the Christian religion'. Cavanagh was 'a base wretch whose polluted hand the aforesaid noble lord does not disdain to shake'. Scollard's letter ended by indicating that he would deal with 'the mother of that wretched family the Moriartys' in his next letter.[10]

John Cavanagh responded to the letters of Testis Oculatus, and asserted that Fr Scollard, 'ashamed of his own name, and not without good cause', was the author. Cavanagh countered Scollard's description of his father as 'a poor fisherman' by agreeing that he was a fisherman and also a coast guard. Scollard's father, wrote Cavanagh, 'was nothing less than a poor herdsman, that was often seen trotting into a market town on the other side of the county selling buttermilk for his employers and, when he could gather them, a firkin of potatoes for himself'. Cavanagh reminded Scollard of the proverb, 'Those that have glass houses should not throw stones.'[11]

In his next letter, Testis Oculatus teased his readers with the phrase 'supposing that I am a priest' and expanded on his personalised attacks on the Moriarty family. He claimed that the 'principal apostate' Thomas, before his conversion, was 'seen in cold and nakedness on the streets selling his back-load of turf which he gathered, justly or unjustly, on the neighbouring mountains'. He wrote that Thomas Moriarty had been dismissed from his position as 'paymaster to the soupers' following complaints against him, and he described Moriarty's brother as 'an overgrown dolt' who had failed the examination to become a clergyman.[12] The letter claimed that Miss Moriarty was harassed and bullied by her brother Thomas over fifteen years, until she finally relented and became 'a contemptible apostate'. Scollard then wrote about the mother of the Moriartys, calling her 'the queen of the hive' and 'Mother Abbess', and claiming that her espousal of Protestantism was a result of pressure from her sons. He cited an acquaintance who asked her why, after a lifetime in the Catholic faith, she now condemned it, to which Mrs Moriarty replied, 'Wisha, my dear, I can't help them d[evil]s, if I did not talk that ways I'd be sint begging and insure I loves the Catholic religion now as well as ivir.'[13]

Several letters from Testis Verus (True Witness) were also published in the *Examiner*, and the author was almost certainly Fr Scollard once again. One letter stated that when Thomas Moriarty returned from 'his begging mission' in England, the converts gathered to collect their 'stipend'. One man suddenly became ill and died, 'scarcely a quarter of a mile from Mr. Moriarty's house'. Testis Verus declared, 'I wish to lay this fact before the public that the world may see that God himself is angry with these people.' This letter claimed that 'money is the mainspring in the "souper deception"' and described how Lt Clifford, 'whom some bad wind blew into Dingle', used to distribute money to converts at his house on Sunday morning.[14]

Lt Herbert Clifford replied at length in a letter to the *Post*. Referring to the 'doings in Dingle', he stated that his activities on the Sabbath Day were exclusively religious. He did not dole out money to 'these poor escaped ones of Rome' but spent his time encouraging the 270 converts of Dingle to 'search the scriptures', to pray and 'to live in peace and goodwill with all their fellowmen of every creed'.[15] Testis replied to Clifford, saying that Catholics were more persecuted than Protestants in west Kerry, 'Go to Ventry and there you will learn on whose side the persecution has been.' Catholic tenants there, who had been cruelly evicted from their homes by court order in times past, were on 'an ocean of grief' and were being attacked by soupers as they walked to and from Dingle, he claimed.[16]

Clifford justified his missionary work by way of a homely analogy:

> If I should see a man deliberately walking over the precipice at Binbawn Head into the sea, insisting that it was the true and only road into Dingle, would it not be right for me to arrest him in his folly and try to put him on the right road?[17]

In December, a letter from Testis Verus condemned the behaviour of converts in Dingle, claiming that 'no later than ten days ago a banditti of these ruffians, exulting in their impiety and irreligion, ran from shop to shop calling *for a farthing's worth of sacrament!*'[18] In an editorial headed 'The Impious Perverts of Dingle', the outraged editor of the *Examiner* wrote, 'A shudder comes over us as we write the words.' He went on:

> These are the boasted converts from Rome! And yet, after all, what boast is the acquisition to any church of ruffians without a conscience to scruple any deed of infamy that may augment their importance in the eyes of their proselytising patrons – without principle, without faith, without religion of any description, without hope in the next world, the soup-pot their only hope in this world. In the depth of its fat content are buried their Faith, their Hope, their Charity. With each draught of the greasy liquor they gulph down their religion, their hopes, their creed of infamy and crime. Keep them, Moriarty and Gayer and the rest of the gang of itinerant liars, keep them, cherish them, they are worthy of you and you of them.[19]

Other newspapers

It was not only local newspapers that reported on incidents in west Kerry. A slightly different version of the farthing incident was noted in the pages of *The Pilot*, a nationalist publication:

> No fiction can exaggerate the barefaced bribery by which the so called 'converts' at Dingle were induced to assume the character of Protestants; and the foul and evil spirit infused into these unfortunate persons, the mode in which they earn their wages and whereby they seek to recommend themselves to their new patrons are evidenced by the elaborate results they offer to those whose communion they have quitted. For example some of the Dingle converts entered the shops of Catholics asking for 'a penny-worth of sacrament' and when summarily ejected by the outraged shopkeeper, a cry of 'persecution' and 'exclusive dealing' is got up and the insolent miscreants whose indecent blasphemy necessarily caused their expulsion are, of course, represented as martyrs for the Protestant faith, victims of the persecuting spirit of popery.[20]

The *Achill Missionary Herald* also carried frequent reports on the angry confrontations in west Kerry, 'A fiery persecution is going on here. For seven Sundays the priests have cautioned their congregations against buying or selling with the converts.'[21] The pulpit campaign was still intense in July 1845, when an anonymous correspondent from Dingle gave a specific date for its beginning, stating that 'people are actually disgusted with the continual Sabbath day cursing which has been practised in Dingle chapel since 4th November last.'[22] The curses included one that would endure 'to the seventh generation'. To a devout and credulous people who believed in the power of clerical curses as much as clerical prayers, this curse was a sombre matter.[23]

As the *Post* entered its seventy-first year of publication, the editor reaffirmed its policy of 'an unswerving and zealous maintenance of every Protestant and constitutional institution in the Empire, and a fearless exposure of the designs of traitorous and bigoted demagogues and the persecution of a tyrant priesthood'.[24] The editor decided to visit Dingle to assess the situation there for himself. Under the heading 'Animus of Popery', he wrote that 'matters are much worse than they have been represented to us.' 'Persecution is now rife', he wrote, 'and enters more into minuter relations of life than we supposed it could in a civilised country in the nineteenth century.' He cited instances of a man who could not buy a pair of shoes and a woman who could not buy fish because of the injunction by Frs Halpin and Scollard against any dealings with converts.[25]

The last editorial of the year in the *Post* was entitled 'The Irish Society in the west – the intolerance of the Romish priesthood and its effects'. The editor welcomed the success of the proselytising campaign and characterised the reaction of the Catholic clergy as one of persecution, terror, tyranny and bigotry. He believed that it was after the conversion of Fr Brasbie that 'the floodgates of Papish zeal and persecution opened'; he asserted that Brasbie 'was libelled from every altar in the county' and in the columns of the *Kerry Examiner*, 'one of the most slavish and unscrupulous organs of the Romish priesthood in Ireland'. The *Post* declared, 'The converts in the barony of Corkaguiny have been subjected to a persecution, which, if not so violent as that of former days, that has led the holy martyrs to the stake and the block, is almost as trying to the constancy of man.'[26]

The editorial referred to cases that had come before the court of Petty Sessions in Dingle. In one case, a milk-woman was convicted of assault, because when she realised that she had just sold milk to the daughter of a convert, the milk-woman 'started up in a fury, and pursued her; having caught her, she wrested the milk, which had been paid for, from her and threw it back into the churn and returned the penny.' Other cases involved two converts being unable to purchase fish due to interference from a Catholic woman, and transactions involving bogwood, turf, nails and snuff being prevented by the injunction of the priests.

The *Post* warned its readers of an attempt to sow seeds of division in the Protestant community whereby 'old Protestants' were distinguished from converts. Sometimes, old Protestants were able to purchase goods on behalf of converts who were refused. Some converts would not have had food on the Christmas table were it not that some 'old Protestants' bought food items for them, on the pretext that they were for their own use.[27] The *Post* encouraged all Protestants to act together and adhere to the policy of 'no peace with popery'.

Another regular writer to the *Post*, styling himself 'The Old Sailor and Coast Guardman', mocked the 'hocus pocus' of Catholic rituals. Referring to the Mass, he wrote, 'I can't fathom that a creature should be able to make the Creator and then eat him.' He then described how the wife of the parish clerk made the altar breads by shaping a wafer out of a paste of flour and water, and placing it in a special piece of equipment – 'a sort of a double shovel with jaws that opened and shut for all the world like an alligator'. This was held over the fire until the paste hardened, and it was then shaped 'into little and big gods or wafers – for it's no gods until the priest's hocus pocus Latin comes out.' He continued, 'Then at Mass, the priest having, as you saw, said some Latin over them, they says the Godhead and Manhood of the Lord Jesus comes into them. Now, isn't this a link or two beyond queerish?'[28]

In a letter to a friend on New Year's Eve 1844, Lt Herbert Clifford described the state of the Dingle converts:

> Our poor converts here are undergoing a cruel persecution by means of exclusive dealing. The priests here have for the eight last Sundays denounced them from the altar and forbid any of their flock buying from or selling to them under pain of damnation – such is the <u>Christianity</u> of the Roman Catholic Church in this place and all Ireland I believe in the 19th century – it is horrible. This is what we got by <u>Emancipation 1829</u>.

Clifford assured his friend that 'they cannot starve our people back, as it is only getting us friends and money in England. We have now upward of 800 souls in the barony reformed from the church of Rome.'[29]

A.M. Thompson

Mrs Thompson vividly described the treatment of converts in the winter of 1844–45, when priests encouraged a policy of 'exclusive dealing', or what we would now call a boycott, towards converts.[30] She wrote that in condemnations from the altars 'Sunday after Sunday', the people were 'lashed into fury' and warned not to have any dealings whatsoever with the converts. This policy had been initiated earlier, but was now 'thoroughly acted out'. Catholics were not to engage in buying or selling with the converts, who then found it almost impossible to buy necessities like potatoes, turf, milk and fish. Thompson wrote that the converts' children were sent to buy milk in the market in the hope they would not be recognised. When they were identified, the milk was taken back and poured away, because it was 'cursed by their touch', and the money was returned to them. The Gayer children were targets of local mobs on occasion – stones were frequently thrown at them, and a lady accompanying them was severely kicked. The elderly mother of Rev. Gayer was hit on the head by a stone. In the market, even a pennyworth of birdseed was denied to a buyer when it was discovered that it was intended for one of the Gayer children.[31]

Converts had to rely on the limited produce of the farms and dairies that had been established for their support, and D.P. Thompson used his influence to help secure a supply of turf and potatoes for them. When he employed a group of thirty Catholics and ten converts on extensive fencing work that would provide employment for three months, a priest came to the place of work and summarily ordered the Catholics not to work alongside the converts. Thompson intervened, asking the Catholics if the priests would come to their support when they were starving, and all the men decided to stay on, in defiance of the priest.[32] Thompson does not name the priest, but he was identified in the *Post* as Fr Halpin, who 'had to draw in his horns and submit in sulky silence not only to his defeat, but to the public reproval of his parish priest, Divine, who, by the by, leaves the dirty work in a great measure to the co-adjutors [curates]'.[33]

Despite the charged atmosphere and the injunctions of the priests, A.M. Thompson was pleased that 'many affecting instances of individual kindnesses appear through the gloom of fanatical bigotry.' Some Catholics got around the rules by bringing milk and fish into the houses of converts after nightfall, leaving the items on the dresser. As there was no buying, selling or communication involved, they were technically not disobeying their priests. Thompson was jubilant because she saw the conflict as proof of the 'reality and extent of the Lord's work'. 'The priests are angry because they know that their dominion is gone,' she wrote. She was confident that 'the natural good sense of the people is righting itself, and if the present moment is not lost, if the converts are enabled to stand out the present storm, victory is sure.'[34]

Reverting to Catholic faith

The *Examiner* carried regular reports of people in west Kerry reverting to their original Catholic faith, and on one occasion this was put in the context of notable conversions to Catholicism in England. An editorial welcomed the much-publicised conversion of John Henry Newman and leading academics of Oxford University; it asserted that these successes more than compensated for the loss of D.L. Brasbie and others to Protestantism. The *Examiner* announced that six families, comprising thirty individuals, had renounced the 'soup gang' and returned to 'the one true faith', and that they were welcomed back by Fr Daniel Healy of Ballyferriter.[35] A correspondent of the *Post* said that the reference to six families was incorrect – that six men had reverted, but not their wives and families. The *Post* also dismissed claims of ten other converts returning as completely unfounded.[36]

Due to the 'indefatigable exertions' of Fr Scollard in Dingle, Patrick O'Donoghue was reported as returning to the 'true faith', along with John Horgan and his wife. Horgan was a Bible reader who had converted about four years earlier.[37] At Ventry, converts Hugh Connor and his wife, 'two of the deluded votaries of the Irish Society', were presented by Fr Scollard to the congregation as penitents who had returned and were to be married under Catholic rites. Fr Scollard conducted a public dialogue with Hugh Connor, who told the congregation that he had converted only because Thomas Moriarty had promised him £8 and an acre of land rent-free, 'a strong inducement to a poor boy like me', but that he had not received these. Connor said that he had never truly believed in his new religion and that none of the converts believed in Protestantism in their hearts, 'It is only the houses that were built for them that are keeping them together.' Connor explained that they were called soupers because, as soon as they accepted a bribe, converts would go every Friday for two or three months to Thomas Moriarty's house or Lord Ventry's house to receive plenty of soup.[38]

15. Intimidation and outrage, 1845

Sudden death of D.P. Thompson

The eventful year of 1845 began with the sudden death of David Peter Thompson. He had gone to Dublin to spend Christmas with family members at Clonskeagh Castle in the south of the city and became ill while there. He was 41 years old and died of gastric fever. The *Post* of 11 January 1845 stated that Clonskeagh Castle was the property of George Thompson, uncle and also father-in-law of D.P. Thompson.

James Raymond Eagar, the editor of another Kerry newspaper, the *Tralee Chronicle*, first published in 1843, was a personal friend of Thompson and wrote a tribute 'in unaffected sorrow':

> Manly, straightforward and generous, it was a matter of no small pride to rank such a man among our supporters [...] Into the transactions of everyday life he carried a spirit of energy, punctuality and integrity which, as a man of business, rendered him unequalled. As a politician he was ardent and uncompromising [...] Many a humble spirit and many a lowly home was blessed by his beneficence [...] He is gone! And take him for all in all, we shall seldom look upon his like again.[1]

The *Post* also carried a warm eulogy to Thompson:

> We have never taken up our pen with deeper feelings of regret than we do on the present occasion to record the departure from amongst us of the gentleman whose name stands at the head of this obituary. In speaking of Mr. Thompson, we must control our feelings, for if we were to speak of him as our hearts dictate, we would exceed the bounds of newspaper panegyric. Of the same politics as ourselves, we always found in Mr. Thompson a zealous and firm supporter. We may truly say that there lived not among us a more honourable man, a truer friend, or a more uncompromising patriot. The cause of true religion and suffering humanity have been deprived in him of a

zealous and kind supporter and patron. His death is indeed a county loss; no man could be more deeply missed in Kerry than he. He will be regretted both in the halls of our gentry and the huts of the peasantry [...] The Ventry family found in him an invaluable and just administrator of their property and to the numerous tenantry a humane and indulgent master.[2]

A long poem in Thompson's memory was published in the *Post*, ending with these lines, 'Weep not for him but pray that we / May be as good and just as he.'[3] The *Achill Missionary Herald* carried this tribute:

Mr Thompson was one of the most popular agents in Ireland and managed a very extensive property in such a manner as procured the goodwill of both landlord and tenant and frequently elicited the praise of the Lord Chancellor. A great part of the Ventry estate being a trust property, I fear his equal as an agent, a friend and neighbour will not readily be found. All Dingle truly may weep for such a man. Reader, pay the tribute of a tear to his memory.[4]

An immediate personal response to Thompson's death is found in a letter written by Lt Clifford, his staunch ally. Clifford wrote, 'We have, I lament to say, just lost our best friend [...] He is unusually regretted and fully so too.' Clifford described Thompson as 'a just and fair agent to employer and tenant, the friend of the Protestant cause and the foe of O'Connell.'[5]

At a libel trial heard in Tralee in March 1845, Rev. Thomas Moriarty described D.P. Thompson as being very supportive of the converts, 'He was active in promoting the happiness of the poor, and he was a man of honour and a gentleman; he purchased potatoes, turf and milk for the poor converts to prevent them being starved.' Moriarty was adamant that Thompson, as a land agent, showed no special favour towards converts, saying that 'he exacted rent from converts in the same manner as he did from Roman Catholics, and even I thought him severe on converts at times.'[6]

There were many people in west Kerry who had suffered under D.P. Thompson's management of the Ventry estate, and it seems that there was some rejoicing in Dingle at his death. One report stated that a priest was 'devilish enough to call on the congregation to rejoice' at the death of Thompson, telling the people that 'God has heard the prayers of his people and poured out the flood of his wrath on him and removed him by a signal judgment.' The writer alleged that 'all this was said yesterday by our new priest, who, we thought, was comparatively a mild pastor.'[7]

In paying tribute to Thompson, Thomas Moriarty described the sermons delivered by priests in Dingle:

> Who has not heard of the insults heaped upon Lieutenant Clifford, Inspecting Officer of the Coast Guards, an officer beloved by his men, Protestant and Roman Catholic, a gentleman respected and esteemed as most benevolent and inoffensive. And will it be believed!! Triumphs were sung on the death of the late, ever to be lamented, D.P. Thompson, Esq. He was indeed a public and a private loss. I know well how he detested hypocrisy and dishonesty in all men, whether Protestants or Roman Catholics. He was a true friend to every honest man under his control, and many a family he raised to independence in this country. He was the widow's friend too. May the Lord comfort his widow. Everyone knows how the Ventry estates improved under his agency. He knew well the state of things in this district and had the manliness to provide turf and potatoes for the poor persecuted converts from the tenants under his charge. This was one of his last acts before leaving for Dublin, hence the triumphs at his death. Alas for religion! Alas for humanity itself – how devoid of both must be the hearts of these men.[8]

Auction at Ballintaggart House

After her husband's death, Anna Maria Thompson and her five children left Dingle. Ballintaggart House was advertised as vacant; it was taken by Charles Gayer and his large family, who moved from Farranakilla House. D.P. Thompson's replacement as agent of the Ventry estate was Richard Chute of Blennerville.[9]

A prominent advertisement announced an 'extensive and magnificent sale by auction' at Ballintaggart House, to take place over four days starting on 8 April 1845. The long list of items for sale gives an indication of the family's lifestyle: seven to eight hundred ounces of solid silver articles, carriages, a choice collection of 709 books, a wine cellar of about eighty dozen bottles, fifty oil paintings, a grand piano 'considered to be one of the finest-toned in Ireland', and all kinds of furniture, utensils and cutlery. The stock for sale included 'twenty-four very beautiful full-grown deer', twenty-seven heifers, eighteen cows in calf, seventeen sheep and a well-bred bull.[10] The *Examiner* noted that two duelling pistols were bought by Rev. Thomas Moriarty, humorously speculating that one was for him and the other for Rev. Charles Gayer.[11]

On the last day of the auction, the deer broke free and scattered around the area. The symbolism was not lost on one of the Dingle priests, who told his congregation that they would be 'scattered to the four winds of heaven, like Mr. Thompson's deers, if they held any communication, either in buying or selling, with the converts'.[12] Ó Mainín referred to local folklore about 'the curse of Thompson's deer' issued by Fr Halpin against converts and also to a tradition that Thompson's sudden death was the result of a curse imposed by Fr Halpin.[13] There is a family memory, which still endures, that Sean-Mhanus Sheehy was about to be evicted from his farm in Ballintaggart, and that it was to be taken over as a colony farm – D.P. Thompson's journey to Dublin was in order to complete the legalities around this. When Fr Halpin was informed of Thompson's intentions, he is remembered as saying ominously, 'Is mó duine a chuaig agus nár tháinig ar ais.' (Many a person who left never came back.)[14] According to Patrick Foley, Thompson had evicted tenants at Cahirdorgan, leaving them 'to perish on the roadside', and had handed over their lands to converts. He was said to have gone to Dublin to secure writs against tenants who refused to attend Protestant services. 'To say the least of him, D.P. Thompson, he was the poor man's scourge,' wrote Foley, quoting a phrase from a poem entitled 'The Exterminator's Song'.[15]

'Dingle Doings'

The first months of 1845 in west Kerry were marked by incidents that represented the zenith of religious conflict and sectarian bigotry in the area. As was customary, the conflict involved provocative sermons in the Catholic churches, responses in newspapers, correspondence with the authorities, anonymous threats and incidents of violence. Confrontations were often given a public airing in the courts; they received widespread coverage in Kerry and further afield. The controversies that swirled around Dingle (the 'Dingle Doings', as they were often referred to in the press) in the wake of the unexpected death of D.P. Thompson enveloped Lord Ventry and his wife, Rev. Gayer and his elderly mother, the local priests and anonymous newspaper correspondents.

On the first day of the year, a letter in the *Post* condemned the language used by a priest, described as 'this gasconading clergyman', against Lord Ventry and his wife and family. The priest was accused of using 'the Billingsgate phraseology of a Maynooth bachelor' and 'language which would do honour to a fish-woman'. The writer asked:

What must an enlightened public think of the unblushing effrontery of a Roman priest who unscrupulously enters the sacred precincts of private life and drags from their retirement a noble lord and his tender-hearted lady and exhibits them the objects of his scurrility and abuse to his poor deluded hearers?[16]

The writer was outraged that a Christian clergyman could 'disgrace the altar on which he stands' by indulging in such language, and he asserted that the priest 'had no regard for the common decencies of life'. He wondered if the priest had ever read St Paul's words on the virtue of charity. While the Ventry family would be remembered for kind and unostentatious acts, such preachers, the writer believed, would be remembered only for 'their anti-Christian, unclerical, unscriptural, unkind, uncharitable, unbecoming, unhandsome, ungenerous, unmanly and unnatural spirit'. The priestly sermons were 'setting fire to the inflammable passions of a naturally warm-hearted, but easily excited, people by the diabolical language which they use on the altars'.[17] This letter set the tone for the public debates that followed.

On 3 January, magistrates John Drummond and Edward Hussey heard a case at Dingle Petty Sessions. A 12-year-old boy named Cornelius Sheehy was charged with striking Mrs Frances Gayer on the head with a stone in Green Lane. She was the mother of Charles Gayer, a widow of over 80 years of age, who was a visitor to Dingle. Rev. Gayer testified that his mother had 'a lump as big as my fist on her head'. Drummond told Gayer that it would be best if Mrs Gayer could come to the court to give evidence, and a policeman was sent to escort her.[18] Gayer said that he had also been a victim of stone-throwing by boys, but that it was difficult to persuade anyone to give evidence against them, 'We may be all murdered and no one would come forward [...] If things are permitted to continue in this state, they may lead to very bad results.'[19] Mr Hussey ruled that there was no proof that stones were intentionally thrown at Mrs Gayer, and the case was dismissed. Gayer asked if he had the right to arrest any boys who were throwing stones at him and hand them over to the police, but the magistrates did not give him a clear ruling on this.[20]

Lord Ventry came under fire in the press when he was accused of displaying a blasphemous image for the entertainment of his family. The image was said to have represented a Catholic sacrament in an offensive manner, and Lord Ventry was told that such conduct was neither manly nor Christian.[21] The image was apparently a lithograph of a priest saying Mass for a sick pig in a poor man's cabin.[22] This image had been published in a short pamphlet that had circulated in the area four years earlier, according to a correspondent of the *Post*. He claimed that the same image was to be found in many Catholic homes in the area; he also pointed out that the priests had indeed said Mass for sick animals, and for fishing boats and milk churns. Therefore, he stated, nobody could have any reason for taking offence.[23]

Petition of January 1845

Charles Gayer responded to the rising tensions by writing to the Lord Lieutenant requesting extra security for converts in the area. He enclosed a memorial or petition signed by 147 heads of families, 'inhabitants of Dingle, Kildrum, Ventry, Donquin, Dunurlin and Kilmacheader', outlining their difficulties. All the signatories were male, except for two widows.[24] The petitioners (or memorialists) stated that they numbered over 800 and were all conscientious converts; they claimed that 'for the last four months in particular, memorialists have been, and are still, suffering grievous persecution and loss.'[25]

The official reply of 14 January was a disappointment to the memorialists. While the Lord Lieutenant regretted 'that any person should be exposed to personal inconvenience, obloquy or insult on the score of religion', he could offer no remedy and advised that 'the ordinary course of law can alone be resorted to them for relief.'[26] Nevertheless, the *Post* reported that 'in consequence of the violent harangues of the Romish priests', the authorities had approved an increase in the police force in Dingle, 'to prevent the mischiefs which are likely to be the result'. Accordingly, a strong party of policemen had left Tralee that morning for Dingle to prevent further incidents.[27]

Threat to the life of Lord Ventry

Another serious incident occurred in early January. This was a death notice issued to Lord Ventry unless he dismissed Rev. Gayer.[28] The *Post* was aghast at this development and believed that 'the design of the miscreants who penned this notice' was to drive Lord Ventry out of the country. It blamed the Dingle curates, 'the Rev. firebrands Halpin and Scollard', who were 'ill-minded men', stirring up the passions of 'a superstitious, priest-ridden and excitable people' in their Sunday sermons. The *Post* was certain that his lordship would not be deterred by 'the pop-gun of any ill-minded bigot' and 'the machinations of wicked men'.[29] A reward of £30 was offered for information on the author of the letter.[30]

A copy of the threatening letter to Lord Ventry is held in the National Archives; it reads as follows:

> Take Notice
> That if you do not send Gayer the bastard out of this country from a quiet and pesible people and discountenance all blagards that deny their holy religion for ~~huere~~ soop this do and you will do right by the eternal God I will drive a brace of balls through your carcass privately otherwise in the noon-day if not.
> Signed by a right good aim
> Parson Goodman is a good man, he interfares with no man's religion. I leave him to you.[31]

The message had the image of a cross and 'Tiprery forever' on the margin of the text. On the back is a note written by Lord Ventry, 'A true copy of a notice received by me, Ventry', followed by the signatures of four witnesses. The reference to 'Tiprery' was an allusion to the fact that several landlords had been victims of violent assaults in Tipperary around that time. It is noteworthy that Parson Goodman was excluded from censure because of his family's standing and reputation in west Kerry. A.M. Thompson's version of this notice is headed 'Take Notis' and has some other spelling differences, such as 'interfaries' for 'interfares'.[32]

The official reaction to this threat was mild. Magistrate John Drummond wrote on 13 January that there was not much that could be done about the threat to Lord Ventry, 'who himself does not appear to feel any considerable degree of alarm'. In Drummond's judgment, 'this disgraceful act was intended rather for the purpose of intimidation than with a view to its actual perpetration.'[33]

Rumours abounded about the authorship of the notice, and Fr Scollard felt obliged to inform his congregation that he was not responsible for it.[34] Criticism of Scollard's sermons continued, some of it from his own congregation. 'A Ventry Catholic' described Scollard's 'cursing Mass' in Dingle church, when the priest, 'with more than ordinary vehemence, discharged his Billingsgate artillery' against Lord and Lady Ventry. Scollard then went on to preach in Ventry, where he 'not only again discharged his poison arrows at the above targets, but at one whose honoured remains were only a few days committed to their kindred dust, the late lamented Mr. Thompson.' The letter went on:

How truly dead to every feeling that should actuate a Christian [...] must that wretched man, and worse than wretched minister, be, who could belie and abuse that departed one whose memory shall ever be fondly cherished by the thousands he has been a blessing to in this neighbourhood.[35]

Robert O'Kelly, parish clerk of Ventry, wrote in defence of Fr Scollard, stating that he had made no reference, directly or indirectly, to the late D.P. Thompson in his sermon.[36] This denial was disbelieved by the *Post*; bitter exchanges continued, with 'Scold-hard' being accused of 'pitiful bigotry', 'base and senseless feelings', 'unblushing falsehood' and 'vindictive feelings'.[37]

Fr Scollard's letter to Lord Ventry
One letter written by Fr Scollard was published by A.M. Thompson under the heading 'Priest Scollard's letter to Lord Ventry proposing terms of peace in the "Dingle Doings"'.[38] This was written on 20 January 1845, just days after the inflammatory sermon described above, and it is possible that its apparently conciliatory tone was influenced by the strong reaction to his sermon. Scollard began by referring to 'this important crisis in the history of Dingle', and he appealed to Lord Ventry to use his 'mighty influence to quell the jarring elements with which we are on all sides beset'. Turning to what he termed 'the persecution of the so-called Dingle "Converts"', Scollard claimed that the converts were deeply insincere and that they had a 'total want of faith in the Protestant religion'. He did not deny that persecution happened, but said that the converts themselves were to blame:

They make their religion principally to insult your numerous tenantry *and long-tried friends*, of which I myself am a witness. The only preventative to this was a total separation from them, and really I don't know how they or their supporters can complain of so simple a remedy.

Scollard then adverted to 'the terms of censure' about Lord Ventry that he had used in his sermon, saying that they were no doubt 'considerably exaggerated' when reported to him, and offering this promise:

But, my Lord, if you allow yourself to be undeceived and give 'fair play' *to all*, I promise that what has been said will be retracted, and that your memory will be enshrined forever in the hearts of a grateful people – the people of Dingle.

Fr Scollard signed off with the customary formality, 'I have the honour to be, My Lord, your Lordship's most obedient servant, John Scollard, C.C.'

There is no record of a response to this, but Thompson wrote that Gayer and Scollard did take part in a public debate 'before a thousand persons', during which Scollard accused Gayer of bribery and corruption, and the converts of hypocrisy and lack of conviction.[39] Scollard claimed that some converts were sending their children back to priests for baptism, but when challenged to name these people, he did not. A.M. Thompson counter-claimed that converts were being offered blankets, clothes and food to return to the Catholic faith; one convert woman who was dying was told that a horse and cart with a feather-bed would be sent for her, and if she was afraid of her husband, twenty stout men would escort her back.[40]

Threat to Rev. Gayer

On 29 January, a report in the *Post* was headed, 'Fearful State of Things in Dingle: Attack on the residence of Lord Ventry and Service of a Threatening Notice on the Rev. Charles Gayer'. Lady Ventry was sitting in her drawing room in Burnham House one night at 11.00 p.m. when a noise was heard at the window. Her son-in-law, Lt Hawkey, R.N., went out to investigate and came upon two men scaling a wall. One of the men pointed a pistol at him and pulled the trigger, but the gun did not discharge. Hawkey fired at the gunman, but the shot missed and the two men escaped.[41] After this, magistrate John Hickson took the decision to send three marines to keep vigil at Burnham House every night. They were from the war steamer the *Lynx*, under Lt John Nott, which was at anchor in Dingle harbour.[42] At the height of the tension of early 1845, there was one instance of light relief in a report of a disturbance that caused quite an alarm in Burnham. The marines eventually traced the noise to a number of fighting cats who had raided the pantry. The *Examiner's* report was headed 'An awful catastrophe at Burnham'.[43]

On Monday, 26 January, Rev. Gayer received a threatening letter. In response to this, the editor of the *Post* wrote 'with feelings of sorrow and of disgust' at how the peace of the county was being disturbed. He laid the blame on 'the preaching and example of men who call themselves ministers of the Most High God, and by their conduct have brought disgrace on that holy and sacred office'.[44] The letter contained a threat to Gayer's life and read as follows:

PARSON GAYER THE BETRAYER,

Will you never cease to do evil and learn to do well: – never, – and conscious of that I now warn you and your family to leave this part of the country at once, where you are beginning to create a civil war, between the inhabitants of this hitherto quiet and peaceable town and neighbourhood, and your ignorant and deluded followers, if you still persevere in remaining among us. Your life, or the lives of one or other of your confederates, must be sacrificed, as there are many who would deem it an honour and a glory to rid the earth of such monsters as yourself, and a certain would-be Noble Lord; and that pay-master general of the Soupers, Lieutenant Clifford, Royal Navy, take heed and carry your hated presence to some other country, or if you do not, mark the consequence; as you have none of Her Majesty's War Steamers in the Dingle Harbour just now, to protect the lives and property of our Tory gentry, nor will they or you ever have the pleasure or gratification of seeing the 'Hecate' and her orange blood-sucking crew in our harbour again, as there was many an anonymous letter sent off against her, until we had the pleasure of seeing and hearing that she could never come in our safe harbour again – as for that rotten Lynx, and her old commander, they are too insignificant to be afraid of her, nor would the few men he commands avail much against the fury of an enraged and justly-incensed populace, though the few sailors he commands are most all of them Roman Catholics, and would in case of emergency help sooner than fight against us; so you see you are beset on all sides; – once again, I tell you beware – beware, and quit this part of the country in time.

Address
Parson Gayer
Fairnakilla House
Dingle[45]

Charles Gayer's response was to place placards around Dingle town with a defiant message:

Having received a notice yesterday in which my life is threatened unless I leave Dingle, I take this way of informing the writer that it has come to hand. I quite agree with him that 'there are many who would deem it an honour and a glory to rid the earth of such monsters as myself and others are.' As in all ages there have been those who, through ignorance and blind zeal have thought as did Saul of Tarsus, that by 'killing those who called upon the name of the Lord Jesus, they were thereby doing God service;' and the reason of which the Saviour gives 'because they have not known the Father nor me,' I would now tell the writer a few things:

1st – That, whatever is the consequence, I am resolved not to leave Dingle.

2ndly – That I fear not him who can *only* kill the body, but *after that* has no more that he can do.

3rdly – That my life is in God's hands, and not his and that it cannot be touched without His permission.

4thly – That I would consider it an honour to be called upon to lay down my life in the service of Him who laid down His life on the cross for my redemption.

5thly – That I forgive him from my heart the evil that he meditates against me, and trust that he may find forgiveness at the hand of God who alone can pardon it, and who has said that 'no murderer hath eternal life abiding in him'.

Charles Gayer

Dingle, Jan. 27, 1845.[46]

Letter of Thomas Moriarty

At the height of the frenzy of January 1845, Thomas Moriarty summed up the grievances of the converts and their ministers in a powerful letter.[47] He began by expressing gratitude to the *Post* for its defence of the converts, who 'have been maligned, misrepresented and abused in a most unchristian manner from the altars and in the pages of the *Kerry Examiner*'. Moriarty indicted the Catholic clergy as distinct from the laity, whom he described as 'naturally very much disposed to peace and goodwill towards us "who are their own flesh and blood"'. Without them, he said, 'we could never have withstood the consequences of such terrible teaching.'

Moriarty went on to make a passionate appeal for freedom of belief and worship. The letter reads like a formal declaration, indicating that the patience of the converts was exhausted and that they were determined to react to what they perceived as extreme provocation. Moriarty's words give an insight into the perspective of his fellow clergymen and the converts:

I am thankful to say that all this time we have preached in our pulpits peace and goodwill towards all – even our enemies, persecutors and slanderers. Our people know this and, thank God, are influenced by it. We have patiently and quietly listened to all that has been falsely said of us and uncharitably done against us. We are at length driven to act on the defensive. We have appealed to the government of our country for protection. All we ask is liberty of conscience, the birthright of every subject of the British empire. Would to God we had it here. But we can never expect it while Roman Catholic priests are allowed with impunity to speak of us and excite people against us, as they do from their altars each Sunday. Our only crime is that we have left their communion and conformed to the Established Church [...]

However, our patience and forbearance may be misunderstood. The constant dropping of water wears the stone and the greatest lies pass for truth with many when constantly repeated. To prevent any such consequence from the weekly repetition of false statements and abuse of us for the last few months, I beg leave to address the public through your pages. I shall state the truth and nothing but the truth. I leave it to others to write under assumed names which betray their want of moral courage as well as their consciousness of a bad cause. What I write you need not be ashamed to publish; I shall state facts well known through this district and capable of proof by most respectable and impartial testimony.

Moriarty continued by giving some instances of the persecution that converts experienced, 'How often is the poor convert on his way to and from the town of Dingle not only insulted and provoked but shouldered, pelted and beaten?' Shopkeepers and traders refused to deal with the converts when they went to purchase 'potatoes, milk, fish and other necessaries of life'. At the funeral of one convert, when the widow, children and other mourners would have expected 'to pass undisturbed through a professedly Christian country', they were instead subjected to insults and jeers from their fellow countrymen, people 'brought into such an unchristian and unnatural state of mind'. On the way home from the burial, Moriarty and the other mourners were 'pelted with clods and stones'.

On another occasion, the skeleton of a horse was dragged out onto the road as Moriarty went by on his own horse, which he said, was well known to be 'skittish'. Two Catholic fishermen were refused lodgings when they went from Ventry to Dunquin to help repair the boats of converts. A young convert who sought a drink of milk for his aged mother was refused by all his neighbours; he had to walk through a snowstorm to request milk from Rev. Moriarty. Another man who was threatened with violence ran into a nearby forge for refuge; he had a red-hot poker brandished in his face and was told, 'Devil, begone'. The convert John Cavanagh was attacked on Ventry strand by a group of men with blackened faces. The windows of the converts' schoolhouse were broken. In the market, when a woman convert asked the price of a fish, she had the fish slapped in her face; a man trying to sell his pig was thumped and pelted with mud.

Moriarty blamed the priests for the unneighbourly behaviour of the people, 'I do bear the people in general testimony that they are driven to it against their own Irish hearts.' He acknowledged instances of Catholics willing to help the converts. He told of one man who bought potatoes as if for himself but then distributed them among the converts. Another was asked by a convert for the loan of a tub in which to salt a pig; he was reluctant to be seen to go against the instructions of the priest, but told his neighbour that if he came around after nightfall, he would find the tub in the corner of the garden.

A new nickname for the soupers was pronounced from the altar every Sunday, according to Moriarty:

> We lived in peace and goodwill with the Roman Catholics of the country in general till these new batteries were opened upon us and certainly our enemies have, according to their Bishop's orders, 'kept up the fire' incessantly for the past four months. This is a desperate effort to put down the reformation by starving and frightening back the poor converts and driving them out of the country; this object is openly avowed.[48]

Responses to Thomas Moriarty's letter

The *Examiner's* response to Thomas Moriarty's letter was to mock the *Post's* headline, 'Fearful State of Things in Dingle', as 'a pompously horrific announcement'. It reprinted the headline in full, followed by five exclamation marks, claiming that the paper connived with Gayer, Moriarty and 'the rest of the magnates of the despairing, drooping, "dumb-foundered" souper warriors of Dingle'. It suggested that the threatening letters and notices were written by Protestant sympathisers, because a good way of 'replenishing the soup cauldron' was to write a notice 'and procure it to be served on Lord Ventry' and then follow it up with a similar letter to Gayer.

It indicated that slandering the whole Catholic population of Dingle was an effective way of adding to 'the exhausted funds of the Irish Society'.[49] The *Examiner* also ridiculed Thomas Moriarty and 'the catalogue of grievances recited by this crafty arch-souper'. It poked fun at the account of his skittish horse, saying it was 'enough to turn a heart of steel into a spring well'. The story of the woman who was slapped in the face with a fish seemed to indicate that she was hankering after the old Catholic ways. 'What did a souper want with fish?' asked the editor, referring to the Catholic tradition of eating fish on Fridays.[50]

These controversies in Dingle and its hinterland were covered by other newspapers in Ireland and Britain, especially the Protestant press. A Belfast paper took up Gayer's complaints against the priests under the headline 'Awful Popish Persecutions at Dingle'. It quoted Gayer's claim that because of exclusive dealing, up to 800 people were 'in danger of starvation, and that in the midst of plenty'. The paper asked, 'When will England arouse herself? When will our Protestant brethren receive, at least, toleration? When will "God arise and his enemies be scattered"? Surely the prayers of God's people will ascend in our brethren's behalf.'[51]

Moriarty's letter was hailed by the evangelical press as evidence of his and Gayer's courage and determination in spreading the light of the gospel in the darkest parts of Ireland. The letter was published in full as an appendix in the book *Ireland and Her Church* by Richard Murray (1845). Charlotte Elizabeth Tonna published long extracts from it in *The Christian Lady's Magazine*, quoting Gayer as stating, 'Nothing can now be had for money – my servant could not get one pennyworth of salt the other day. Only for the potatoes from the Colony Farm, the people would be in a deplorable state.' Nevertheless, Gayer was confident that 'popery is going fast downhill, and Babylon will soon fall.'[52] Tonna informed readers that Thomas Moriarty was one of the 'first fruits of the rich harvest' and referred to 'the martyr-spirit' of Mr Gayer. Her tone was more strident and belligerent than Moriarty's, and it reveals how events in Dingle were presented to readers of the more extreme evangelical publications:

Tell us of battle fields and crowns of conquest! Look at the wilds of Kerry and the warriors of this world will appear but as aimless madmen; their proudest triumphs as a feverish dream. There *is* war; there the prophetic Beast makes war upon the saints and there the Lord girds his people to the battle and in the midst of the tumult adds daily to the Church such as shall be saved. There, hunger and thirst, cold and nakedness, cruel mockings and scourgings, and the hatred of all whom they most fondly love is the actual lot of the poor believers [...] The Sun of Righteousness is rising on those western shores of the western isle [...] Who will hasten to the help of the Lord against the mighty? Who will uplift the hand in prayer and stretch it forth in bounty, for the persecuted children of dear Erin, brought back to the light in which of old their fathers walked rejoicing? Many we trust will respond to the call, and great will be the bliss of such when the harvest is called in.[53]

Insult and invective

During the month of February, the extraordinary level of inflammatory invective and insult continued. The poor of Dingle continued to play their roles in the grand opera that was taking place. In one report, a dying woman named Carney, who lived in the colony, wished to return to Catholicism. A writer to the *Post* claimed that she received blankets, food and clothing for herself and her children from the priests as an inducement to return.[54] In a letter to the *Examiner*, Maurice Crean wrote that he had witnessed an unseemly squabble that took place at Mrs Carney's bedside when Rev. Gayer 'threatened her and her children with immediate expulsion from *his* house (as he called it)'. When Gayer was confronted by a priest and by Maurice Crean, he became subdued; he withdrew only when police inspector Gillman arrived and ascertained that it was Mrs Carney's wish to have the priest at her bedside. According to Crean, Gayer then placed watchmen on the house and took possession of the door key. Crean also claimed that dying converts were given the drug laudanum to prevent them from returning to Catholicism.[55]

Two people died in a tragic house fire in Dingle in late January, and the family was left destitute. Sailors from the *Lynx*, along with Lt Clifford and Sub-inspector Gillman, helped to quell the fire.[56] Lady Ventry came to the assistance of the family, who were Catholics. The *Post* pointed out, 'These are the kind-hearted individuals whom Scollard and Halpin hold up as tyrants and uncharitable to their flocks every Sabbath.'[57] 'A Ventry Catholic' wrote to the *Post* again, describing Fr Scollard as 'that poor old cursing curate', and conceding that he had softened of late but still referred to Thomas Moriarty as the 'bull-dog'.[58] 'A Dingle Souper' mocked 'Fr Scold-hard', who was 'trying *hard* to starve us back to the bosom of the mother church and won't let us get a potato, a turf or a drop of milk in the market in the good old town'.[59]

The *Examiner* dismissed the grievances and threats described by the evangelicals and converts as 'fabrications'. One correspondent listed all that had recently occurred 'in this little romantic town of ours': 'threatening notices served; police force increased; applications made for a military force; several attempts made to represent our peaceable peasantry in a state of rebellion'.[60] The *Post* was gratified to receive support from the *Cork Constitution*, which wrote:

> All the atrocities disclosed are the natural fruits of the iniquitous system in which the perpetrators are brought up and of the Satanic spirit inculcated by their priest. Aye, Satanic spirit. Is that epithet too strong? Do any of our conciliating friends object to it? Will they peruse the letter and articles to which we have alluded and favour us with a phrase that will suit them better?[61]

The *Post* was also pleased to receive support from the *Dublin Evening Mail*, which expressed the hope that the Dingle pastors would receive a generous response from 'the wealthy and humane community of the Established Church at large'. A start was already made in the distant parish of Kilmood, Co. Down, where 1,100 people signed a letter of support for Rev. Gayer and made a collection for the Dingle converts.[62]

'An Old Protestant' accused the priests of west Kerry of displaying 'depravity and insensibility to religion'. On the previous Sunday, Ventry chapel became 'rather a bear-garden than a temple of the living God', when the priest started 'to abuse and malign all the converts of this district in the most opprobrious and uncharitable language'. He went further and condemned their relatives who had not converted and even their dead ancestors. 'Yea, he wrought himself up into such a state of anger and phrenzy that he actually stamped and blasphemed at that altar where a few minutes before he *pretended* to have sacrificed and partaken of the body and blood, soul and divinity of our Lord and Saviour Christ.' The writer observed, 'So much for the tender mercies of popery.' He cited other examples of harsh sermons in Dingle and Dunquin, and concluded that 'Christianity and humanity are clean gone, driven out by popery [...] These men are not the ministers of Christ.'[63]

Cartoon in the *Post*

The *Post* was becoming more belligerent in its tone, with the editor openly describing himself as 'a Protestant journalist' while berating the *Chronicle*.[64]

He declared, 'No less than four large families have joined the Church of Ireland lately in Dingle. So much for the boasting of the Catholic priesthood. Verily the Dingle mission is of God and the hand of man cannot prevail against it.'[65] It was rare to see cartoons in the Kerry newspapers of this time, but one issue carried a cartoon with the caption, 'A far west ecclesiastic of the Church Militantary waging war to the knife against the Dingle converts, eight hundred in number'. The cleric is seated on a donkey, with the stamp 'AD 666' and 'The Pope's Own Light' on his tail. A speech bubble from the cleric reads, 'I'll give the soupers just six months to live and not one other day. Repeal!' 'Parson Gayer and 800 souls' is written on one banner flowing from the cleric's head.

In the text accompanying the cartoon, the cleric was described as 'a regular Don Quixote in his profession, arrayed *cap-a-pee*, in the trappings of the Scarlet Lady'. The text refers to 'maledictions from the altar' and 'clamorous harangues, which, while they serve the purpose of exciting the ignorant multitude, add fuel to the flames of persecution already raging with a frightful impetuosity'. The reason for these sermons was obvious, said the *Post*; it was because 'the converts or soupers, as they are classically termed, have given a mortal wound to the Beast and thus the proverb is strikingly exemplified: "The devil is never so angry as when you tread on his tail."'[66] The *Examiner* condemned the image as 'a woodcut of a most infamous character' and predicted that the *Post* would be prosecuted by the clergyman.[67] Fr Scollard was undoubtedly the subject of the satire, but he does not appear to have responded and no prosecution was initiated.

An anonymous letter written by a visitor to Dingle described 'priestly or Popish persecution' there. The author was 'Tell Truth', and the letter was a diatribe against Catholics and a sideswipe against 'old Protestants', who were seen as too lenient towards Catholicism, 'the deadly viper'. The author stated, 'Popery bellows dreadfully when her dominion is falling, the denunciations of her firebrands are truly awful, as are their diabolical machinations.' He referred to 'one of the priests termed Scold-hard, of cursing notoriety', and he berated Fr Divine for calumniating Rev. Gayer from his pulpit. 'Tell Truth' believed that 'popery is tottering on one knee and will ere long be driven into the broad Atlantic'; he predicted that Rev. Gayer would be 'cherished by many a fine, honest, Irish heart'.[68]

John Drummond's letters

There is evidence that the evangelicals were dissatisfied with the response of some magistrates to their claims of persecution. When seventy-one windows were broken in Rev. Gayer's house and school, 'six young scoundrels' were charged with the offence. The perpetrators were described as aged between 7 and 10.[69] They were supported in court by Fr Scollard, who succeeded in winning an adjournment of the case.[70] 'Liberal Protestants' were advised to take careful note of this evidence that priests supported the outrages inflicted on the converts.[71] The eventual outcome of the case was that each boy received a fine of tenpence or a week's imprisonment.[72] They went off cheering at what they perceived to be a light fine. The boys were described as 'ill-taught curs' in the *Post*, which told magistrates that they were too lenient and that they should 'act somewhat more summarily in their dealings with such wanton outrages'. It stated that repairs to the windows cost £2 (40s), but the six fines totalled only 5s.[73]

Consideration was given to sending soldiers to Dingle, and Col Clarke of Tralee barracks, accompanied by H. Hawkshaw, county inspector of police, visited Dingle 'to engage barracks for some troops to be quartered in that locality'.[74] However, Clarke reported that there was no suitable accommodation for troops in Dingle; he thought that naval protection in the form of a war steamer with a detachment of marines on board would be best.[75]

In reports to his superiors, magistrate John Drummond, who was based in Tralee, found fault on both sides. He wrote to Edward Lucas, the under-secretary in Dublin Castle, confirming that the Dingle area had been for some time 'in an uneasy and unsatisfactory state' and that the cause was 'religious disputes and quarrels' over conversions. He described Fr Scollard as 'a young and most zealous curate' who, 'in order to distinguish himself and to check any further changes, appears to be acting in a very exciting and improper manner'.[76]

Drummond was more critical of Rev. Gayer's actions and his 'superabundant zeal to make proselytes to his own faith'. He wrote, 'I have reason to think that in his abhorrence of popery, he has brought to bear motives and influences which ought never to be employed in so solemn, so sacred and so delicate a subject as a man's religious belief.' Significantly, Drummond expressed criticism of Gayer's personality based on his observations of him during court cases, which 'have not infrequently been conducted by him in a manner disrespectful to the magistrates presiding and unbecoming the character and conduct of a clergyman'. There are few glimpses of Gayer's personality in the records, but observations like Drummond's suggest that his manner was arrogant and abrasive.

Drummond's comments on the Dingle converts were also significant:

The <u>worldly condition</u> of those persons is materially and manifestly improved; this looks very like bribing and hence the name of <u>soupers</u> generally given to these persons. It is this general and prevailing, and I am afraid, <u>not altogether unfounded</u>, belief that gives the intensity and bitterness to that utter scorn with which these reported converts are, for the most part, regarded by their Roman Catholic brethren. They are believed and universally assailed with the charge of <u>'selling their souls'</u> as they term it. Nor is it to be overlooked that among so poor and destitute a population as that of Dingle, a very small degree of benefit, whether in the shape of a comfortable house, rent-free, or in the shape of even, regular and steady employment is, of itself, sufficient to induce many miserable creatures to profess a faith very different from what they really believe.[77]

Undoubtedly, the issue of whether the conversions were sincere or not was difficult for contemporaries to assess, but magistrate Drummond's view – that it looked very like bribery was involved – was a reasonable one. Drummond told Lucas that the persecutions and insults to which converts were subjected were 'much exaggerated' and were no more than 'annoyances and inconveniences'. He recognised that stories of persecution were useful to Gayer on his fund-raising tours throughout Britain and Ireland, 'as the means of procuring contributions which otherwise he never would obtain'.

Drummond did not anticipate any serious breach of the peace. He suggested that a war steamer based in Dingle, in place of the *Hecate*, would act as 'a measure of salutary precaution' and a check on the zealots on both sides.[78] The security of Lord Ventry and Rev. Gayer had already been provided for, and he believed that the authorities could not do any more. He expressed confidence in the ability of his fellow magistrates, Mr Hussey and Mr Hickson, to deal with any occurrences.

Drummond wrote again on 12 March about the grievances of converts.[79] This was in response to a request from Edward Lucas, who asked him to provide information on whether the converts 'experience more difficulties than other persons in purchasing in the market or otherwise the necessary articles of consumption for daily use'.[80] Drummond informed Lucas that exclusive dealing originated in 'some hint or recommendation' from the Catholic priests, and Fr Scollard in particular, but it had been 'short-lived and altogether unsuccessful, as such attempts usually are'. It was Drummond's considered opinion that exclusive dealing, 'imperfect and defective as it appears to have been during that short period of its feeble existence, is now at an end'.

In another significant observation, Drummond stated that some Catholics were 'determined not to permit themselves to be dictated to, even by their priests, in a matter that they most justly and properly conceived the priests had no right or proper authority to intermeddle with'. Drummond was highly sceptical of the converts' stories of intimidation; he repeated his belief that they were presenting themselves as 'harassed and persecuted' in order 'to excite the sympathy and draw forth the <u>pecuniary aid</u> of persons who sympathise in their imaginary afflictions' – people who lived far away and were not in a position to establish the truth of the claims.[81] Drummond's correspondence was private, but it would have had a powerful impact if it had been public.

Such was the atmosphere of toxic mistrust and tension that prevailed in Dingle in March 1845, when a widely publicised libel case taken by Charles Gayer against the *Kerry Examiner* was heard at the Spring Assizes in Tralee.

16. The great libel trial: Rev. Charles Gayer v. the *Kerry Examiner*

In November 1844, the fiery Patrick Robert Byrne wrote a highly intemperate assessment of the Protestant mission in west Kerry, under the heading 'Infamous perversion of facts as well as of persons in Dingle':

> It is really astonishing to what extreme lengths the spirit of falsehood and fabrication will carry the hypocritical dealers in cant, the whole tribe of pharisaical traffickers in tea, tracts and fraud. In fact, so frequent are the lies, so accumulated are the impostures uttered and resorted to by all and each of these false teachers, these wolves in sheeps' clothing, and the unfortunate dupes that compose their flock, that if we could wield as many pens simultaneously as there are quills in a porcupine, we should be able to meet the one-hundredth part of them, so as to refute the one and expose the infamy contained in the other [...] A lie is never out of place or out of season with them; in summer and winter, in autumn and spring it blossoms on their lips and in every climate of the world they expect to gather in its fruits and gather in its golden harvest.[1]

This editorial was a response to a report in the *Belfast Commercial Chronicle* of a meeting in Belfast. Charles Gayer was supposed to speak at the meeting as part of a fund-raising tour on behalf of the Dingle mission, but he was unable to attend because of illness. Byrne took delight in declaring, 'We have the delinquent by the ear and, sick as it appears he is, we bring him back to Kerry to punish him here also for the lie, provided the sickness with which he is already visited as if by a superior power, will permit him to revisit the former seat of his fanaticism and fraud.'

The lie of Charles Gayer, according to Byrne, was the claim that eight hundred people in Dingle had converted from Catholicism to Protestantism. Byrne challenged this figure and quoted Lt Clifford's claim that the number of converts was 250. The discrepancy in figures was easily explained: Gayer referred to the wider area of west Kerry, whereas Clifford referred to Dingle town only. Byrne went on to claim that Gayer's illness was as a result of his lie: like the biblical Ananias, who was struck dead when he lied, Gayer was struck down by a vengeful God.

At the fund-raising event in Belfast, Rev. William McIlwaine of St George's church spoke on behalf of Gayer. McIlwaine displayed some items he called 'curious appendages' as examples of Catholic practices.[2] These included scapulars and badges of the order of St Joseph. The *Examiner* added that other items were 'rude crucifixes and some beads' and a stole (part of a priest's vestments) which belonged to Denis Leyne Brasbie. McIlwaine also read from Catholic pamphlets, recited a ballad written about Brasbie and read one of Brasbie's letters to his former parishioners.

Gayer's health recovered, and he proceeded to Edinburgh on his speaking tour. Byrne resumed his attack on the man he termed 'an itinerant impostor [...] endeavouring to sustain his disreputable career in the districts of Dingle and Ventry [...] the scriptures in the hand and the tongue heavily encumbered with lies'.[3] The Bible was being used by 'remorseless villains who thumb over its sacred pages for diabolical purposes', wrote Byrne. He condemned Gayer's 'disreputable career' as 'a self-styled minister of heaven' and the 'abominable system of lying' that he promoted. 'We followed this Gayer to Belfast', wrote Byrne, 'and detected him in a lie.' The notice advertising Gayer's meeting in Gibb's Royal Hotel on Prince's Street in Edinburgh was reprinted in the *Examiner*. It announced that Gayer would give details of 'the work of reformation [...] where a Roman Catholic priest and eight hundred persons have left the church of Rome'. This notice, according to Byrne, made it appear that 'one fine morning, a priest and 800 Catholics marched in a body beyond the jurisdiction of the "Popish priests" and took up their abode with the soup-bloated tribe encamped within the precinct of the Dingle colony of traitors to their faith, their souls and their maker.'[4] These reports were the last straw for Charles Gayer, and they were the basis of a libel case that was heard in Tralee courthouse in March 1845.

P.R. Byrne had ample opportunity to apologise and settle the dispute, but at first he showed no inclination to do so. When proceedings were initiated in January 1845, he announced, 'We have been served with a writ from the Court of Exchequer, at the suit of the Rev. Charles Gayer – holy, meek and patient man.' Byrne claimed that he was mystified as to the cause for complaint; he defiantly resolved to continue to expose Gayer's 'fanatical doings' and the 'infamy, corruption and wickedness' of the proselytising campaign. Byrne referred to the converts 'seated round the great pot whose greasy contents they had been so long swilling'. He disparaged those who provided the evangelicals with financial support as 'the old gulls in petticoats and the old gulls in pantaloons [who] continued with a bountiful hand to pour the good things of this life into the midst of the pious crew'.[5]

Three weeks later, Byrne was more conciliatory, possibly under legal advice. He conceded that the articles published in November contained 'language which in moments of cool reflection we certainly should not have penned and for which we hasten to express our regret'. He outlined the pressures on him as a busy newspaper editor, 'It is written against time, and therefore we are deprived of the opportunity of amending what we may consider faulty, what may be considered harsh or intemperate. We fling off our thoughts in the warm influence of the moment and it is then not to be wondered at, if sometimes we wound where we never intended it.'[6] After the repeated insults directed at the evangelicals, the apology rang hollow; Charles Gayer continued with the case.

Tralee courthouse, March 1845.

The libel case was heard under Judge Johnson in Tralee courthouse over three days, 13 to 15 March 1845. The court was in session from 9.00 a.m. to 9.00 p.m. on the first two days, and the verdict was given at 5.00 p.m. on the third day. Rev. Charles Gayer sued the *Kerry Examiner* and its editor, Patrick Robert Byrne, for libel and claimed damages of £1,000 in respect of two articles in the *Kerry Examiner* on 22 and 26 November 1844. Gayer was represented by Mr Freeman, Q.C.; Mr Bennett, Q.C.; Mr Keller, Q.C.; and Mr Leahy, while Byrne was represented by Sir Colman O'Loghlen, Bart.; Right Hon. David Pigott, Q.C.; and Mr Gallwey. The special jury was composed of six Catholics and six Protestants, and these were named in the report of the trial. The foreman was Bryan McSwiney, a Catholic.

The case was reported in detail in an 'extraordinary edition' of the *Tralee Chronicle* on 15 March 1845, the day on which the trial ended. It was surprising that the *Chronicle*, which usually devoted little attention to the religious conflict in west Kerry, was the paper that reported the case most fully. The editor was justifiably proud of 'the fullness and fidelity' of the lengthy report, which involved 'considerable expense' and stretched his resources to the limit. He paid tribute to his hard-working staff, and apologised for some typographical errors that arose as a result of dealing with 'a ponderous mass of manuscript'.[7] The value of having such an authentic account was not lost on the evangelicals; they promptly published the *Chronicle* account as a pamphlet entitled *Persecution of Protestants in Ireland in the year 1845, as detailed in a full and correct report of the trial at Tralee, on*

Thursday, March 20th, 1845 for a libel on the Rev. Charles Gayer, with preface and appendix. This was published in Dublin by Philip Dixon Hardy and Sons, of the Religious Book and Tract Depository for Ireland. This company shared the same address as the Priests Protection Society at 23 Upper Sackville Street, Dublin. The date cited in the title was incorrect, as the trial took place from 13 to 15 March.[8] Philip Dixon Hardy was a prominent evangelical, and author and editor of the *Dublin Penny Journal*.

It was strange (but not remarked on at the time) that although Gayer and Byrne were in court, neither gave evidence, nor did any Catholic clergyman. The trial generated great interest; clergymen of both persuasions attended, as did 'a vast number of ladies of the first respectability', something that was regarded as unprecedented in Tralee.[9] Bennett began by relating the history of Charles Gayer's work in Dingle and drew attention to 'his exemplary conduct, his piety, his charity and benevolence in that country'. Bennett said that in Gayer's efforts to expand his mission by building churches and schools, 'it would almost appear as if the Almighty had, with especial favour, crowned his labour' and that 'there was neither terror, threat, force nor any other means but simply the exertion of charity'. Bennett told the court that Gayer 'fed the hungry, clothed the naked and gave comfort to persons of all persuasions [...] he was beloved of persons of all persuasions in that district.'

Prosecution witnesses

Twenty witnesses were called by the prosecution, including five Anglican ministers and one Presbyterian minister. Rev. Thomas Moriarty was the first witness, and his cross-examination was lengthy, taking up six pages of the pamphlet. He said that he was connected to the Irish Society for ten years – that he was 32 years old and had converted at the age of 18, well before the arrival of Rev. Gayer. He was a confident and articulate witness, and his statement summarised the progress of the Protestant mission up to then. Moriarty confirmed that he was curate of Ventry and Dunquin since 1838, and that he had spoken at public fund-raising meetings in various locations in Ireland and in England, including Limerick, Belfast, Cork, Dublin, London, Derby, Lincoln, Liverpool, Bedford and Bath.

Moriarty told the court that Gayer was rector of Ventry, curate of Kilmalkedar, rector of Dunurlin and assistant curate of Dingle. He listed the buildings that had been constructed since Gayer's arrival: a church, schoolhouse and parsonage in Dunurlin; a schoolhouse at Kilmalkedar, attached to the residence of the master; a schoolhouse, a master's residence and a room for the clergyman at Dunquin; a glebe, school and church at Ventry; a schoolhouse and master's residence on the Blasket Island; a new schoolhouse in Dingle. Moriarty told the court that these six schoolhouses were the finest in Munster and they employed trained teachers.

Moriarty said that there were three scripture readers in Ventry and fifteen Irish teachers. In Ventry, there were thirty-eight families of converts, about 180 or 190 individuals; in Dunquin and the Blaskets combined, there were twenty-five families, about 120 people, not including those who had returned to Catholicism. In Moriarty's estimate, there were three hundred converts in total in Ventry, Dunquin and the Blasquetts, and 150 students in the schools. He proudly stated, 'Yes, all my services are in Irish: I preach in Irish, baptise children in Irish and bury the dead in Irish. I am an Irishman.'

Moriarty confirmed that eight hundred people, including men, women and children from all classes of society, had converted to Protestantism in recent years 'in the entire district of Dingle'. Cottages had been erected for the converts on account of 'their great difficulty to support themselves in consequence of persecution', when people refused to engage in business with them. As examples of the kind of persecution meted out to converts, Moriarty cited a man named Riordan who could not get sufficient business as a shoemaker and so was obliged to revert to Catholicism, then finding that his business revived. Another shoemaker named Corkery also lost most of his customers when he converted.

Moriarty said that he was not aware of any threats to the lives of converts, but that he had experienced fear for his own life when he was 'pelted, abused, hooted at and surrounded by an excited mob'. People said of the converts that 'they were the children of the devil and hell', and that ''twas a pity to let them pass the road.' He had seen converts 'pelted with clods and stones', and was himself subjected to 'several opprobrious names and expressions'. 'I am so accustomed to such language now that I take no notice of it,' he told the court. He was aware of one particular nickname applied to him:

> I am called 'lying Tom' (loud laughter) – if you know Irish it is 'Thomas an ehig', that is literally, 'Tom of the lies' (much laughter). I am also called 'souper' and so are other members of my family (loud laughter). We get plenty of soup there, my Lord.

In accepting that he and Gayer gave 'temporal relief' to converts, Moriarty stated that it was only because these people could not support themselves as a result of their conversion. In times of general distress, he said that they gave relief to all who were in need, 'I assisted Gayer in giving relief to all classes and in doing so we gave meal, potatoes and turf irrespective of religious persuasion. I remember the time of a storm in Dingle when Mr. Gayer repaired the boats of some fishermen and thatched their houses; these fishermen were mostly Catholics.' Moriarty acknowledged that some people asked for favours in return for conversion, including a man named Sheridan who had 'offered himself to me if I would buy him'. Moriarty spelled out his response to such cases, 'I always felt it to be my duty to admonish them and caution them against such motives.'

When asked if all the converts were from the poorer classes, Moriarty named some who were not: his own father, brother and sister, and Robert Conway Hickson (who lived in Dublin but was originally from Dingle) and his brother. Other converts named were Mr Hamilton, who was in Trinity College preparing for the ministry, and Mr Foley, who was already a minister; and finally, Peter Bodkin Hussey of Farranakilla, who was a barrister and a man of substance. Some shopkeepers were interested in converting, according to Moriarty, but few did so because it would jeopardise their businesses.

Another witness was Rev. Edward Lee Sandiford, curate of Dunurlin, who stated that there were seven families of converts in Dunurlin and fifteen in Kilmalkedar. He was aware that they were persecuted, and he also had experience of people coming to him asking what they would receive in return if they came to his church. He informed them that that was not a proper motive for converting. Sandiford accepted that he personally was not very active or successful in gaining converts but 'endeavoured to procure peace'.

Sandiford was a newcomer to the area, but Rev. Thomas Goodman was a member of a long-established family of Ballymore. He identified himself as vicar of the parish of Dunquin and perpetual curate of Dingle since 1824. He said that there were now eighty-four families of converts, comprising approximately 365 persons, in Dingle. Before those conversions, there had been 319 'old Protestants' in Dingle. In Goodman's opinion, Rev. Gayer had shown Christian charity to all people regardless of religious persuasion; he said that 'the excitement' reached a peak about three months before the trial, when 'exclusive dealing' had begun. Asked about the term 'souper', Goodman claimed that he could not say precisely what it meant, 'I think it is applied to a person who would eat meat or soup on a Friday (much laughter.)' He also gave a surprisingly blunt answer to a question about the

Irish Society, 'I know nothing whatever of the Irish Society.' This assertion is difficult to accept, as he must have known of its activities. Perhaps he meant that he had no involvement with the society, or that he did not wish to answer questions about it. Goodman said that he did not think that there was an organised system of conversion in the area, and he did not know how much money was spent on conversions. He had heard of only one family who had returned to Catholicism, adding, 'I suppose the reason of that is because they were not sincere.' Goodman seems to have been a reluctant and uncomfortable witness.

Dr R. Hickson, a Catholic, was one of the Dingle dispensary doctors and also physician to Rev. Gayer. He stated that he was not aware of any particular acts of kindness by Gayer, although he had heard people speak about them. He was aware that converts were called 'soupers' and 'all kind of names', but in his opinion, converts were 'generally very unoffending' and he had never seen them as 'aggressors'.

James Gloster was a convert and scripture reader who lived in Dunquin. He worked for Rev. Moriarty and received £24 a year. He told the court that there were twenty-five convert families between Dunquin and the Blasket Island. Before his conversion seven years earlier, he had worked as a teacher for Fr Casey, with whom he had a good relationship. Gloster was teaching the children of the Coast Guards when he was attracted to Protestantism. He acquired a copy of the Douai Bible with permission from Fr Casey and said that 'it was the word of God that led me to seek for myself from that out.' Some relatives of Gloster also converted, and their livelihoods as masons and fishermen were badly affected. Gloster gave graphic details of the treatment he experienced from other acquaintances after his change of religion:

> When I became a convert, the thatch of my house was taken off and my windows were broken. Those who were my dearest friends became my bitterest enemies and none of them would speak to me. One of my cousins who was once my dearest friend before I left the Church of Rome and who knew me from the time of my infancy is now as great an enemy to me as any of them. He passes me almost every day yet he never speaks a word to me, except he'd call out 'soup' or some other nickname after me; stones were often flung at me and clods. When I was a Roman Catholic, I was a schoolteacher and my wife a mantua-maker, but I lost the favour of my friends. My family have often stones thrown at them and are called names

too. One time I met a party of them when going home on the road. They tried to push me into the glen but I folded my arms and forced my way through them. I was one night coming from Dingle and a cousin of mine, a convert also, was with me. We went into the house of a cousin of his, who I thought was a friend of mine and they beat us. His servant boys also beat us. I have cousins that are Roman Catholic; they don't speak to me. James Kennedy is the man who would not speak to me.[10]

When asked about the sincerity of conversions in general, Gloster responded, 'I can't pry into a man's heart, but I do think none but a sincere person would conform when persecution was to the masthead.' As a scripture reader, Gloster said that he did 'not do anything else but read the word of God for those who are willing to read it, and no other exertions but that are made'.

Another man who gave evidence on behalf of Gayer was Daniel Sullivan, a scripture reader who lived in one of the colony houses in Ventry, and whose wife remained a Catholic. Michael Lynch, another scripture reader, said that there were thirty-seven houses altogether in the colonies of Dingle. J. Brosnahan was a smith and a Catholic; he stated that Charles Gayer was 'a humane man' who, during a period of distress, bought provisions and sold them at half-price to Protestants and Catholics alike. Rev. William McIlwaine of St George's church in Belfast described the items he had exhibited when he deputised for Gayer, and he read out the ballad entitled 'Brasbie's Reformation'.

The case for the defence

When Mr Pigott opened the case for the defence, he claimed that Gayer, in his lectures in Belfast and Edinburgh, implied that the eight hundred conversions happened all at once, rather than over a period of eleven years. Pigott admitted that the *Examiner* articles were written in 'exceedingly warm language' and said that Byrne had 'deep and poignant regret' for his language. He argued that Byrne had already given an ample apology for his language, and that the matters dealt with were 'legitimate subjects of commentary in the public press'. Pigott asserted that there was great public interest in the evangelical campaign in Kerry, which had become known 'through the entire empire as an extensive system of conversion of a most extraordinary and comprehensive nature'. Pigott's case was that, as an editor, Byrne had a duty and obligation to inform his readers on such matters.

Pigott quoted from the apology published in the *Examiner* of 4 February 1845, saying that it met the legal requirement of an apology at 'the earliest opportunity'. He stressed that Byrne's full apology was published in three national newspapers, including the *Freeman's Journal*, a month before the trial began, but that this was deemed inadequate and unacceptable to Gayer. Byrne was now willing to publish a further statement to the effect that his original comments were 'libellous and illegal' and that Gayer was 'incapable of any acts of lying, hypocrisy, imposture and fraud'.

Defence witnesses

Most of the witnesses who gave evidence on behalf of P.R. Byrne were sometime converts of dishonourable character. For example, Timothy Lynch admitted that, for his own advantage, he had 'humbugged' or tricked many evangelicals into believing that he was a sincere convert. He had been a National School teacher in Ballyferriter and went to Liverpool in 1841; from there, he moved to Dublin, where he met Matthew Moriarty, brother of Thomas. He was introduced to two women, Mrs Peebles and Miss Bellingham, who employed him as an Irish teacher. He freely admitted that he led the women to believe that he was 'a great Protestant'. Lynch later returned to Dingle and likewise hoodwinked Charles Gayer, who promised him a salary of £12 if he converted and became a Bible reader. At the time of the libel trial, Lynch had reverted to Catholicism; he had been employed by Fr Divine as a National School teacher since April 1844. Mr Freeman pointedly asked if he taught the 180 pupils in his school about matters of morality, truth and honesty.

Another disreputable witness was Maurice Power, a fish-jolter or trader. He said that he was approached by one of Mr Gayer's scripture readers with the promise of money to buy a horse. Power said that he worked for Gayer for twenty weeks without pay and concluded, 'I would not go with them "soupers" now for all the money they could give me, that's all I have to say about the set, and a bad set they are.' Power became confused and incoherent under questioning; he stated, 'Sure 'tisn't for the sake of my soul I went at all; 'twas for the sake of the bribe.' Pressed by Freeman, Power broke into Irish but was told, 'Come, none of your Irish here.' The editor of the *Chronicle* added his comment on this exchange, saying that Power 'spoke with volubility that actually stunned the ears of his hearers'.

Power said that when he converted, he had asked for a horse, because 'nothing less than a horse would satisfy me.' Asked if he would sell his soul to any religion for a horse, he replied, 'I would, I might stop along with you for two or three days.' He also got potatoes, and when he was asked if he had paid for them, his answer was, 'Arrah, why should I, sir, whin I was going to church? (roars of laughter).' Power said that his daughter went to church 'because she got clothes for it'. When Power was asked if he considered it a bad thing to change from being a Catholic to being a Protestant, he paused; the reporter of the *Chronicle* observed, 'Here the witness hesitated, cast a glance at the Rev. Mr. Divine, the Roman Catholic priest of Dingle, comically scratched his head and evidently appeared in a complete "fix".' When Mr Freeman told him to stop looking around at others in the court, Power replied, to more loud laughter, 'Sure, I see yourself looking about you every way.' When Power was stepping down, he addressed Fr Divine in Irish. The *Chronicle* reporter understood him to say, 'If they'd take it in Irish, Father, I'd give it to them finely.' The suggestion throughout was that these witnesses had been coached and were being closely observed in court by Fr Divine. It was pointed out that Fr Divine, from time to time, consulted with counsel for Byrne.

The farcical exchanges continued with the evidence of John Power, another fish-jolter who attended Protestant services for a time. He was asked, 'What induced you to go to church?' His reply was, ''Twas my belly, of course, what else?' When asked what had induced him to go back to Mass, Power answered, 'What would make me but the love of God?' Power admitted to being a drunkard, and when asked if he was ever called a souper, he responded, 'Wisha, faith, sir, it is a good name and I'd be glad to be called it every day if I got a good bowl of it.' According to Power, he received £5 or £6 in total from Gayer, as well as clothes, potatoes, a free house and the promise of a horse if he continued to attend the Protestant church.

James Kearney (Carney), who was a retired sailor and member of the Coast Guard, gave an account of his wife's experience. The couple lived in the colony on John Street. When Mrs Kearney became very ill, she reverted to Catholicism and asked for Fr Scollard to visit her to administer the last rites. According to James Kearney, when Rev. Gayer heard this he told the woman, 'Mrs Kearney, that greasy oil can be of no more service to your soul than it could be to the sole of my boot.' Gayer sent 'keepers' to stand on guard in case of further visits by the priest. Kearney told the court that he 'became a Protestant in order to get work – 'twas not from any great conscience. I kept up the pretence for two years and latterly I was getting fond of it.' James Kearney got a house and a small garden but said, 'My conscience changed when I did not get the money.' By the time of the court case, he was a Catholic again; he said that it was Fr Scollard who had told him to attend the court that day, although his wife was near death.

Thomas Horgan of Ventry was also a Protestant for a time. He received money from Rev. Gayer and a house rent-free from Rev. Moriarty, and he stated that 'it was these advantages induced me to go with them and stay with them.' Other witnesses such as Edward Hussey gave specific details of money received 'for going to church'. Maurice Ferriter of Dunurlin said that he had heard a convert refer to the Catholic Church as 'the whore of Babylon' and the Pope as the anti-Christ.

Mr Freeman's address to the jury

In summing up for the prosecution, Mr Freeman spoke for an incredible four and a half hours; his speech was a tour de force, taking up twenty-five pages of the pamphlet. From the passion of his delivery and the care he took to persuade the jury, it seems clear that the outcome of the trial was not taken for granted and Freeman was leaving nothing to chance. He was an accomplished orator, and his words must have made a huge impact on the jury. He deplored the scandalous, divisive aspects of the conflict between the Christians of Dingle:

> They worship the same God, they admit the same doctrine, they recognise the same authority, they approach the same temple, they enter the same portal, they may rise to the same summit by different staircases, yet they look forward to the same ultimate goal of hope.

Freeman argued that vigorous debate on religious matters should not stoop to personal insults. The position of editor of a newspaper was a responsible one, he said, 'but the more serious his duty, the more should always be the caution with which he exercises that duty. No man is to be made the sport, the object of insult, of injury, of anonymous slander, of vindictive imputation which he has no means to repel.' He quoted more extracts from the *Kerry Examiner*, written in the febrile months of January and February 1845, arguing that Byrne was not at all repentant and that 'the violent mercurial heat of his temperament continues unabated'.

Freeman's address had many rhetorical flourishes:

> Gracious God! Is this a free country? Are we to be borne down by the tyranny of anybody or the oppression of persons of any persuasion? [...] If Roman Catholic clergymen were hooted and

pelted through the Protestant districts of the north, insulted, reviled, called by indecent names so disgusting they could not be mentioned in a court of justice, what would be the feeling of Roman Catholics?

He did not hold back on his attack on Byrne himself, referring to his 'double-distilled malignity', 'deliberate malice' and 'utter heartlessness'. Byrne was 'a miserable scribbler' who had written about Gayer 'with all the venom an exasperated mind can feel'. Freeman expressed outrage at one particular insult that Byrne directed against Gayer, which read, 'His indeed is a course of life in which all respect for truth and decency seems to be studiously sacrificed for the sake of the daily sustenance which his animal wants desire.' Nevertheless, Freeman also conceded that Byrne was capable of 'eloquent writing and beautiful imagery'.

The witnesses for the defence were scorned and ridiculed by Freeman, who posed the question, 'Gracious God! Is there a man on earth who could believe their testimony?' He had particular criticism for Timothy Lynch, 'That being, whose words excited unmingled, withering disgust in the minds of every one who heard him, he is now the instrument of education, of instruction of the rising generation! [...] Can that man administer instruction to the poor, steeped as he is in the moral filth of infamy and crime?' He described Lynch as 'a double-sold apostate, a foul liar to his God and an abominable perjurer'. Referring to the defence witnesses in general, Freeman asked the jury, 'Gentlemen, when they admit themselves to be so debased, so blackened, so darkened, with every crime that can debase man, can you think of attaching the slightest credence to what they say?'

Judge Johnson's address

Freeman was not above flattery, and stated, 'I have never known a corrupt, an unfair or a dishonest verdict to come from a Kerry Jury.' The judge's charge to the jury began with praise for the zeal and efficiency of the legal teams on both sides, which he saw as a confirmation of 'the high reputation of the Munster bar'. He cautioned the jury that they were adjudicating only on the libel issue and on whether the apology offered was prompt and full. They were not adjudicating on 'this movement of reformation, as it is called' in west Kerry, and the case was not about the numbers of converts, their motives for conversion or whether witnesses were truthful or not. He explained the law of libel and echoed Freeman's expression of confidence in the jury, saying that he had never had a complaint against a Kerry jury. It was clear that Judge Johnson was expecting a guilty verdict.

Verdict and reaction

After two hours of deliberation, the jury found Patrick Robert Byrne guilty on all counts. He was ordered to pay £40 damages and sixpence in costs. The final costs and expenses were calculated later and came to over £450, since Byrne was liable for the fees and expenses of the legal teams on both sides. This was a potentially crippling debt for him. One juror said they would have awarded £1,000 damages except that they did not believe the defendant could pay this amount. A second jury member agreed, but another interjected, 'That is not the feeling of all the jurors.' The fact that six Catholics were on the jury would 'serve to silence an ancient calumny on the Irish Catholics', according to the *Cork Examiner*.[11]

Rev. William McIlwaine was pleased at the verdict, 'The independent honest verdict of the twelve men who tried this case has set a seal to these attested facts which no sophistry can, to any reflecting mind, either mystify or falsify.' McIlwaine described the court proceedings as taking place

> under the eye of not a few of the Romish priesthood, whose scrutinising and not-to-be-mistaken glance was fixed unceasingly on all the parties concerned, from the foreman and the jury to the trembling, pallid, perjured witnesses, who left the table of testimony with a hardly suppressed groan of disgust and indignation from all in whose breasts even a lingering love of truth and reverence for an oath survived.[12]

McIlwaine hoped that one result of the trial would be that the Catholics of Kerry would not be 'so heartless and unchristian' as to allow the persecution of Protestants to continue.[13] He noted that on the first day of the trial there were excited, noisy crowds around the court house, but by the last day, 'shame appeared to have taken possession of them, and well it might. All parties were silent and still.'[14]

In the introduction to *Persecution of Protestants*, the pamphlet based on the *Chronicle*'s coverage of the trial, Philip Dixon Hardy described the libel of Gayer as one part of a 'disgraceful system of persecution [...] whose object obviously was, and we regret to add, still is, to exterminate freedom of religious opinion in that remote district'.[15] Hardy posed this question:

> Could it be believed that there was any part of her Majesty's dominions in which men can be, and daily are, with impunity, ruthlessly and unceasingly insulted, oppressed and injured for no

other reason than that they have ventured to think for themselves and have publicly conformed to the religion by law established in England and Ireland?

He asserted that

> the whole of this dreadful and disgraceful state of things is attributable *to the preaching of the priests of the Roman Catholic Church from their altars* and that when the Roman Catholic priests do not excite their flocks against the Protestant converts, their Roman Catholic neighbours are well disposed to them and they live in peace and goodwill with each other.[16]

Hardy was dismayed that a grant of £28,000 a year for Maynooth seminary had just been approved by parliament, supporting the training of priests such as those in west Kerry.[17] He also noted that Tralee was full of priests on the first day of the trial, but by the end they had all left.[18]

Newspaper reaction

Patrick Robert Byrne responded defiantly to the trial verdict. 'One thing is certain', he wrote, 'the system is exploded and its depravity exposed.'[19] He was bloodied but unbowed, 'We have been mulcted in heavy costs, but our moral triumph has been great, and therein we find both joy and consolation.' As he saw it, 'bribery of the most shameful character, hypocrisy and dissimulation in all their most depraved forms, were exhibited to the view of the astonished audience [...] The veil by which they had hitherto been so industriously concealed had been torn off.'[20] Byrne's strategy was to depict what was undeniably a disaster as a propaganda triumph, and he was pleased to see that the issue of press freedom came to the fore. He acknowledged the support of other newspapers, 'Our provincial brethren in particular are standing by us with devoted energy and zeal [...] They have all stood by us, honourably and nobly, in our hour of anxiety, difficulty and trouble.'[21]

The *Cork Examiner* was a staunch supporter of Byrne. It railed against the 'five-shilling converts' and 'the apostles who substitute soup for scripture and flesh-meat on Friday for faith'. Describing the extreme poverty of the Dingle area, the paper asked how its inhabitants could be expected to resist 'tempters with gold in their hands, holding out visions of good food, good houses, good clothes, with a horse, a cow or a pig'.[22] It commended Byrne for striking 'a vigorous blow at an infamous and demoralising *system*', and saw him as 'a bold, honest and intrepid public servant' who had rendered 'a great and lasting service to the community'.[23] It differentiated between the motives of the evangelicals and the system they adopted:

> Why, if this be the modern mode of spreading the Gospel, the Bank of Ireland would beat the bench of bishops, a potato store would purchase the whole flock of the Dingle apostle, and an old clothes shop would be more than a match for ten Gayers and a score of Moriartys! Can this farce last? Is it possible that this humbug can any longer be sustained by the credulity of even the most arrogant gulls. Mind! It is of the system we speak, for with the motives of any reverend gentleman we dare not meddle.

The *Cork Examiner* recommended that Catholics everywhere should be made aware of 'this religious man-trap [...] and the snares of the tempter. The Catholic community must bestir themselves and crush this evil before it spreads this poison.'[24]

Byrne argued that the judge's charge to the jury was 'one-sided' and inappropriate, 'Every point in our favour was omitted, every point that could be made to tell against us was twisted and twisted again, tossed and turned about, made to assume every phase and form to produce the "desired effect" in the jury box.'[25] An echo of this criticism of the judge could be seen in the *Freeman's Journal* report, which pointed out, without comment, that Judge Johnson had served as secretary of the Kildare Place Society for some years.[26] The suggestion was that he was therefore biased in favour of the evangelicals.

Byrne was pleased to publish numerous extracts from supportive newspapers. The *Waterford Chronicle* wrote in forceful language about 'the filth of the malicious tongues of infidel iconoclasts who vent their felon blasphemies against the holiest influences of the ancient religion'. It commended Byrne by saying, 'If any man ever deserved the thanks of a nation, Mr. Byrne does.' This paper also suggested that the Catholics on the jury could have prevented the guilty verdict.[27] The *Dublin Monitor* wrote that when Charles Gayer came to Dingle, he worked among fishermen, 'who are proverbially ignorant'. It continued, 'They are that class in society who are most uneducated and most superstitious and to these qualities was added in the case of Dingle, the extremest indigence.' The *Monitor* concluded:

So long as there is plenty of money, so long will persons be willing to take the advantages which it affords; but when that fails, the whole system falls to the ground. It is impossible under such circumstances to look on the Dingle mission in any other light than the fabric of a day which falls to the ground when the scaffolding is removed [...] Money can do all things except make an honest man out of a rogue. Money has done much in Dingle – more than the Bible we may safely say.[28]

The *Belfast Vindicator* announced that 'Belfast will take its own distinguished place in this as in every cause of religion and of country. The *Kerry Examiner* must not, shall not, be put down.' It opened a subscription in support of Byrne and his 'debt of honour and of virtue', and asked:

> Is it not horrible that in whatever part of the country want and desolation set in, demons in human shape will be found to follow in the wake of famine, and buy for money, for a mess of pottage, immortal souls which they train in irreligious hypocrisy and a profane traffic of the rights of conscience?[29]

The Cork-based *Southern Reporter* praised Byrne for 'the fidelity of his paper to the cause of the people and his honest exposure of a vile system of demoralising imposture'.[30] It believed that money was at the root of all the conversions in Dingle, and advised, 'Misery is a market in which any religious capitalists may traffic [...] Let the Gayers and Moriartys be left to depend upon texts of scripture and nothing else, and it will then be seen what progress they will make, and what fidelity they will find among those who were seduced by their captivating eloquence.'[31] The *Freeman's Journal* was pleased to acknowledge receipt of £5 from a Mr Lynch in aid of Byrne, and the *Waterford Chronicle* acknowledged £5 contributed by Sir Charles Wolseley of Wolseley, Staffordshire, who expressed his 'disgust of the reptiles of Dingle who disgrace the name of Christian'.[32] The *Mayo Telegraph*, the *Galway Vindicator*, the *Tipperary Vindicator* and the *Kilkenny Journal* were other newspapers that supported Byrne.[33]

The Tablet

A correspondent who signed himself 'D.S.L.' wrote from Killarney to *The Tablet*, an English Catholic journal, in late March. He described the revelations at the trial as so alarming and disgusting that 'they must fill every true friend of morality and religion with sadness.' The writer was certain that reports of the trial would be circulated widely in the evangelical press, and he wanted to inform Catholics and 'the dispassionate portion of the Protestant world' in England about the trial, as an 'antidote to poison'.

D.S.L. began with an overview of the Dingle area, 'one of the most impoverished and least improved regions of Ireland':

> It is a wild and romantic place; its majestic cliffs and sunny sands are washed by the unmingled waters of the Atlantic and it is inhabited by a hardy and thrifty race whose chief means of support is that precarious one derived from fishing. The people trace their descent from the Spaniards and there is much in their more regular features and olive complexions to sustain the tradition and distinguish them from the other races of the country. They generally speak Irish and in one of the districts where scripture light is said to have diffused itself, word of English is rarely spoken or understood.

> Before the Union, the linen trade flourished in Dingle, but the brief prosperity which native manufactures produced has only rendered subsequent decay and indigence more oppressive. The parish of Dingle contains about 7,000 inhabitants of which about 4,500 are in the town [...] Ventry – another seat of proselytism – might be described in language similar to Dingle. It is about four and a half miles to the westward. Its scenery is ruder, its population still poorer. It contains about 2,600 inhabitants. Dunurlin contains about 2,000 inhabitants.

> The principal proprietor of this district is Lord Ventry. The present lord is a zealot in religion and applies all his influence to the propagation of his own doctrines. The estate is under the management of the court of Chancery and the late agent Mr. D.P. Thompson was understood to be a gentleman equally devoted in his zeal for proselytism and was said not to have been very scrupulous in the exercise of his extensive influence to promote these views. He has lately died, but not until he had practised a long and effective control over the destinies of his unhappy people.

> Dingle was severely visited by the cholera; and two or three summers of scarcity succeeding the former fearful visitation, these poor

fishermen were cruelly wrung by famine and want. In these circumstances the benevolent dispositions of Mr. Gayer are represented as extending the hand of relief to all Christians indiscriminately [...] This open-handed benevolence, however, was not without its spiritual result, for in due time and as a consequence, we begin to find these poor creatures giving up their old faith and attaching themselves to that of Messrs. Gayer and Moriarty.[34]

D.S.L. conceded that he could not justify the language used by Byrne in his reports of November 1844, but he pointed out that Byrne had offered an apology. He explained that Byrne was brought 'before the wealth and might of the Protestant power of the land', and noted that five clergymen and three scripture readers gave evidence in court. He observed, 'The sleek and well combed appearance of these reverend crusaders better would have graced the lawn of the cathedral pulpit than suited the coarse mantle and slender scrip of the self-sacrificing self-subduing missionary. The evidence of these persons is naturally directed to extol the charity, meekness and humility each of the other.' He commented on Rev. McIlwaine, 'This Belfast parson had quite the air and perfume of a lady's man.'

In summing up aspects of the evidence given, D.S.L. took particular exception to a statement attributed to Charles Gayer, and he vividly conveyed its impact on those present in the gloomy courthouse:

I can never forget the impression with which I and every Catholic in the court heard that part of Kearney's evidence in which he states the spiritual advice and ghostly comfort with which Mr. Gayer approached the death-bed of his repenting victim. 'That greasy oil,' says he, 'Mrs. Kearney, is no more use for the salvation of your soul than for the sole of my boot.' The court at this period was crowded to suffocation. It was seven o'clock in the evening and the darkness was relieved by the dimness of a few flickering tallow candles when this evidence of blasphemy and heretical ignorance upon a most sacred rite of Catholic worship fell upon the jury. Every Catholic present thrilled with horror and alarm, which the very darkness and silence rendered almost more palpable![35]

D.S.L. admitted that witnesses for the defence were untrustworthy and disreputable, and that they had not improved 'either in morality or in religious knowledge by their long sojourn under the tents of cedar', but he nevertheless chose to believe their statements about their 'pseudo-conversions'. He wrote of the evangelicals that 'it is for the children that they angle – the parents are but the bait'. He pointed out how 'schools and churches and residences for clergymen spring up as if by magic from the resources furnished by all parts of the empire', and he urged Catholics to be equally generous in responding to the challenges presented by the Bible campaign in west Kerry. The bishop of Kerry had set an example, he wrote, by setting up 'Presentation convents for the education of poor girls at his own sole expense almost in every hamlet of his extensive diocese'. D.S.L. ended by expressing his hope that religious orders such as the Redemptorists or Christian Brothers would respond to his call.

William O'Neill Daunt

William O'Neill Daunt was a convert to Catholicism, a close associate of Daniel O'Connell's and a prominent Repeal supporter. As the trial was taking place in Dingle, he was about to publish a book, and he took this opportunity to add a long footnote stating that it was only because of 'the rigid acceptation of the law' that Byrne was convicted. He highlighted the evidence that people had received inducements from Gayer and Moriarty; these were 'the uncontradicted oaths of competent witnesses', he wrote. O'Neill Daunt referred to the money, free houses and employment that were given to converts, but he chose to pass over the dubious moral character of the witnesses. He believed that the trial had exposed wholesale bribery by the evangelicals, and he scorned the 'spiritual recklessness' and the 'ludicrous character of the proselytising system'. O'Neill Daunt further claimed that fifteen Dingle converts, after they had found their circumstances had not improved as much as they had expected, had approached the Presbyterian minister of Milltown to ask what terms he could offer them to join his congregation.[36]

Indemnity fund in aid of P.R. Byrne

Within weeks of the trial, a committee was set up to help P.R. Byrne to cover his substantial expenses. The committee was headed by Bishop Egan of Kerry, and five of the members were parish priests: Dr John McEnery, PP of Tralee and vicar-general of the diocese; Fr Thomas O'Sullivan of Killarney; Fr Eugene McCarthy of Ballyheigue; Fr B. O'Connor of Milltown; and Fr Eugene O'Sullivan of Killorglin. None of the Dingle priests were on the committee. The other members were Maurice O'Connell, MP, of Derrynane; Kean Mahony of Castlequin, Caherciveen; and Maurice Brennan.[37]

A fund was established to support Byrne, who had exposed 'a foul and unchristian system' and found himself liable for 'damages and costs to a ruinous degree'. People were urged to respond promptly, cheerfully and liberally, because 'Mr. Byrne's cause is the cause of all and each of us.' An advertisement for the fund was published in almost every issue of the *Examiner* over several months. The first parish collection took place outside Lixnaw church in north Kerry in early April; £6 9s 6d was collected.[38] Various parish priests sent in donations, and a man was sent around the county to collect subscriptions.[39] A list showed that over £43 had been subscribed from people 'in and around Killarney', including £5 each from Bishop Egan, Maurice O'Connell and John O'Connell of Grena.[40] Byrne declared himself flattered and gratified by the support he received; he grandiosely claimed that the cause was much greater than him or his paper, 'It is the cause of religion and morality throughout Ireland against scheming hypocrites who take advantage of the poverty of our fellow creatures.'[41] Byrne was particularly 'proud, joyful and happy' to announce that the Liberator, Daniel O'Connell, had contributed £5 to the fund.[42]

However, Byrne expressed great disappointment at the contributions from the Dingle area, especially since he had expected that there would be 'grateful reminiscence of our suffering, now for the second time, for the well-being of the good people of Dingle'.[43] He was here referring to his two convictions for libel. The priests of west Kerry, Frs Divine, Halpin, Scollard and Healy, contributed a total of £7 17s, while S. McKenna and 'a friend' gave £1 each, but no other individual subscribers in west Kerry were listed. According to Byrne, the amount collected from Dingle was barely enough to cover the costs of transporting the witnesses from there to Tralee for the trial. 'MUCH, MUCH MORE INDEED WAS EXPECTED FROM DINGLE,' he wrote in upper case.[44] A parish priest in north Kerry sent £2 15s from his poor parishioners, saying that 'they feel ashamed of those who have remained back and never will they forget or forgive the ingratitude of Dingle to you who fought so bravely for them and for the county.'[45] This lack of financial support from Dingle was surprising. It suggests that the strident campaigning of P.R. Byrne and the *Kerry Examiner* was not widely supported in west Kerry, or that people may have been weary of the continuing war of words between the Christian denominations. Ultimately, Byrne lodged £253 12s 6d with the county sub-sheriff to cover expenses related to the trial; he informed readers that £200 was still outstanding.[46]

There was no evidence of any moderation in P.R. Byrne's language after the libel case. He continued with attacks on converts, including an article headed 'The arch-soupers at their "greasy" work again'. This feature copied a report from the *Southern Reporter*, claiming that Gayer and Moriarty had gone to Cork to raise funds but had met with little success. The article stated that the 'reformation' was 'at a standstill' in Dingle, and had received 'a blow from which it cannot recover'.[47] Gayer and Moriarty came back from Cork with no money, but with supplies of soap, candles, madder and hemp, leather, shovels, wax, awls, knitting needles and yarn. These everyday items were examples of goods that the converts could not buy in Dingle shops. Byrne gloated that matters were 'looking blue for the mission in Dingle'.[48] He later wrote, 'We have given a fatal stab to proselytism and it is to us no small source of delight to witness its convulsive heavings, its writhings, its throes and agonies.'[49]

Other reactions to the libel trial

Referring to the composition of the jury, the *Post* believed that Gayer 'could hardly have had a more adverse jury' but the weight of evidence made a guilty verdict inevitable. It claimed that the trial vindicated 'the purity of the Dingle colony'. The paper also added that some Protestants, who had formerly suspected that bribery was involved in the Dingle conversions, were influenced by the revelations at the trial and 'are now changed from that state of lukewarmness unto zealous partisans of the good cause'. The *Post* considered some individual witnesses and concluded:

> It is indeed miserable sophistry to attempt to establish that all the work of conversion in Dingle and elsewhere is the result of a wholesale system of bribery because those few hypocritical scoundrels were induced from mercenary motives to become Protestants and had returned to Romanism when they found the expected supplies not forthcoming.[50]

The *Post* also stated that persecution of converts had greatly increased since the trial, and that they continued to be insulted and pelted with clods and stones as they walked through Dingle town.

The *Dublin University Magazine*, a prestigious publication, also devoted considerable attention to the libel trial. It commented, 'Ireland is ripe for conversion. This the Romish clergy well know. This is no age in which a Mass performed in an unknown tongue can be regarded by any class of people as a reasonable service.' This was written in the context of a debate on a controversial bill for the endowment of Maynooth seminary, which the magazine saw as 'an attempt to crutch up a tottering superstition'.[51]

There were references to the Tralee libel case in the House of Commons. In opposing the bill supporting Maynooth, Mr Colquhoun, MP, drew the attention of Prime Minister Robert Peel to the behaviour of the Dingle priests; he referred specifically to the evidence of Timothy Lynch.[52] P.R. Byrne delighted in being 'the humble instrument of bringing this monstrous system under the notice of the British legislature'.[53] Byrne relished all the attention given to the trial, because it was 'making havoc on the hopes and prospects of the irreligious gang' and was a sign that 'the day of reckoning is at hand.'[54]

The first indication of Rev. Gayer's reaction to the trial was in a letter written on 7 April. He stated that 'the priests are furious here at present, cursing every Sabbath the converts and any Roman Catholics who will deal with them. Not a drop of milk can now be purchased by a convert and we are obliged to purchase several cows to supply their wants and the want of milk is the greatest.'[55] It is likely that a letter to the *Achill Missionary Herald* in late April was written by Charles Gayer. The writer described the hardships of the converts in Dingle and asked, 'Is this Christianity to starve your neighbour or is it anti-Christianity? The poor Roman Catholics who have no bad feeling towards the converts, except such as is instilled by the priests' lectures, seem to feel very much the curse said to rest to the seventh generation on their children and there is much canvassing of the subject among them.' The letter went on, 'We are to be inundated by sisters of charity or sisters of mercy, and it is said a monkery is to be got up, to keep the poor Roman Catholics from reading their Bibles and selling their souls.'[56]

In a comment on the trial, Thomas Moriarty said that the evangelicals 'had come out of that fiery ordeal with honour to their cause and to themselves'. He blamed the priests for manipulating witnesses and believed that even 'the poor little editor of the paper, Paddy Byrne, was a mere puppet in their hands.' Some Catholics, he said, were surprised by the evidence presented in court, and 'the judge, the jury and court were indeed disgusted, distressed and grieved in their hearts to see such an exhibition of moral degradation.'[57]

The trial and the events that gave rise to it evoked a popular response too, as shown in this extract from a ballad by 'Foxy Pat':

> At Ventry hunger pressed me sore –
> It may be called the starving shore.

To Dingle I proceeded strait
And squatted at the Parson's gate;
I got my soup, was told to stay,
If I would go to church next day.
Reluctantly I then agreed –
'Twas hunger drove me to the deed –
And hunger makes more converts here
Than all the talk of Parson Gayer.
In Dingle I have seen strange scenes,
The town paraded by marines,
The Moriarties talking loud
And Brasbie hooted by the crowd.
Tralee assizes soon came on
And there we certainly had fun.
The soupers told the truth I vow,
Some for a horse or for a cow,
A pair of shoes, an old great coat,
Or some old boards to mend about,
Were tempted to abjure their creed
And yielded in a time of need [...]

Don't mind the lying Orange press,
The Dingle mission's great success
Is all a humbug, you will find,
And just got up to raise the wind [...]

We never can due thanks return
To honest, injured Mr. Byrne.[58]

17. In the shadow of the blight

Lady Chatterton's visit, 1838

When Georgiana Lady Chatterton visited west Kerry in 1838, the religious conflict was in its early stages, so it is perhaps understandable that she did not refer in detail to it. She was a well-travelled Englishwoman who was aware of the conflicts and divisions in Irish society, but she chose not to dwell on them in her book, *Rambles in the South of Ireland in the year 1838*. While in west Kerry, she concentrated on the scenery, the antiquities and her encounters with interesting individuals, but it is possible that her experiences there helped her to reach this general conclusion about the Irish people:

> There are faults everywhere. The Protestants, Roman Catholics, landowners and peasants, high and low, rich and poor, are all more violent, more full of party spirit, in short more angry than in any other country. It seems as if there were something in the atmosphere of Ireland which is unfavourable to the growth of common sense and moderation in its inhabitants, even those who go there with their brains stocked with that most useful quality.[1]

Two other women writers visited Corca Dhuibhne in 1845. They both referred to the religious conflict there, although neither referred to the libel trial that took place a short time before their visits. One was an American named Asenath Nicholson, and the other was Lydia Jane Fisher.

Asenath Nicholson's visit, 1845

Asenath Nicholson was a widow living in New York, where she was involved in philanthropic work. She wrote, 'It was in the garrets and cellars of New York that I first became acquainted with the Irish peasantry and it was there I saw they were a suffering people.'[2] Nicholson took the remarkable initiative to visit Ireland to see for herself what conditions were like. She arrived in May 1844, and she spent fifteen months travelling around the country, often on foot. In the opening chapter of her book, she described her departure from New York and declared her objective, 'It was not the rich, the honoured or the happy I was hoping to meet [...] It was the poor and the outcast.'[3] Nicholson was a devout evangelical, and she distributed Bibles and religious tracts as she went around the country. This meant that she was treated with suspicion by some Catholics, while her democratic principles and her open, trusting disposition made her unwelcome among some evangelical Protestants.[4]

It is clear that hospitality was a quality which Nicholson prized highly, and she was pleased to be received with great warmth and generosity in Killarney and in other parts of south Kerry. The one night she spent in Tralee was a complete contrast, however.[5] It began inauspiciously, after she made it known that she preferred private lodgings to a hotel. The house to which she was directed turned out to be 'a whiskey den' and she left immediately, but not before her gloves and handkerchief were stolen. In the second house, her sleep was disturbed by a drunken man. She spent 'a miserable night, took a miserable breakfast in a miserably dirty room' and then found that she was a victim of fraud when she tried to arrange transport to Dingle. Even with the help of a policeman and an intermediary, a resolution to the dispute could not be reached; she eventually left Tralee on foot, stubbornly walking 8 miles 'in torment, with blistered feet' before being persuaded to accept a place on a horse-drawn car. In Dingle, she stayed with the carman's sister and 'found the same accommodations, the same food, and the same kindness as in all houses of the poor'.

Asenath Nicholson arrived in Dingle on 4 April 1845 and spent ten days in the area. To her, it was 'the celebrated town of Dingle, a "city on a hill"'. The scriptural reference was to Matthew 5:14, which reads, 'You are the light of the world. A city that is set on a hill cannot be hidden.' She was clearly well aware of the evangelical campaign underway there, 'Distant as it is from all the world beside, yet it has in the last few years said to all who would hear: "Turn aside and look at me." Its bay is full of interest and its people more so.'

Nicholson gratefully accepted the offer of a tour of Dingle town by a local Catholic woman 'of much good nature and some intelligence', who first took her to visit a priest, most likely the parish priest, Fr Michael Divine. He received her with suspicion, 'His every look and taciturnity seemed to say: "What brought you here?"' She understood the reasons for his lack of warmth:

IN THE SHADOW OF THE BLIGHT

He was the first I had met who showed reserve, but Dingle had been struggling with party creeds and as the 'soupers', as the Protestant converts are called, were getting quite numerous, the priest has all his sensibilities awake to keep the prowler from making further inroads into his fold. A newcomer from a foreign country might be the 'very wolf in sheep's clothing' to beguile more of the faithful, and, as I was afterwards informed, he therefore kept more caution. I was sent empty away.[6]

Nicholson then received an invitation, sent via a gardener, to visit the wife of the rector, Catherine Gayer, identified as 'Mrs. G.'. But when Nicholson called and gave her name to a servant at the door, she was told the mistress of the house was very busy. She was perplexed and 'disgusted' at this treatment, and was walking away when she received a summons to return. Nicholson's account gives a rare view into the Gayer family home at Ballintaggart. It was, to say the least, a testy conversation between the two women. Mrs Nicholson was 'immediately asked' what her 'message to Ireland' was. After she explained it, and mentioned that she had called on the priest, the following exchange took place:

CG: And what did you call on him for? I will never go near any of them. They are a persecuting people.

AN: I thought they were the subjects we were to strive to benefit. And how can we do them good by keeping aloof?

CG: When they come to us, we always receive them kindly but we do not proselyte. Though we are accused of going after them we do not. Neither do we bribe them, as it is said of us, by feeding them and promising high wages.[7]

Mrs Gayer pointed out a man working in the field; she said that he was paid eight pence a day and was glad to have it. 'Do you call that bribing him?' she asked. Although she was a guest in the house, the spirited Nicholson responded, 'I call that oppression.' Mrs Gayer retorted, 'Well, he is glad to do it.' The guest was then asked if she made a practice of 'going among Catholics'. Her reply was that she went among the poor without distinction, and often found that she was better received by Catholics than by her fellow Protestants.

One of the peculiar aspects of the meeting of the two women was that Rev. Gayer and another man, identified only as 'Mr. C.', were present in the room but did not take part in the conversation. Nicholson acidly described the men as acting 'as if dinner were cooling and the sooner this Jesuitical spy shall have done, the better'. Nicholson was also aware that the 'tidy-looking Catholic girl' who was her guide had been left standing in the hall for an hour while she conversed with Mrs Gayer. When she asked for the girl to be given a seat or dismissed, Mrs Gayer replied, 'No matter, they always stand.' It is not clear who she meant by 'they' – it could refer to poorer people, Catholics or local people. Nicholson was honest enough to record her disappointment at not being offered a meal in the Gayer house, and she left feeling despondent:

> I was grieved, not for the personal treatment, but grieved that so noble, so apostolic a work was in the hands of those whose hospitality, whose humility, whose courteousness to strangers and whose self-denial were so far behind the principles they professed to inculcate.[8]

Nicholson's spirits were restored by her experience of a Methodist family named Jackson, with whom she lodged and found 'happy Christian love'. She visited some of the converts and was disappointed to find that their 'great change' seemed to have no deep conviction. She detected no evidence of a spiritual transformation; all they could tell her was, 'We do not worship images.' But Nicholson acknowledged that at least they had received 'the unadulterated word of God', and even if they did not fully understand it, she believed that it might have a beneficial effect at a later time.

She went on to visit the colony at Ventry, where she wrote that 'a former priest' was living. Denis Brasbie had left for Dublin by this time; she either confused Thomas Moriarty with Brasbie, or mistakenly believed that Moriarty was a former priest. On seeing some maps in the mission school, she asked the young female teacher if the girls studied geography. She was told that the maps were for the boys and that the girls were 'daughters of the lower orders' who 'must be educated according to their station'. Nicholson was critical of the teacher, saying that she could not see any evidence that her 'dark understanding had ever been enlightened by the spirit of God'. She visited some converts in their houses and later found out that they had been told not to receive her again.

On a visit to the convent school in Dingle with her friend Mrs Jackson, Nicholson found that three hundred 'children of the poor' were being taught 'in the most thorough manner', with high standards in grammar, geography, history and needlework. One of the three nuns teaching there told Nicholson, 'Though they are the children of the poor, we do not know what station God may call them to fill. We advance them as far as possible while they are with us.' The nun told the visitors that the girls in the Protestant schools learned only reading, writing and arithmetic. Mrs Jackson commented, 'What a rebuke is this on the practice of Bible Christians!'[9]

Asenath Nicholson later visited the colony of Rev. Edward Nangle in Achill, where she also met with hostility. Nangle took a dislike to her; he observed that she was 'evidently a person of some talent and education', but that her main object was 'to create a spirit of discontent among the lower orders'. He concluded, 'There is nothing in her conduct or conversation to justify the supposition of insanity and we strongly suspect that she is the emissary of some democratic and revolutionary society.'[10] Nicholson responded to this criticism by saying that she had visited Achill with the best intentions, as she had every right to do, and as a guest of Mr Nangle 'in his own parlour', she had been treated 'not merely *uncivilly* but *degradingly* and *wickedly*'.[11]

Lydia Fisher's letters, 1845

During the summer of 1845, Lydia Jane Fisher wrote a series of twelve letters to her sister describing her travels in Kerry, including Dingle and west Kerry. Lydia was a Quaker, born in the village of Ballitore, Co. Kildare, and she was the daughter of Mary Leadbeater (née Shackleton), an accomplished author and poet. Lydia was married to Joseph Fisher, a Limerick merchant and mill owner. The letters were published in book form by Webb and Chapman in Dublin in 1847.

In August 1845, Lydia Fisher sailed into Dingle from Valentia and admired the cliffs and crags at the mouth of the harbour. One cluster was known as the 'Smoothing Irons', and Lydia wrote, 'They are exactly of that form and I suppose Fion-ma-Coul's wife was wont to use them in her laundry.' She gave her sister a short account of the history of Dingle, 'seated on the hilly slopes and backed by lofty mountains'.[12] She lodged at Miss Walsh's on Green Lane, near a fine, clear spring well that many people visited during the day. In general, Lydia Fisher found a great deal of 'poverty, laziness and filth' in Dingle. She also witnessed drunkenness, and described the people as 'most primitive in their notions and habits'. She commented on the harsh living conditions and lifestyles of the people, noting, 'Yet hard as are their privations and labour, they make out time to yield observance to the claims of friendship.' One evening on a road outside the town, Lydia met about twenty young women dressed in 'holiday garments' but looking sad. She learned that eight of the women were emigrating to America, and their friends were accompanying them part of the way. It was an 'American wake'.

Lydia Fisher's first impressions of Dingle were coloured by the weather, 'A wet Sunday in Dingle! Can anything be more doleful!' She described St James's church as 'a small building with an octagon tower, turreted, that seems more suited to a baronial residence of feudal times than to an humble place of worship'. The Catholic church or chapel was larger, but it was decorated outside in what she saw as 'a paltry taste'. She passed the time watching people coming from Mass, and when she saw a funeral passing by, she remarked on the small number attending. The waiter, 'Bailly junior', told her that 'it was one of them turncoats who never had big funerals, for only their own sort went with them.' He told her that there were nearly 1,000 converts in the area, crediting the work of the Irish Society. After the religious conflict was explained to her, Fisher commented succinctly, 'Pity such excellent intentions should produce distrust and dissension.'[13]

Fisher visited the ancient sites of Kilmalkedar and Gallarus, and sheltered from the rain in 'a Protestant school for the children of "the Soupers", as the converts are called'. An old woman took great interest in the material of her gown and petticoat. 'I felt very awkward while undergoing the inspection, for I could not speak a word of Irish,' she wrote. Fisher described Ventry strand in lyrical terms:

> It is fully three miles long, firm, flat and extensive, its shores curving boldly in from the sea and its sands bright and clear. It now looked lovely under the summer sun, the lazy waves creeping gently in, and swaying the canoes and fishing boats on their tranquil waters, seeming as if its peace was never broken by a louder cry than that of the curlew or the sea-gull's plaintive wail.[14]

She found Ventry Protestant church attractive but regretted that it had no steeple, 'The clergyman's house and the school add to the dignity of this little place, which is better built and more cleanly than the neighbouring villages.' Ballyferriter also had 'a neat church and schoolhouse', but Fisher lamented that the Catholic chapel was shabby and neglected. 'I love to see all places of worship kept in respectful order and repair,' she wrote. She climbed Sybil Head and wished that she could convey to her sister 'any idea of this glorious landscape – but alas, I am not gifted with a pen of fire!' Below Sybil Head and the peaks known as the Three Sisters, Fisher saw the remains of Ferriter's Castle, which had fallen down in a western gale a few weeks earlier and was only a heap of stones. 'The people regret it very much', wrote Fisher, 'and declare that its fall portends some direful calamity to the neighbourhood.'[15]

After a fortnight in Dingle, Lydia Fisher told her sister that she regretted her earlier use of the term 'dirty Dingle' and said she must have been in 'a horrid bad humour' when she wrote it. By the end of her stay, she saw Dingle as 'this romantic little town' that would in the future 'be pictured in my mind's eye and refresh my imagination with recollections of nature's sublime handywork!'[16]

'Counter-reformation'

Although Anna Maria Thompson saw the result of the libel case as a complete vindication of Charles Gayer, she described the trial as 'in some respects very unfortunate' because of the more intense hostility it engendered towards the mission. The publicity had made a martyr of P.R. Byrne, and the Catholic Church was galvanised into a reaction.[17] One response came from a Dublin priest, Fr Andrew O'Connell, of St Michael and St John parish. He announced in July 1845 that a fund-raising committee was being established to promote Catholicism in west Kerry. He and three professional men in Dublin made up the committee: James O'Brien, Q.C., of St Stephens's Green; Thomas Galway of Lr Mount Street; and James O'Ferrall of Baggot Street.[18] Their initial statement claimed that advantage had been taken of 'the state of destitution and consequent ignorance of the population' of Dingle and west Kerry, and that 'seven or eight hundred individuals have been seduced from the faith of their forefathers.' It explained that 'men of considerable talents, intimately acquainted with the language and habits of the people, have devoted themselves to an organised system of proselytism.' The converts were described as people who were 'wholly illiterate, unacquainted with the English language, and who professed their adhesion to the Protestant faith without any knowledge of its tenets or belief in its truth'.[19]

The objective of this Dublin group was to raise funds to counteract the success of the Protestant mission; they sought to establish an order of nuns, such as the Sisters of Charity or Sisters of Mercy, who would set up a school and visit the homes of the poor. The members of the committee also wished to set up a Christian Brothers' schools for boys in Dingle and Ventry, and to send more clergymen into the area to support the parish clergy and ensure that there was a closer involvement with the people on a daily basis.

In May, the *Post* announced that there was a plan to bring 'the stealthy foot and whispering voice' of an order of nuns to Dingle. 'Is it love to the poor or hatred to Protestantism which is about to open a *Beguinage* in Dingle?' it asked. The *Post* welcomed an open conflict, 'The Bible against the Beguine any day.' (The term 'Beguine' referred to a community of ascetic and philanthropic women in the Netherlands in the thirteenth century.) But it hoped, 'when this new artillery is brought into play, that the old clumsy weapons of cursing and denunciation will be laid aside.' The *Post* wondered about what people in their cabins would think when they heard the sisters 'whispering about the meekness and peaceful spirit of their holy religion, while in their chapels their spiritual guides thunder and roar like demons against their fellow creatures'.[20]

The initiative taken by the four Dublin men could be seen as the beginning of a counter-reformation in response to the 'Second Reformation' of the evangelicals. In due course, it resulted in a Christian Brothers boys' school being established in Dingle. It also led to a Catholic mission being held in Dingle, in 1846, under the direction of a team of visiting Vincentian priests. This devotional revival involved intense prayer, church services and sacraments as a means of reinvigorating Catholics in their faith. It was held over a six-week period in August–September 1846. The headline of the first report in the *Kerry Examiner* chose to depict it as a direct response to the success of the Protestant campaign: 'The Dingle Mission: The Poison and the Antidote'.[21] This Catholic mission coincided with the return of the potato blight on a scale much more extensive and ominous than the partial crop failure of 1845.

Fr Scollard and Fr Halpin

Fr John Scollard was again the centre of attention in the early summer of 1845. He supported the editor of the *Examiner* and praised him for 'handsomely kicking the *Post*'. The *Post* responded to 'the cursing curate of Ventry' by identifying him as the person who had written to the *Examiner* under the pseudonym 'Testis'. The paper concluded, 'Pshaw, but he excites our contempt.'[22] The *Achill Missionary Herald* continued to carry reports from Kerry stating that the persecution was going on 'with greater vigour than ever' and that a letter was in circulation which 'the poor people say is from the Pope himself'.[23] The *Herald* referred to 'the curse to the seventh generation' that was continually issued from the pulpits by a priest it described as 'saggart ah wattah' (*sagart a' bhata*, or the priest of the stick).[24]

Incidents of assault continued in Dingle. John Cooke, a teacher in the Protestant school, was attacked by a mob as he crossed Milltown bridge.[25] A man named Crane, who was described in the *Post* as 'the confidential servant and agent' and 'man Friday' of Fr Scollard, was convicted of assaulting converts and was bound to the peace for seven years. Crane was reported to have gone around intimidating converts and noting any Catholics who had business dealings with them.[26] However, one person saw a sign of a change in Fr Scollard's sermons: 'a poor persecuted souper' from Ventry wrote that the priest was moderating his cursing and concentrating more on promoting exclusive dealing.[27]

The same writer noted that 'poor old Halpin' was 'waxing worse and worse every day'.[28] He reported that Fr Halpin 'spat forth his Romish venom with more than ordinary vehemence and precision'.[29] He also asserted that Halpin named and cursed Catholics who had any dealings with the converts. When a man named John Feinaghty sold cattle to Matthew Moriarty, Halpin expressed the wish that his 'health and substance may melt as the froth on the river'. The priest condemned three named women of his congregation who had purchased potatoes on behalf of convert relatives: Mary Lyne, for her father; Mrs William Shea, for her husband; and Widow Kennedy, for her two sons. The Ventry letter writer said that Mrs Kennedy had a role in the community as 'our village doctoress'; he claimed that Halpin stated that he would not anoint (i.e. administer the last rites to) anyone who had sent for her for medical care. This meant that she would lose her livelihood. 'The cursed are still Romanists and those for whom they purchased are converts,' added the letter writer, who concluded that Halpin was 'a wretched man [...] steeped in callousness' and 'free from every feeling that would ennoble either soul or body'.[30] It is likely that the condemnations of priests were counter-productive, and that the arrogance and authoritarianism of their tirades from the altar would have outraged and alienated members of their congregations, even to the extent of driving them into the arms of the evangelicals.

Fr Halpin does not appear to have been deterred by criticism, and his sermons continued to make waves in the press. In October, he condemned magistrates who had convicted people for attacks on converts. He may also have been the unnamed priest accused of grossly insulting a young woman, a visitor to Dingle, simply because she had visited the Protestant school.[31]

When Mrs Gayer was hooted and hissed by a mob in Dingle one Sunday, the blame was laid on 'the extreme violence of the language' of Halpin's sermon that morning. The *Post* added that the reason for Halpin's vehement language was that he was trying to ingratiate himself with the bishop, having been dismissed years earlier from the position of parish priest on account of 'some irregularities'.[32]

Transfer of Fr Scollard

In August 1845 came a surprising announcement. Fr John Scollard was being removed from Dingle 'in consequence of the complaints of his own flock', according to the *Post*, which optimistically anticipated better times in Dingle as a result:

> The *reverend* gentleman has kept that town in a state of extreme ferment from his hebdomadal altar attacks on all the respectable Protestants of that locality, particularly the magistrates. This event will also, we have no doubt, assist in quieting the town and tend to allay the religious animosity which now unfortunately prevails in that locality, as Mr. Scollard and his violent harangues were in a great measure the source and cause from which that unchristian feeling emanated.[33]

Although there were no other newspaper reports about Scollard's removal, neither was there any denial of the claims of the *Post*. It could be that the bishop disapproved of the continuing personalised attacks of Scollard and Halpin, although the latter was not moved from Dingle. Fr John Scollard was appointed to Lisselton in north Kerry, and by 1848, he was in Dromtariffe parish in Co. Cork, part of the diocese of Kerry. By 1850 he had moved to Liverpool diocese. There is no further information on the circumstances of this move.[34] He was replaced in Dingle by Fr William McCarthy, and 'a liberal Catholic' was pleased to record that the new priest's first sermon 'breathed peace and goodwill to all, a doctrine, we must allow, rather novel in Dingle chapel'. The writer looked forward to 'a new and milder system', and the editor of the *Post* to 'some quietness for the persecuted converts'.[35]

Lord Monteagle and *The Times*

On 5 June 1845, *The Times* of London published details of an extraordinary claim made by Lord Monteagle (Thomas Spring-Rice) of Mount

Trenchard, Co. Limerick. Monteagle had served in government as Chancellor of the Exchequer from 1835 to 1839, and his words carried weight. In the House of Lords, Monteagle claimed that a Protestant missionary in Achill had interrupted a public Catholic religious service at which large numbers were in attendance. The minister had 'stepped forward, insulted the consecrated wafer which the priests were exhibiting to the people and scornfully appealed to them, asking if that was their God or not'. The crowd was incensed, according to Monteagle, and rushed at the missionary, who was only saved by the intervention of the Catholic clergy. In *The Times* of 17 June, Rev. Edward Nangle emphatically denied that any such incident had taken place in Achill; nevertheless, his publication, the *Achill Missionary Herald*, often derided Catholic beliefs by referring to the 'wafer God' and 'the pasty idol'.[36] Catholics were described as 'worshippers of the wafer', and the first issues of the *Herald* had an image of the altar bread alongside Hindu statues under a banner reading, 'There be no Gods that are made with hands.'[37]

For some reason, Thomas Moriarty mistakenly believed that Monteagle had claimed that this incident occurred in Dingle. He wrote to *The Times* to deny it utterly, saying that such conduct would disgrace any Christian and that neither he nor Charles Gayer had ever so acted and never would, 'Our whole cause of ministration in this district has been quite the reverse of that described by my Lord Monteagle [...] We have studiously avoided giving offence.' The fact that there were no reports in Kerry newspapers of any such incident is confirmation that Moriarty was in error.

Moriarty's letter is significant because it summarised for British readers the grievances of the Protestants of Dingle, including the boycott that obliged them to import potatoes and turf by sea. He depicted their struggle as one for survival and appealed to the editor of *The Times*:

What think you, sir, of the spirit which influences the Roman Catholic priests to ask their hearers to pray that a wasting from God may come upon us, and that we may be scattered like the froth of the sea, perish like the young birds in the frost and the snow etc., and not only we, but all who strengthen us in the place, even several Protestant gentry have been abused and denounced for being friendly to converts [...]

Will you not, sir, insist upon protection for us or at least inquiry into the real state of affairs? Do we live in the nineteenth century? Do we live under British law? Shall we not be allowed liberty of conscience whether we are right or whether be wrong? Are we to be driven from our native land or persecuted back again to the Roman communion and allegiance to the Pope? I ask you, sir, would not both houses of Parliament and the press of Europe ring with the clamour that would be justly raised by Protestants as well as Roman Catholics, if Roman Catholic priests and converts to their system were treated by us as we are treated by them?

Are Roman Catholic priests to act as they do here with impunity? Where is the honest indignation of a free press and of all lovers of liberty of conscience?[38]

Moriarty wrote that the 'quiet and kind people' of west Kerry, to whom the converts were 'united by blood or kindred', disliked the conduct of their priests, and some of the people dealt openly or secretly with converts.

By July 1845, there were strong indications that the effort to provide food for converts was putting great strain on their ministers. A report written on 12 July stated, 'Our last potato was expended last Sunday. The potato boat arrived from Baltimore [Co. Cork] just in time to rescue the famished multitude. I need not, nor will not, add another word.'[39] The report was anonymous, but it is likely to have been written by either Gayer or Moriarty. It went on to say that people 'are actually disgusted with the continual Sabbath Day cursing which has been practised in Dingle chapel since 4 November last'. The writer echoed the questions posed by Thomas Moriarty, 'Are we in the nineteenth century? Do we live under British or papal Roman law?' He claimed that the eight hundred converts in the barony were struggling to source food, and that they were 'fed day by day almost as miraculously as Elijah was fed by ravens'.[40]

Incidents at Milltown bridge

In June and July 1845, several violent incidents flared up at the bridge at Milltown, the point of access by road from areas west of the town. The census of 1841 recorded 387 people living in hovels there, having been evicted from their holdings. In July 1845, affidavits were sworn before magistrate John Hickson in connection with attacks on the converts as they passed over the bridge.[41] On one occasion, the funeral of a convert was going from Ventry into Dingle for burial in the churchyard there. By the time it reached Milltown bridge, the funeral party consisted of three hundred people, and they were verbally abused by a mob and stoned by children as they passed. Rev. Thomas Moriarty and his brother Matthew stayed at the back of the cortege to prevent any retaliation from their side, 'having good reason to know that the young people were only set on to provoke such, if possible, and to give the adults an apparent reason for coming forward to mob the converts'. The stone-throwing continued as the cortege went towards the quay, where a police presence was enough to deter the perpetrators.[42]

Thomas Moriarty blamed the priests for exciting the people and appealed for the establishment of a police barracks at Milltown. He also wrote a private letter to magistrate John Hickson giving his view that 'the government cannot allow such a state of things; nothing less than four policemen stationed there can afford us sufficient protection.' Charles Gayer offered to cover the expenses of establishing the barracks and warned that 'someone will be injured, if not murdered' if it was not set up. Sub-inspector Gillman was dubious, 'I know the converts are greatly insulted, but they have not been injured to my knowledge to the extent that would make it a subject for special reporting.' Nevertheless, the County Inspector of Police, Hugh Hawkshaw, corresponded with the Inspector General of Police, who eventually authorised a temporary barracks with four policemen for Milltown.[43]

'This thoroughly potato district'

In the autumn of the fateful year of 1845, the advance of a disease in the potato crop in mainland Europe was being tracked in the Kerry papers.[44] In early October, 'the distemper on the potato crop' was noted, with one account stating that 'Kerry has not to any great extent, if at all, been reached by the pestilence.'[45] However, by the end of that month, the *Post* reported that 'rot is being daily found to have exhibited itself' and 'accounts from Dingle and Killorglin are very unfavourable.'[46]

At this time, Charles Gayer was in a state of despair for his followers, as shown in a letter from him published on 20 October. It contained an extraordinary admission of helplessness, even despair, from a man who had always been so confident and strident in his language. Gayer seems to have anticipated a famine, and even his own death:

> The markets here are closed against us. And we are almost worn out in trying to provide food and fireing for our poor people. I have just been told that the failure in the potato crop is very great, that a man

will hardly dig in a day what will do his family for it. A famine seems before us; let the Lord do as seemeth him good – it would be better for us to be in the hands of the Lord than as we are at present, in the hands of man.

Our enemies are trying to 'wear us out'; no stone is left unturned to try and persecute us in every way, but the Lord still supports us, without which we must resign in the unequal contest. The constant harassing excitement in which we are kept must be felt to be known. We have none to take part in it, which makes it heavier upon us; only that I believe the Lord is at hand and that I hope soon to see the goodness of the Lord in the land of the living, I verily believe I could not stand the ceaseless anxiety of mind to which Moriarty and I are subject at present.

Dreadful as a famine would be, I think it would be even a relaxation to our minds; any change in fact would be a relief.[47]

For Charles Gayer to wish for a famine as a means of affording some improvement in his circumstances is extraordinary. In using the term 'famine', he was perhaps remembering periods of food shortage in the early 1840s, when he had procured food supplies and won approval as a benefactor of the people. In October 1845, he could not have imagined the scale of the potato blight and the devastation that was to come.

Before he left on a lecture tour in England, Thomas Moriarty wrote two letters alerting the public to the state of the potato crop west of Dingle, and expressing his own fears for the future. The first letter appeared in the *Post* on 25 October, when it was reported that in the Dingle area, 'the rot has commenced in the pits.' What was termed 'the potato rot', or in Irish 'an dubh' (the blackness), was 'the all-engrossing subject of public attention' by this time. Through the years of the Great Famine, Thomas Moriarty wrote many letters to the local papers, keeping officials and the public informed of the tragic state of west Kerry. In Moriarty's first letter about the blight, the sense of urgency is palpable:

'The Potato Plague' has visited this district and appears to be making fearfully rapid strides. The worst feature of it here is the *rotting in the pits*, which is just being discovered by the people. I saw pits being opened today on my way to Dingle; my brother has seen others during the week and in all cases the potatoes were rotten or in a state of decay. I fear that this is the case generally throughout the district and the impression on the minds of most people is that we shan't have a sound potato in three months. If this be so, what will become of the population of this remote district, who so entirely depend on the potato for their subsistence? I would not be an alarmist without reason and I state facts and my impression is that we shall have a famine. I think that steps should be taken in time to meet the fearful day. At any rate, immediate inquiry should be instituted and the real state of the case reported to the government.[48]

Thomas Moriarty wrote again a few days later, in a perplexed and fearful state of mind:

I regret to have to inform you that the potatoes are getting worse and worse every day. The people are bewildered and don't know what to do. The infection appears to increase and spread through the potatoes still in the ground, while such as have been put into houses and pits, apparently sound, are rotting very fast. Indeed I think it next to impossible to preserve what are still sound, by any means in our power. 'Tis hard to account for such a state of things. There is something very mysterious in it.

Potatoes were never apparently better than this year, and when the people rejoiced in the abundance of their staple food, as well as in the good prices for butter, pigs etc., in a moment as it were, their fair prospects are blighted and their hopes are scattered to the wind. 'Tis heartrending to witness the state of mind of poor families crying and lamenting over their losses and their prospects.

I sincerely hope that something may be done to prepare for what is coming, and may the Lord deliver us from plague, pestilence and famine.[49]

Thomas's brother Matthew wrote from Ventry Cottage, expressing the same sense of foreboding:

In a word, sir, so frightful is the extent to which the plague is raging in this quarter as that the farmers have quite given up digging them, and as to what are dug, they are in quite a hopeless state, left in the field exposed to the element, it being now quite evident that any kind of enclosure increases the plague.

As facts speak for themselves, I will give you two that will, I think, give you an idea of the sad state to which we are now brought in this immediate locality. Within a stone's throw of where I write, a poor conacre man was yesterday throwing out of his house seven or eight pecks he had a little more than a week ago put in, seemingly quite sound.

A few days since about a mile from this, I saw two pigs in a very fine looking field of potatoes. I went to the owner and told him the pigs would root all his potatoes. And his answer was, I know they will, sir, I don't care as they are not worth digging. Not willing to believe them quite gone, I told him to bring me a spade to try them. He did so and after trying many a ridge, alas! alas! I found his tale too true.[50]

Many newspapers had published suggestions for dealing with the rotting potatoes, and Matthew gave his opinions on these:

As to the various and varying methods of turning the rotted and rotting potatoes to account, proposed by the many disinterested persons who every day write on the subject, you might as well talk to our poor people in this remote district of the principle on which the Archimedean screw propels, as they neither understand the theory or have within their reach the means of putting it into practice. What do they know about soda, nutmeg, arrowroot, jelly and the many other ingredients talked of as necessary for the food, so much and so justly recommended by those who have tried it? As much as about 'the man in the moon'.

Such, sir, is the sad state to which we are being brought in this thoroughly potato district, and what think you will be the consequence. 'Tis too awful to anticipate. God only knows.

Hoping the Lord may, in due time, preserve for our use the kindly
fruits of the earth.[51]

Another unnamed correspondent of the *Post*, who also wrote from west
Kerry, introduced religious controversy when he expressed concern for the
poor but animosity towards the priests:

> Is it true? Can it be possible? And yet how can we doubt it? We have
> it on good authority that the Romish priests in Dingle district are
> making a 'harvest' on the alarm and credulity of the poor people by
> saying Masses for the potatoes, as they are in the habit of doing for
> fishing boats! cattle! &c. What a heartless scheme it is when the poor
> people's potatoes are gone, to take their money also!! Fie upon it!!
> The potatoes are their chief support; they are decaying in the ground,
> rotting in the pits and all but gone. They see misfortune, if not
> starvation, staring them in the face; they are alarmed for themselves
> and their little ones, and, lamentably credulous and superstitious as
> they are, they run to the priests – *but not without money!* – to have
> their potatoes saved by Masses or some kind of charms!!! The priests
> take advantage of this and make merchandise of it!!! The poor people
> are to be pitied; their spiritual state is awful and their temporal
> prospects are at present frightful.[52]

This writer believed that the normal dues exacted from the people should
be enough for the priests and that it was 'cruel and unnatural' to 'drain the
pockets of the poor' during the prevailing crisis. 'Why trade upon their
superstition?' he asked.

In November, there was a growing sense of alarm in reports about the
potato crop. A commission was established by the government, and in an
ominous instruction, the Church of Ireland primate of Ireland announced
that 'the second prayer appointed to be used in time of famine' should be
read in church services. Referring to 'the dawning of what may be a
universal famine', *The Packet* newspaper stated, 'A dire calamity is, we fear,
impending over our unhappy country. The accounts from all the rural
districts arriving day after day are of a nature sufficiently fearful to chill the
most sanguine heart.' The *Post* saw the crop failure as 'this national calamity'
and published a letter which claimed that it was 'a divine judgment'.[53]

Thomas Moriarty in England

In early November, Thomas Moriarty left Kerry on a fund-raising tour. In the Rotunda in Dublin, he made 'an eloquent and successful appeal' on behalf of the Dingle converts, 'who are, we regret to hear, likely to suffer severely by the loss of the potato crop'.[54] Moriarty then travelled to England, where he spoke in places such as Stratford-on-Avon, Cheltenham and Bristol. He gave two lectures in the town hall in Stratford-on-Avon, after which 'a liberal sum' was collected. His speeches did not elaborate on the potato blight and its effects, but concentrated more on what was required for the missionary work.[55]

In Cheltenham, Rev. F.W. Robertson introduced Moriarty to a well-attended meeting of the Literary and Philosophical Institution.[56] Robertson, an Oxford graduate, was a curate in Cheltenham from 1842 to 1846 and had a reputation for being intense, zealous and ascetic. He is said to have learned by heart the whole New Testament in English and in Greek. He later became famous as a preacher in Brighton. Robertson had paid a brief visit to Dingle in the summer of 1845; he remembered the area as 'particularly bleak and desolate, quite cold and uninviting', although he appreciated that 'an earnest and good work was going on.' He heard one young clergyman preach as effectively as any graduate of an English or Irish university, and was surprised to learn that 'he had received the whole of his education at that little colony of Dingle in the wilds of Kerry.' Robertson described the people as living in 'extreme privation', and he believed that Catholics were in a state of 'mental prostration' before the priests. He also criticised the 'faulty policy' and 'the many wrongs inflicted upon Ireland' by English rulers down through the centuries, and he claimed to understand why 'the concentrated wrath induced by the wrath of six centuries was still deeply implanted in the breast of the Irish peasantry.'[57]

Moriarty then spoke and described the progress of the mission, informing the audience that six young men were being educated for the ministry. He defended his Catholic neighbours, saying that although they were 'deep in error', they were sincere and zealous in their error, 'so that perhaps they were not so much to blame after all'. He gently rebuked Robertson for his 'rather bleak and inhospitable' description of the Dingle area and pointed out that, in his short visit, he had no time to view the wonderful scenery around Ventry. According to the *Cheltenham Chronicle*, Moriarty told the audience that he believed the English had 'better heads than the Irish, but he would not yield to any people the possession of larger hearts than those of his countrymen'.

Moriarty gave a short account of the history of Protestantism in Ireland, saying that it had failed to make progress among the people only because it was presented 'in an English garb'. According to the *Chronicle*, 'Had it been presented to them in their vernacular tongue, he felt confident that they would have embraced it.' He pointed out the absurdity of Protestants over the centuries condemning the use of Latin in Catholic services while themselves using unintelligible English among Irish speakers. He praised the work of Rev. Gayer, but added that, because Gayer did not speak Irish, 'he could not reach their hearts so effectually in the English tongue, against which they had many prejudices.' A collection was taken up at the end of this meeting and 'a considerable sum was realised'.[58]

In Bristol, Thomas Moriarty told the audience that the purpose of his visit to England was, 'if possible, to collect £400 for payment of a debt incurred for finishing the parsonage, schoolhouse and church at Ventry'.[59] He told the large audience that Ventry church was the first and only church in Ireland where services and sacraments were conducted exclusively in Irish, and that when he was a schoolboy, 'there was no sign of Protestantism except at Dingle', but now there were growing congregations at Ventry, Dunquin, Dunurlin and Kilmalkedar.

He again stated that the Protestant church had failed in Ireland because it was 'a Sassenagh church' that had neglected the Irish language. The Dingle and Ventry Mission was different because 'the great principle upon which they acted was the preaching of the gospel in Irish.' For Moriarty, this was 'a common sense principle, nay, a pentecostal principle, that the people should hear in their own tongue the wonderful works of God'. He told the audience that he was so accustomed to speaking Irish, he felt like a fish out of water when called to address them in English. However, he also pointed out that the English language was taught in the mission schools and that they 'were thus civilising as well as seeking to evangelise the population'. Moriarty also gave a summary of the libel case, referring to P.R. Byrne as being 'in the pay of the Romish priests'.[60]

Crisis meeting in Dingle

While Thomas Moriarty toured England, a public meeting was held in Dingle on 4 December to establish the scale of the potato crop failure. On the platform there were several Protestant ministers and several priests, as well as local officials. The meeting could be seen as a rallying of all factions in the face of a crisis, but underlying tensions came to the fore and it ended in conflict. Fr Divine was present, as well as Fr George O'Sullivan and Fr

Thomas Healy. Revs Charles Gayer and Thomas Goodman attended, and Matthew Moriarty represented his brother. The general consensus of the meeting was that one-third of the crop was already lost, and that the remainder would be exhausted by the end of April 1846, by which time it was expected that the people would be in a desperate state.

Matthew Moriarty spoke towards the end of the meeting. He claimed to be 'something of a practical farmer', familiar with the area west of Dingle. In his estimation, the situation was worse than had been stated, because only one-third of the crop that he had seen was sound. Matthew Moriarty's choice of words provoked loud disagreement. This is how his contribution was reported:

> He was not at all raising the question how the crop might have been saved or finding fault with the people's ignorance as to saving the crop, but he spoke of things as they are. There is now no help for the past neglect of his countrymen which had been the cause of a great part of the disease.[61]

This statement was greeted with cries of 'No! No!' from the public and from Fr George O'Sullivan. But Moriarty continued:

> But it *had* been caused by their ignorance (loud cries of 'no, no' from the same quarter) as to how they should treat the crop. He might be contradicted, but he had only one object in view. If those who said 'no, no' thought otherwise, they knew more of him than he did of himself. His object was to bring before the chairman, as the representative of the meeting, the state of the crop. Through his own neglect, a great portion of his crop had been lost. The disease came on so suddenly that everyone was taken by surprise. He did not want to charge the poor people with wilful neglect; it was their interest and that of the gentlemen present, if from no other motive than that of self, to endeavour to save the crop. The fact was that they did not know how to treat the crop. He was waiting and they were waiting for information from persons competent to give it.[62]

For a prominent convert to use words like 'ignorance' and 'neglect' about his neighbours was inviting a negative reaction, even when he included himself among the ignorant. Mr Trant spoke after Moriarty and was more judicious. He disagreed with Moriarty's view that the spread of the disease was due to neglect on the part of the people. Trant said that 'no country on the face of the earth possesses a more hard-working people, a less negligent people than those of Corkaguiny.' Matthew Moriarty responded 'hear, hear' and attempted to clarify his views:

> There was no real difference between him and Mr. Trant. Their object was one and the same. He had not attributed wilful neglect to the people, but simply neglect arising from ignorance – ignorance not in the *general* sense of the word, but ignorance of the mode of treating the disease.[63]

Matthew Moriarty's words were poorly chosen. His views were a little too nuanced for the end of a tense four-hour public meeting, and it is likely that his brother would have expressed himself more diplomatically. At the end of the meeting, a committee was set up to monitor and report on the potato blight; the absent Thomas Moriarty was named as one of its members. On the Sunday after the meeting, Fr Halpin gave a sermon in Ventry in which he condemned Matthew Moriarty for saying that the people had caused the blight by their ignorance and neglect. This prompted Matthew to reply, in 'self-justification', saying that he was being misrepresented by Halpin, who, he claimed, had given the congregation an inaccurate account of what he had said. Moriarty wrote that Halpin had concluded his sermon with a personal and religious attack on him, which placed his life in danger.[64]

It seems tragically appropriate that the year 1845 ended with acrimony between a priest and a prominent convert who would later become an ordained Protestant minister. The spirit of civility and co-operation which men of the cloth on both sides shared on that public platform in early December appeared to be fragile. These men would co-operate in unprecedented ways during the Famine years ahead, but they remained bitter rivals – and this rivalry would lead to many more outbreaks of hostility in later years.

In the dying days of December 1845, Rev. Charles Gayer responded to a request from the Mansion House Committee for information on the effects of the potato blight in his district. This committee, with Lord Cloncurry as chairman, was gathering information from around the country, in anticipation of extreme food shortages by the spring of 1846. Charles Gayer, described as 'the principal of the well-known missionary settlement at Dingle', wrote with a great sense of foreboding:

I believe that there will be a *very great* scarcity, if not absolute want, about the first of April. I know some persons who had a sufficiency for their own use for the year and they have lost all by rot. I had six acres of potatoes this year without losing one by the disease, but I believe I was nearly the *only exception* in this district. It is my firm belief that unless some provision is made for the poor of this neighbourhood, during the summer, the consequences will be dreadful.[65]

In an appeal for prompt government action, an editorial referred to the 'lamentable detail' of Gayer's letter and his ominous warning of what lay ahead. Decisions taken by the government in early 1846 meant that the spring and summer were not as disastrous as predicted, but the total failure of the potato crop in the autumn of 1846 ushered in an unprecedented catastrophe. One of the many victims of the Great Famine was Charles Gayer himself, who died of typhus in February 1848.

18. Afterword

The story of the Protestant mission in west Kerry during and after the Great Famine is a complex subject meriting more detailed discussion than is possible here. The controversial question of whether food relief by Protestant missionaries during the Famine was for the sake of conversion is also too complex to be addressed here. Protestant ministers and Catholic priests of the area co-operated in relief work and played a significant part in food distribution during the tragic years of starvation, disease and death – *an droch-shaol*, or the 'bad times', as the Famine years were known.

When the government ended outdoor relief in August 1847, Charles Gayer wrote about his relief work in Dingle:

> Thousands are now thrown upon what I brought and when it is out, I fear there will be dreadful misery and starvation. I hope to make my store last for another week and unless some further aid can be got by that time, I fear the people will be driven to plunder and then will lie down and die. There is no district in Ireland, I am sure, like this. I am giving food to *at least* three thousand people daily.[1]

When the time came to harvest the corn on the colony farms, the *Post* reported that two hundred Catholic labourers, out of 'a kindly and grateful feeling', came to the assistance of the converts as a way of showing their appreciation for Rev. Gayer's efforts 'to relieve the wants of the poor of all religions'.[2] Charles Gayer claimed that Protestant missionaries kept the people of the Great Blasket alive in 1847; it is sobering to contemplate what a profound and tragic loss would have ensued if the Great Blasket had been depopulated then rather than a century later.

In late September 1847, Charles Gayer initiated another form of public works: the building of what were first termed light-towers and later beacon towers. As Dingle was a 'blind harbour', ships often had difficulty in sailing safely into port. These towers were to serve a useful purpose, warning mariners to lower their sails to enter the mouth of the harbour in safety. By

November, four of these towers were near completion and had already helped to guide one vessel to safety.[3] A contemporary drawing shows five towers around the harbour.

Private tragedies befell the Gayer family in 1846 and 1848. Catherine died in 1846 at the age of 42, leaving nine children, and Charles's mother died in the same year. On the memorial plaque to Charles Gayer in St James's church, Catherine is described as 'his true and faithful partner in life and labours'. In June 1847, Charles married Mabel D'Esterre Parker of Co. Cork, who was eighteen years younger than him.

Typhus and relapsing fever were rampant during the Great Famine. Transmitted by lice, they both spread wherever people congregated for food distribution and on public works. Although it was possible to recover from 'famine fever', as these diseases were called, they were the cause of many deaths. Because of their close interaction with the poor, clergymen of all persuasions fell victim to typhus. Rev. Robert Traill of Schull, Co. Cork, a second cousin of Charles Gayer and a prominent campaigner on behalf of the starving people of his area, died of typhus in 1847, as did Rev. Archibald Macintosh of Castleisland in 1848.[4] On 20 February 1848, Rev. Charles Gayer died of typhus at the age of 43. He was buried beside Catherine in the graveyard of St James's church in Dingle.[5] Their son Edward, who died in 1840 at the age of 9, was in the same tomb, as were Charles's mother Frances and Catherine's parents. The nine surviving Gayer children were cared for by Charles's brother, Arthur Edward, a Dublin barrister and a supporter of the Dingle mission. Some four months after the death of Charles Gayer, his wife Mabel gave birth to a daughter, whom she named Dorcas.

The plaque in memory of Charles Gayer in St James's church has this inscription:

A few of the many friends who knew and valued the untiring zeal, disinterested labour and faithful simplicity for which for XV years he preached the Gospel of the Grace of God and Promoted the temporal and eternal interests of the People of this district have united to place This Tablet.

Thomas Moriarty wrote this moving response to the untimely death of his friend:

This is indeed a most afflicting dispensation – we can hardly realise it as yet; it appears like a terrible dream. The ways of God are wonderful and past finding out by us. How many, alas, have lost in him their best earthly friend. Think of his own nine children, now orphans indeed, without father or mother. But the Lord will never leave them, and will be to them a father and will raise up for them many friends.[6]

All nine children of Charles and Catherine Gayer eventually left Ireland, with four settling in Australia. One son was named Ventry, and among the many Gayer descendants in Australia, eight were given Ventry as a middle name.[7] In time, the family erected a plaque in memory of Arthur Edward Gayer in St James's church. This reads in part, 'For many years he took an active part in advancing the Christian Mission, which his devoted brother, the Rev. Charles Gayer, had begun in Dingle. Erected by his brother's children, who were left orphans and who received from him a father's love and care.'

Thomas Moriarty left west Kerry in 1862 to take up the position of rector of Tralee, which he occupied until 1869. He died at Day Place, Tralee, on 26 April 1894 at the age of 82. He was buried beside St Anna's church in Millstreet, where he was rector from 1879 to 1894, succeeding his son, also Thomas, who was minister there from 1874 until his death in 1879.[8]

During the Famine years, Patrick Robert Byrne used his prominent position as newspaper editor to champion the cause of the destitute and to call public officials to account. His fearless, passionate writing in the *Kerry Examiner* stirred the consciences of his readers and influenced the course of events.[9] In 1856, the combative Byrne became embroiled in a dispute with James R. Eagar, editor and owner of the *Tralee Chronicle*; with yet another libel case pending, the *Kerry Examiner* ceased publication in March 1856. A fund was set up to assist P.R. Byrne and his family in beginning a new life in Dublin.[10] The *Tralee Chronicle* was published until 1881, and the *Kerry Evening Post* survived until 1917.

On 29 May 1849, Fr Michael Divine, parish priest of Dingle, died as a result of cholera contracted while he worked among his parishioners. He was one of about seven priests of Kerry diocese who died of disease during the Famine years. Michael Divine had served in Dingle parish since 1839; before that, he had been in Castletownbere, Co. Cork. In St Mary's Catholic church in Dingle, a plaque to his memory reads:

Possessing in an eminent degree the spirit and virtues of his sacred profession, he laboured without ceasing as a true minister of Christ and dispenser of the Mysteries of God and in the end died a martyr to his Pastoral zeal, having inhaled the Poison of death in administering the last consolations of Religion to the plague stricken members of his flock during the cholera visitation.

There was a dark symmetry to the deaths of Charles Gayer and Michael Divine. Both men died as a result of their efforts to preserve the lives of others. In the book *Céad Bliain*, the two plaques to their memory are pictured together, with the caption 'Cairde ina mBearta, Eascairde ina mBriathra' (Friends in their deeds, enemies in their words).[11]

In his account of Charles Gayer's funeral, Thomas Moriarty saw the beacon towers as fitting memorials to him:

His death is universally admitted to be the greatest public loss that could befall this district, while to his own family and the poor converts it is irreparable. We observed nothing but respect and sympathy from all the people as the immense funeral passed through Dingle. The day was fine and a great body of the country people were in the town after Mass. Many of the Roman Catholic poor joined the mourning body of converts and it was truly observed that it pleased God not to take him till they too (the Roman Catholic poor) could cry after him, as they had good reason to do. The beacon towers he had nearly finished, to guide vessels to the blind harbour of Dingle, though they are, as it were, his own tombstones, will ever remain monuments of his concern for the Roman Catholic poor, who alone were employed at them. 'It is not tomorrow or after,' said a poor woman in my hearing, 'but for years to come, Mr. Gayer will be missed out of Dingle.' How true![12]

It is noteworthy how Moriarty stated that only Catholic labourers were employed on building the beacon towers. Only one tower now stands, on Carhoo Hill, still guiding vessels into Dingle. It is known as Eask Tower, or Burnham Tower, and it can be accessed by a pathway through the fields. The tower was originally eight metres high and was raised to about twelve metres around 1900.

Notwithstanding Thomas Moriarty's hope, only faint memories of Charles Gayer have survived, and these are not marked by any warmth. However, in the late twentieth century there were signs of a greater appreciation of Gayer's humanitarian work. Fr Mícheál Ó Mainín, who had written about the Protestant mission in *Céad Bliain* in 1973, revisited the subject in 1996. He acknowledged the beneficial deeds of Thomas Moriarty during the Famine, 'When the real crisis came, Parson Moriarty helped everyone on the Blasket, irrespective of their religion.' Fr Ó Mainín also acknowledged that Rev. Gayer 'did Trojan work to relieve people during the Famine' and offered this qualified tribute, 'I don't think one would be justified in vilifying Charles Gayer or Parson Moriarty. Charles Gayer displayed some heroic qualities, however misled he may have been in his religious views.'[13]

In due course, Rev. Gayer was succeeded by Rev. Samuel Lewis, and Fr Divine by Fr Eugene (Owen) O'Sullivan. Tragically, the deep-rooted enmities endured, and bitter words were exchanged between these two clerics and between people on both sides of the religious divide in west Kerry for many more years. Ultimately, the 'Protestant crusade' (as Fr Ó Mainín described it) ended following a vigorous, concerted response from the Catholic clergy (the 'counter-reformation'), the reduction in donations from Britain and the emigration of large numbers of converts. The decline in numbers attending the mission schools and churches led to their closure, and eventually to the loss of some of the buildings. The church near Kilmalkedar still stands, now transformed into a modern home. A plaque over the door has the date 1860; the building represented one final, perhaps defiant, flourish, as the evangelical mission was undoubtedly in sharp decline by then.

A.M. Thompson's later life

In 1846, A.M. Thompson published her detailed account of the Protestant mission in west Kerry, and her book has become a standard source for historians. The edition of 1846 has an introduction dated 10 November 1844, just two months before her husband's sudden death. This edition was followed by another, in 1847, containing updated information and appendices. Pagination in the 1846 edition goes from page 25 to page 45. Thompson regretted having to omit those twenty pages and apologised for the 'mutilated state' of the book, explaining that, at a late stage, some persons referred to had withdrawn permission to publish.

However, at least one copy of the complete book, with the missing pages, was published; it is available on the online catalogue of the National Library of Ireland, with the date of publication given as 1845. The missing section gave an account of the experience of an unnamed young convert and members of his family, 'persons of a better class' than other converts.[14] The young convert was likely Daniel Foley, who later became a distinguished academic.[15]

Reactions to A.M. Thompson's book

When A.M. Thompson's book on the evangelical campaign was published in 1846, it received a cool response in the *Athenaeum*, a London literary magazine, which referred to Dingle as 'a decayed town in the south of Ireland', 'Mrs. Thompson is a firm believer in the reality of these conversions and writes of them in a thoroughly controversial spirit – not quite in accordance with our notions of the temper and tone that beseem a lady.'[16]

Two surviving copies of A.M. Thompson's book are of particular interest. One is held in Dingle Library, and it has a two-page note written by An Seabhac, the author Pádraig Ó Siochfhradha (1883–1964), a native of Ballingoleen (Baile an Ghóilín), near Burnham. He wrote, 'Níl ach beagán dá bhfuil sa leabhar seo bunaithe ar fhírinne.' (Very little of what is in this book is based on truth.) According to An Seabhac, the conversion campaign was not as successful as Thompson depicted in the book, but because the funding came from subscribers in England and elsewhere, she felt obliged to render a positive report, to show that the money was well spent, 'Níor mhór deagh-chuntas a chur amach ar a fheabhas a bhí an obair ag dul chun cinn.' (It was necessary to send out a positive report on how well the work was progressing.)

Another copy of Thompson's book, held in Kerry County Archive, Tralee, has notes written on the margin by Fr John O'Sullivan.[17] Many of the notes contradict her statements criticising priests, and O'Sullivan wrote 'lie' in several places. For example, beside Thompson's claim that Rev. Gubbins lived in a humble cabin, O'Sullivan has written, 'A scandalous lie! He had comfortable lodgings in the town of Dingle.' Another note challenged Thompson's claim that Catholic priests fled when cholera struck, 'Oh, Oh, – I spent thirteen nights in succession attending country calls in that year, slept during the day.' He disputed some minor details of the account of the excommunication ritual of 1837, but he did not deny that it had occurred as described. Neither the priest nor the excommunicated woman was named in Thompson's book, but a note by O'Sullivan identified himself and Ellen Waters. Throughout the book, O'Sullivan identified some individuals for whom Thompson had not given full names.

Anna Maria Thompson left Corca Dhuibhne after her husband's death, and her subsequent movements are difficult to trace. In the preface to the

1847 edition of her book, she gave her address as Floraville, Donnybrook, Co. Dublin. In 1850, she published *Ellen of Dingle*, in which she recounted how she first moved from Tralee to Dingle in 1835. She described Dingle as 'the locality where, in the latter days, it was first proved that the fortifications of Romanism were not proof against the Lord's word'.[18] She had founded an orphanage in Tralee, and she transferred this to Burnham House when she moved. Ellen (whose surname is not given) was an orphan child, born around 1823, who helped with the care of the Thompson children. Ellen died of consumption, or tuberculosis, and the tract held her up as a model of Christian piety and forbearance. Thompson summarised the mission situation in Dingle in 1850 as follows, '*five large, well-attended churches, nine* schools containing 1,800 scholars, a body of upwards of a thousand God-fearing adults, male and female'. Seven converts had become Protestant ministers. She wrote, 'It was my privilege to be a resident there during the entire time of this marvellous work.'[19]

A.M. Thompson published another book in 1858 with the title *The Galley Slave and His Daughter: A Tale founded on French Protestant History*. There is no Irish dimension to this book, except that the publishers were Madden and Oldham of Grafton Street, Dublin. The bibliographers Rolf and Magda Loeber mention other works by Thompson, and indicate that, in 1880, she was living in Uptown Park, Slough, Berkshire.[20]

Today in west Kerry

In Dingle town, a short cul-de-sac off Strand Street is still known as the Colony, and there is a plaque explaining the name. In the Mall, a plaque inscribed 'Dingle Parochial School 1845' marks the location of the Church of Ireland school. The building is currently the office of Sacred Heart University of Fairfield, Connecticut, which has a campus in Dingle. St James's church holds a Sunday service throughout the year, and the Gayer family resting place is in the adjoining graveyard. Burnham House is now part of Coláiste Íde Secondary School, and Ballintaggart House and Farranakilla are still in use. Across the bay, Eask Tower, the only surviving beacon tower, is a prominent hilltop feature. Until recently, a wooden finger-post projected from it, directing seafarers to Dingle harbour.

Some colony houses and the college building can be identified in Ventry today, but there are only traces of the rectory and church there. On the Great Blasket, the ruins of the mission schoolhouse can be seen. In Ballyferriter, the imposing building that was the parsonage of Rev. George Gubbins still stands, looking westwards towards Ceann Sibéal. Only some hidden stones remain from the church that stood beside it. In the townland of Cloghaneduff, between Murreagh and Kilmalkedar, an imposing and isolated Protestant church has recently been transformed into a private dwelling.

Thomas Moriarty's challenge

The tone of religious discourse in west Kerry in the 1830s and 1840s was undoubtedly vitriolic and divisive, and the converts and their spiritual leaders were certainly subjected to sustained verbal abuse and social isolation. However, it was mainly a war of words, a propaganda conflict, erupting only occasionally in physical violence against converts. Up to the end of 1845, nobody had died in west Kerry on account of their religious beliefs, whereas several converts had been killed in the Kingscourt district of the Irish Society. As early as July 1830, Rev. Robert Winning of Kingscourt stated that 'three of our men have already been murdered.'[21] In 1840, Rev. Edward Norman, then curate of Kingscourt, claimed that teachers of the Irish Society had been persecuted in every possible way, and 'four teachers had been hurried into eternity by assassination.'[22] In a recent study, Marion Rogan states, 'Five Irish Society teachers from the Kingscourt District were murdered at the height of the Irish Society's activity in the district. In the absence of corroborating evidence from unbiased sources, not all of these murders can be attributed definitively to working as Irish Society teachers.'[23] Even though nobody was killed in west Kerry, religious intolerance remained a blight on the area for many decades, and converts and their descendants sometimes experienced discrimination. They deserve to be remembered today with respect and magnanimity rather than simply by the disparaging term 'soupers', or 'lucht a' tsúip'.

This plea of Thomas Moriarty's in the summer of 1845 was a challenge to his contemporaries in west Kerry, 'Shall we not be allowed liberty of conscience?' The religious conflict that tragically darkened the lives of many in Corca Dhuibhne arose out of deep-seated fears, prejudices and suspicions of different values and world-views. Religious intolerance is a worldwide phenomenon today, but a spirit of pluralism and respect for the beliefs of others has grown in Ireland; happily, relations between the Christian denominations are now marked by mutual respect and tolerance, and freedom of conscience is valued as a human right.

Fifty years ago, Desmond Bowen ended his account of the religious conflict in west Kerry as follows, 'Little is heard about Protestantism in this part of Kerry in the years following the famine, as the tide of Protestant emigration grew and many of the converts quietly and slowly returned to Catholicism.'[24] The subject of Protestant emigration warrants further study, as does the nature of Catholic activities to win back converts, and all the other developments that led to those quiet, slow and doubtless painful decisions, and the long silence of Protestant voices, other voices, in west Kerry.

Appendices

Appendix 1: Petition to the Bishop of Kerry, 1826

The petition of Catholic parents sent to Dr Cornelius Egan, Bishop of Kerry, in 1826 was described as 'an extraordinary document' and 'a voluntary and unprompted remonstrance'.[1] Bishop James Doyle, who was referred to in the petition, was bishop of Kildare and Leighlin; he was known as JKL. He was ecumenical in attitude, and in 1824 he had advocated the union of the Anglican and Catholic Churches.

The petition read as follows:

To the right Rev. Cornelius Egan Roman Catholic Bishop of Kerry etc etc:

We the undersigned being members of the Roman Catholic Church in your bishopric beg leave to approach you with all the respect and deference due to our spiritual father and to implore your pastoral indulgence on a subject of much anxiety to us and of great importance to the bodies and souls of our dear children.

In almost every parish of this county free schools have been established by our charitable gentry with the assistance of the generous English, in which all who choose to attend are taught how to earn their bread with honesty and to live in quietness and kindness with their neighbours, and every sort of books necessary for this purpose are supplied without the least cost. As many of our clergy supported and recommended these schools, as we know the masters are good scholars, and men who have obtained certificates of character from their priests, and as we see that the pupils of these schools get on rapidly in knowledge and good behaviour, we are desirous that our beloved children should have the benefits which are enjoyed by our neighbours.

For some time past however, the clergy have required us to take our little ones away from these schools, telling us there is danger of losing our religion by sending them, or that though they can see no harm whatever in our doing so, yet they must obey the orders of their bishop in forbidding us. Some of us being unwilling to deprive our children of such great blessings have been denied the rites of that holy church in which it is our wish to live and die; some have had their names called Sunday after Sunday from the sacred altar and thus been exposed to the scorn and persecution of our neighbours, whilst our little ones have been the object of insult and abuse – and all this because we wish our dear children to become sensible, industrious and honest Catholics.

Most reverend sir, we do not presume to dictate to our clergy but we think it very strange that they should now call that bad what they once called good; we do not know how the sending our children to these schools in which God's word is taught can injure their religion if our church is built upon a rock against which 'the gates of hell shall not prevail', especially while they have the use of the Roman Catholic version of scripture, and their masters are willing to instruct them in the catechism when school has closed. Nay, many of our children who attend the scripture schools are most perfect in the catechism of our holy church.

We approach your paternal feet, holy father, humbly imploring that you will instruct your clergy to relax that hostility which many of them direct against the scripture schools and to suspend those denunciations and penalties which are dealt to us merely because we love our children and wish to see them honest men, loyal subjects, good Christians and faithful Catholics. In short, PERMIT US TO KNOW SOMETHING OF THE WORD OF GOD, so much spoken of in these days.

Do not suffer us to be branded heretics or rotten Catholics and to have our hearts wounded and our livelihood taken away without deserving it, and at last be driven from the church in which we were reared, to one which our Bishop Doyle says is not very different but which does not interfere with the natural rights of parents to educate the children which almighty God has given them. Some of our neighbours have gone over, from being opposed, and we do not see them less happy than they were.

Holy father and most reverend sir, we beg you to forgive our presumption, and to grant us, in a general order to the clergy, the reasonable indulgence we thus seek, that we may remember you in our prayers and thanksgivings to almighty God and that the blessing of them that are ready to perish may come upon you.

We are, Most Reverend Father,
Though poor and ignorant,

Your faithful children.[2]

Appendix 2: Petition of 147 converts, 1845

On 9 January 1845, a petition, or memorial, signed by 147 converts in the Dingle area was sent to the Chief Secretary. This significant document is held in the National Archives, with the signatures of fifty-six people and the marks of ninety-one others (62 per cent) who could not write their names. It is possible that some of these were able to read. (NAI, Outrage Papers Kerry, 12/3967. The text of the petition, without the names, and the reply are also given in *Persecution of Protestants*, Appendix 1, p. 88.) They were converts and heads of families. Two women, Honora Murphy and Mary Connor, signed the petition; both of them were widows and therefore heads of families. The number 147 corresponds closely to the number of convert families cited by Rev. Thomas Moriarty in March 1846. Addressing a meeting of the Irish Society in the Rotunda, he quoted references to 'upwards of eighty families' of converts. 'That was a mistake', he stated, 'the number being one hundred and fifty, amounting to seven or eight hundred persons.' (*KEP*, 25 March 1846).

The official reply to the memorial by E. Lucas in Dublin Castle was sent to Rev. Charles Gayer on 14 January. As already noted in Chapter 15, Lucas stated that the Lord Lieutenant regretted the situation of the converts but advised them to resort to the ordinary course of law.

Text of memorial of January 1845:

MAY IT PLEASE YOUR EXCELLENCY – The memorial of the undersigned inhabitants of the parishes of Dingle, Kildrum, Ventry, Donquin, Dunurlin and Kilmacheadar on behalf of themselves and their families.

HUMBLY SHEWETH – That memorialists with their families were formerly in the communion of the Roman Catholic Church; that memorialists, from what they believe and profess to be conscientious motives, have withdrawn from the communion of the Roman Catholic Church and joined that of the Protestant Established Church; that memorialists have suffered reproach and persecution, more or less, from time to time; but that for the last four months particularly memorialists have been, and still are, suffering grievous persecution and loss as converts from the Church of Rome; that when memorialists pass through the town of Dingle and the surrounding district they are insulted and provoked to a breach of the peace by many persons shouting at them, using opprobrious and threatening language and sometimes throwing stones; that memorialists have often had convictions before the magistrates and assistant barrister, for waylaying, assaulting and threatening in cases where they knew or could discover the parties so offending; that memorialists themselves have not been charged with any such crime before the magistrates or assistant barrister; that memorialists cannot purchase the necessaries of life in the markets and shops, the people refusing to sell to them or have any dealings with them as converts from the Roman Catholic Church; that memorialists have reason to know and believe that this state of things is entirely owing to the preaching of the priests of the Roman Catholic Church from their altars; that memorialists are constantly exhorted by their respective ministers in public and in private to peace and goodwill towards all men, even their persecutors and slanderers; that memorialists desire to testify that their Roman Catholic neighbours are well disposed towards them and that they are in peace and goodwill with each other when Roman Catholic priests do not excite them against memorialists; that memorialists do not feel themselves and their families in the enjoyment of that safety and liberty which is the right of every subject of Her Gracious Majesty; that sad consequences are apprehended if such a state of things be allowed to continue; that memorialists are prepared to prove these statements by their own and other most respectable testimony; that memorialists appeal under these circumstances to a humane government on behalf of themselves and their families, who altogether amount to over 800 souls. And memorialists will ever pray.

Signatures to the petition of 1845, with X signifying those unable to write:

Thomas Moriarty	Maurice Connor X	Maurice Donleavy X
Matthew Moriarty	Patrick Landers	Dennis Quill X
Daniel Sullivan	Patrick Fitzgerald	Daniel Kennedy X
John Cavanagh	Maurice Connor X	Michael Sullivan X
James Kennedy	Richard Smith X	James Jordan
Thomas Horgan	John Sullivan	Patrick Giheen X
Simon Upton	Eugene Donleavy X	John Shea X
William Shea X	Michael Lyne X	James Giheen X
Nicholas Francis X	Patrick Giheen X	Timothy Connor X
Thomas Cahalane X	John Murphy	James Gloster
Patrick Kennedy X	Thomas Connor	Michael Kennedy X

John Connor
Timothy Connor X
Thomas Keating X
Maurice O'Brien
James Kennedy
Maurice Fitzgerald
James Connell
Maurice Shea X
Tim Denahy X
Thomas Fitzgerald X
Robin Fitzgerald X
Honora Murphy
 widow X
John Seavers
John Moriarty X
Patrick Kennedy X
Patrick Long X
Patrick Connor X
John Sheehy X
Maurice Kavanagh X
Timothy Shea X
John Dawly X
Thomas Connor X
Michael Kavanagh X
Peter Fitzgerald X
John Lyne X
Thomas Kennedy
John Francis X
Mary Connor widow
 X
Hugh Connor X
Bartholomew
 Kennedy X
John Lawlor X
John Herlihy X
John Riordan
John Giheen X
Eugene Donleavy
Patrick Kennedy X

John Sullivan
John Leacy
Daniel Connor X
Jerry Leehy X
Edmond Moriarty X
Richard Thomas X
David Moriarty X
Edward Hickson
James Moriarty
Richard Hickson
James Carney X
William Carney X
Callaghan McCarthy
Daniel Clifford
John Slatery X
William Thomas
Daniel Lehane
Daniel Slattery
James Huggard
Eugene McCarthy
Thomas Conway
Peter Finn
John Thomas
Batt Lovett X
Timothy Coffey
Matthew Hair X
Patrick McCarthy
Thomas McCarthy
Michael [?] Lynch
Daniel Connell X
Thomas Fitzgerald X
Charles Connor
Laurence Buckley
Patrick Cullinane
Michael Foley X
John Daly X
Patrick Curnane
Thomas Halloran X
Andrew White X

James Riordan X
Daniel White X
Jeremiah Griffin X
James Fitzgerald X
George Bryan X
James Murphy X
Thomas West X
John Moore X
Patrick Doody X
John Moriarty X
Thomas Lynes X
Richard Stretton
John Breen X
Maurice Scanlan X
David Fitzgerald X
James Griffith X
Joseph Marcum
Batt Browne
Thomas Horgan X
William Leahy
Silvy Shea
Patt Gloster X
John Conohan
Thomas Breen X
Patrick Connor
Nicolas Baker X
Patrick Shea X
Richard Finn X
Daniel Welsh X
Batt Moore
Michael Murphy X
Larry Sullivan
Michael Shea X
Richard Walker X
John Foley [Fahy?] X
Michael Connor
Maurice Welsh X
Martin Sullivan X
Michael Walsh.

Bibliography

Newspapers and journals

Achill Missionary Herald and Western Witness
Bath Chronicle
Cheltenham Chronicle
Chester Chronicle
Christian Examiner
Chute's Western Herald
Connaught Telegraph
Cork Constitution
Cork Examiner
Cork Reporter
Cork Southern Reporter
Dublin Weekly Register
Irish Ecclesiastical Gazette
Kerry Evening Post
Kerry Examiner and Munster General Observer
Nenagh Guardian
Southern Reporter
Statesman and Dublin Christian Record
The Athenaeum
The Belfast Protestant Journal
The Bristol Mercury and Western Counties Advertiser
The Pilot
The Tablet
The Times
The Warder
Tralee Chronicle
Tralee Mercury
Tyrone Constitution
Western Courier, West of England Conservative and Plymouth and Devonport Advertiser
Western Herald
Westmoreland Gazette
Worcester Journal

Archives, theses and parliamentary papers

National Archives of Ireland (NAI)
Outrage Papers Kerry 1845: 12/1055, 12/3967, 12/5165, 12/14263, 12/14381, 12/17335.
CSORP/1824/278/2.

National Library of Ireland manuscripts
O'Hara Papers, NLI MS 20,323. Letter of 26 September 1839 by Charles Gayer, and Clifford letter of 11 January 1845 to Major O'Hara.
NLI Ms 24,445: Lithographed Report by Charles Gayer of the Irish Missionary Settlement at Ventry, Co. Kerry [in form of a letter] with illustration, 26 September 1839.

Representative Church Body Library, Dublin
Monkstown, Co. Dublin, Parish records, P 838.
Ventry Burial Records, P 677/27/1.

Trinity College Manuscript Library
MS 6932/22, Letter of Rev. John Jebb, 17 November 1830.

St Columba's College Archive, Whitechurch, Co. Dublin
'Narrative by Viscount Adare'.

Kerry Diocesan Archives, Killarney
Diary of Archdeacon John O'Sullivan, 1850 (typescript copy).

National Gallery of Ireland
Catalogue No. 7808, 'Scripture Readers in Ventry'.

Unpublished PhD thesis
Marion Rogan, 'The "Second Reformation" in Ireland, 1798–1861: case study of Rev. Robert Winning and the Kingscourt District' (unpublished PhD thesis in History, Maynooth University, 2019).

Parliamentary Papers
First Report of the Commissioners of Public Instruction (1835).

Articles and essays

'A Sketch of the Reformation in Dingle and Ventry', *The Christian Guardian and District Visitors' and Sunday School Teachers' Magazine* (Nov. 1842).
[Anonymous], 'Popery and Protestantism in Ireland', *Christian's Monthly Magazine and Universal Review*, vol. 1 (January to June 1844).
Broderick, Eugene, 'Bishop Robert Daly: Ireland's "Protestant Pope"', *History*

Ireland, vol. 14, 6 (November–December 2006).

Bunbury, Turtle, 'The calm before the Big Wind of 1839 was particularly eerie', *Irish Times* (16 October 2017).

Creedon, Ted, 'The Coast Guard on the Dingle Peninsula', *JKAHS*, 2nd ser., vol. 20 (2020), pp 3–32.

Curtin, Gerard, 'Religion and Social Conflict in West Limerick, 1822–1849', *Old Limerick Journal* (Winter 2003).

de Brún, Pádraig, 'A census of the parish of Ferriter, January 1835', *JKAHS*, no 7 (1974).

de Brún, Pádraig, 'Kildare Place Society in Kerry', *JKAHS*, series of articles in issues of 1979 to 1984.

de Brún, Pádraig, 'A Ventry Convert Group, 1842', *JKAHS*, no 13 (1980).

de Brún, Pádraig, 'An tAthair Brasbie', *JKAHS*, no 2 (1969).

de Brún, Pádraig, 'Some lists of Kerry Priests, 1750–1835', *JKAHS*, no 18 (1985).

Evangelical Magazine and Missionary Chronicle, vol. 24, (November 1816).

Graham, Dan, 'The "Colony" at Dingle', *The Kerry Magazine*, no 4 (1992–93).

Irish Ecclesiastical Journal, no 2 (25 August 1840).

Irish Intelligence: The Progress of the Irish Society of London, vols 1–5.

Mac Conghail, Muiris, 'Scoil an Mhisiúin san Oileán Tiar: Conas a fuair Tomás Ó Criomhthain an léamh agus an scríobh?', *Bliainiris* 7 (2007).

Mac Suibhne, Breandán, review of Patricia Byrne, *The Preacher and the Prelate: The Achill Mission Colony and the Battle for Souls in Famine Ireland* (Dublin, 2018), in *Irish Times* (23 June 2018).

McDonagh, Oliver, 'The Economy and Society', in W.E. Vaughan (ed.), *A New History of Ireland, Vol. V: Ireland under the Union 1801–70* (Oxford, 1989).

McNamee, Brian, 'The Second Reformation in Ireland', in *Irish Theological Quarterly*, vol. 33, no 1, (January 1966).

Miller, David W., 'Landscape and Religious Practice: A Study of Mass Attendance in Pre-Famine Ireland', *Éire-Ireland*, vol. 40, 1 & 2 (Spring/Summer 2005), pp 90–106.

Miller, David W., 'Soup and Providence: Varieties of Protestantism and the Great Famine', in Enda Delaney and Breandán Mac Suibhne (eds), *Ireland's Great Famine and Popular Politics* (New York and Abingdon, Oxon, 2016).

Moriarty, Rev. Thomas, 'The Irish Bible', in Charles Bullock (ed.), *The Day of Days*, Vol XII (London, 1883).

Murphy, Clíona, 'Nova Scotia, Ireland and the British Empire in the writings of Charlotte Elizabeth Tonna, 1829–46', in Tom Dunne and Laurence M. Geary (eds), *History and the Public Sphere: Essays in Honour of John A. Murphy* (Cork, 2005), pp 100–13.

Murphy, Clíona, 'The Trial at Tralee: the Reverend Charles Gayer and the *Kerry Examiner*, proselytism or persecution?', in Maurice J. Bric (ed.), *Kerry History and Society* (Dublin, 2020), pp 409–32.

Ní Bhriain, Máirín, 'Imeachtaí na Teanga', in Mícheál Ó Ciosáin (eag.), *Céad Bliain 1871–1971* (Baile an Fheirtéaraigh, 1973).

Ó Conaire, Breandán, 'Mar is cuimhin liom Tomás Dhónaill Uí Chriomhthain: Agallamh le Seán Ó Criomhthain', in Breandán Ó Conaire (ed.), *Tomás an Bhlascaoid* (Indreabhán, Conamara, 1992).

Ó Dubhshláine, Mícheál, 'Na Ventrys', in Pádraig Ó Fiannachta (eag.), *An Clabhsúr: Iris na hOidhreachta 11* (An Daingean, 2002).

Ó hAilín, Tomás, 'Seanchas ar Léamh agus Scríobh na Gaeilge i gCorca Dhuibhne', *JKAHS*, no 4 (1971).

Ó Mainín, Mícheál, 'Is mairg do thréig an t-aon chreideamh cóir', in Mícheál Ó Ciosáin (eag.), *Céad Bliain, 1871–1971* (Baile an Fheirtéaraigh, 1973).

Ó Mainín, Mícheál, 'A Post-Mortem on the Protestant Crusade in Dingle', *JKAHS*, no 29 (1996).

Ó Mainín, Seán, 'Scoileanna an Oileáin', in Aogán Ó Muircheartaigh (eag.), *Oidhreacht an Bhlascaoid* (Baile Átha Cliath, gan dáta).

Ó Raghallaigh, Eoghan, 'Daniel Foley (Domhnall Ó Foghludha)', in James McGuire and James Quinn (eds), *Dictionary of Irish Biography* (Cambridge, 2009).

O'Rourke, Canon, *The Battle of the Faith in Ireland* (Dublin, 1887).

Rafferty, Oliver, 'David Moriarty's episcopal leadership in the diocese of Kerry, 1854–77', in Maurice J. Bric (ed.), *Kerry: History and Society* (Dublin, 2020).

Presbyterian Review and Religious Journal, vol. 18, no 3 (October 1845).

Scott, Rev. William, 'Last Hour of Thomas Dowling, Irish Reader', *Irish Intelligence*, vol. 3 (1850).

The British Magazine and Monthly Register of Religious and Ecclesiastical Information, vol. 35 (February 1849).

The Christian Guardian and Church of England Magazine (1846).

The Christian Lady's Magazine, vol. 23 (January–June 1845).

The Christian's Monthly Magazine, vol. 1 (1844).

The Churchman: a magazine in defence of the Church and Constitution (February 1843 and March 1843).

The Missionary Repository for Youth and Sunday School Missionary Magazine, vol. 8 (1844).

The Protestant Magazine, published under the direction of the committee of the Protestant Association, vol. 7 (1845) and vol. 16 (1854).

Whelan, Irene, 'The Stigma of Souperism', in Cathal Poirtéir (ed.), *The Great Irish Famine* (Cork, 1995).

Books

A sermon on the death of honourable Judge Foster preached in Harold's Cross Church on Sunday July 17ʰ July [1842] by Rev. Robert J. M'Ghee, A.M.

A sketch of the missionary and other operations of the Irish Society established in 1818 (London, 1852).

Alcock, Deborah, *Walking with God: A Memoir of the Venerable John Alcock* (London, 1887).

Alumni Dublinenses 1593–1860.

An appeal on behalf of the Irish Society (Cambridge, 1842).

An Irish and English Spelling Book (Dublin, 1825).

Bowen, Desmond, *Souperism: Myth or Reality?* (Cork, 1970).

Bowen, Desmond, *The Protestant Crusade in Ireland 1800–70* (Dublin, 1978).

Burke, Sir Bernard, *A Genealogical and Heraldic History of the Landed Gentry of Ireland*, 10th edn (London, 1904).

Byrne, Patricia, *The Preacher and the Prelate: The Achill Mission Colony and the Battle for Souls in Famine Ireland* (Dublin, 2018).

Campbell, Rev. W. Graham, *The Apostle of Kerry, or The Life of the Rev Charles Graham* (Dublin, 1868).

Chatterton, Lady, *Rambles in the South of Ireland in the year 1838* (London, 1839).

Colthurst, Elizabeth, *Tales of Erin* (London, n.d.).

Colthurst, Elizabeth, *The Little Ones of Innisfail, or The Children of God* (London, n.d.).

Comharchumann Dhún Chaoin Teoranta, *Logainmneacha Dhún Chaoin, Co. Chiarraí* (Dún Chaoin, 2017).

Davitt, Michael, *The Fall of Feudalism in Ireland* (London, 1904).

de Brún, Pádraig, *Filíocht Sheáin Úi Bhraonáin* (Baile Átha Cliath, 1972).

de Brún, Pádraig, *Scriptural Instruction in the Vernacular: The Irish Society and its Teachers, 1818–1827* (Dublin, 2009).

de Mórdha, Mícheál, *An Island Community: The ebb and flow of the Great Blasket Island*, tr. Gabriel Fitzmaurice (Dublin, 2015).

Dill, Rev. Edward Marcus, *The Mystery Solved or Ireland's Miseries: The Grand Cause and Cure* (Edinburgh, 1852).

Dixon Hardy, Philip (ed.), *The Persecution of Protestants in Ireland in the year 1845* (Dublin, 1845).

Doyle, Aidan, *A History of the Irish Language from the Norman Invasion to Independence* (Oxford, 2015).

Edgar, John, *Trials and Triumphs of Irish Missions* (Belfast, 1846).

First Annual Report of the Priests' Protection Society (Dublin, 1845).

Fisher, Lydia Jane, *Letters from the Kingdom of Kerry in the year 1845* (Dublin, 1847).

Fitzpatrick, W., *et al.*, *What Ireland Needs: The Gospel in the Native Tongue* (London, 1880).

Foley, Patrick, *History of the Natural, Civil, Military and Ecclesiastical State of the County Kerry in Baronies: Corkaguiny* (Dublin, 1907).

Foley, Patrick, *The Ancient and Present State of the Skelligs, Blasket Islands, Donquin, and the West of Dingle* (Baile Átha Cliath, 1903).

General Rules of the Irish Society of London, Published by the Irish Society of London for promoting the education of the native Irish through the medium of their own language, instituted 25 March 1822 (London, 1822).

Gregg, Robert Samuel, *Faithful Unto Death: Memorials of the Life of John Gregg, D.D.* (Dublin, 1879).

Hansard (1845), pp 1079–80.

Holy Cross 150 History Group, *Holy Cross Church, Kenmare 150: A Social and Local History* (Kenmare, 2014).

Leslie, Rev. James B., *Ardfert and Aghadoe Clergy and Parishes* (Dublin, 1940).

Lewis, Samuel, *A Topographical Dictionary of Ireland*, vol. 1 (London, 1840).

Long, Bernie, *Ventry Calling*, tr. Gabriel Fitzmaurice (Cork, 2005).

Loeber, Rolf, and Magda Loeber, *A Guide to Irish Fiction 1650–1900* (Dublin, 2006).

Mac Conghail, Muiris, *A Kerry Island Library* (Dublin, 2006).

Mac Conghail, Muiris, *The Blaskets: People and Literature* (Dublin, 2001).

MacMahon, Bryan, *The Great Famine in Tralee and North Kerry* (Cork, 2017).

MacWalter, J.G., *The Irish Reformation Movement in its religious, social and political aspects* (Dublin, 1852).

Magee, Seán (ed.), *Ballinteer, Co. Dublin: A Local History from Rural to Suburban* (Dublin, 2017).

Moffitt, Miriam, *Soupers and Jumpers: The Protestant Missions in Connemara, 1848–1937* (Dublin, 2008), p. 16.

Monck Mason, Henry Joseph, *Reasons and Authorities and Facts, Afforded by the History of the Irish Society Respecting the Duty of Employing the Irish Language as a More General Mode for Conveying Scriptural Instruction to the Native Peasantry of Ireland* (Dublin, 1848).

Monck Mason, Henry Joseph, *History of the Origins and Progress of the Irish Society* (Dublin, 1846).

Murphy, Janet, and Eileen Chamberlain, *The Church of Ireland in Kerry: a record of church and clergy in the nineteenth century* (2011; e-book available at www.lulu.com).

Murphy, Maureen (ed.), *Ireland's Welcome to the Stranger: Asenath Nicholson* (Dublin, 2002).

Nicholson, Asenath, *Ireland's Welcome to the Stranger, or An Excursion through Ireland in 1844 & 1845 for the purpose of personally investigating the condition of the poor* (London, 1847).

Ó Criomhthain, Tomás, *Allagar na hInise*, eag. Pádraig Ua Maoileoin (1977).

Ó Conaire, Breandán (eag.), *Tomás an Bhlascaoid* (Indreabhán, Conamara,

1992).

Ó Ciosáin, Mícheál (eag.), *Céad Bliain, 1871–1971* (Baile an Fheirtéaraigh, 1973).

Ó Siochfhradha, Pádraig (An Seabhac), *Triocha-céad Chorca Dhuibhne* (Baile Átha Cliath, 1938).

O'Donovan, Patrick F., *Stanley's Letter: The National School System and Inspectors in Ireland, 1831–1922* (Galway, 2017).

O'Neill Daunt, William J., *Ireland and Her Agitators* (Dublin, 1845).

O'Rourke, Canon John, *The Battle of the Faith in Ireland* (Dublin, 1887).

O'Sullivan, Thomas F., *Romantic Hidden Kerry* (Tralee, 1931).

Quarterly extracts from the Correspondence of the Irish Society.

Register of Ecclesiastical Intelligence, published with *Church of England Magazine*, vol. 15 (1843).

Report of the Colony at Dingle 1841 (1842)

Report of the Dingle Colony 1843 (Bristol, 1844).

Report of the Proceedings of the Church Congress held in The Free Trade Hall, Manchester, October 1863 (Manchester, 1864).

Ryan, John, *Popery Unmasked: A Narrative of twenty years of Popish persecution* (London, 1845).

Scott, Rev. George, *The Irish Society's Missions at Doon, Dingle, Ventry and Dunurlin* (Dublin, 1854).

Sewell, William, *Journal of a Residence at the College of St. Columba in Ireland* (London, 1847).

Sheehy, Maurice, *The Dingle Peninsula: 16 walks through its heritage* (1991).

Shields, Hugh, *Tunes of the Munster Pipers*, vol. 1 (Dublin, 2016).

Smith, Charles, *History of Kerry* (1756).

Thackeray, W.M., *The Book of Snobs* (New York, 1852).

The 20th Report of Irish Society for the promotion of the education of the Native Irish through the medium of their own language for the year ending 17 March 1838 (Dublin, 1838).

The 34ᵗʰ Annual Report of the Irish Evangelical Society under the Board of British Missions for year ending 30ᵗʰ April 1853.

The Tenth and Eleventh Reports of the Committee of the Irish Evangelical Society for the Years 1825 and 1826 (Dublin, 1825 and 1826).

Thompson, Mrs D.P., *A Brief Account of the Rise and Progress of the Change in Religious Opinion now taking place in Dingle and the west of the county of Kerry, Ireland* (Dublin, 1847).

Thompson, Mrs D.P., *Ellen of Dingle: A Narrative of Facts* (London, 1850).

Tonna, Charlotte Elizabeth, *The Works of Charlotte Elizabeth*, vol. 1 (New York, 1848).

Whelan, Irene, *The Bible War in Ireland: The 'Second Reformation' and the Polarization of Protestant–Catholic relations, 1800–1840* (Dublin, 2005).

Wilson, Joseph (ed.), *Innisfail; or the Irish Scripture Reader* (London, 1841).

Endnotes

PREFACE

[1] Mrs D.P. Thompson, *A Brief Account of the Rise and Progress of the Change in Religious Opinion now taking place in Dingle and the west of the county of Kerry, Ireland* (1846) [AMT], p. iv. All references here are to the 1846 edition, unless otherwise stated. Another edition, with additional material, was published in 1847. See Afterword for more details on Anna Maria Thompson's life and work.

[2] See http://www.odonohoearchive.com/romantic-hidden-kerry/.

INTRODUCTION

[1] David W. Miller, 'Soup and Providence: Varieties of Protestantism and the Great Famine', in Enda Delaney and Breandán Mac Suibhne (eds), *Ireland's Great Famine and Popular Politics* (New York and Abingdon, Oxon 2016), p. 61.

[2] Thomas F. O'Sullivan, *Romantic Hidden Kerry* (Tralee, 1931), p. 191.

[3] *Achill Missionary Herald and Western Witness* [*AMH*], 28 October 1841.

[4] Mrs D.P. Thompson, *A Brief Account of the Rise and Progress of the Change in Religious Opinion now taking place in Dingle and the west of the county of Kerry, Ireland* (Dublin, 1847), p. 223.

[5] Breandán Mac Suibhne, review of Patricia Byrne, *The Preacher and the Prelate: The Achill Mission Colony and the Battle for Souls in Famine Ireland* (Dublin, 2018), in *Irish Times*, 23 June 2018.

[6] Mícheál Ó Mainín, 'Achrann Creidimh in Iarthar Dhuibhneach', in Mícheál Ó Ciosáin (eag.), *Céad Bliain, 1871–1971* (Baile an Fheirtéaraigh, 1973), p. 40.

[7] Muiris Mac Conghail, 'Scoil an Mhisiúin san Oileán Tiar: Conas a fuair Tomás Ó Criomhthain an léamh agus an scríobh?', *Bliainiris*, 7 (2007), p. 43.

[8] Muiris Mac Conghail, *A Kerry Island Library* (Dublin, 2006), pp 40–1.

[9] AMT, p. 125.

[10] Pádraig Ó Siochfhradha (An Seabhac), *Triocha-céad Chorca Dhuibhne* (Dublin, 1938), p. 105.

[11] *Kerry Evening Post* [*KEP*], 30 March 1844.

[12] *KEP*, 24 July 1844.

[13] The figure 600 was cited in *AMH*, 28 October 1841. The figure 700 was cited in a court case of 1845, as discussed in Chapter 16. In July 1845, *AMH* cited the figure of 800.

[14] Fr John O'Sullivan, curate of Dingle, in *Freeman's Journal* [*FJ*], 1 February 1837.

[15] Rev. Anthony Denny in *KEP*, 30 March 1844.

[16] Lt Herbert Clifford, Dingle Coast Guard, *KEP*, 20 November 1844. Beenbawn (Binn Bán) is near Dingle harbour.

[17] *KEP*, 29 January 1845.

[18] *KEP*, 9 July 1845.

[19] Cited in Henry Joseph Monck Mason, *History of the Origins and Progress of the Irish Society* (Dublin, 1846), p. 78.

[20] *Ibid.*, p. 77.

[21] Ó Criomhthain said that Brian Ó Ceallaigh encouraged him to write 'chun go mbeinn beo agus mé marbh' (so that I may be living when I am dead). See Tomás Ó Criomhthain, *Allagar na hInise*, ed. Pádraig Ua Maoileoin (1977), p. x.

CHAPTER 1

[1] The term 'Second Reformation' is attributed to Archbishop Magee of Dublin. See Brian McNamee, 'The Second Reformation in Ireland', in *Irish Theological Quarterly*, vol. 33, no 1, (January 1966), p. 39.

[2] Desmond Bowen, *Souperism: Myth or Reality?* (Cork, 1970), p. 79.

[3] *Ibid.*, p. 39.

[4] Oliver McDonagh, 'The Economy and Society', in W.E. Vaughan (ed.), *A New History of Ireland, Vol. V: Ireland under the Union 1801–70* (Oxford, 1989), p. 236.

[5] Quoted in Desmond Bowen, *The Protestant Crusade in Ireland 1800–70* (Dublin, 1978), p. 89.

[6] *Ibid.*

[7] Irene Whelan, 'The Stigma of Souperism', in Cathal Poirtéir (ed.), *The Great Irish Famine* (Cork, 1995) p. 136.

[8] *Ibid.*, pp 136–7.

[9] Irene Whelan, *The Bible War in Ireland: The 'Second Reformation' and the Polarization of Protestant–Catholic relations, 1800–1840* (Dublin, 2005), p. 96. The Society for Irish Church Missions (ICM) became well known as a proselytising society, but it was not founded until 1849.

[10] Bowen, *Protestant Crusade*, p. 128.

[11] Letter of Rev. John Jebb to Rev. Charles Foster, 17 November 1830, Trinity College Dublin, MS 6392/22. Further information on Rev. John Jebb can be found in Janet Murphy and Eileen Chamberlain, *The Church of Ireland in Kerry: a record of church and clergy in the nineteenth century* (2011; e-book available at www.lulu.com), pp 92–3. John Jebb went on to serve in England, where there is a memorial to him in Hereford Cathedral.

[12] See Monck Mason, *History of the Origins*, p. 75. The date 1827 is wrongly cited for this meeting in *A Sketch of the Missionary and Other Operations of the Irish Society* (London, 1852), pp 11–12.

[13] J.G. MacWalter, *The Irish Reformation Movement in its religious, social and political aspects* (Dublin, 1852), p. 172.

[14] *Tralee Mercury* [*TM*], 1 April 1829.

[15] *TM*, 22 April 1829.

[16] Robert Samuel Gregg, *Faithful Unto Death: Memorials of the Life of John Gregg, D.D.* (Dublin, 1879), p. 38. See Chapter 7 for Thomas Moriarty's own account of this incident.

[17] *Ibid.*, pp 34–5.

[18] Whelan, *Bible War*, p. 266.

[19] McNamee, 'Second Reformation', p. 41.

[20] Mícheál Ó Mainín, 'Is mairg do thréig an t-aon chreideamh cóir', in *Céad Bliain*, pp 62–3. Citing a manuscript in National Library of Wales, NLW Ms 5345B=A27.

[21] *Ibid.*, p. 65.

[22] Charles Bullock, 'Preface', in W. Fitzpatrick *et al.*, *What Ireland Needs: the Gospel in the Native Tongue* (London, 1880), p. 18.

[23] *KEP*, 21 May 1842.

[24] John Edgar, *Trials and Triumphs of Irish Missions* (Belfast, 1846), p. 9. Emphasis in original.

[25] *Ibid.*, p. 10.

[26] Rev. W. Graham Campbell, *The Apostle of Kerry, or The Life of the Rev. Charles Graham* (Dublin, 1868), p. 46.

[27] *Evangelical Magazine and Missionary Chronicle*, vol. 24 (November, 1816), p. 444.

[28] *The Tenth Report of the Committee of the Irish Evangelical Society for the Year 1825* (Dublin, 1825), p. 19.

[29] *Ibid.*, p. 20.

[30] *Ibid.*

[31] Quoted in Pádraig de Brún, *Filíocht Sheáin Úi Bhraonáin* (Dublin, 1972), p. 21, n.48a. More information on McCrea can be found in this book.

[32] IES, *Tenth Report*, p. 21.

[33] *Ibid.*

[34] *Eleventh Report of the Committee of the Irish Evangelical Society for the Year 1826* (Dublin, 1826), p. 25.

[35] *Ibid.*, p. 32. Italics in original.

[36] See IES, *Eleventh Report*, p. 25.

[37] *Ibid.*

[38] *Ibid.* See Appendix 1 for the full text of the petition.

[39] *Chute's Western Herald* [*CWH*], 7 May 1828.

[40] *Ibid.*

[41] *CWH*, 26 April 1828.

[42] *CWH*, 7 May 1828.

CHAPTER 2

[1] Pádraig de Brún, *Scriptural Instruction in the Vernacular; the Irish Society and its Teachers, 1818–1827* (Dublin, 2009), p. 483. Emphasis in original. This statement was revised in 1842, as detailed by de Brún in a footnote.

[2] Henry Joseph Monck Mason, *Reasons and Authorities and Facts, Afforded by the History of the Irish Society Respecting the Duty of Employing the Irish Language as a More General Mode for Conveying Scriptural Instruction to the Native Peasantry of Ireland* (Dublin, 1848), p. 13. Various editions of Irish Bibles are on display in Ionad an Bhlascaoid Mhóir, Dún Chaoin.

[3] Whelan, *Bible Wars*, p. 115.

[4] Monck Mason, *History of the Origins*, p. 9.

[5] de Brún, *Scriptural Instruction*, p. 489.

[6] *Ibid.*, p. vi.

[7] *Ibid.*, p. v.

[8] Fitzpatrick *et al.*, *What Ireland Needs*, p. 152.

[9] Monck Mason, *History of the Origins*, p. 2.

[10] Monck Mason, *Reasons and Authorities*, pp 3–4.

[11] Monck Mason, *History of the Origins*, p. 4.

[12] *Ibid.*, p. 4

[13] *Ibid.*, p. 9.

[14] *Ibid.*, pp 12–13.

[15] *Saunders Newsletter*, 12 March 1856, cited in Desmond Bowen, *Protestant Crusade in Ireland*, p. 228.

16 *KEP*, 19 April 1828.

17 Whelan, *Bible Wars*, p. 115.

18 Eugene Broderick, 'Bishop Robert Daly: Ireland's "Protestant Pope"', *History Ireland*, vol. 14, 6 (November–December 2006).

19 Monck Mason, *History of the Origins*, p. 10.

20 Royal Irish Academy [RIA] Library, HT (Box) 430/4.

21 de Brún, *Scriptural Instruction*, p. 113.

22 de Brún, *Scriptural Instruction*, p. 14. This book has a full account of Connellan's life, pp 14–39.

23 *Ibid.*, p. 113, n.5.

24 Máirín Ní Bhriain, 'Imeachtaí na Teanga', in *Céad Bliain*, p. 114.

25 See Tomás Ó hAilín, 'Seanchas ar Léamh agus Scríobh na Gaeilge i gCorca Dhuibhne', *Journal of the Kerry Archaeological and Historical Society (JKAHS)*, no 4 (1971), p. 132, n.13 and p. 138.

26 Monck Mason, *Reasons and Authorities*, p. 16.

27 Monck Mason, *History of the Origins*, pp 23–4.

28 *A Sketch of the Missionary*, p. 9.

29 *Presbyterian Review and Religious Journal*, vol. 18, no 3 (October 1845), pp 317–18. Emphasis in original.

30 *Ibid.*, p. 319.

31 Patrick Foley, *History of the Natural, Civil, Military and Ecclesiastical State of the County of Kerry in Baronies: Corkaguiny* (Dublin, 1907), p. 215.

32 *Essex Herald*, 4 June 1850.

33 Monck Mason, *Reasons and Authorities*, p. 20.

34 *Ibid.*, p. 20.

35 Monck Mason, *History of the Origins*, p. 24.

36 Deborah Alcock, *Walking with God: A Memoir of the Venerable John Alcock* (London, 1887), p. 219.

37 *Ibid.*, p. 124.

38 *Ibid.*, p. 126.

39 *Ibid.*, p. 124.

40 Rev. Thomas Moriarty, 'The Irish Bible', in Charles Bullock (ed.), *The Day of Days*, Vol XII (London, 1883), p. 117. See also de Brún, *Scriptural Instruction*, p. 87 for the names of some of these manuscript men. The term Irishian is defined as 'a lover or student of the Irish language; (more generally) a student of or expert in Irish culture'. (Lexico.com) The earliest use of the word Irishian was by the author Gerald Griffin (1803–1840). The spellings Iresian and Iretian are also found.

41 *General Rules of the Irish Society of London* (London, 1822). Published by the Irish Society of London for promoting the education of the native Irish through the medium of their own language, instituted 25 March 1822.

42 *Ibid.*, p. 6.

43 *Ibid.*, p. 9–10.

44 *Ibid.*, p. 23.

45 *Ibid.*, p. 8.

46 *Ibid.*, p. 10.

47 *Ibid.*, p. 11.

48 Bowen, *Protestant Crusade*, p. 225.

49 Miriam Moffitt, *Soupers and Jumpers: The Protestant Missions in Connemara, 1848–1937* (Dublin, 2008), p. 16.

[50] Bowen, *Souperism*, p. 80.

[51] Moffitt, *Soupers*, p. 92.

[52] Bowen, *Protestant Crusade*, p. 225.

[53] *Irish Ecclesiastical Gazette* [*IEG*], 1 May 1856, p. 28.

[54] Whelan, *Bible War*, p. 173.

[55] *Ibid.*, p. 177.

[56] *Ibid.*, p. 172.

[57] Monck Mason, *History of the Origins*, p. 25.

[58] *Ibid.*, p. 25.

[59] *Ibid.*, p. 25.

[60] Monck Mason, *History of the Origins*, p. 26.

[61] *Ibid.*, pp 27–8. See also his *Reasons and Authorities*, p. 24.

[62] Irish Evangelical Society, *Tenth Report* (1825), p. 20.

[63] *Ibid.*, p. 21.

[64] *Quarterly extracts from the Correspondence of the Irish Society* [*QE*], no 14 (1 October 1824), p. 118.

[65] *QE*, no 16 (1 April 1825), p. 16.

[66] *Ibid.*, p. 5.

[67] *Ibid.*, p. 6.

[68] *Ibid.*, p. 4.

[69] *QE*, no 17 (1 July 1825), p. 20.

[70] *Ibid.*, p. 20.

[71] *QE*, no 20 (1 April 1826), p. 63.

[72] *Ibid.*, p. 63.

[73] *Ibid.*, p. 64.

[74] *Ibid.*, p. 63. Jagoe seems to have become a minister later, as a Rev. A. Jagoe is listed as an inspector of the Irish Society in Cong, Co. Mayo, in 1856. *A Sketch of the Missionary*, p. 56.

[75] *QE*, no 20 (1 April 1826).

[76] *QE*, no 22 (1 October 1826), p. 78.

[77] *QE*, no 23 (1 January 1827), p. 84.

[78] *Ibid.*, p. 85.

[79] *QE*, no 23 (1 January 1827), p. 86.

[80] *QE*, no 27 (1 January 1828), p. 117.

[81] *QE*, no 28 (1 July 1828), p. 127.

[82] *QE*, no 31 (1 July 1829), p. 149.

[83] *Ibid.*, p. 149.

[84] *QE*, no 38 (1 October 1831), p. 204.

[85] *QE*, no 48 (20 October 1834), p. 289.

[86] *QE*, no 50 (20 July 1835), p. 305.

[87] *QE*, no 53 (20 July 1836), p. 329.

[88] *QE*, no 54 (20 October 1836), p. 1.

[89] *The Works of Charlotte Elizabeth*, vol. 1 (New York, 1848), p. 401. The author was Charlotte Elizabeth Tonna, an English woman who lived in Ireland for a time. She was a devoted evangelical with strong anti-Catholic beliefs, and she greatly admired the Irish Society's work. She married Captain George Phelan in 1813, and after his death in 1837, she married Lewis Tonna. She was a successful novelist, a champion of women's rights and, under the name 'Charlotte Elizabeth', the influential editor of a number of evangelical magazines, including *The Christian Lady's Magazine*. See also Clíona Murphy, 'Nova

Scotia, Ireland and the British Empire in the writings of Charlotte Elizabeth Tonna, 1829–46', in Tom Dunne and Laurence M. Geary (eds), *History and the Public Sphere: Essays in Honour of John A. Murphy* (Cork, 2005), pp 100–13.

90 *An Irish and English Spelling Book,* Preface, p. iv. Italics in original.

91 Monck Mason, *History of the Origins,* p. 15.

92 *Ibid.,* p. 14.

93 *Ibid.*

94 *Ibid.*

95 *Ibid.,* p 15.

96 *An Appeal on behalf of the Irish Society* (Cambridge, 1842), p. 8 and p. 12.

97 Aidan Doyle, *A History of the Irish Language from the Norman Invasion to Independence* (Oxford, 2015), p. 120.

98 Muiris Mac Conghail, *The Blaskets: People and Literature* (Dublin, 2001), p. 42.

99 Whelan, *Bible Wars,* p. 260. Whelan cites a 1993 interview with the poet Nuala Ní Dhomhnaill as the source of this observation.

100 Breandán Ó Conaire, 'Mar is cuimhin liom Tomás Dhónaill Uí Chriomhthain: Agallamh le Seán Ó Criomhthain', in Breandán Ó Conaire (ed.), *Tomás an Bhlascaoid* (Galway, 1992), p. 206, 'Fuaireadar san an t-eolas a bhi acu uirthi ó Léitheoirí an Chait Bhric, a bhí go flúirseach i nDún Chaoin agus in iarthar Chorca Dhuibhne blianta móra fada sarar tháinig Tomás isteach sa tsaol so riamh.' (They received their knowledge from the speckled-cat readers, who were numerous in Dunquin and western Corca Dhuibhne many years before Tomás ever came into this world.)

101 [Anonymous], 'Popery and Protestantism in Ireland', in *Christian's Monthly Magazine and Universal Review,* vol. 1 (January to June 1844), p. 281. Good Friday is Aoine an Chéasta, literally 'Friday of the Crucifixion' in Irish.

102 *Tralee Chronicle [TC],* 30 March 1844.

103 *Ibid.*

104 *The Hampshire Chronicle,* 5 September 1857. Cited in Ó Conaire, *Tomás an Bhlascaoid,* p. 52.

105 *KEP,* 30 April 1845.

106 Canon Hayman, 'A Reminiscence', in Fitzpatrick *et al., What Ireland Needs,* pp 54–66, at p. 58.

107 Canon Hayman, 'A Second Reminiscence', in Fitzpatrick *et al., What Ireland Needs,* p. 84. Italics in original.

108 *The Works of Charlotte Elizabeth,* p. 401.

109 *KEP,* 24 May 1843.

110 Elizabeth Colthurst, *The Little Ones of Innisfail, or The Children of God* (London, n.d.), p. 78. Innisfail was from Inis Fáil, Isle of Destiny, a poetic name for Ireland, popularised by Thomas Moore's composition 'Song of Innisfail'.

CHAPTER 3

1 See de Brún, *Filíocht,* p. 93 and p. 104.

2 [Anonymous], 'Popery and Protestantism in Ireland', in *The Christian's Monthly Magazine and Universal Review,* vol. 1 (January to June 1844), p. 279.

3 *Essex Herald,* 4 June 1850.

4 *Ibid.*

5 Joseph Wilson (ed.), *Innisfail; or the Irish Scripture Reader* (London, 1841), p. 1. To avoid confusion, this book is referred to as Wilson, *Innisfail* and Elizabeth Colthurst's book is

referred to as Colthurst, *Little Ones of Innisfail*.

6   Wilson, *Innisfail*, p. 12.

7   *Ibid.*, p. 17.

8   *Ibid.*, p. 97–8.

9   *Irish Intelligence, The Progress of the Irish Society of London*, vol. 2 (1849), pp 99–103. This source incorrectly names the secretary as 'Miss Mason'. Catherine Hartland Mahon was the daughter of Rev. Arthur Mahon of Cavetown House, Co. Roscommon, and she was one of the main fund-raisers for the Bible campaign in Dingle and west Kerry. She married Col Archibald Inglis in 1844 and lived in Kerse Hill, Falkirk, Scotland.

10 *Ibid.*, p. 100.

11 Edward Norman, 'Thomas Dowling, the Irish Inspector', in Fitzpatrick *et al.*, *What Ireland Needs*, p. 121.

12 Norman, 'Thomas Dowling', p. 122.

13 *The Kerry Examiner and Munster Observer* [*KEx*], 3 November 1843.

14 *The Christian's Monthly Magazine*, vol. 1 (1844), p. 279.

15 Cited by de Brún, *Scriptural Instruction*, p. 213. Details of Dowling's movements cited here are from this source.

16 *Ibid.*, p. 213.

17 *Ibid.*, p. 216.

18 *Ibid.*, p. 213.

19 Cited in *What Ireland Needs*, p. 80.

20 Rev. William Fitzpatrick, 'Bishop Gregg and the Irish Society', *What Ireland Needs*, pp 41–2.

21 Norman, 'Thomas Dowling', p. 123.

22 *Ibid.*, p. 123.

23 Wilson, *Innisfail*, pp 17–18.

24 *Ibid.*, p. 18.

25 *Irish Intelligence*, vol. 2 (1849), p. 101.

26 *The Christian's Monthly Magazine*, vol. 1 (1844), p. 279.

27 Monck Mason, *History of the Origins*, p. 39.

28 Norman, 'Thomas Dowling', p. 125.

29 *Irish Intelligence*, vol. 2 (1849), p. 101.

30 *Ibid.*, p. 102.

31 *Céad Bliain*, p. 49.

32 Wilson, *Innisfail*, pp 18–19. The 'precious minister' was Rev. Charles Gayer, and the 'noble friend' was probably Lord Ventry, the main landlord of west Kerry and an ardent supporter of the proselytising campaign.

33 Wilson, *Innisfail*, pp 21–2. 'G——r' refers to Rev. Charles Gayer, and the curate may have been Rev. Goodman, long-time minister of the area who spoke Irish fluently.

34 *The Statesman and Dublin Christian Record* [*Statesman*], 19 March 1841, p. 4.

35 Wilson, *Innisfail*, p. 231.

36 *Irish Intelligence*, vol. 2 (1849), p. 102.

37 Wilson, *Innisfail*, pp 29–33.

38 *Ibid.*, p. 36.

39 *Ibid.*, pp 23–4.

40 *Ibid.*, p. 25.

41 Alcock, *Walking with God*, p. 129.

42 *Irish Intelligence*, vol. 1 (1848), p. 9. The quotation may be from the wife of Denis Dunlevy, a convert who died in 1841. See Chapter 9 for more information on Denis Dunlevy.

43 Norman, 'Thomas Dowling', pp 127–31.

44 *Ibid.*

45 Wilson, *Innisfail*, p. 42.

46 AMT, p. 50.

47 *KEP*, 13 June 1849.

48 *Ibid.*

49 *KEP*, 2 June 1849.

50 *Ibid.*

51 Rev. William Scott, 'Last Hour of Thomas Dowling, Irish Reader', in *Irish Intelligence*, vol. 3 (1850), p. 171. Written on 10 October 1850.

52 *Ibid.*

53 *Ibid.*, p. 174.

54 *Ibid.*

55 See https://churchrecords.irishgenealogy.ie/churchrecords/display-pdf.jsp?pdfName=k-461-1-1-010. I am grateful to Dr Pádraig de Brún for this information.

56 Norman, 'Thomas Dowling', p. 131.

57 *Ibid.*

CHAPTER 4

1 Mícheál Ó Dubhshláine, 'Na Ventrys', in Pádraig Ó Fiannachta (eag.), *An Clabhsúr: Iris na hOidhreachta 11* (An Daingean, 2002), pp 54–108

2 National Archives of Ireland [NAI], CSORP/1824/278/2. See also Ó Dubhshláine, 'Na Ventrys', p. 71.

3 *FJ*, 24 October 1827.

4 *TM*, 9 June 1838.

5 *KEP*, 16 June 1839.

6 Charles Smith, *History of Kerry* (1756), p. 33 and p. 96.

7 Michael Davitt, *The Fall of Feudalism in Ireland* (London, 1904), p. 30.

8 W.M. Thackeray, *The Book of Snobs* (New York, 1852), pp 44–50.

9 *TM*, 14 February 1829.

10 *TM*, 31 July 1830.

11 *TM*, 13 July 1831.

12 *TM*, 16 July 1831.

13 *TM*, 30 July 1831.

14 *Western Herald* [*WH*], 17 May 1832.

15 *Belfast Newsletter*, 21 September 1832.

16 *WH*, 9 May 1833.

17 *TM*, 16 April 1834. Cloghane is at the foot of Mount Brandon, on the north coast of the Dingle peninsula.

18 *TM*, 16 April 1834.

19 *KEP*, 19 April 1834.

20 *KEP*, 21 June 1834. See also *WH*, 23 June 1834.

21 *KEP*, 21 June 1834.

22 *FJ*, 13 January 1836.

23 See *FJ*, 15 November 1839; *FJ*, 18 December 1839.

24 *KEP*, 25 November 1840.

25 Sir Bernard Burke, *A Genealogical and Heraldic History of the Landed Gentry of Ireland*, 10th edn (London, 1904), p. 587.

[26] *KEP*, 19 June 1830.

[27] *KEP*, 25 November 1840. See also *TM*, 9 June 1838, *KEx*, 10 May 1842 and *FJ*, 13 January 1836 for further detail on the Ventry estate.

[28] *KEP*, 25 November 1840.

[29] *Ibid.*

[30] *KEP*, 5 June 1841.

[31] See for example *TM*, 9 February 1839.

[32] *TM*, 20 July 1839.

[33] *The Warder*, 11 December 1841. Neither Hawthorn nor Coolnaleen House can be identified exactly.

[34] *KEx*, 11 August 1840.

[35] *Ibid.*

[36] *Ibid.* Emphasis in original.

[37] *KEP*, 19 August 1840.

[38] *Connaught Telegraph*, 2 September 1840.

[39] *Ibid.*

[40] *KEP*, 16 September 1840.

[41] *KEP*, 29 August 1840.

[42] *KEP*, 2 September 1840.

[43] Quoted in *KEP*, 16 September 1840.

[44] *KEx*, 22 September 1840.

[45] *KEP*, 25 November 1840.

[46] *KEx*, 10 May 1842.

[47] *Ibid.*

[48] *KEx*, 17 May 1842. See *KEx*, 20 May 1842 for a second column written from Tralee gaol.

CHAPTER 5

[1] *KEP*, 30 January 1833.

[2] Foley, *History of the Natural*, p. 212.

[3] AMT, p. 1.

[4] *Ibid.*, p. 2.

[5] *Ibid.*, pp 9–10.

[6] *Ibid.*, p. 11.

[7] *Ibid.*, p. 50.

[8] *Ibid.*, p. 169.

[9] *Ibid.*

[10] Murphy and Chamberlain, *Church of Ireland*, p. 70.

[11] Pádraig de Brún, 'A census of the Parish of Ferriter, 1835', *JKAHS*, no 7 (1974), p. 46.

[12] Whelan, *Bible Wars*, pp 254–5.

[13] Letter of Rev John Jebb, 17 November 1830, TCD Ms 6932/22.

[14] Murphy and Chamberlain, *Church of Ireland*, p. 71. The Goodman home was in Ballyameen, Ballymore, several kilometres from the town of Dingle.

[15] AMT, p. 5.

[16] TCD Ms 6932/22. Emphasis in original.

[17] *KEP*, 11 July 1832.

[18] *KEP*, 6 April 1839.

[19] Hugh Shields, *Tunes of the Munster Pipers*, vol. 1 (Dublin, 2016), p. xii.

20 Murphy and Chamberlain, *Church of Ireland*, p. 71.

21 See Samuel Lewis, *A Topographical Dictionary of Ireland*, vol. 1 (London, 1840), p. 460. Captain Bowie is referred to in *Chute's Western Herald*, 11 and 29 December 1828. For more information on the Coast Guard see Ted Creedon, 'The Coast Guard on the Dingle Peninsula', *JKAHS*, 2nd ser., vol. 20 (2020), pp 3–32.

22 AMT, p. 6. See also Murphy and Chamberlain, *Church of Ireland*, p. 93 for more details on his career.

23 AMT, p. 6.

24 Whelan, *Bible Wars*, p. 256.

25 AMT, p. 7.

26 *Cork Southern Reporter*, 28 August 1838.

27 *TM*, 22 September 1832.

28 *TM*, 20 October 1832.

29 AMT, p. 8.

30 Diary of Archdeacon John O'Sullivan, Kerry Diocesan Archives, p. 79. Haceldama, the field of blood or potter's field, was the place where Judas took his own life. See Matthew 27:3-8 and Acts of the Apostles 1:18-19.

31 Diary of Archdeacon John O'Sullivan, Kerry Diocesan Archives, pp 79–80.

32 *KEP*, 24 October 1832.

33 *KEP*, 27 October 1832.

34 NAI, CSO/RP/1832/5265. See also NAI, CSO/RP/1832/4761.

35 AMT, p. 7.

36 See David W. Miller, 'Landscape and Religious Practice: A Study of Mass Attendance in Pre-Famine Ireland', *Éire-Ireland*, vol. 40, 1 & 2 (Spring/Summer 2005), pp 90–106.

37 Statistics from *First Report of the Commissioners of Public Instruction* (1835), pp 164–80. I am grateful to Breandán Mac Suibhne for drawing my attention to this source.

38 Oliver Rafferty, 'David Moriarty's episcopal leadership in the diocese of Kerry, 1854–77', in Maurice J. Bric (ed.), *Kerry: History and Society* (Dublin, 2020), p. 392.

39 *KEP*, 26 February 1836.

40 AMT, p. 48.

41 *KEP*, 20 February 1836.

42 *First Report of the Commissioners of Public Instruction* (1835).

43 *The Standard*, 28 October 1838, cited in Murphy and Chamberlain, *Church of Ireland*, p. 93.

44 *KEP*, 12 January 1839.

45 Thomas Moriarty, letter of 10 December 1838, in 'Narrative by Viscount Adare', St Columba's College Archive, p. 2. This manuscript is a compilation of letters and documents relating to the evangelical campaign in west Kerry. On the opening page, Viscount Adare wrote, 'The following references to letters and short analyses of their contents will help to illustrate the progress of affairs.'

46 *KEP*, 6 March 1839.

47 *Ibid.*

48 *KEP*, 15 May 1839.

49 *Report of the Proceedings of the Church Congress held in The Free Trade Hall, Manchester, October 1863* (Manchester, 1864), p. 114. Online.

50 *AMH*, 28 May 1840, p. 59.

51 *AMH*, 26 March 1840, p. 36.

52 *KEP*, 24 July 1841.

53 *The Little Ones of Innisfail*, pp 9–15.

[54] *Ibid.*, p. 13.

[55] Letters written by George Gubbins in 1845 describing his work in Ballingarry can be found in *Christian Guardian and Church of England Magazine* (1846). See also Gerard Curtin, 'Religion and Social Conflict in West Limerick, 1822–1849', *Old Limerick Journal* (Winter 2003), pp 43–54.

[56] Murphy and Chamberlain, *Church of Ireland*, p. 93. I am grateful to Anthea Kennedy Gayer Mitchell for genealogical information on the Gayer family.

[57] AMT, p. 10.

[58] *Ibid.*, p. 12. Emphasis in original.

[59] *Ibid.*, pp 10–13.

[60] MacWalter, *Irish Reformation*, p. 171 and pp 172–3.

[61] *KEP*, 30 April 1845.

[62] AMT, p. 46.

[63] *QE*, no 55 (January 1837), p. 350. Written in November 1836 by an anonymous correspondent.

[64] *QE*, no 56 (July 1837), p. 360.

[65] *QE*, no 58 (January 1838), p. 373. Written in November 1837.

[66] *KEP*, 21 January 1837.

[67] *Ibid.*

[68] *FJ*, 1 February 1837.

[69] *KEP*, 15 February 1837.

[70] *Ibid.*

[71] *TM*, 18 February 1837.

[72] *KEP*, 22 February 1837.

[73] 'Sketch of the Reformation in Dingle and Ventry', in *The Christian Guardian and District Visitors' and Sunday School Teachers' Magazine* (November 1842), p. 434.

[74] AMT, p. 47.

[75] 'Sketch of the Reformation in Dingle and Ventry', p. 434.

CHAPTER 6

[1] *20th Report of Irish Society for the promotion of the education of the Native Irish through the medium of their own language for the year ending 17 March 1838* (Dublin, 1838) p. 15.

[2] *Ibid.*, p. 16.

[3] *Ibid.*, p. 24.

[4] Patrick F. O'Donovan, *Stanley's Letter: The National School System and Inspectors in Ireland, 1831–1922* (Galway, 2017), p. 12.

[5] For further details on KPS, see O'Donovan, *Stanley's Letter*, pp 12–18.

[6] For more details, see Pádraig de Brún, 'Kildare Place Society in Kerry', *JKAHS*, no 14 (1981), pp 37–93. This is one of a series of articles on the Kildare Place Society in each issue of the journal from 1979 to 1984.

[7] *KEP*, 8 August 1829.

[8] *TM*, 28 October 1829.

[9] *TM*, 4 November 1829.

[10] *Ibid.*

[11] *Ibid.*

[12] See Ní Bhriain, 'Imeachtaí na Teanga', pp 103–9 for more information on hedge schools in Corca Dhuibhne.

[13] Foley, *History of the Natural*, pp 122–3.

14 *20th Report of the Irish Society* (Dublin, 1840), p. 17.

15 *Ibid.*

16 *KEP*, 21 June 1837.

17 AMT, p. 18.

18 All in AMT, pp 18–21. 'Carminole' refers to Coumeenole near Slea Head, an area that was considered very remote and inaccessible. The scenic road around Slea Head did not exist at this time.

19 AMT, p. 22. Copy annotated by Fr John O'Sullivan, Kerry County Archives, Tralee.

20 AMT, p. 23.

21 *KEP*, 3 June 1837.

22 *KEP*, 17 June 1837.

23 *KEP*, 21 June 1837.

24 *TM*, 7 June 1837.

25 *KEP*, 21 June 1837.

26 *Ibid.* See also Revelations 13:11-18.

27 *KEP*, 16 June 1838.

28 O'Sullivan, *Diary*, pp 62–3. Author's translation, 'And thus was Father John protected.'

29 *Ibid.*, p. 12.

30 *Ibid.*, p. 36.

31 *Ibid.*

32 *TM*, 20 April 1839.

33 *Ibid.*

34 AMT, p. 23.

35 See Holy Cross 150 History Group, *Holy Cross Church, Kenmare 150: A Social and Local History* (Kerry, 2014) for a detailed treatment of the life and work of Archdeacon John O'Sullivan.

36 *FJ*, 19 November 1874.

CHAPTER 7

1 *The British Magazine and Monthly Register of Religious and Ecclesiastical Information*, vol. 35 (February 1849), pp 153–4. Online.

2 See Ó Siochfhradha, *Triocha-céad Chorca Dhuibhne*, p. 54, 'Is annamh a thugann Béarlóirí aon ainm eile air ach Ventry […] Póilíní, gardaí cósta agus lucht phuist agus 'na dteannta san, an Missionary Society, a thosnuigh ag obair ann tuairim na bl. 1835 a thug Ventry air i n-ionad Cantra.' (English speakers rarely use any name other than Ventry […] It was the police, coast guards and postal staff, along with the Missionary Society which began working there around 1835, who named it Ventry instead of Cantra.) Cantra was Ceann Trá.

3 Wilson, *Innisfail*, p. 209.

4 *Ibid.*, p. 210.

5 *Ibid.*, pp 212–13.

6 *Ibid.*, p. 214.

7 *Ibid.*, pp 216–17.

8 *Ibid.*, pp 218–19. See also AMT, p. 65.

9 Wilson, *Innisfail*, p. 221.

10 *Ibid.*, p. 223.

11 *Ibid.*, p. 107.

12 *Ibid.*, p. 224.

[13] *Ibid.*, p. 219

[14] *Ibid.*, pp 223–4.

[15] *Ibid.*, p. 219.

[16] *Ibid.*, p. 223.

[17] AMT, p. 49.

[18] *Ibid.*, p. 51.

[19] Circular letter of Charles Gayer, written on 26 September 1839, published in *The Warder*, 30 November 1839. A copy is also found in NLI, O'Hara Papers, MS 20,323 and in the Adare Narrative in the archives of St Columba's College, Dublin.

[20] *Ibid.*

[21] AMT, p. 54.

[22] *The Warder*, 30 November 1839.

[23] *KEP*, 20 March 1839.

[24] *Ibid.*

[25] MacWalter, *The Irish Reformation*, pp 194–5. O'Sullivan also gives the date 13 November 1838 for the laying of the foundation stone. (*Romantic Hidden Kerry*, p. 536.)

[26] Monck Mason, *History of the Origins*, p. 81

[27] See Elizabeth Colthurst, *Tales of Erin* (London, n.d.), pp 97–102.

[28] *Ibid.*, p. 96.

[29] *Ibid.*, pp 101–2.

[30] *The Kerryman*, 21 September 1963.

[31] National Gallery of Ireland, Catalogue No. 7808.

[32] For further biographical information on these individuals, see Pádraig de Brún, 'A Ventry Convert Group, 1842', *JKAHS*, no 13 (1980), pp 143–8.

CHAPTER 8

[1] Ó Mainín, 'Achrann Creidimh', p. 44, n.6.

[2] Biographical information here is taken mainly from Rev. James B. Leslie, *Ardfert and Aghadoe Clergy and Parishes* (Dublin, 1940), pp 20–1. In Trinity College records, Denis Moriarty is described as 'agricola' or farmer. See *Alumni Dublinenses 1593–1860*, p. 598. Mac Conghail states that Denis Moriarty was a miller. See Mac Conghail, 'Scoil an Mhisiúin'.

[3] Thomas Moriarty letter, *IEG*, 10 December 1881, p. 14.

[4] Leslie, *Ardfert*. One account said that the young Moriarty went to disturb a Protestant service and 'while waiting for the moment when he should commence his interruptions, received such impressions from the truth he heard, as ultimately led to his conversion'. Rev. Edward Marcus Dill, *The Mystery Solved or Ireland's Miseries: the Grand Cause and Cure* (Edinburgh, 1852), p. 282. Online.

[5] *IEG*, 10 December 1881, p. 14.

[6] *KEx*, 2 November 1841, citing the *Kilkenny Journal*.

[7] Leslie, *Ardfert*, p. 20.

[8] *IEG*, 17 December 1881, p. 14.

[9] *KEP*, 25 March 1846.

[10] *IEG*, 31 December 1881, p. 21.

[11] *Ibid.*, p. 22.

[12] *Presbyterian Review and Religious Journal*, vol. 18, no 3 (October 1845), p. 322.

[13] *Ibid.*, p. 323.

[14] *KEP*, 21 October 1837.

15 Patrick Foley, *The Ancient and Present State of the Skelligs, Blasket Islands, Donquin and the West of Dingle* (Dublin, 1903), p. 57. Foley claimed that Moriarty studied for the priesthood, but I have found no other evidence to support this.

16 Breandán Ó Conaire, 'Mainistir na Súpanna', in Ó Conaire (eag.), *Tomás an Bhlascaoid*, p. 48.

17 *QE*, no 61 (17 January 1839).

18 *Ibid.*

19 Mac Conghail, *Blaskets*, p. 41.

20 Adare Narrative, St Columba's College Archive, Co. Dublin. Monsell lived in Clarina, Co. Limerick.

21 *Ibid.*

22 *Ibid.*

23 *Ibid.*

24 *Ibid.* Rev. Gayer letter of 12 January 1839.

25 *Ibid.*

26 *Ibid.*

27 AMT, p. 61n.

28 *Ibid.*

29 *KEP*, 12 January 1839. See also Turtle Bunbury, 'The calm before the Big Wind of 1839 was particularly eerie', *Irish Times*, 16 October 2017.

30 Adare Narrative. A 'cliabh' was a basket for carrying turf.

31 *KEP*, 2 December 1840.

32 *TM*, 20 February 1839.

33 *TM*, 9 February 1839.

34 *KEP*, 20 February 1839.

35 *KEP*, 27 February 1839.

36 *KEP*, 20 February 1839.

37 *Ibid.*

38 *Ibid.*

39 *KEP*, 23 February 1839.

40 *KEP*, 16 March 1839. Spelling and grammar as in original. The suggestion in this notice that Moriarty should have become a miller rather than a preacher could indicate that his father was indeed a miller, as stated by Muiris Mac Conghail.

41 *KEP*, 20 March 1839. Lawlaider was from the Irish *lámh láidir*, or physical force.

42 *KEP*, 2 December 1840.

43 *Ibid.*

44 AMH, 25 June 1840, pp 70–1.

45 *Ibid.* Moriarty was familiar with the Catholic custom of stations, holding community Masses in private houses, and he seems to have adopted the term for his own household gatherings.

46 *Ibid.*

47 *Irish Ecclesiastical Journal*, no 2 (25 August 1840), pp 21–2.

48 *Statesman*, 19 March 1841.

49 *KEP*, 30 March 1844.

50 *Ibid.*

51 *Ibid.*

52 *Ibid.*

53 *TC*, 22 June 1844.

54 *Ibid.*

[55] Ó Mainín, 'Achrann Creidimh', p. 46, n.9.

[56] AMT, p. 85. 'Paddy Connor', who defied the priest and proclaimed the Bible openly in Dingle, was the son of Séamus Bán.

[57] Monck Mason, *History of the Origins*, 2nd edn, p. 118.

[58] *Cork Examiner*, 26 July 1843.

[59] *Ibid.*

[60] *Freeman's Journal*, 18 March 1842.

[6⁻] *Kilkenny Journal* cited in *KEx*, 12 November 1841. The editor of the *Examiner* characterised Moriarty's visit as 'a Quixotic expedition to Kilkenny'.

[62] Adare Narrative, Letter of 4 February 1840.

[63] *Ibid.*

[64] Adare Narrative.

[65] *Ibid.*

[66] *Ibid.*

[67] *Ibid.* In a cliff cave known as 'Nancy Brown's parlour' near Dingle, the inscription 'J. Sewell 1841' has been noted. See Maurice Sheehy, *The Dingle Peninsula: 16 walks through its heritage* (1991), p. 23.

[68] William Sewell, *Journal of a Residence at the College of St. Columba in Ireland* (London, 1847), p. 6. Online. See also Bryan MacMahon, 'An Irishman's Diary', *Irish Times*, 2 April 2018.

[69] *A sketch of the missionary and other operations of the Irish Society established in 1818* (London, 1852), pp 12–13. Online.

[70] *Ibid.*, p. 36.

[71] Monck Mason, *History of the Origins*, p. 92.

[72] *Western Courier, West of England Conservative and Plymouth and Devonport Advertiser*, 27 November 1850.

[73] *Cork Constitution*, 8 December 1853.

[74] *KEP*, 27 September 1854. Ragged Schools were independent charitable schools established for the education of destitute children. The Ragged School movement was supported by Charles Dickens and by the Earl of Shaftesbury.

[75] *KEP*, 19 November 1859.

[76] Rev. George Scott, *The Irish Society's Missions at Doon, Dingle, Ventry and Dunurlin* (Dublin, 1854), p. 32.

[77] *KEP*, 20 June 1855.

[78] See Bernie Long, *Ventry Calling*, tr. Gabriel Fitzmaurice (Cork, 2005), p. 23.

CHAPTER 9

[1] *TM*, 1 May 1839.

[2] *Ibid.*

[3] *Ibid.*

[4] *TM*, 13 July 1839.

[5] *TM*, 17 July 1839. The *Tralee Mercury* ceased publication with the issue of 20 July 1839.

[6] *KEP*, 27 July 1839.

[7] *Southern Reporter*, 20 May 1840.

[8] *Ibid.*

[9] *KEP*, 24 June 1840.

[10] All reports in *KEP*, 8 May 1841. Rev. Edward Spring moved to Dunurlin from Castletownbere in the autumn of 1840. See *Westmoreland Gazette*, 21 November 1840.

11 *TM*, 2 March 1839.
12 *Ibid*. The quotation marks here were in the original letter. This is the earliest specific reference that I have seen to soup being offered as an inducement to conversion.
13 *KEP*, 6 March 1839.
14 *TM*, 23 March 1839.
15 *Ibid*.
16 *TM*, 30 March 1839.
17 *Ibid*.
18 *KEP*, 6 April 1839.
19 *Ibid*.
20 *TM*, 20 April 1839.
21 *Ibid*.
22 *The Warder*, 30 November 1839.
23 *Ibid*.
24 *Chester Chronicle*, 6 December 1839.
25 *Ibid*.
26 *KEP*, 7 December 1839.
27 *KEP*, 11 December 1839.
28 *Ibid*. This issue also carried the full text of Fr Divine's letter to the *Chester Chronicle*.
29 *KEP*, 14 December 1839.
30 *Ibid*.
31 *The Pilot*, 16 December 1839.
32 *KEP*, 21 December 1839.
33 *KEP*, 8 January 1840.
34 *Cork Southern Reporter*, 2 January 1840, citing *Leicester Mercury*.
35 *KEP*, 28 December 1839.
36 *KEP*, 23 September 1840.
37 *KEx*, 27 November 1840.
38 *Ibid*.
39 Colthurst, *Little Ones of Innisfail*, p. 98.
40 *KEx*, 4 December 1840.
41 *KEP*, 2 December 1840.
42 Cited in *KEP*, 2 December 1840.
43 See *KEP*, 5, 9, 12 and 16 December 1840.
44 *KEP*, 5 December 1840.
45 *KEP*, 5 and 12 December 1840. Emphasis in original.
46 *KEx*, 11 December 1840.
47 *Ibid*.
48 *KEx*, 15 December 1840.
49 *KEP*, 16 December 1840.
50 *KEx*, 25 December 1840.
51 *KEx*, 1 January 1841.
52 AMT, p. 68.
53 *Ibid*., pp 68–70.
54 *KEP*, 24 July 1841.
55 AMT, pp 56–61.
56 Colthurst, *Tales of Erin*, p. 4.
57 *Ibid*., p. 4.
58 *KEP*, 28 April 1841. Names were not cited in this report.

[59] Colthurst, *Little Ones of Innisfail*, p. 91. Colthurst names the boat *Crusader*, but newspapers name it *Brothers*. The missionaries did have another boat named *Crusader*.

[60] AMT, p. 58.

[61] *Ibid.*, p. 59.

[62] *Ibid.*, p. 60.

[63] Colthurst, *Tales of Erin*, p. 9. This would be known as the 'caoineadh' in Irish.

[64] AMT, p. 60.

[65] Colthurst, *Tales of Erin*, pp 10–11.

[66] AMT, p. 61.

[67] Colthurst, *Tales of Erin*, p. 12.

[68] Representative Church Body Library, Ventry Burial Records, P 677/27/1.

[69] *KEx*, 9 July 1844.

CHAPTER 10

[1] *KEP*, 17 June 1840.

[2] *KEP*, 28 December 1839.

[3] Wilson, *Innisfail*, pp 116–17.

[4] AMT, p. 47.

[5] AMT, annotated by Fr John O'Sullivan, Kerry County Archives, Tralee. Confirmation of this is found in Canon John O'Rourke, *The Battle of the Faith in Ireland* (Dublin, 1887), p. 532n, 'It was in Dingle the proselytisers and the converts were first called Soupers. This soubriquet was first given to them by Rev. John (afterwards Archdeacon) O'Sullivan, then stationed there.' I am grateful to Pádraig de Brún for this reference.

[6] *KEx*, 30 March 1841. Italics in original. It is possible that the letter writer was Fr John Halpin, curate of Dingle.

[7] *Ibid.*

[8] *KEx*, 13 July 1841. 'Meow' was a veiled reference to the term 'cat breac' for a convert.

[9] *Ibid.*

[10] Asenath Nicholson, *Ireland's Welcome to the Stranger, or An Excursion through Ireland in 1844 & 1845 for the purpose of personally investigating the condition of the poor* (London, 1847), pp 351–2. (See Chapter 17 for more on Nicholson's visit.)

[11] *Dublin Weekly Register*, 1 February 1845.

[12] Miller, 'Soup and Providence', p. 65.

[13] *KEx*, 22 October 1841.

[14] *KEP*, 27 October 1841.

[15] *Ibid.*

[16] *KEP*, 7 April 1841.

[17] *KEP*, 3 November 1841.

[18] *Ibid.*

[19] *KEx*, 11 January 1842.

[20] *KEP*, 10 November 1841.

[21] *KEP*, 13 November 1841.

[22] *AMH*, 28 October 1841, p. 125.

[23] *KEx*, 22 September 1842.

[24] *TC*, 30 March 1844.

[25] *Ibid.*

[26] *Report of the Dingle Colony 1843* (Bristol, 1844), p. 4. Online.

[27] AMT, pp 144–5.

28 Foley, *History of the Natural*, Preface, p. viii. Emphasis in original.

29 *KEx*, 26 November 1844.

CHAPTER 11

1 See Patricia Byrne, *The Preacher and the Prelate: The Achill Mission Colony and the Battle for Souls in Famine Ireland* (Dublin, 2017).

2 AMT, pp 131ff.

3 *The Christian Examiner*, 1 August 1841, pp 243–4.

4 *Ibid.*

5 *Ibid.*, p. 243.

6 *AMH*, 25 November 1841, p. 138.

7 *Christian Examiner*, 1 August 1841, p. 244. Quoting Gayer Letter of 12 December 1840.

8 *AMH*, 25 March 1841, p. 26.

9 Colthurst, *Little Ones of Innisfail*, p. 122.

10 See Dan Graham, 'The "Colony" at Dingle', *The Kerry Magazine*, no 4 (1992–93), p. 11.

11 NLI, Lawrence Collection, Call No: L_CAB_06165.

12 *Christian Examiner*, 1 November 1841, p. 341ff.

13 *Christian Examiner*, 1 December 1841, p. 376. Gayer's letter is included in AMT, pp 134–8.

14 *Ibid.*

15 AMT, p. 142.

16 *Ibid.*, p. 141.

17 *AMH*, 30 December 1841, p. 144.

18 Monck Mason, *History of the Origins*, p. 80.

19 *Report of Dingle Colony*, 1841, NLI Ms 24,445.

20 *Ibid.*

21 *Ibid.*

22 *AMH*, 25 November 1841, p. 138.

23 *Ibid.*

24 Colthurst, *Little Ones of Innisfail*, pp 105–15.

25 *Register of Ecclesiastical Intelligence*, September 1843, p. 20. Published with *Church of England Magazine*, vol. 15.

26 *Ibid.*

27 AMT, Appendix, pp 171–91. Lists of donations are not included in AMT, but are included in *Report of the Dingle Colony*, 1843, NLI Ms 24,445. The report is also available online.

28 NLI Ms 24,445.

29 *KEx*, 3 November 1843.

30 *Ibid.*

31 Ó Mainín, 'Achrann Creidimh', p. 48.

32 O'Sullivan, *Romantic Hidden Kerry*, p. 502 and p. 504.

33 AMT, p. 84.

34 *An Appeal on behalf of the Irish Society* (Cambridge, 1842), p. 11. This publication lists five bishops, seven earls, two viscounts and three lords as vice-patrons of the Irish Society.

35 Quoted in Monck Mason, *History of the Origins*, pp 87–8

36 O'Sullivan, *Romantic Hidden Kerry*, p. 557.

37 See Comharchumann Dhún Chaoin Teoranta, *Logainmneacha Dhún Chaoin, Co. Chiarraí* (Dún Chaoin, 2017), pp 47–50.

[38] AMT, pp 125–7.

[39] *Ibid.*, p. 125.

[40] *Ibid.*, pp 125–6

[41] *Ibid.*, p. 126.

[42] *Ibid.*, p. 127

[43] *KEP*, 19 February 1845.

[44] *Ibid.*

[45] *Ibid.*

[46] Foley, *Ancient and Present State*, p. 62.

[47] AMT, p. 139.

[48] *KEP*, 8 March 1843.

[49] *KEP*, 5 August 1843.

[50] *Ibid.*

[51] *TC*, 5 August 1843.

[52] *KEP*, 8 August 1843.

[53] *KEP*, 29 March 1843.

[54] *Ibid.*

[55] *TC*, 25 March 1843.

[56] *KEP*, 24 May 1843.

[57] *Irish Intelligence*, vol. 2 (1848), p. 92.

[58] *The Churchman: a magazine in defence of the Church and Constitution*, February 1843, pp 122–7, and March 1843, pp 179–86.

[59] *The Churchman*, February 1843, pp 122–3. The name 'Dingle-i-couch' came from the old Irish name for Dingle, Daingean Uí Chúis.

[60] *Ibid.*, p. 127.

[61] *The Churchman*, March 1843, p. 183.

[62] *The Churchman*, February 1843, p. 125.

[63] *The Churchman*, March 1843, p. 183.

[64] *Ibid.*, p. 185.

[65] *Ibid.*

[66] *Ibid.*, p. 186.

CHAPTER 12

[1] *AMH*, 28 April 1847, p. 39.

[2] AMT, p. 94.

[3] Ó Conaire, *Tomás an Bhlascaoid*, p. 17.

[4] Foley, *Ancient and Present State*, p. 42.

[5] *Ibid.*, p. 185n and p. 186n.

[6] *Churchman*, March 1843, p. 181.

[7] *Irish Intelligence*, vol. 1 (1848), p. 173.

[8] *Ibid.*, p. 172–3.

[9] *The British Magazine and Monthly Register of Religious and Ecclesiastical Information*, vol. 35 (February 1849), p. 156.

[10] AMT, p. 96.

[11] *Ibid.*

[12] AMT (1847), p. 181.

[13] Wilson, *Innisfail*, p. 130. The following details are from this book, pp 129–41.

[14] *Ibid.*, p. 131.

15 *Ibid.*, pp 134–5.

16 *Ibid.*, p. 136.

17 *Ibid.*, p. 139.

18 *Ibid.*, p. 135.

19 Colthurst, *The Little Ones of Innisfail*, p. 18.

20 Colthurst, *Tales of Erin*, p. 88. This is a longer and slightly different version of the poem, with fifty-two four-line stanzas telling the story of the mission to the Blaskets.

21 Wilson, *Innisfail*, p. 131.

22 *Ibid.*, p. 139.

23 Thomas Moriarty letter of 10 December 1838, Adare Narrative.

24 AMT, pp 96–7.

25 See Seán Ó Mainín, 'Scoileanna an Oileáin', in Aogan Ó Muircheartaigh (eag.), *Oidhreacht an Bhlascaoid* (Baile Átha Cliath, gan dáta). Muiris Mac Conghail also records the belief that Patrick Connor was the son of Séamus Bán. (Mac Conghail, 'Scoil an Mhisiúin', p. 44.)

26 *Churchman*, March 1843, p. 183.

27 AMT, p. 98.

28 *British Magazine*, p. 157.

29 Charles Gayer letter of 2 October 1839, Adare Narrative.

30 *Ibid.*

31 *TC*, 30 March 1844.

32 Charles Gayer letter of 2 October 1839, Adare Narrative.

33 AMT, p. 99.

34 *KEP*, 28 December 1839. The 'craythur' was poitín or whiskey; 'crubeens' were pigs' feet.

35 Foley, *Ancient and Present*, p. 60.

36 *The Warder*, 30 November 1839.

37 AMT, p. 99.

38 Foley, *Ancient and Present*, p. 60.

39 AMT, pp 112–13.

40 de Brún, 'A census of the parish of Ferriter, January 1835', *JKAHS*, no 7 (1974), p. 52. The census was entitled, 'A list of the population of Dunqun [*sic*], Dunurlin, Marhin, parish of Kilmilkedar and Kilquane, being the district or parishes belonging to the Revd. John Casey P.P.'. Mícheál de Mórdha's study adds considerable information on each family on the Great Blasket, including the family of Maurice Guiheen. (Mícheál de Mórdha, *An Island Community: the ebb and flow of the Great Blasket Island*, tr. Gabriel Fitzmaurice (Dublin, 2015), pp 184–210.)

41 AMT, p. 98.

42 *Churchman*, March 1843, pp 182–3. This letter is broadly the same as a letter cited by Thompson as dating from 1840. (AMT, p. 101.) It appears that A.M. Thompson's account does not always have accurate dates.

43 *Little Ones of Innisfail*, pp 19–20.

44 *A sermon on the death of honourable Judge Foster preached in Harold's Cross Church on Sunday July 17th July [1842] by Rev. Robert J. M'Ghee, A.M.*, p. 23. For a discussion on Rev. Robert James McGhee and 'his bombastic and sometimes hysterical attacks on the Church of Rome', see Bowen, *Protestant Crusade*, pp 113–17.

45 *KEx*, 23 September 1842.

46 *KEx*, 9 September 1842.

47 *KEx*, 30 September 1842. See also *KEP*, 28 September 1842.

[48] AMT, pp 104–5. Tomás Ó Criomhthain referred to 'Bean Thompson […] i dtigh na scoile lena gúna breá breac' (Mrs Thompson […] in the schoolhouse in her fine bright dress). He also criticised Mrs Thompson for writing that the women were chewing 'seaweed', when he felt she should have specified that it was 'dileasc' (dilisk or dulse), an edible seaweed. (Ó Criomhthain, *Allagar na hInise*, pp 149–50, cited in James Stewart, 'An Allusion in Allagar na hInise', *Éigse,* no 20 (1984), pp 226–7. I am grateful to Pádraig de Brún for this reference.)

[49] AMT, p 109.

[50] *Ibid.*, p. 112.

[51] *Ibid.*, p. 110.

[52] *Ibid.*, p. 114.

[53] See de Mórdha, *Island Community*, pp 200–10.

[54] MacWalter, *Irish Reformation*, p. 195.

[55] AMT, p. 107.

[56] *Churchman*, March 1843, p. 183.

[57] AMT (1847), p. 91.

[58] *Ibid.*, p. 95.

[59] de Brún, 'A Ventry Convert Group, 1842', p. 148. See also Mac Conghail, *A Kerry Island Library*, p. 44. In the 1847 edition of her book, A.M. Thompson quoted extracts from the journal kept by James Jordan during the year 1846. This material is outside the scope of this book.

[60] AMT, p. 102.

[61] Mac Conghail, *Bliainiris*, p. 44.

[62] AMT, p. 103.

[63] Foley, *Ancient and Present*, p. 50.

[64] Colthurst, *Tales of Erin*, pp 92–102.

[65] Colthurst, *Little Ones of Innisfail*, p. 18.

[66] AMT, p. 104.

[67] *Ibid.*, p. 109.

[68] *Churchman*, March 1843, p. 183.

[69] *KEx*, 3 May 1844.

[70] Ó Conaire, p. 63, quoting Dingle and Ventry Mission Association Report for 1847.

[71] *Ibid.*, p. 70–1.

[72] Ó Conaire, 'Mainistir na Súpanna', in *Tomás an Bhlascaoid*, pp 43–79.

[73] *Ibid.*, p. 72. Ó Conaire cites figures that show the decline in attendance from eighteen in 1852 to eight in 1863.

[74] Mac Conghail, *Kerry Island Library*, p. 42.

[75] Mac Conghail, *Bliainiris*, pp 39–71.

[76] *Ibid.*, p. 53.

[77] Mac Conghail, *Kerry Island Library*, p. 41.

[78] Mac Conghail, 'Scoil an Mhisiúin', p. 48.

[79] Census of 1901. Online.

[80] de Mórdha, *Island Community*, p. 232, citing Mac Conghail, 'Scoil an Mhisiúin'.

[81] Wilson, *Innisfail*, pp 129–30.

[82] Colthurst, *Little Ones of Innisfail*. Preface.

[83] *Ibid.*

[84] *The Missionary Repository for Youth and Sunday School Missionary Magazine*, vol. 8 (London, 1844), pp 41–4.

CHAPTER 13

1 *KEx*, 20 November 1844. Boherbue, Co. Cork, is part of Kerry diocese. Mr Casey was Fr John Casey, who was parish priest of Ballyferriter and lived in Murreagh (An Muiríoch).

2 *AMT*, p. 125.

3 *KEP*, 10 December 1842. Pádraig de Brún noted that 'Brasby's Lane' was also cited in Griffith's Valuation in 1853. Pádraig de Brún, 'An t-Athair Brasbie', *JKAHS*, no 2 (1969), p. 38, n.4. This chapter draws on this source.

4 *KEP*, 15 December 1838.

5 *KEx*, 22 September 1840.

6 *FJ*, 1 September 1841.

7 *FJ*, 19 November 1841.

8 The following details are from *AMT*, pp 156–62.

9 *AMT*, p. 159.

10 Foley, *Ancient and Present State*, p. 62.

11 These unsubstantiated folk memories were cited by de Brún, 'Brasbie', pp 48–9.

12 *AMT*, p. 160.

13 *AMT* (annotated copy), Kerry County Archives, p. 156.

14 *KEP*, 24 July 1844.

15 *AMT*, p. 159.

16 William J. O'Neill Daunt, *Ireland and Her Agitators* (Dublin, 1845), pp 115–16. This book has a report from the *Cork Constitution* of 27 July 1844 with the heading 'Doings in Dingle'. This heading came to be used regularly for news from Dingle.

17 *First Annual Report of the Priests' Protection Society* (Dublin, 1845) p. 9.

18 NAI, Outrage Papers Kerry 1845, 12/14381. Report of Lt Edward Miller, 11 August 1844.

19 NAI, Outrage Papers Kerry 1845, 12/14263.

20 *KEx*, 26 July 1844.

21 *KEx*, 30 July 1844.

22 *KEx*, 27 August 1844.

23 *KEP*, 15 March 1845.

24 *Ibid.*

25 *KEx*, 26 July 1844.

26 *KEP*, 24 July 1844.

27 *KEx*, 26 July 1844.

28 *KEP*, 31 July 1844.

29 *KEP*, 20 November 1844.

30 Brasbie letter to *Statesman*, 27 February 1845, published in *KEP*, 8 March 1845.

31 *KEP*, 31 August 1844.

32 *AMH*, 25 August 1844, p. 91.

33 *KEP*, 8 March 1845.

34 *KEx*, 20 August 1844.

35 *KEx*, 10 September 1844.

36 *KEP*, 5 October 1844.

37 Letter reprinted in *KEP*, 8 February 1845.

38 *AMH*, 27 March 1845, p. 30. Also in *KEP*, 8 March 1845.

39 *KEP*, 31 August 1844.

40 *Ibid.*

41 *KEx*, 28 January 1845.

[42] *KEx*, 7 February 1845.

[43] *Ibid.*

[44] *KEP*, 12 February 1845

[45] *KEx*, 14 February 1845.

[46] *KEP*, 5 October 1844.

[47] See *KEP*, 14 May 1845 and *Cork Examiner*, 17 October 1845.

[48] *Tyrone Constitution*, 3 October 1845.

[49] de Brún, 'Brasbie', p. 50.

[50] See *Nenagh Guardian*, 10 May and 13 September 1845.

[51] *KEP*, 12 April 1845.

[52] *KEx*, 18 February 1845.

[53] *KEx*, 7 March 1845.

[54] *Nenagh Guardian*, 19 April 1845, quoting *Statesman*.

[55] *KEP*, 28 May 1845.

[56] *KEP*, 21 June 1845.

[57] *Nenagh Guardian*, 9 August 1845. Letter dated 30 July.

[58] Report in *Dublin Weekly Register*, published in *KEx*, 21 January 1845.

[59] *KEx*, 6 May 1845.

[60] de Brún, 'Brasbie', p. 48. De Brún published a list of pamphlets written by Brasbie and published by the Priests Protection Society, p. 54. Unfortunately, none of the Irish translations has survived.

[61] *Nenagh Guardian*, 23 January 1847.

[62] Published in *The Protestant Magazine, published under the direction of the committee of the Protestant Association*, vol. 16 (1854), pp 303–6.

[63] See also *KEP*, 22 November 1845.

[64] Cited in de Brún, 'Brasbie', p. 51.

[65] *Protestant Magazine* (1854), p. 304.

[66] *Ibid.*, p. 305.

[67] *Ibid.*

[68] *KEP*, 24 June, 1848, cited in de Brún, 'Brasbie', p. 52.

[69] Monkstown Parish records, P 838, Representative Church Body Library, Dublin. As A.M. Thompson lived in Floraville, Donnybrook after she left Dingle, it is possible that Brasbie lodged with her at the time of his marriage.

[70] *Protestant Magazine* (1854), p. 306.

[71] de Brún, 'Brasbie', pp 52–3.

[72] I am grateful to genealogist Richard M. Doherty for this information.

[73] de Brún, 'Brasbie', p. 49. Author's translation.

[74] *KEP*, 26 June 1847.

[75] *KEP*, 12 October 1844.

[76] AMT, pp 161–4.

[77] *The British Magazine and Monthly Register*, vol. 35, p. 14.

[78] AMT, p. 162.

[79] *Ibid.*

[80] *Ibid.*, p. 163.

[81] *AMH*, 31 October 1844, p. 117.

[82] *KEP*, 28 December 1844.

[83] AMT, p. 163.

[84] *KEP*, 12 October 1844.

[85] *KEP*, 28 December 1844.

[86] *Statesman*, 15 November 1844.

[87] *KEP*, 19 March 1845.

CHAPTER 14

[1] *KEP*, 21 December 1844.

[2] *Ibid.*

[3] *KEx*, 17 December 1844.

[4] AMT, p. 52, annotated copy in Kerry County Archives.

[5] See letter in *KEP*, 29 January 1845.

[6] *KEx*, 18 October 1844.

[7] *KEP*, 12 October 1844.

[8] *Ibid.*

[9] *KEx*, 25 October 1844.

[10] *Ibid.*

[11] *KEP*, 2 November 1844.

[12] *KEx*, 15 November 1844.

[13] *Ibid.*

[14] *KEx*, 8 November 1844.

[15] *KEP*, 13 November 1844.

[16] *KEx*, 22 November 1844.

[17] *KEP*, 20 November 1844.

[18] *KEx*, 17 December 1844.

[19] *Ibid.*

[20] *The Pilot*, 21 May 1845.

[21] *AMH*, 26 December 1844, p. 137.

[22] *AMH*, 30 July 1845, p. 83.

[23] *AMH*, 29 April 1845, p. 41.

[24] *KEP*, 21 December 1844.

[25] *KEP*, 14 December 1844.

[26] *KEP*, 28 December 1844.

[27] *Ibid.*

[28] *Ibid.* The author of this piece was most likely Lt Herbert Clifford, assuming the voice of an old sailor.

[29] Letter of Lt Herbert Clifford of Dingle to Major O'Hara, 31 December 1844, NLI, O'Hara Papers, MS 20,323.

[30] See AMT, pp 164–6.

[31] AMT, p. 180.

[32] *Ibid.*, pp 165–6.

[33] *KEP*, 28 December 1844.

[34] AMT, pp 165–7.

[35] *KEx*, 17 December 1844.

[36] *KEP*, 22 January 1845.

[37] *KEx*, 7 February 1845.

[38] *KEx*, 31 January 1845.

CHAPTER 15

[1] *TC*, 11 January 1845.

2 *KEP*, 11 January 1845.
3 *KEP*, 15 January 1845.
4 *AMH*, 30 January 1845, p. 8. Copied in *KEP*, 15 February 1845.
5 O'Hara Papers, NLI, MS 20323, letter of 11 January 1845 to Major O'Hara.
6 *The Persecution of Protestants in Ireland in the year 1845* (Dublin, 1845), pp 19–20.
7 *AMH*, 30 January 1845, p. 8.
8 *KEP*, 29 January 1845.
9 *KEP*, 22 February 1845.
10 *KEP*, 2 April 1845.
11 *KEx*, 18 April 1845.
12 *KEP*, 23 April 1845.
13 Ó Mainín, 'Achrann Creidimh', p. 56.
14 I am grateful to Fr Jim Sheehy, great-great-grandson of Sean-Mhanus, for this memory.
15 Foley, *History of the County Kerry*, pp 225–6.
16 *KEP*, 1 January 1845.
17 *Ibid.*
18 *KEP*, 8 January 1845.
19 *Ibid.* See also *TC*, 11 January 1844.
20 *KEP*, 8 January 1845.
21 *KEx*, 7 January 1845.
22 *KEP*, 8 January 1845.
23 *KEP*, 11 January 1845.
24 NAI, Outrage Papers Kerry 1845, 12/3967. *Persecution of Protestants*, Appendix 1, p. 88, has the text of the memorial, without names. The text of the memorial and the names are listed in Appendix 2 here.
25 *Ibid.*
26 *Ibid.*
27 *KEP*, 25 January 1845.
28 *KEP*, 11 January 1845.
29 *Ibid.*
30 *KEP*, 25 January 1845.
31 NAI, Outrage Papers Kerry 1845, 12/5165.
32 AMT, Appendix I, p. 192.
33 Drummond letter of 13 January 1845, NAI, Outrage Papers Kerry 1845, 12/1055.
34 *KEP*, 1 February 1845.
35 *KEP*, 22 January 1845.
36 *KEx*, 28 January 1845.
37 *KEP*, 29 January 1845 and 1 February 1845.
38 AMT, Appendix II, pp 193–4.
39 *Ibid.*, p. 194. There were no newspaper reports to corroborate this account of a public debate.
40 *Ibid.*, p. 195.
41 *KEP*, 29 January 1845.
42 NAI, Outrage Papers Kerry 1845, 12/3967.
43 *KEx*, 21 February 1845.
44 *Ibid.*
45 AMT, Appendix V, p. 206.
46 AMT, p. 208.
47 *KEP*, 29 January 1845. Also in AMT, Appendix IV, pp 195–206.

[48] *KEP*, 29 January 1845. Moriarty was referring to Bishop Egan's letter appointing Fr. Brasbie to Kilmalkedar.

[49] *KEx*, 31 January 1845.

[50] *Ibid.*

[51] *The Belfast Protestant Journal*, 18 January 1845.

[52] *The Christian Lady's Magazine*, vol. 23 (January–June 1845), p. 241.

[53] *Ibid.*, p. 253–4.

[54] *KEP*, 1 February 1845. The case of Mrs Carney (or Kearney) featured in the libel case of March 1845, which is dealt with in Chapter 16.

[55] *KEx*, 28 January 1845.

[56] *KEP*, 1 February 1845.

[57] *KEP*, 8 February 1845.

[58] *KEP*, 1 February 1845.

[59] *KEP*, 5 February 1845.

[60] *KEx*, 31 January 1845.

[61] Cited in *KEP*, 5 February 1845.

[62] *Dublin Evening Mail*, cited in *KEP*, 8 February 1845.

[63] *KEP*, 12 February 1845.

[64] *Ibid.*

[65] *KEP*, 8 February 1845.

[66] *KEP*, 15 February 1845.

[67] *KEx*, 18 February 1845.

[68] *KEP*, 15 February 1844.

[69] *KEx*, 4 March 1845.

[70] *KEP*, 15 February 1845.

[71] *KEP*, 1 March 1845.

[72] *KEP*, 29 March 1845.

[73] *Ibid.*

[74] *KEP*, 8 February 1845.

[75] Col Clarke letter of 14 February 1845, NAI, Outrage Papers Kerry 1845, 12/3967.

[76] Drummond letter of 24 February 1845, NAI, Outrage Papers Kerry 1845, 12/3967.

[77] *Ibid.* Emphasis in original.

[78] *Ibid.*

[79] Drummond letter of 12 March 1845, NAI, Outrage Papers Kerry 1845, 12/5165.

[80] Edward Lucas letter of 26 February 1845, NAI, Outrage Papers Kerry 1845, 12/3967.

[81] Drummond letter of 12 March 1845, NAI, Outrage Papers Kerry 1845, 12/3967.

CHAPTER 16

[1] *KEx*, 22 November 1844.

[2] *Statesman*, 15 November 1844.

[3] *KEx*, 26 November 1844.

[4] *Ibid.*

[5] *KEx*, 10 January 1845.

[6] *KEx*, 4 February 1845.

[7] *TC*, 22 March 1845.

[8] This pamphlet is available online at Google Books. Unless otherwise stated, the details of the trial given here are from the account of the *Tralee Chronicle* in an 'Extraordinary Edition' published on 15 March 1845. The *Post* of 19 March also published a report of

the trial, acknowledging the work of reporters of the *Chronicle*.

9   *KEP*, 19 March 1845.

10 *Ibid*.

11 Cited in *KEx*, 28 March 1845.

12 *Persecution of Protestants*, Appendix III, p. 89.

13 AMT, p. 176.

14 *Ibid*., p. 174.

15 *Persecution of Protestants*, Preface, p. i.

16 *Ibid*.

17 *Ibid*.

18 *KEP*, 31 May 1845.

19 *KEx*, 18 March 1845.

20 *KEx*, 21 March 1845.

21 *KEx*, 28 March 1845.

22 *Cork Examiner*, 19 March 1845.

23 *Cork Examiner*, 24 March 1845.

24 *Ibid*.

25 *Ibid*.

26 *FJ*, 20 March 1845.

27 Cited in *KEx*, 28 March 1845.

28 Cited in *KEx*, 25 March 1845.

29 Cited in *KEx*, 15 April 1845.

30 Cited in *KEx*, 15 April 1845.

31 Cited in *KEx*, 29 April 1845.

32 Cited in *KEx*, 15 April 1845.

33 *KEx*, 29 April 1845.

34 *The Tablet*, 29 March 1845.

35 *Ibid*.

36 William J. O'Neill Daunt, *Ireland and her Agitators* (Dublin, 1845), p. 187n.

37 *KEx*, 15 April 1845.

38 *Ibid*.

39 *KEx*, 22 April 1845.

40 *KEx*, 25 April 1845.

41 *Ibid*.

42 *KEx*, 6 May 1845.

43 *KEx*, 30 May 1845. This was a reference to his earlier imprisonment as a result of his campaign against D.P. Thompson.

44 *Ibid*.

45 *KEx*, 13 June 1845.

46 *KEx*, 4 November 1845.

47 Cited in *KEx*, 29 April 1845.

48 *KEx*, 6 May 1845.

49 *KEx*, 30 May 1845.

50 *KEP*, 29 March 1845.

51 Cited in *KEP*, 25 June 1845.

52 Hansard, 23 June 1845, pp 1079–80.

53 *KEx*, 30 May 1845.

54 *KEx*, 3 June 1845.

55 John Ryan, *Popery Unmasked: a Narrative of twenty years of Popish persecution* (London,

1845), p. 228. Online.
56 *AMH*, 24 April 1845, p. 41.
57 *KEP*, 30 April 1845.
58 *KEx*, 15 April 1845, citing *Cork Southern Reporter*.

CHAPTER 17

1 Lady Chatterton, *Rambles in the South of Ireland in the year 1838* (London, 1839), vol. 1, pp 17–18. See 'The bizarre life of Lady Chatterton' on www.patrickcomerford.com for more information on the life of Lady Chatterton. She was born in London and, at the age of 17, married Sir William Chatterton of Castlemahon, Co. Cork.

2 Nicholson, *Ireland's Welcome*, Preface, p. iii. See also Maureen Murphy (ed.), *Ireland's Welcome to the Stranger: Asenath Nicholson* (Dublin, 2002).

3 Nicholson, *Ireland's Welcome*, p. 1.

4 See Murphy (ed.), *Asenath Nicholson*, Editor's Introduction, p. viii.

5 Nicholson's experiences in Tralee are in *Ireland's Welcome*, pp 348–50; her experiences in Dingle and west Kerry, pp 351–62.

6 *Ibid.*, pp 351–2.

7 *Ibid.*, p. 352.

8 *Ibid.*, p. 353.

9 *Ibid.*, p. 356.

10 *AMH*, 25 June 1845, p. 69.

11 Nicholson, *Ireland's Welcome*, p. 438. Emphasis in original.

12 *Ibid.*, p. 27.

13 *Ibid.*, pp 35–6.

14 *Ibid.*, p. 54.

15 *Ibid.*, p. 56.

16 *Ibid.*, p. 53.

17 See AMT, p. 178ff.

18 *KEP*, 20 September 1845.

19 AMT, p. 178.

20 *KEP*, 7 May 1845.

21 *KEx*, 11 August 1846.

22 *KEP*, 14 May 1845. See also *KEP*, 28 May 1845.

23 *AMH*, 25 June 1845, p. 69.

24 *AMH*, 29 May 1845, p. 57.

25 *KEP*, 7 June 1845.

26 *KEP*, 28 May 1845.

27 *KEP*, 25 June 1845.

28 *Ibid.*

29 *KEP*, 5 July 1845.

30 *Ibid.*

31 *KEP*, 8 October 1845.

32 *KEP*, 22 October 1845. John Halpin was parish priest of Iries, or Eyeries, Co. Cork, from 1823 to 1832, so his appointment as curate in Dingle may have been a form of demotion. He died in Dingle in 1849, aged 74. (Pádraig de Brún, 'Some lists of Kerry Priests, 1750–1835', *JKAHS*, no 18 (1985), p. 138 and p. 163.)

33 *KEP*, 27 August 1845. Hebdomadal means weekly.

34 See *KEx*, 30 December 1845, 5 May 1848 and 29 March 1850.

[35] *KEP*, 15 November 1845.

[36] See, for example, *Protestant Magazine*, vol. 7 (August 1845), pp 329–31.

[37] *AMH*, Frontispiece, vols 1–3.

[38] *The Times*, 26 June 1845. Cited in *KEP*, 9 July 1845.

[39] *AMH*, 30 July 1845, p. 83.

[40] *Ibid.*

[41] NAI, Outrage Papers Kerry 1845, 12/17335.

[42] *Ibid.*

[43] *Ibid.*

[44] See *TC*, 20 and 27 September 1845.

[45] *Cork Reporter*, cited in *KEP*, 1 October 1845.

[46] *KEP*, 29 October, 1845.

[47] *AMH*, 20 October 1845, p. 116.

[48] *KEP*, 25 October 1845.

[49] *KEP*, 29 October 1845.

[50] *Ibid.*

[51] *Ibid.*

[52] *Ibid.*

[53] All reports from *KEP*, 8 November 1845.

[54] *Ibid.*

[55] *Worcester Journal*, 13 November 1845. Other reports of his lectures appeared in *Banbury Guardian*, 13 November 1845 and *Bath Chronicle*, November 1845.

[56] *Cheltenham Chronicle*, 20 November 1845.

[57] *Ibid.*

[58] *Ibid.*

[59] *The Bristol Mercury and Western Counties Advertiser*, 6 December 1845.

[60] *Ibid.*

[61] *TC*, 13 December 1845.

[62] *Ibid.*

[63] *Ibid.*

[64] *KEP*, 17 December 1845.

[65] *FJ*, 15 January 1846.

CHAPTER 18

[1] Cited in *KEP*, 8 September 1847. Emphasis in original.

[2] *KEP*, 1 September 1847.

[3] *KEP*, 13 November 1847.

[4] Bryan MacMahon, *The Great Famine in Tralee and North Kerry* (Cork, 2017), p. 183.

[5] I am grateful to archaeologist Laurence Dunne for information on the location of the Gayer family grave.

[6] *KEP*, 5 February 1848.

[7] Information from Anthea Kennedy Gayer Mitchell of Australia, a direct descendant of Charles and Catherine Gayer. For further information on the family, see the entry by Anthea Kennedy Gayer Mitchell on https://www.irishancestors.ie/reverend-charles-gayer-1804-1848/.

[8] See Murphy and Chamberlain, *Church of Ireland*, pp 76–7 and pp 231–2 for more details.

[9] See MacMahon, *Great Famine*, for reports of the *Kerry Examiner* during the Famine.

[10] *KEP*, 28 May 1856.

11 *Céad Bliain*, pp 54–5.
12 *KEP*, 5 February 1848.
13 Mícheál Ó Mainín, 'A Post-Mortem on the Protestant Crusade in Dingle', *JKAHS*, no 29 (1996), pp 109–10.
14 AMT, p. 25.
15 See entry by Eoghan Ó Raghallaigh on Daniel Foley (Domhnall Ó Foghludha) in James McGuire and James Quinn (eds), *Dictionary of Irish Biography*, vol. 3 (Cambridge, 2009), pp 1037–8. To the best of my knowledge, the 1845 edition of A.M. Thompson's book has not been referenced by any previous writers.
16 *Athenaeum*, no 973, 20 June 1846, p. 628.
17 I am grateful to Pádraig de Brún for drawing my attention to this copy.
18 Mrs D.P. Thompson, *Ellen of Dingle: a Narrative of Facts* (London, 1850), p. 16. This 88-page tract has not been cited before in accounts of the Dingle mission. It is available on Google Books.
19 *Ibid.*, pp 16–17.
20 Rolf Loeber and Magda Loeber, *A Guide to Irish Fiction, 1650–1900* (Dublin, 2006), pp 128–9.
21 Whelan, *Bible War*, p. 181 and p. 190.
22 *KEP*, 2 December 1840.
23 Marion Rogan, 'The "Second Reformation" in Ireland, 1798–1861: case study of Rev. Robert Winning and the Kingscourt District' (unpublished PhD thesis in History, Maynooth University, 2019), p. 267.
24 Bowen, *Souperism*, p. 88.

APPENDICES
1 Edward Robert Petre, *The Catholic Claims Rejected: An Answer to the Letters of 'An English Catholic'* (York, 1826), p. 45.
2 *Ibid.*, Appendix 1, pp 92–3. Petre added, 'Here follow the signatures of 428 persons on behalf of upwards of 1,300 children.' J.B. McCrea later wrote that there were 435 petitioners representing 1,422 children. (*KEP*, 7 May 1828.)

Index